Advance
Square Pegs a

"I have taught student development theory for the majority of my faculty career. For a long time, I had to teach using theoretical frameworks that are outdated and not representative of the diverse student populations on college campuses today. *Square Pegs and Round Holes* provides a much-needed expansion of theories and perspectives to understand better the lives and experiences of the multiple, intersectional, and complex populations left out of traditional student development theories. As an instructor, I no longer have to rely solely on theories void of diverse perspectives. Students entering higher education preparation programs desire to learn more about diverse populations and grapple with social justice issues. This text answers that call by bringing together seminal minds in the field who center marginalized populations' experiences and voices. As a practitioner-based field that relies on theory to guide practice, we must use theories and perspectives that are inclusive. Texts like this one challenge our thinking, research, and practice in ways that help us 'know better so that we can do better!'"—*Joy Gaston Gayles; Professor; Senior Advisor for the Advancement of Diversity, Equity, and Inclusion; and President Elect, Association for the Study of Higher Education (ASHE)*

"*Square Pegs and Round Holes* does an exceptional job of honoring and acknowledging past and current theoretical perspectives. Simultaneously, the book pushes the boundaries of how we need to reconceptualize our understanding of the complex nature of identity development and the lived experiences of historically minoritized groups in higher education. Furthermore, it positions the construct of race as central to understanding marginalization across different identity groups. Finding ourselves amid a reckoning with racial injustice and other -isms in the United States, this book's timeliness is appreciated and welcomed as we seek new perspectives to help us serve and understand a growing and evolving diverse segment of the college-going population."—*Salvador B. Mena, Vice Chancellor of Student Affairs, Rutgers University–New Brunswick*

"Hallowed past practices in the field of student development have often failed to engender student empowerment and success among the diverse students that universities serve. Help has finally arrived in the form of *Square Pegs and Round Holes* which offers invaluable perspectives on how to reframe and enhance narrow and outmoded practices in this field."—*Ruth J. Simmons, President, Prairie View A&M University*

"This text privileges the experiences of those of us left out of early 'mainstream' student development theories. Chapters offer critical insight regarding the many ways-of-being of postsecondary students with models and frameworks to guide and further our understanding of student development. *Square Pegs and Round Holes* is particularly timely given current social stresses and pandemic—the implications of which will impact our students, our institutions, and our communities for years to come."—*Stephanie J. Waterman*, *Associate Professor, Leadership, Higher and Adult Education; Coordinator, Student Development/Student Services Stream, Ontario Institute for Studies in Education, University of Toronto*

"*Square Pegs and Round Holes* is an important asset to the field of higher education and student affairs. Uniquely centering critical race theory as the organizing frame for alternative student development models and perspectives presented, the book empowers practitioners and faculty with updated tools for understanding the intersectional, contextualized, and diverse identities of today's college students. While this book thoughtfully critiques the shortcomings of traditional theories, it does not reject them entirely. Rather, it builds new space for emerging voices that tell a more complete story about the complexity of student experiences and identities."—*Alexa Wesley*, *Associate Director for Research and Policy, NASPA–Student Affairs Administrators in Higher Education*

SQUARE PEGS AND ROUND HOLES

SQUARE PEGS AND ROUND HOLES

Alternative Approaches to Diverse College Student Development Theory

Edited by Fred A. Bonner II,

Rosa M. Banda, Stella L. Smith, and

aretha f. marbley

Foreword by Rev. Dr. Jamie Washington

Afterword by Amelia Parnell

1996-2021 25TH ANNIVERSARY

Sty/us
PUBLISHING, LLC.

STERLING, VIRGINIA

Library of Congress Cataloging-in-Publication Data
Names: Bonner, Fred A., editor. | Banda, Rosa M., editor. | Smith,
    Stella L., editor. | marbley, aretha f., editor.
Title: Square pegs and round holes : alternative approaches to diverse
    college student development theory / Edited by Fred Arthur
    Bonner II, Rosa M. Banda, Stella L. Smith, and aretha f. marbley;
    Foreword by Jamie Washington ; Afterword by Amelia Parnell.
Description: First edition. | Sterling, Virginia : Stylus Publishing,
    [2021] | Includes bibliographical references and index. |
Identifiers: LCCN 2020053531 (print) | LCCN 2020053532
    (ebook) | ISBN 9781620367728 (paperback) | ISBN
    9781620367711 (hardback) | ISBN 9781620367735 (pdf) |
    ISBN 9781620367742 (ebook)
Subjects: LCSH: Student affairs services--Administration. |
    Multicultural education. | Academic achievement. | Education,
    Higher--Aims and objectives.
Classification: LCC LB2342.9 .S68 2021 (print) | LCC LB2342.9
    (ebook) | DDC 378.1/97--dc23
LC record available at https://lccn.loc.gov/2020053531
LC ebook record available at https://lccn.loc.gov/2020053532

13-digit ISBN: 978-1-62036-771-1 (cloth)
13-digit ISBN: 978-1-62036-772-8 (paperback)
13-digit ISBN: 978-1-62036-773-5 (library networkable e-edition)
13-digit ISBN: 978-1-62036-774-2 (consumer e-edition)

Printed in the United States of America

All first editions printed on acid-free paper
that meets the American National Standards Institute
Z39-48 Standard.

Bulk Purchases

Quantity discounts are available for use in workshops and
for staff development.

Call 1-800-232-0223

First Edition, 2021

Square Pegs and Round Holes: Alternative Approaches to Diverse College Student Development Theory *is dedicated to the legions of higher education and student affairs graduate students who I have engaged with in classroom settings from Louisiana, Ohio, New Jersey, and Texas. These engagements have taken place in departmental and programmatic contexts conveying a diverse set of monikers—AHE, CSA, CSP, and SAAHE. Each student has in very profound and unique ways contributed to how I have crafted my academic life and career as a college professor. Invariably, over the years I would end my class sessions with the statement, "Go forth and do great things." This book is a testimony to the great things that they have done.*

—Fred A. Bonner II

CONTENTS

PART SIX: ALTERNATIVE FRAMEWORKS AND MODELS FOR BI- AND MULTIRACIAL AND NATIVE AMERICAN COLLEGE STUDENT POPULATIONS

PART SEVEN: ALTERNATIVE FRAMEWORKS AND MODELS FOR NONTRADITIONAL COLLEGE STUDENT POPULATIONS

"I'm not feeling that this framework speaks to my experience as a queer man of color."

"It feels to me like this was written to address a 19-year-old college student. I have a 19-year child."

"This model does not take into account the difference in sexual orientation and gender identity."

"I know I'm a person of color, but this framework seems to be more about Black people."

I start this foreword the way I start much of my writing, with the voices of the people who will be served by this book. After nearly 37 years in higher education, I am still fascinated by the voices, perspectives, and experiences that are not represented in many or our core models theoretical frameworks. I learned a long time ago that curriculum must be a window and a mirror. Students need to be able to look out the window and see experiences and perspectives different from their own. However, curriculum must also be a mirror so that students might see a reflection of themselves. I believe this is also true of theories and models. If the core theoretical frameworks and models that are used to inform our practice were not written or developed with "me" in mind, I am then likely to be underserved.

When I started in student affairs, I was excited to see that my graduate programs included racial identity development models. The primary models we studied were Cross's, for people of color, and Helms's, for White folks. I could see myself and my journey as a Black person through Cross's stages of pre-encounter, encounter, immersion, internalization, and commitment. While some things felt a little off, I was able to fit my experience into this round hole. I also felt like Helms's model spoke well to the White people I had encountered, particularly during my undergraduate years. I did not see the limitations in the models at that time. As a Black person coming to consciousness about what it meant to be Black, I was excited, and I felt like I found ways to understand my own experience and that of others like me who

I would serve as a professional. I did not realize that the models presented all people of color as the same. They failed to consider the intersecting identities for Black people, and there also seemed to be very little discussion of how the other minoritized folks of color might have a different process.

It was not until some 16 years after my master's degree that I was introduced to critical race theory (CRT). CRT provides the foundation needed to address and examine the similarities and difference based upon being a member of a racialized minority. It's also useful for inviting a more critical look at other identities.

The contributors to *Square Pegs and Round Holes: Alternative Approaches to Diverse College Student Development Theory* demonstrate how Blacks are not monolithic and invite the reader to also consider the experiences of Latinx, Asian American, bi- and multiracial, and Native American people as distinct and deserving of attention. As I consider the impact of not having these distinctions, I am aware that I attempted to treat all students of color the same. I developed programs and addressed concerns with a very limited and skewed perspective. It was a perspective that was based in systemic racism and the "Black and White" binary. I was, in fact, attempting to put square pegs in round holes. When the pegs did not fit, I did not examine the problem with the theories—I made the pegs the problem and thus too hard to support. In this time of racial unrest and deliberate attempts to become more effective antiracist practitioners, this book is a critical resource.

In addition to doing the important work of centering race in this book, the contributors also address the ever-expanding learning as it relates to gender and sexuality. The theories of the 1980s and 1990s do not begin to address the complex and nuanced understandings that we have today. The experience of lesbian, gay, bisexual, transgender, queer, intersex, asexual, and more (LGBTQIA+) folks was not represented. Most of the models and frameworks of gender and sexuality were based on the experiences of White, cis, middle class, gay men. These models were not intersectional, they did not engage the fluidity of sexualities and gender, and they were based in binary thinking. Part Five of this book helps address these issues in a powerful way.

The final part of the book addresses the experience of nontraditional students. This offers us a look at not only the students but also their locations. Again, most frameworks and models that have been a part of our canon have been based on the experience of students at predominantly and historically White institutions and students ages 18 to 24 years old. There have been very few models that address the differences in the developmental experience for students who are older than 24, or those attending community colleges, historically Black colleges and universities, Hispanic-serving institutions, or Tribal colleges. As a result, the faculty, staff, and administrators serving those populations often have to extrapolate from work that does not take into account the unique experiences that come with a difference in academic environment and age.

Each part of this book will provide you with new insights, new questions, and opportunities to meet the needs of often misunderstood populations. A major take-away for me is that each chapter is framed as offering "Alternative Frameworks and Models." This says to me that these scholars are offering more resources and tools for the work. They are not suggesting that we throw away everything that's been done. Nor have they suggested that previous frameworks models are not useful. They are simply stating that we need to have alternatives for a growing and changing demographic, so that we are not forcing square pegs in round holes.

Rev. Dr. Jamie Washington
President and Cofounder,
The Social Justice Training Institute

INTRODUCTION

Fred A. Bonner II, Rosa M. Banda, Stella L. Smith, and aretha f. marbley

*S*quare Pegs and Round Holes: Alternative Approaches to Diverse College Student Development Theory will serve as a distinctive work among books that seek to offer new and viable alternatives to higher education and student affairs practitioners who seek to understand the development of diverse college student populations on their respective campuses. This volume builds on the frameworks established in past and contemporary scholarship that focused on student development theory. Contributors will use critical race theory (CRT) (Ladson-Billings, 1999; Solórzano et al., 2000; Tate, 1997) as an analytical frame and theoretical and methodological foundation for developing alternative student development frameworks and models. CRT is a useful framework for the examination of the impact of race because it accounts for the role of racism in U.S. education and works toward the elimination of racism as a part of a larger goal of eliminating all forms of subordination in education (Yosso, 2002).

Specifically, CRT will allow contributors to situate race-related encounters at the center of their proposed alternative framework or model, done in an effort to deconstruct and challenge commonly held assumptions about diverse college student development. In the tradition of CRT, each contributor will offer an alternative model or framework that can be applied to the diverse population upon which the chapter is framed. According to Patton et al. (2007), "Therefore, it is important to expand the critical framework to include the intersections of race, gender, sexual orientation, and other characteristics deemed salient by each individual" (p. 47).

Currently, there are few books on the market that foreground the unique subject matter focus, and they will be included in this text. However, few if any of the extant works use CRT as the organizing center to explore college student development, particularly diverse college student populations—a major gap in the extant literature that this book will address.

The primary audiences we are attempting to reach include higher education and student affairs practitioners as well as faculty who seek to understand how to facilitate the development of diverse college student populations. *Square Pegs and Round Holes* is significant in that it addresses the long-standing dilemma of how diverse college students develop, while at the same time offering viable frameworks and models that can be readily applied to key developmental processes as they matriculate in academe. Additionally, this book provides a focused dialogue on the topic of "development" in an attempt to assist those in the academy who are responsible for the successful matriculation of all college students regardless of cultural affiliation and identity. While diverse students might represent the square pegs, this book rejects the notion that they must fit into the round holes that traditional frameworks and models represent. The contributors view these alternative models as working in tandem with rather than supplanting extant theory that has historically informed the field of student development. The secondary audience the book will focus on includes students enrolled in graduate-level courses in higher education and student affairs administration, sociology programs, and other social science courses that explore issues of race and other intersections of identity. Examples of critical venues for this volume include courses on the sociology of race, diversity and multiculturalism, college student development, counseling and advising, social justice, and others. *Square Pegs and Round Holes* serves as an additional tool in a world that requires more than a hammer for the building and construction process.

References

Ladson-Billings, G. J. (1999). Preparing teachers for diverse student populations: A critical race theory perspective. *Review of Research in Education, 24*, 211–247. https://doi.org/10.2307/1167271

Patton, L. D., McEwen, M., Rendón, L., & Howard-Hamilton, M. F. (2007). Critical race perspectives on theory in student affairs. In S. R. Harper & L. D. Patton (Eds.), *Responding to the realities of race on campus* [Special Issue] (New Directions for Student Services, no. 120, pp. 39–53). Wiley. https://doi.org/10.2307/1167376

Solórzano, D., Ceja, M., & Yosso, T. (2000). Critical race theory, racial microaggressions, and campus racial climate: The experiences of African American college students. *Journal of Negro Education, 69*(1/2), 60–73. https://doi.org/10.17763/haer.79.4.m6867014157m707l

Tate, W. F. IV. (1997). Critical race theory and education: History, theory, and implications. *Review of Research in Higher Education, 22*, 195–247. https://doi.org/10.2307/1167376

Yosso, T. J. (2002). Toward a critical race curriculum. *Equity & Excellence, 35*(2), 93–107. https://doi.org/10.1080/713845283

PART ONE

THE NEED FOR ALTERNATIVES IN COLLEGE STUDENT DEVELOPMENT THEORY

I

ALTERNATIVE COLLEGE STUDENT DEVELOPMENT FRAMEWORKS

An Exploration Across Race, Gender, and Sexuality

Fred A. Bonner II, Rosa M. Banda, Stella L. Smith, and aretha f. marbley

Ow American college students learn, grow, and develop has been a key focus of higher education research and scholarship since the very inception of postsecondary education in this country. According to Evans et al. (2010),

> From the paternalistic faculty authority figure who supervised Harvard students in 1636 to the contemporary student affairs professional who uses developmental theory to understand and enhance students' personal growth and learning, student development has always existed in some form as a goal of educators. (p. 5)

While higher education from the vantage point of academic affairs has focused on critical topics such as achievement, persistence, retention, and completion, student affairs has been positioned to address matters particularly related to student development. As Rodgers (1990) so aptly summarized, student affairs is characterized by a concern for the "whole" person (p. 27). Thus, college student development, particularly college student development theory is recognized as a body of scholarship that guides student affairs and higher education practices (Patton et al., 2016).

Much like the lessons learned related to student academics, such as the need to vary learning contexts and modalities in order to address the styles of myriad learners, student affairs professionals also have made critical adjustments. They have attempted to meet the needs of diverse student populations who bring multiple and competing identities to the campus context. Consequently, student affairs professionals have determined that the "one size fits all" approach to the application of student development theory is at best problematic and at worst inappropriate. According to McEwen (2003), "Theories are evolving, both in their own development and in how we use them in student affairs. Yet we must remember that theories are not pure; they are not perfect; they were not created and do not exist in a vacuum" (p. 23).

One of the noted difficulties in applying extant college student development theory, in both the academic and student affairs settings, has been the lack of congruence between diverse college student development and the application of traditional student development theory. This chapter, as a contribution to the book *Square Pegs and Round Holes*, attempts to initiate the dialogue about alternative student development theory by first providing a brief overview of a few key foundational college student development theories. Next, alternative developmental frameworks are advanced, whether included as an original model or the implementation of a *nonconventional* framework that more closely approximate the cultures, mores, and traditions of diverse college student populations. McEwen (2003) asserts that "theory must be examined in terms of its *implicit* worldview and those worldviews, or cross-cultural perspectives that are absent" (p. 20).

This chapter explores alternative frameworks, models, perspectives, and theories that higher education and student affairs administrators can use to inform their practice as it relates to the development of diverse student populations. Building on theory, as well as conceptual and theoretical frameworks established in past underscoring of student development, we offer needed departures from these traditional theories and ultimately foreground more authentic renderings for college student populations who represent diverse cultural, ethnic, and racial communities (Astin, 1997; Evans et al., 2010).

Moving College Student Development Theory From the Margins to the Mainstream

The origin of college student development is rooted in the work of Kurt Lewin (1936) and his famous equation $B = f(P \times E)$. The formula states that behavior (B) is a function (f) of the interaction (x) of person (P) and environment (E). In addition to Lewin's groundbreaking work, student development was also the work of Nevitt Sanford in 1966, who asserted, "Several conditions are found (or not found) in the college environment can have a major impact on students' growth and development. These include the concepts of challenge and support, involvement, marginality and mattering, and validation" (as cited in Evans et al., 1998, p. 25).

College student development theories are partitioned into clusters referred to as "families" (Knefelkamp, 1978, p. xi). According to Jones and Abes (2010),

> This umbrella term [families] incorporates those theories that are developmental and focus on the individual, including social identities; those that examine students in the collegiate context such as student success, engagement, and learning; theories that explain the relationship of campus environments to student development and success; and those focused on organizations and institutions of higher education. (p. 152)

These families of theories not only served to establish clear lines of demarcation within the context of college student development but also functioned as cynosures to galvanize the field. Miller and Winston (1983) posited,

> From these theory families, three core student development principles emerged: (1) human development is both continuous and cumulative; (2) development is a matter of movement from the simpler to the more complex; and (3) human development tends to be orderly and stage-related. (pp. 13–14)

However, despite the order that using these family groupings as organizing centers brought to the student development movement, concerns mounted that were part and parcel of the rapidly shifting diversity context on college and university campuses. Torres et al. (2009) discussed the importance of acknowledging extant theory; however, they also advanced the importance of looking to newer theoretical approaches that positioned the engagements and experiences of marginalized populations (e.g., by race, ethnicity, disability, sexual orientation). These scholars also spoke to the criticality of addressing the contextual variables (people, place, and situation) that perpetuate marginalization and oppression.

Therefore, as the college student development movement has evolved, key moments and shifts across the higher education landscape have moved this evolution on an array of divergent pathways. One such evolutionary movement focused on gender and its implication on how college students, particularly female college students, developed during their college matriculation experiences is reflected in the work of Belenky et al. (1986). Another movement was the focus and subsequent shift that occurred due to the increasing cultural, ethnic, and racial diversity experienced across academe after 1960. College student scholars and theorists whose work is emblematic of this movement include Bernal (2002), Cross (1978), Helms (1990), Horse (2005), Kim (2012), Phinney (2000), Root (1998), Ruiz (2008), Torres (2003), and Wijeyesinghe (2001).

Prior to these movements that attempted to foreground college student development among diverse and marginalized groups, the central tendencies were to advance extant theories that privileged the experiences of populations and researchers who were ostensibly White, male, and elite. Forerunners in the college student development movement were Chickering (1969) and Reisser (Chickering & Reisser, 1993) and Lawrence Kohlberg (1958). Chickering (1969) and Chickering and Reisser (1993) developed seven vectors that theorized the tasks that students go through while developing their identity. Kohlberg (1958), an American psychologist, developed a theory of stages of moral development. Although the theories proffered by these two theorists became staples in the college student development movement, they were not without their shortcomings, particularly their lack of diverse college students. Thus, the engagements and experiences of these student populations were relegated to the so-called theoretical margins. For example, Chickering's norming population was elite male students who attended Goddard College, and Kohlberg's prototypical usage of lower- and middle-class males comprised 100% of the study participants included in the development of his theory of moral development. It is no question that the critical work of these two theorists along with Erik Erikson (1993), William Perry (1999), Sanford (1962), and other mainstream theorists grounded the field; however, this grounding was accomplished primarily to the exclusion of diverse college student cohorts. In today's higher education environment, increasing numbers of diverse students entering higher education has moved the needle in a direction toward conceptual and theoretical frameworks that are more inclusive of the myriad cultural, ethnic, and racial differences present on college and university campuses.

Racial, Gender, and Sexual Identity Development in Higher Education

Theory has been used by higher education professionals, especially those who serve in the field of student affairs, to understand how college students learn, grow, and develop. According to McEwen (2003), "People turn to theory—both formal and informal—to make the many complex facets of experience manageable, understandable, meaningful, and consistent rather than random" (p. 6). In addition, a deeper level of clarity is achieved when the selection and application of college student development theory aligns with students' cultural, ethnic, and racial backgrounds and experiences. More than 3 decades ago, Stage (1991) posed the following questions:

> How can students be encouraged to adopt an appreciation of those different from themselves? Can students learn to place greater value on responsibility toward fellow humans and less on their own accretion of wealth? How can the college campus be made comfortable for all students, including those outside the mainstream? (pp. 60–61)

These questions posed in her article uncovered common elements of theory needed to establish a college student development framework. Now, as then, her questions serve as a clarion call for those invested in providing a robust postsecondary experience for all students.

Torres et al. (2009) posited,

> Although it is important to recognize commonalities among existing theories, several newer theoretical approaches to understanding identity are emerging. These approaches foreground both marginalized populations (e.g., by race, ethnicity, disability, or sexuality) as well as the societal structures and dynamics that produce and perpetuate marginalization and oppression (e.g., racism, heterosexism, ableism). (p. 583)

Alternative Theoretical Perspectives: Racial Identity Development

The recognition of newer theoretical approaches has not only advanced college student development theorizing but also opened it up to an array of diverse analytical and conceptual perspectives. These alternative frames are providing student affairs practitioners and scholars with an unobstructed range of motion, thus allowing them to align and contextualize their application of theory across all student populations. In her article titled *A Comparison of European and African-Based Psychologies and Their Implications for African American College Student Development,* V. D. Johnson (2003) discussed the importance of implementing models and tools that are congruent with African American culture to explore the African American college student experience. According to Johnson, "The task is to create theories, models, and instruments that are Afrocentric in design and analyzed by those who are Afrocentric in their understanding of the developmental needs of African American college students" (p. 827).

Some of the earlier attempts to disrupt the dominant narratives that grounded the ways we theorized about college student development took place in the area of racial and ethnic identity (McEwen, 2005). A litany of scholars (Helms, 1995; Parham & Helms, 1981; Phinney, 2003; Sellers et al., 1998; Wijeyesinghe & Jackson, 2001) are noted for their work on ethnic and racial identity development. However, it is the scholarship advanced by William Cross and his theory of psychological nigrescence that has gained the widest acclaim. According to Sneed et al. (2006),

> Nigrescence theory (Cross, 1971, 1991) was developed based on Fanon's (1963, 1967a, 1967b) thinking about racial or cultural identity development and liberation struggles. Nigrescence theory originally tracked the identity development stages that Black American adults traverse in movement away from an identity that places low or even negative salience on Black identity toward the achievement of an identity that places positive emphasis on race and Black culture. In addition to Fanon's influence, the original model borrowed from the anthropological and sociological literature on identity conversions and social movements (Gerlach & Hine, 1970; Wallace, 1956, 1970). (p. 70)

Due to space limitations, an exhaustive overview of Cross's model is not offered here; consequently, readers are encouraged to seek additional references that provide a comprehensive explanation of the model and the various stages Cross outlined in the framework that Black individuals traverse in their development and progression toward a positive identity (Sneed et al., 2006). However, this brief discussion of Cross's model does offer a point of departure to underscore the importance of contextualized theorizing as a resource for the construction of alternative college student development frameworks. Much like the ophthalmologist who oscillates between lenses, asking "A or B? B or A? Clearer or about the same?" Cross's theory provided higher education and especially the college student development movement with a way to see the experiences of Black students more authentically. This work is being further expanded in contemporary enclaves. One such expansion is the insightful article by V. D. Johnson (2001) that used the Nguzo Saba as an alternative framework to contextualize the racial identity developmental experiences of African American college students. According to V. D. Johnson (2001), "Student affairs researchers and practitioners simply have to look to what African Americans collectively say about themselves. No other practice or ideology presents this better than the holiday of Kwanza and its value system of the Nguzo Saba" (p. 412).

Alternative Theoretical Perspectives: Gender Identity Development

A review of the extant scholarship in the area of gender identity development reveals an array of scholars who positioned their work in camps with identifying monikers that included gender role, feminist identity, and womanist identity. Cannon, Crenshaw, Collins, Downing, Helms, O'Neil, and Ossana are but a few on the list of stalwarts in the field who gained prominence for their theorizing as it related to some aspect of gender and gender identity development. Perhaps one of the most noted forerunners in the area of gender and its importance to developmental theory is Carol Gilligan. Gilligan's (1986) extension of Lawrence Kohlberg's theory of moral development and her own scholarship *In A Different Voice* (Gilligan, 1993) have for decades served as guideposts for those conducting research in the area of gender, gender identity, and women's moral identity development. Gilligan's work represented a way to reimagine and redefine moral development in a way that positioned women in the foreground.

McLeod (2013) indicated that

> according to Gilligan (1977), because Kohlberg's theory was based on an all-male sample, the stages reflect a male definition of morality (it's androcentric). Men's morality is based on abstract principles of law and justice, while women's is based on principles of compassion and care. (p. 3)

In addition, Kakkori and Huttunen (2010) noted,

> The most famous opponent of Kohlberg is the feminist thinker Carol Gilligan, who presents both philosophical and empirical counterclaims against Kohlberg's cognitivist theory of moral development. Gilligan's main criticism is that Kohlberg constructs what he considers "the highest stage of moral development" from a male viewpoint and thus it is not neutral and impartial at all. (p. 1)

Kerber (1986) asserted that "Gilligan's theory of women's moral development has taken root in native soil" (p. 324). Evans et al. (1998) asserted that "several theorists in the twentieth century singled out women as a group and portrayed women's experiences as inferior and qualitatively different from that of men" (p. 187). Consequently, Gilligan's viewpoint and rationale for pushing scholarship past Kohlberg's male-dominated theory and theoretical underpinnings were underscored by Evans et al. (1998), who affirmed her statements regarding her "beliefs that Kohlberg's theory was biased in regard to women" (p. 191).

Additional researchers who influenced the college student development literature, particularly gender and gender identity related to the development of feminist and womanist perspectives, are Anzaldua, Bloom, Collins, Crenshaw, hooks, Painter, and Spivak (Schiller, 2000). The contemporary focus on gender identity has moved beyond discussions centered on traditional female/male binary distinctions and taken on more complex and multilayered perspectives that include *cis* and *trans* gender distinctions. According to Alexander (2008),

> Acknowledging the presence of the transgendered is useful not only for understanding those who are differently gendered or whose presentation or experience of gender falls outside our "norms," but also for helping us interrogate the constructs of gender that we often take for granted as "natural" or "normal." (p. 130)

Space limitations preclude a more comprehensive discussion of gender and the role that both scholars and scholarship have played in the college student development movement. What the extant literature reveals are the many parallel as well as intersectional points along the college student development continuum in which gender, gender identity, sexual identity, feminist, and womanist scholarship function independently and synergistically.

Narratives centered on gender, gender identity, and how they are engaged in societal contexts would be incomplete without the influential work of Anzaldúa (1999). Pereles (2013) stated,

> In *Borderlands/La Frontera*, Anzaldúa offers a personal and brutally honest account of her own life spent between and across borders: as a woman of color, as a lesbian, as a Tejana, and as someone confronting daily the legacy of conquest. (p. 163)

Anzaldúa's (1999) work provides a certain authenticity and verisimilitude that makes for seamless coupling with extant historical and contemporary theory and theorists. Martinez (2002) provided the following critical perspective on how theory advanced by W. E. B DuBois and Anzaldúa could function as concomitants:

> While African Americans and Latina/os are often linked in sociological research in discussions of major societal ills such as residential segregation, drug usage, and imprisonment rates, researchers have paid little if any attention to the links between Black and Latino/thinkers. This paper provides an analysis of the work of 19th century African American thinker,

W.E.B. Du Bois, in relation to the work of 20th century Chicana feminist thinker, Gloria Anzaldúa and argues that their work is related and resonant as they construct significant forms of oppositional culture or consciousness within a matrix of domination (Feagin & Mitchell, 1995; Collins, 2000, p. 174). (p. 162)

Martinez's melding of Anzaldúa's and DuBois's conceptual and theoretical frames provides scaffolding on which college students' identity, in general, and gender identity, in particular, can unfold. The application of these conceptual and theoretical perspectives in seemingly nontraditional ways can offer an alternative pathway to both amplify and explain how college students learn, grow, and develop. Other theories could plausibly be coupled to yield analytical and heuristic tools for the purpose of divining developmental templates to address the evolving higher education student demographic profile—especially as it relates to gender identity development. One of the leading voices associated with gender and sexual identity is Audre Lorde (1982), and her words are quite powerful: "If I didn't define myself for myself, I would be crunched into other people's fantasies for me and eaten alive" (p. 137). Thus, what these theoretical frames provide as they work in tandem are alternatives that allow college students and those tasked with college student development to do just that: Define themselves for themselves.

Alternative Theoretical Perspectives: Sexual Identity Development

The previous section that provided insight on gender identity development closely aligns with the evolution of the sexual identity development movement. Many of the frameworks and models along with key scholars and theorists cross the gender and sexual orientation border. In essence, the extant research focused on gender and sexual orientation is mutually reinforcing and shares not only similar origins but also similar epistemologies. Collectively, the theoretical frames that have codified sexual identity have included foci on gay and lesbian identity, bisexual identity, heterosexual identity, and general sexual identity (Yarhouse, 2001). Some of the noted theorists are Cass, D'Augelli, Dillon, Fassinger, Klein, Mueller, Savoy, and Washington (McEwen, 2005). Beginning in the 1970s, identity development models emerged related to gay identity (and later lesbian identity) and the so-called coming out process. Cass (1979, 1984) suggested that during the teenage years or early twenties that nonheterosexuals move through varied identified stages that share common characteristics (Gonsiorek, 1995; Renn & Bilodeau, 2011).

Sexual identity development among college student populations is routinely associated with Cass's (1979) model (originally called homosexual identity formation) that was based on her clinical work with gays and lesbians in Australia (Evans et al., 2010). While this stage model provided an initial framework to study and theorize about gay and lesbian identity development, it was not without its shortcomings. Cass noted some of these challenges, and others were initiated by the rising tide of diversity experienced across the higher education waterfront. Bilodeau and Renn (2005) explained that "there is growing scholarly recognition of the experiences and diversity of sexual orientation beyond 'heterosexual,' 'gay,' and 'lesbian' identities" (p. 27).

In a more contemporary vein, scholars have transitioned the discourse about LGBTQ cohorts away from the lopsided perspective that all individuals who fit into this population can be subsumed into descriptive and developmental frames labeled "gay," "White," and "male." The field-shifting scholarship of E. P. Johnson (2005) and his advancement of quare theory offers a counternarrative affirming the experiences of LGBTQ individuals of color. According to Means and Jaeger (2013),

> Quare theory (Johnson, 2005; Johnson & Henderson, 2005), Black queer studies (Johnson & Henderson, 2005), Queer of Color Critique (QCC) (Ferguson, 2004), and Black Lesbian Feminism (Lorde, 1984, 1988) all are related critical theories and offer a comprehensive framework for understanding the experiences of LGB individuals of color. (p. 48)

In addition, situated in the camp of sexual identity frameworks and providing an alternative developmental rendering is the scholarship of Patricia Hill Collins, Kimberle Crenshaw, and Lisa Bowleg. Each of these scholars holds as concomitants gender and sex in articulating their respective theories.

A hallmark of the research on college student development in general and sexual identity development in particular has been the criticality of using multiple theoretical and perspectival frames. In her seminal research that explored lesbian identity development, Abes (2009) found that by dismantling rigid lines of theoretical demarcation she was able to theorize on the borderlands between and across theory. She asserted, "In the context of college student identity development, it is important to live with tensions to more fully describe the complexity of development" (p. 149). Regarding her decision to create a "borderland" between theories, she said, "Among the issues it raised are whether it is appropriate to simultaneously apply theoretical perspectives that differ in fundamental assumptions as well as to retell participants' stories through multiple theoretical perspectives" (p. 148).

Readers are encouraged to review the extant literature for a more comprehensive discussion about sexual identity development and the various other theoretical foci (e.g., bisexual, heterosexual, and transgender identity development) that are emergent on our college and university campuses. The challenges (i.e., increasing diversity, non-Western ideologies, ongoing essentialist versus constructionist debate, multiplicity of theoretical lenses) related to college student sexual identity development are looming; however, if we take an active approach that recognizes the diversity of college students' background and experiences, we will be well on our way to meeting their developmental needs writ large.

References

Abes, E. S. (2009). Theoretical borderlands: Using multiple theoretical perspectives to challenge inequitable power structures in student development theory. *Journal of College Student Development, 50*(2), 141–156. https://doi.org/10.1353/csd.0.0059

Alexander, J. (2008). *Literacy, sexuality, pedagogy: Theory and practice for composition studies*. Utah State University Press.

Anzaldúa, G. (1999). *Borderlands: La Frontera, the new Mestiza*. Aunt Lute Books.

Astin, A. W. (1997). *What matters in college? Four critical years revisited*. Jossey-Bass.

Belenky, M. F., Clinchy, B. M., Goldberger, N. R., & Tarule, J. M. (1986). *Women's ways of knowing: The development of self, voice, and mind*. Basic Books.

Bernal, D. D. (2002). Critical race theory, Latino critical theory, and critical raced-gendered epistemologies: Recognizing students of color as holders and creators of knowledge. *Qualitative Inquiry, 8*(1), 105–126. https://doi.org/10.1177/107780040200800107

Bilodeau, B. L., & Renn, K. A. (2005). Analysis of LGBT identity development models and implications for practice. In R. L. Sanlo (Ed.), *Gender identity and sexual orientation: Research, policy, and personal* [Special Issue] (New Directions for Student Services, no. 111, pp. 25–39). https://doi.org/10.1002/ss.171

Cass, V. C. (1979). Homosexual identity formation: A theoretical model. *Journal of Homosexuality, 4*, 219–235. https://doi.org/10.1300/J082v04n03_01

Cass, V. C. (1984). Homosexual identity formation: Testing a theoretical model. *The Journal of Sex Research,* 20, 143-167.https://doi.org/10.1080/00224498409551214

Chickering, A. W. (1969). *Education and identity*. Jossey-Bass.

Chickering, A. W., & Reisser, L. (1993). *Education and identity* (2nd ed.). Jossey-Bass.

Cross, W. E. Jr. (1978). The Thomas and Cross models of psychological nigrescence: A review. *Journal of Black Psychology, 5*(1), 13–31. https://doi.org/10.1177/009579847800500102

Erikson, E. H. (1993). *Childhood and society*. WW Norton & Company.

Evans, N., Forney D. S., & Guido-DiBrito, F. (1998). *Student development in college: Theory, research, and practice.* Jossey-Bass.

Evans, N. J., Forney, D. S., Guido, F. M., Patton, L. D., & Renn, K. A. (2010). *Student development in college: Research, theory, and practice* (2nd ed.). Jossey-Bass.

Gilligan, C. (1986). Reply by Carol Gilligan. *Signs: Journal of Women in Culture Aad Society, 11*(2), 324–333. https://doi.org/10.1086/494226

Gilligan, C. (1993). *In a different voice: Psychological theory and women's development.* Harvard University Press.

Gonsiorek, J. C. (1995). Gay male identities: Concepts and issues. In A. R. D'Augelli & C. J. Patterson (Eds.), *Lesbian, gay, and bisexual identities over the lifespan: Psychological perspectives* (pp. 24–47). Oxford University Press.

Helms, J. E. (1990). *Black and White racial identity: Theory, research, and practice.* Greenwood Press.

Helms, J. E. (1995). An update of Helms' White and people of color racial identity models. In J. G. Ponterotto, J. M. Casas, L. A. Suzuki, & C. M. Alexander (Eds.), *Handbook of multicultural counseling* (pp. 181–198). SAGE.

Horse, P. G. (2005). Native American identity. In H. Kyound Ro & E. M. Broido (Eds.), *Listening to marginalized voices: Paradigmatic, philosophical, and ethical bases of inclusive inquiry practices in student affairs* (New Directions for Student Services, no. 109, pp. 61–68). Wiley. https://doi.org/10.1002/ss.154

Johnson, E. P. (2005). "Quare" studies or (almost) everything I know about queer studies I learn from my grandmother. In E. P. Johnson & M. G. Henderson (Eds.), *Black queer studies: A critical anthology* (pp. 124–157). Duke University Press.

Johnson, V. D. (2001). The Nguzo Saba as a foundation for African American college student development theory. *Journal of Black Studies, 31*(4), 406–422. https://doi.org/10.1177/002193470103100402

Johnson, V. D. (2003). A comparison of European and African-based psychologies and their implications for African American college student development. *Journal of Black Studies, 33*(6), 817–829. https://doi.org/10.1177/00219347030 33006006

Jones, S. R., & Abes, E. S. (2010). The nature and uses of theory. In J. H. Schuh, S. R. Harper, & S. R. Jones, *Student services: A handbook for the profession* (5th ed., pp. 149–167). Wiley.

Kakkori, L., & Huttunen, R. (2010). The Gilligan-Kohlberg controversy and its philosophico-historical roots. In M. Peters, P. Ghiraldelli, B. Žarníc, & A. Gibbons (Eds.), *Encyclopaedia of philosophy of education* (pp. 1–27). Springer.

Kerber, L. (1986). Some cautionary words for historians. *Signs, 11*(2), 304–310. http://www.jstor.org/stable/3174051

Kim, J. (2012). Asian American racial identity development theory. *New perspectives on racial identity development: Integrating emerging frameworks* (pp. 138–160). New York University Press.

Knefelkamp, L. L. (1978). *A reader's guide to student development theory: A framework for understanding, a framework for design* [Unpublished Manuscript]. Iowa State University.

Kohlberg, L. (1958). *The development of modes of moral thinking and choice in the years ten to sixteen.* [Unpublished doctoral dissertation]. University of Chicago.

Lewin, K. (1936). *Principles of psychological topology.* McGraw-Hill.

Lorde, A. (1982). *Sister outsider: Essays and speeches.* Crossing Press.

Martinez, T. A. (2002). The double-consciousness of Du Bois & the "mestiza consciousness" of Anzaldúa. *Race, Gender & Class, 9*(4), 158–176. http://www.jstor.org/stable/41675281

McEwen, M. K. (2003). The nature and uses of theory. In S. R. Komives & D. Woodard (Eds.), *Student services: A handbook for the profession* (4th ed., pp. 153–178). Jossey-Bass.

McEwen, M. K. (2005). The nature and uses of theory. In M. E. Wilson & L. Wolf-Wendel (Eds.), *ASHE Reader on College Student Development Theory* (pp. 5–24). Pearson Custom Publishing.

McLeod, S. A. (2013). Kohlberg's stages of moral development. *Simply Psychology.* www.simplypsychology.org/kohlberg.html

Means, D. R., & Jaeger, A. J. (2013). Black in the rainbow: "Quaring" the black gay male student experience at historically black universities. *Journal of African American Males in Education, 4*(2), 46–62.

Miller, T. K., & Winston Jr., R. B. (1983). *Administration and leadership in student affairs; Actualizing student development in higher education.* Routledge.

Parham, T. A., & Helms, J. E. (1981). The influence of Black students' racial identity attitudes on preferences for counselor's race. *Journal of Counseling Psychology, 28*(3), 250–257. https://doi.org/10.1037/0022-0167.28.3.250

Patton, L.D., Renn, K.A., Guido, F.M., & Quaye, S.J. (2016). *Student development in college: Theory, research, and practice* (3rd ed.). Jossey-Bass.

Perry, W. G. (1999). *Forms of ethical and intellectual development in the college years: A scheme.* Jossey-Bass.

Phinney, J. S. (2000). Ethnic and racial identity: Ethnic identity. In A. E. Kazdin (Ed.), *Encyclopedia of Psychology* (Vol. 3, pp. 254–259). American Psychological Association.

Phinney, J. S. (2003). Ethic identity and acculturation. In K. M. Chun, P. Balls Organista, & G. Marín (Eds.), *Acculturation: Advances in theory, measurement, and applied research* (pp. 63–81). American Psychological Association. https://doi.org/10.1037/10472-006

Renn, K. A., & Bilodeau, B. (2011). Lesbian, gay, bisexual, and transgender identity development theories. In B. Bank (Ed.), *Gender and higher education* (pp. 55–62). Johns Hopkins University Press.

Rodgers, R. F. (1990). Recent theories and research underlying student development. In D. G. Creamer (Ed.), *College student development: Theory and practice for the ACPA Media Publication No. 49* (pp. 27–79). American College Personnel Association.

Root, M. P. (1998). Experiences and processes affecting racial identity development: Preliminary results from the Biracial Sibling Project. *Cultural Diversity and Mental Health, 4*(3), 237–247.

Ruiz, V. L. (2008). *From out of the shadows: Mexican women in twentieth-century America*. Oxford University Press.

Sanford, N. E. (1962). *The American college: A psychological and social interpretation of the higher learning*. Wiley.

Schiller, N. (2000). A short history of Black feminist scholars. *The Journal of Blacks in Higher Education, 29*(2000), 119–125. https://doi.org/10.2307/2678863

Sellers, R. M., Smith, M. A., Shelton, J. N., Rowley, S. A., & Chavous, T. M. (1998). Multidimensional model of racial identity: A reconceptualization of African American racial identity. *Personality and Social Psychology Review, 2*(1), 18–39. https://doi.org/10.1207/s15327957pspr0201_2

Sneed, J. R., Schwartz, S. J., & Cross, W. E. (2006). A multicultural critique of identity status theory and research: A call for integration. *Identity, 6*(1), 61–84. https://doi.org/10.1207/s1532706xid0601_5

Stage, F. K. (1991). Common elements of theory: A framework for college student development. *Journal of College Student Development, 32*(1), 56–61.

Torres, V. (2003). Influences on ethnic identity development of Latino college students in the first two years of college. *Journal of College Student Development, 44*(4), 532–547. https://doi.org/10.1353/csd.2003.0044

Torres, V., Jones, S. R., & Renn, K. A. (2009). Identity development theories in student affairs: Origins, current status, and new approaches. *Journal of College Student Development, 50*(6), 577–596. https://doi.org/10.1353/csd.0.0102

Wijeyesinghe, C. L. (2001). Racial identity in multiracial people: An alternative paradigm. In C. L. Wijeyesinghe & B. W. Jackson (Eds.), *New perspectives on racial identity development: A theoretical and practical anthology* (pp. 129–152). New York University Press.

Wijeyesinghe, C. L., & Jackson III, B. W. (2001). *New perspectives on racial identity development: A theoretical and practical anthology*. New York University Press.

Yarhouse, M. A. (2001). Sexual identity development: The influence of valuative frameworks on identity synthesis. *Psychotherapy: Theory, Research, Practice, Training, 38*(3), 331–341. https://doi.org/10.1037/0033-3204.38.3.331

2

MODELING ALTERNATIVE COLLEGE STUDENT DEVELOPMENT FRAMEWORKS

Increasing Access and Inspiring College Success

Saundra M. Tomlinson-Clarke, Petra A. Robinson, and Sattik Deb

Culturally diverse societies with visions of ensuring all students accessible pathways to and through higher education are faced with challenges for creating equitable opportunities to learn and to achieve. Today, the United States might boast that its population is far more educated than ever. Indeed, increasingly more students from noncollege-educated families are realizing a college degree is mandatory for social mobility and for gaining equal footing with their peers (Dyce et al., 2013; Fallon, 1997; London, 1996; Pratt & Skaggs, 1989). Statistics show increased high school graduation rates with upward trends in enrollments at colleges and universities. Hispanic and African American participation in higher education is increasing at a much faster rate than that of Whites (Carnevale & Strohl, 2013). Although these data may suggest positive gains, there is still much work to do to advance access and equity (Perna & Kurban, 2013). Hispanic/Latinx student and African American student graduation rates (75.2% and 70.7%) are still lower than rates for White (86.6%) and Asian (88.7%) students (DePaoli et al., 2015). Also, White students continue to enroll in the top colleges and universities in the United States, while those from minoritized and underrepresented backgrounds have moved into the seats vacated by Whites in open-access institutions that are frequently crowded and often underfunded (Carnevale & Strohl, 2013).

In advancing U.S. educational reform initiatives, educational leaders have partnered with schools and communities to develop early intervention strategies designed to enhance learning and development. To this end, efforts have not significantly increased the numbers of racially/ethnically diverse students in the educational pipeline. Black, Latinx, and Native American students continue to experience difficulties negotiating pathways to higher education, remaining underrepresented at many predominantly White colleges and universities (DePaoli et al., 2015; Samel et al., 2011; Thompson et al., 2006). Educational disparities between White and Black students, White and Latinx students, White and Native American students, and wealthy and low-income students are a focus of concern.

Educational researchers and practitioners are met with the formidable challenge of developing alternate theoretical frameworks that advance strategies for decreasing the disparities between student groupings on measures of academic success (i.e., grade point averages, standardized test scores, dropout rates, enrollment in rigorous courses, graduation rates, college enrollment rates). Alternate student development frameworks are needed to guide programs and services that more effectively assist racialized and minoritized students to successfully negotiate pathways to and through higher education. *Racialized* refers to socially constructed identities and societal practices that influence sense of self, range of choices, and achievement (Nasir, 2012). The term *minoritized* refers to "the ongoing social experience of marginalization, even when groups subject to racial-ethnic discrimination achieve a numerical majority in the population" (Chase et al., 2014, p. 671), yet these groups continue to be subject to societal and institutional exclusionary practices. As we become a more globally and technologically driven society with resultant changes in the demographics of our national as well as our student population across the entire pre-K–20 spectrum, it is imperative that we pay close attention to the assumptions we hold or have held in relation to how students experience school. As educators, scholars, and overall stakeholders who are committed to student success, we propose creative approaches that do not subscribe to a singular traditional view of student development. These creative approaches are developed by incorporating learning from existing models and frameworks. Embracing alternative approaches for college student development also includes a focus on ways to increase access and inspire college success.

To achieve this goal, it is important to have a comprehensive understanding of student development theories (SDTs), traditional frames of reference, as well as alternate theories and models to support all students in their achievements. Recognizing that academic institutions have their own organizational cultures (Lucas & Murry, 2011), higher education practice must guide the college SDT body of scholarship (Patton et al., 2016). In other words, SDT should serve as a framework of principles and as a foundation for working with students from diverse backgrounds and experiences as well as serve to articulate the values of the profession that guide practice. To further our understanding of the overall context of student development frameworks, in this chapter, we subscribe to the idea that student development is a philosophy that has guided student affairs in practice and has served as a rationale for specific programs and services since the profession's inception (Rodgers, 1990). SDT seeks to complement academic progress and development. Alternative frameworks provide theory that guides practice designed to promote student learning and development, assisting all students to experience equitable and accessible opportunities to achieve academic excellence.

Pathways to and Through Higher Education

The latest national data from the National Center for Educational Statistics (NCES) suggested that high school graduation rates are trending upward across the nation. Approximately 85% of high school seniors during the 2016–2017 year graduated, an increase from 82.3% in 2014–2015 and 81% in 2013–2014 (NCES, 2017, 2018). The graduation rate has inched up annually over the last few years, largely due to the educational obtainment strides made by marginalized and underrepresented student groups. For example, graduation rates for minority students significantly improved since 2006, with a 15% gain for Hispanic/Latino students and a 9% gain for Black students. Most states met or exceeded the national graduation average, including a few that were already very close to reaching the 90% mark.

Based on enrollment predictions, more than 20.4 million students were expected to attend U.S. colleges and universities in 2017 (National Student Research Clearinghouse, 2017). These increases in college enrollment are reported to be a result of declining dropout rates for White, Black, and Hispanic students between 2000 and 2015, as well as increases in the number of students enrolling in college following high school (NCES, 2016). Of students attending college, 43.4% completed college at starting institution, and 54.8% completed college within 6 years. By comparison, in the 1970s for example, approximately 12% of adults over the age of 25 held a bachelor's degree or higher. By 2012, that percentage increased to 31% (Blumenstyk, 2015). Also, reflecting the increasing diversity of the United States, many predominantly White institutions report a student body composed of predominantly students of color. Harvard was one of several predominantly White institutions that reported a high diversity index, indicating that the majority of students in the classes of 2020 and 2021 were non-White (Fernandes, 2017).

The 1960s saw the beginning of significant changes in higher education in light of the turmoil of the Vietnam War, the civil rights and women's rights movements, and the greater diversification of the college student populations (Evans et al., 2009). Today's college students, however, are different from student cohorts of previous generations in important ways. This generation of students has grown up in an environment that has seen a more racially and linguistically diverse population; an increasing number of immigrants; and increasingly diverse cultural, economic, and geographic backgrounds. Further, this generation is accustomed to advanced technology and as such is extremely comfortable with and relies heavily on technology and social media to inform themselves and to communicate with others (Seemiller & Grace, 2016).

The Need for Alternate Frameworks: A Closer Look

Acknowledging educational gains is important, yet to suggest there have been equal gains across people of all demographics and backgrounds would be naïve at best and disingenuous at worst. Educational attainment gains across the nation have been "uneven across income levels, racial and ethnic lines, and sexes" (Blumenstyk, 2015, p. 12) showing that the national education systems have not kept pace with increased demographic change in society. A closer look at the data indicates that high school graduation rates vary greatly from state to state, and many educational gains reported are due to local reforms, not necessarily broad socioeconomic trends (DePaoli et al., 2015). Although graduation rates increased for low-income students over the past 3 years, this student subgroup still lags well behind their more affluent peers. The 2012–2013 adjusted cohort graduate rates (ACGR) for low-income students reached 73.3%, up 3.3 percentage points from 2010–2011 but still more than 8 points behind the national overall rate (DePaoli et al., 2015). ACGR is a measure of the adjusted cohort of full-time ninth graders in a particular school year that graduate within 4 years. In addition, any progress that has been made has not been universal, as many states still fell below the national average, with states such as Arizona, Illinois, and New York reporting drops in high school graduation rates (DePaoli et al., 2015). California is one of four states identifying as majority-minority, with "minority" populations that exceed 50% (DeVore, 2015; U.S. Census Bureau, 2015). Gao and Johnson (2017) reported that "most of California's high school students are not prepared for college. . . . Only 45% of the graduating class of 2016 completed the college preparatory courses required for admission to CSU [California State University] or the University of California," and predictions based on current high school and college completion rates suggest that "only 30% of California 9th graders will earn a bachelor's degree" (p. 1). Furthermore, Gao and Johnson (2017) reported that students in California who are academically prepared are not finding successful pathways in and through college.

Along with reported increases in college enrollment, examining the demographic profile of today's college student population is useful in determining which students are gaining access to higher education and which students are excluded from higher education. Recent statistics indicate that there are more female students than male students and more full-time students than part-time students enrolled in college. Also, Blumenstyk (2015) noted that the age range of students indicated that 11.8 million students were under the age of 25, and "more than a third of college students are aged twenty-five years and older, and that this population of students has been growing at a faster rate than the number of younger students" (p. 13).

Examining students' successful pathways through college indicated college completion rates for White and Asian students as 62% and 63.2%, respectively, followed by Hispanic/Latinx graduates (45.8%) and Black graduates (38%). College completion rates refer to first-time students who enter postsecondary institutions and subsequently obtain a degree at any U.S. degree-granting institution. Interestingly, the percentage of first-time undergraduate students who completed their program of study at the same 4-year institution within a specified period of time—college graduation rate—by race/ethnicity indicated that Asian students had the highest graduation rate (51%), followed by White students (47.5%), Hispanic/Latinx students (35.6%), and Black students (28.7%). Of the racial/ethnic groupings, Black students attending 4-year public institutions had the lowest 6-year completion rate (45.9%), with Black men reported to have the lowest completion rate (40.0%) and the highest stop-out rate (41.1%) (Lumina Founation, 2017). Based on these data, Black and Latinx students are underrepresented in the college student population and, when enrolled, are less likely to complete college at their starting institution when compared with White and Asian students. Furthermore, Black men have the lowest college retention rates when compared to White and Asian students and Black women (Farmer & Hope, 2015; Harper, 2012).

Comparing student groups solely by enrollment and completion rates may provide general data; however, between-group comparisons neglect important individual and institutional characteristics as well as the relationship between the individual and the institution that impacts personal development and academic achievement. These and other contextual factors such as social and cultural capital (Strayhorn, 2010) are associated with an individual's ability to successfully negotiate pathways to and through higher education. However, using simple metrics such as enrollment and graduation rates without a solid understanding of their meaning in divergent contexts may distort as much as they might inform (Sullivan et al., 2012).

Furthermore, differing completion and enrollment rates by race, ethnicity, gender, income, or other measures of diversity should in no way be used to suggest a standard to which other students are compared. In other words, White and Asian students' enrollment and completion rates should not be used as the standard to which Black and Latinx students are assessed. Furthermore, comparisons by race, ethnicity, gender, or other dimensions of personal identity limit understanding of students' individual experiences. Comparative approaches tend to focus on deficits rather than strengths of the compared group, resulting in homogeneous stereotyping as well as ignoring the achievements of racialized and minoritized students. Theories based on comparison research often result in deficit or deficient models of development that only serve to reinforce culturally biased assumptions and call into question the relevancy of traditional student development approaches for understanding minoritized students' experiences and their development. It is necessary to explore between and within group differences and individual student's experiences in developing alternate frameworks. Stewart (2013) stated,

> A cultural deficit approach masks heterogeneity within and across the racial and ethnic groups that comprise racially minoritized students. Consequently, racially minoritized students appear to be generally deficient in cultural capital, underprepared and at risk for attrition. . . . Given this situation it is vital to construct an understanding of racially minoritized students that does not use a cultural deficit approach. (p. 184)

Students must be appreciated and understood based on their self-definition, not as a comparison against any other prescribed ideal. An understanding of students' diverse identities and the way they make meaning of their own experiences and development must be an integral aspect of any theoretical framework for it to be culturally relevant.

Adopting an open systems approach to SDT considers the educational system as an integrated and dynamic entity. Understanding success for underserved students within a higher education context requires a deeper understanding of the educational and socioeconomic inequalities that exist prior to college, as well as the need for student personnel who are engaged in the challenge of applying new theoretical models that are able to bridge the transiton between secondary and higher education. Therefore, social scientists, policymakers, and educators should incorporate home and school contexts in efforts to fully understand inequity in society and in our educational systems. Students also must have voice, which allows opportunities to create alternative or counternarratives based on students' experiences (Shedd, 2015). With the exception of researchers who examine the process of self-authorship (Baxter Magolda, 2001, 2004; Hernández, 2016; Pizzolato et al., 2012; Torres & Hernández, 2007), few theoretical frameworks have sought to understand student development based on identities and meaning as defined by the student.

Overview of Traditional SDT

Responding to the need to guide practice, the evolution of SDT suggests distinct schools of thought. Emerging from mid-20th-century research in psychology and sociology, SDT is not free from limitations or cultural bias; rather, the theoretical frameworks reflect the predominant values of the profession based on the time period in which the theory was developed. Given this reality, one primary limitation with which we are concerned is the limitation of SDTs for understanding racialized and minoritized students. Just as there is no one-size-fits-all approach to life and to student success, we seek to problematize any theory-to-practice model that ignores systematic barriers that marginalize students, particularly the experiences of students of color. Although we acknowledge the increase in the number of racial identity development theories, it is problematic to accept them as one-size-fits-all approaches because there is inadequate attention to other aspects that influence development (Pattton et al., 2016), especially as they relate to contextual and historical legacies of oppression. This means that for their success, and with the goal of developing socially responsible students and global citizens, there is the need for an expansion of traditional models that go beyond statistical measures and deficit approaches that center on contemporary and self-determined identities of students.

Jones and Stewart (2016) provided a useful review of the history of SDT organized into three waves. The issues for concern and the professional values that influenced practice during each wave are evident and reflected in the theoretical framework of that time. The first wave focused on foundational SDTs and placed an emphasis on the development of the whole student. Key theoretical aspects identified are the knowledge base needed for practice, and the psychological social processes associated with development, with emphasis on the individual in context. Given the current diversity of our college student population, these models are viewed as limiting and relatively inefficient in that the totality of an individual or experience above and beyond a particular period of time or circumstance is not considered. Early SDT and models offer a very limited scope typically based on development within a vacuum that is the college experience. Evans et al. (2009) stated that most foundational theories assume the existence of an objective reality that holds regardless of time or circumstance. Moreover, foundational SDTs often failed to see development as part of a larger continuum and therefore defined student development through siloed and compartmentalized periods of time. As a result, contextual considerations and factors outside of the college experience were not considered. Limitations of the first wave of theoretical frameworks also include the absence of student diversity, with theory based on the experiences of White males from privileged social and economic backgrounds (Jones & Stewart, 2016). Evans et al. (2009) argued that student development research based on small, homogenous samples precluded generalizability to other populations.

The second wave emerged with a change in the demographic profile of the United States and an accompanying need to better understand the social identities and experiences of diverse students attending institutions of higher education. Feelings of alienation and attrition for Black students (Allen, 1985; Astin, 1993; Astin & Bayer, 1971; Mallinckrodt & Sedlacek, 1987; Sedlacek, 1987; Taylor, 1986) and the negative effects of the so-called chilly climate for women (Britton & Elmore, 1977; Hall & Sandler, 1982; Ossana et al., 1992; Pascarella et al., 1997) are well documented in earlier higher education research. In addressing the negative impact of the campus climate as well as structures of inequality that affected persistence and retention for minoritized students, there was a need to look beyond developmental theories and toward holistic theoretical frameworks. The holistic nature of traditional approaches, however, may present limitations when working with today's students since individual differences may be inadvertently ignored. Kimball and Ryder (2014) suggested that alternate approaches to student development must capture "social history," "institutional history," and "life story" in understanding a student's experience and include "the ability to see multiple perspectives, which is crucial to the [professional's] ability to respond to the unique needs of each individual student" (p. 301).

Jones and Stewart (2016) called attention to Baxter Magolda's (2001, 2009) research on self-authorship, whereby the three dimensions of development (i.e., cognitive, interpersonal, intrapersonal) result in a process of internally defined meaning-making. More recently, researchers (Hernández, 2016; Pizzolato, 2003; Pizzolato et al., 2012; Torres & Hernández, 2007) examined the complex process of self-authorship for marginalized student populations who are challenged to make meaning and to develop a sense of self as they are confronted by inequitable social systems (e.g., racism, power, and privilege).

The third-wave theories discussed by Jones and Stewart (2016) are described as critical and poststructural perspectives, focusing on institutional and structural systems as well as the ways in which power and oppression operate to include some groups while excluding other groups. The development of identities is at the forefront, and knowledge is reconsidered with respect to role of context, intersectionality, and individual agency. Role of context includes where people live and function as well as the historical context. Other researchers have referred to this as the historical era or time and space dimensions of personal identity (Arredondo & Glauner, 1992; Arredondo et al., 1996). Intersectionality assumes identity fluidity, challenging notions of a single, unidimensional or fixed identity, and assists in "understanding how both privilege and marginality shape and inform each other in individuals' identity meaning makings and in the context of their environments" (Jones & Stewart, 2016, p. 25). Individual agency advances the process of self-authorship, creating spaces and opportunities for individuals to make meaning and define themselves within their social context.

Reconceptualizing SDT

Although factors such as socioeconomic inequality (Robinson & Roksa, 2016) and student precollege characteristics (Kuh et al., 2007) are associated with outcomes in college, most student development research has focused solely on the college experience (Gillett-Karam, 2016). Based on findings from research on student persistence and retention (Astin, 1993; Stage, 1989; Tinto, 1993), Newman and Newman (1999) identified "three classes of factors" (p. 484) (i.e., precollege characteristics, institutional factors, student personal-emotional development) associated with successful degree completion:

1. *Precollege characteristics* (college-oriented high school, parents' educational background, family's educational values, and goals, the intention to attend college, clarity of career goals, and high school course work and grades);
2. *Institutional factors* related to the college or university, including availability of financial aid or other financial support, academic climate, availability of tutoring, student orientation to the faculty, acceptance into a degree-granting program, availability of required courses, housing and roommate arrangements and access to a mentor and/or academic advisor;

3. *Student personal-emotional development*, such as level of identity resolution, the ability to balance various demands, degree of homesickness, feelings of alienation or social isolation, academic self- concept, academic self-efficacy, and the ability to seek out support. (p. 484)

Critical and poststructural perspectives, as discussed by Jones and Stewart (2016), advance theory and practice toward alternate student development frameworks for work with racialized and minoritized student populations. A focus on educational access and equity provides the foundation for alternate theoretical frameworks. Critical are the experiences of racialized and minoritized students as well as the complexity of interrelated factors associated with choice and achievement. Relying solely on traditional SDTs, in an attempt to understand the experiences of racially minoritized students, tends to provide a narrow lens for conceptualizing student development (Stewart, 2013).

Influenced by the writings of bell hooks (1994), Jones and Stewart (2016) wrote that "theory becomes healing only when the focus of theorizing is centered on issues and questions that elevate larger historical, social, and cultural structures that pattern a diverse array of lived experiences" (p. 17). Jones and Stewart (2016) further noted that theories frame the practice of the profession and reflect the social historical context, the nature of the questions that are the focus of concern, and the values of the theorists developing the framework. Therefore, a historical lens guides reflective practice by aligning the work with knowledge of the professional values reflected by the times (Kimball & Ryder, 2014). If the higher education profession values equity, justice, and democracy, and if we truly care about the success of all students, then reflective practice should reconceptualize theory to reflect these values (Gillett-Karam, 2016), which are a result of the historical and sociocultural context in which we live.

Alternate theoretical frameworks provide the components to guide us in our reflective practice (Figure 2.1). Alternate theoretical frameworks use unique and creative models that identify the best ways in which we can support our students and help them develop skills to assist with optimal development and success beyond their college career. Alternative SDTs and student development models appreciate the interrelationship among factors that create successful pathways for preparing students with the abilities, skills, and readiness for college access and success in a global workforce. In order to ensure the personal development and academic success of racialized and minoritized students, it is necessary to examine structural inequities and inequitable polices that work to exclude minoritized students, and to develop strength-based models to empower students toward optimal

Figure 2.1. Alternative theoretical frameworks.

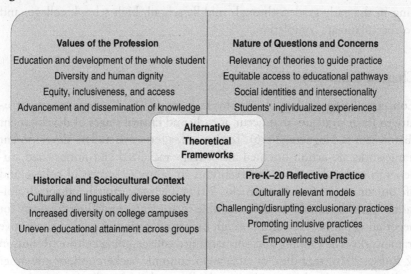

personal development and academic achievement (Tomlinson-Clarke & Hernández, 2019).

Highlighting the importance of multiple intersections of students' identities (especially those that may be considered untraditional), alternate theoretical frameworks help us to better understand the ways in which intersectionality influences education and development ultimately, success in life. Sawyer et al. (2013) posited that it is not only necessary but also vital that we expand research efforts to understand the intersectionality of identities in the workplace. As we provide inclusive and equitable opportunities for our students, we must consider these intersections and complexities in relation to our hopes of student access, resiliency, and success.

In addition, Boykin and Noguera (2011) highlighted the need for students to be prepared with 21st-century skills to achieve higher-order learning outcomes. Specifically, students must achieve knowledge-transfer skills by which they are able to reflect on what they have learned, "generating knowledge and applying their knowledge and skills to solve real-world problems" (Boykin & Noguera, 2011, p. 5). The challenge to prepare students who possess the educational and social emotional readiness to meet the challenges of a 21st-century labor market remains. An alternate model reconceptualizes SDT as a continuum from precollege through vocation, with institutions of higher education serving as the locus through the formation of partnerships with local school districts as well as with prospective employers. Therefore, we ascribe to alternate frameworks that focus on students' experiences beginning in the early grades, through middle school, high school, college, and postbaccalaureate completion.

Chapter Summary

Conceptualizing student development from pre-K–20 supports opportunity to learn strategies that occur at early and critical stages of development (Blankstein & Noguera, 2016). To this end, alternative student development frameworks are action oriented and engage racialized and minoritized students in early educational interventions to promote successful college and life outcomes (McCoy & Rodricks, 2015). Cultural capital and social capital networks are available and accessible to students, providing supports for negotiating pathways to and through higher education. A goal of alternative frameworks is developing and normalizing a college-going culture (Robinson & Roksa, 2016) regardless of race, socioeconomic background, or any other traditional metrics that serve to marginalize students.

Given the need to have an accurate and informed understanding of racially minoritized students' experiences in education (Stewart, 2013), alternate theories of student development are crucial for engaging in culturally informed practice. Early intervention programs eliminate boundaries, encourage student persistence, provide clear pathways to and through college, and foster students' academic and social-emotional development across the educational continuum. Therefore, understanding student development beginning in the early years is important to developing effective strategies that create a college-going culture. Theoretical frameworks extend beyond a point in time that begins with the college years and must include all aspects of education early intervention models. Rather than focus on deficit or deficient models of development, alternate frameworks encompassing pre-K–20 education are built on strength-based perspectives that serve to empower students to make choices from a success framework.

Although there are numerous programs and services designed to identify and offer students opportunities for learning that increase the likelihood of college attendance and graduation, the question remains as to whether the theoretical frameworks underlying these programs actually address the needs of racialized and minoritized students. Theories that adequately address the experiences of underrepresented students are needed if we are to provide programs and services to better serve these populations (Stewart, 2013). Through the use of alternative frameworks, we are better able to create equitable learning environments and opportunities that enhance student success to and through higher education.

References

Allen, W. (1985). Black student, White campus: Structural, interpersonal, and psychological correlates of success. *The Journal of Negro Education, 54*(2), 134–147. https://doi.org/10.2307/2294928

Arredondo, P., & Glauner, T. (1992). *Personal dimensions of identity model.* Empowerment Workshops, Inc.

Arredondo, P., Toporek, R., Pack Brown, S., Jones., J., Locke, D. C., Sanchez, J., & Stadler, H. (1996). Operationalization of the multicultural counseling competencies. *Journal of Multicultural Counseling and Development, 24*(1), 42–78. https://doi.org/10.1002/j.2161-1912.1996.tb00288.x

Astin, A. W. (1993). *What matters in college? Four years revisited.* Jossey-Bass.

Astin, A. W., & Bayer, E. (1971). Antecedents and consequents of disruptive campus protests. *Measurement and Evaluation in Guidance, 4,* 18–30. https://doi.org/10.1080/00256307.1971.12022476

Baxter Magolda, M. B. (2001). *Making their own way: Narratives for transforming higher education to promote self-authorship.* Stylus.

Baxter Magolda, M. B. (2004). Evolution of a constructivist conceptualization of epistemological reflection. *Educational Psychologist, 39*(1), 31–42. https://doi.org/10.1207/s15326985ep3901_4

Baxter Magolda, M. B. (2009). Promoting self-authorship to promote liberal education. *Journal of College and Character, 10*(3), 1–6. https://www.tandfonline.com/doi/pdf/10.2202/1940-1639.1079

Blankstein, A. M., & Noguera, P., with Kelly, L. (2016). *Excellence through equity: Five principles of courageous leadership to guide achievement for every student.* ASCD.

Blumenstyk, G. (2015). *American higher education in crisis? What everyone needs to know.* Oxford University Press.

Boykin, A. W., & Noguera, P. (2011). *Creating the opportunity to learn: Moving from research to practice to close the achievement gap.* ASCD.

Britton, V., & Elmore, P. B. (1977). Leadership and self-development workshop for women. *Journal of College Student Personnel, 18,* 318.

Carnevale, A.P., & Strohl, J. (2013). *Separate & unequal: How higher education reinforces the intergenerational reproduction of white racial privilege.* Georgetown Public Policy Institute.

Chase, M. M., Dowd, A. C., Pazich, L. B., & Bensimon, E. M. (2014). Transfer equity for "minoritized" students: A critical policy analysis of seven states. *Educational Policy, 28*(5), 669–717. https://doi.org/10.1177/0895904812468227

DePaoli, J. L., Fox, J. H., Ingram, E. S., Maushard, M., Bridgeland, J. M., & Balfanz, R. (2015). *Building a grad nation: Progress and challenge in ending the high school dropout epidemic.* Civic Enterprises.

DeVore, C. (2015, June 21). Of the four-majority-minority states in America, minorities do the best in Texas. *Forbes.* https://www.forbes.com/sites/chuckdevore/2015/06/21/america-majority-minority-by-2044-with-four-states-already-there-minorities-do-best-in-texas/#4288526287cb

Dyce, C. M., Albold, C., & Long, D. (2013). Moving from college aspiration to attainment: Learning from one college access program. *High School Journal, 96*(2), 152–165. http://www.jstor.org/stable/23351967

Evans, N. J., Forney, D. S., Guido, F. M., Patton, L. D., & Renn, K. A. (2009). *Student development in college: Theory, research, and practice.* John Wiley & Sons.

Fallon, M. V. (1997). The school counselor's role in first generation students' college plans. *The School Counselor, 44*(5), 384–393. http://www.jstor.org/stable/23897872

Farmer, E. D., & Hope, W. C. (2015). Factors that influence African American male retention and graduation: The case of Gateway University, a historically Black college and university. *Journal of College Student Retention: Research, Theory and Practice, 17*(1), 2–17. https://doi.org/10.1177/1521025115571074

Fernandes, D. (2017, August 2). The majority of Harvard's incoming class is non-white. *Boston Globe.* https://www.bostonglobe.com/metro/2017/08/02/harvard-incoming-class-majority-nonwhite/5yOoqrsQ4SePRRNFemuQ2M/story.html

Gao, N., & Johnson, H. (2017). *Improving college pathways in California.* Public Policy Institute of California. http://www.ppic.org/publication/improving-college-pathways-in-california/

Gillett-Karam, R. (2016). Student Affairs: Moving from student development to student success. In C. C. Ozaki & R. L. Spaid (Eds.), *Applying college change theories to student affairs practice* (New Directions for Student Affairs, no. 174, pp. 9–21). https://doi.org/10.1002/cc.20205

Hall, R. M., & Sandler, B. R. (1982). *The classroom climate: A chilly one for women?* Project on the Status and Education of Women, Association of American Colleges.

Harper, S. R. (2012). *Black male student success in higher education: A report from the National Black Male College Achievement Study.* University of Pennsylvania, Center for the Study of Race and Equity in Education.

hooks, b. (1994). *Teaching to transgress: Education as the practice of freedom.* Routledge.

Hernández, E. (2016). Utilizing critical race theory to examine race/ethnicity, racism, and power in student development theory and research. *Journal of College Student Development, 57*(2), 168–180. https://doi.org/10.1353/csd.2016.0020

Jones, S. R., & Stewart, D-L. (2016). Evolution of student development theory. In E. S. Abes (Ed.), *Critical perspectives on student development theory* [Special Issue] (New Directions for Student Services, no. 154, pp. 17–28). Wiley. https://doi.org/10.1002/ss.20172

Kimball, E. W., & Ryder, A. J. (2014). Using history to promote reflection: A model for reframing student affairs practice. *Journal of Student Affairs Research and Practice, 51*(3), 298–310. https://doi.org/10.1515/jsarp-2014-0030

Kuh, G. D., Kinzie, J., Buckley, J. A., Bridges, B. K., & Hayek, J. C. (2007). Piecing together the student success puzzle: Research propositions, and recommendation. *ASHE Higher Education Report, 32*(5), 1–182.

London, H. B. (1996, November–December). How college affects first generation students. *About Campus, 1*(5), 9–13. https://doi.org/10.1002/abc.6190010503

Lucas, C. J., & Murry Jr., J. W. (2011). *New faculty: A practical guide for academic beginners* (3rd ed.). Palgrave-Macmillan.

Lumina Foundation (2017, March 2). *Untold barriers for Black students in higher education: Placing race at the center of developmental education.* https://www.lumina foundation.org/resources/barriers-for-black-students-in-higher-ed

Mallinckrodt, B., & Sedlacek, W. E. (1987). Student retention and the use of campus facilities by race. *NASPA Journal, 24*(3), 28–32. https://doi.org/10.1080/00 220973.1987.11072005

McCoy, D. L., & Rodricks, D. J. (2015). Critical race theory in higher education: 20 years of theoretical and research innovations. *ASHE Higher Education Report, 41*(3), 1–117. https://doi.org/10.1002/aehe.20021

Nasir, N. S. (2012). *Racialized identities: Race and achievement among African American youth.* Stanford University Press.

National Center for Education Statistics. (2016). *Advancing diversity and inclusion in higher education: Key data highlights focusing on race and ethnicity and promising practices.* U.S. Department of Education. http://www2.ed.gov/rschstat/research/pubs/advancing-diversity-inclusion.pdf

National Center for Education Statistics. (2017). *Table 1. Public high school 4-year adjusted cohort graduation rate (ACGR), by race/ethnicity and selected demographic characteristics for the United States, the 50 states, and the District of Columbia: School year 2015–16.* Common Core of Data: America's Public Schools. https://nces.ed.gov/ccd/tables/ACGR_RE_and_characteristics_2015-16.asp

National Center for Education Statistics. (2018). *Public high school graduation rates.* https://nces.ed.gov/programs/coe/pdf/coe_coi.pdf

National Student Research Clearinghouse (2017). *Term enrollments.* https://nsc researchcenter.org/current-term-enrollment-estimates-fall-2017/

Newman, P., R., & Newman, B. M. (1999). What does it take to have a positive impact on minority students' college retention? *Adolescence, 34*(135), 483–492.

Ossana, S. M., Helms, J. E., & Leonard, M. M. (1992). Do "womanist" identity attitudes influence college women's self-esteem and perceptions of environmental bias? *Journal of Counseling & Development, 70*(3), 402–408. https://doi.org/10.1002/j.1556-6676.1992.tb01624.x

Pascarella, E. T., Hagedorn, L. S., Whitt, E. J., Yeager, P. M., Edison, M. I., Terenzini, P. T., & Nora, A. (1997). Women's perceptions of a "chilly climate" and their cognitive outcomes during the first year of college. *Journal of College Student Development, 38(2),* 109–124.

Patton, L. D., Renn, K. A., Guido, F. M., & Quaye, S. J. (2016). *Student development in college: Theory, research, and practice.* Jossey Bass.

Perna L. W., & Kurban, E. R. (2013). Improving college access and choice. In L. W. Perna & A. Jones (Eds.), *The state of college access and completion: Improving college success for underrepresented group* (pp. 10–33). Routledge.

Pizzolato, J. E. (2003). Developing self-authorship: Exploring the experiences of high-risk college students. *Journal of College Student Development, 44*(6), 797–812. https://doi.org/10.1353/csd.2003.0074

Pizzolato, J. E., Nguyen, T.-L. K., Johnston, M. P., & Wang, S. (2012). Understanding context: Cultural, relational, psychological interactions in self-authorship development. *Journal of College Student Development, 53*(5), 656–679. https://doi.org/10.1353/csd.2012.0061

Pratt, P. E., & Skaggs, C. T. (1989). First generation college students: Are they at greater risk for attrition than their peers? *Research in Rural Education, 6*(2), 31–34.

Robinson, K. J., & Roksa, J. (2016). Counselors, information and high school college-going culture: Inequalities in the college application process. *Research in Higher Education, 57*(7), 845–868. https://doi.org/10.1007/s11162-016-9406-2

Rodgers, R. F. (1990). Recent theories and research underlying student development. In D. Creamer & Associates (Eds.), *College student development: Theory and practice for the 1990s* (pp. 27–79). American College Personnel Association.

Samel, A. N., Sondergeld, T. A., Fischer, J. M., & Patterson, N. C. (2011). The secondary school pipeline: Longitudinal indicators of resilience and resistance in urban schools under reform. *The High School Journal, 94*(3), 95–118. https://doi.org/10.1353/hsj.2011.0005

Sawyer, K., Salter, N., & Thoroughgood, C. (2013). Studying individual identities is good, but examining intersectionality is better. *Industrial and Organizational Psychology-Perspectives On Science and Practice, 6*(1), 80–84. https://doi.org/10.1111/iops.12012

Sedlacek, W. E. (1987). Black students on White campuses: 20 years of research. *Journal of College Student Personnel, 28*(5), 484–495.

Seemiller, C., & Grace, M. (2016). *Generation Z goes to college.* Jossey-Bass.

Shedd, C. (2015). *Unequal city: Race, schools, and perceptions of injustice.* Russell Sage Foundation.

Stage, F. K. (1989). Motivation, academic and social integration, and the early drop-out. *American Educational Research Journal, 26*(3), 385–402. https://doi.org/10.2307/1162979

Strayhorn, T. (2010). When race and gender collide: Social and cultural capital's influence on the academic achievement of African American and Latino males. *The Review of Higher Education, 33*(3), 307–332. https://doi.org/10.1353/rhe.0.0147

Stewart, D-L. (2013). Racially minoritized students at U.S. four-year institutions. *The Journal of Negro Education, 82*(2), 184–197. https://doi.org/10.7709/jnegroeducation.82.2.0184

Sullivan, T., Mackie, C., Massey, W., & Sinha, E. (2012). *Improving measurement of productivity in higher education.* National Research Council of the National Academies.

Taylor, C. A. (1986). Black students on predominantly White campuses in the 1980s. *Journal of College Student Personnel, 27*(3), 196–202.

Thompson, C. E., Alfred, D. M., Edwards, S. L., & Garcia, P. G. (2006). Transformative endeavors: Implementing Helms's racial identity theory to a school-based heritage project. In R. L. Toporek, L. H. Gerstein, N. A. Nadya, G. Roysircar, & T. Israel (Eds.), *Handbook for social justice in counseling psychology: Leadership, vision, and action.* (pp. 100–116). SAGE.

Tinto, V. (1993). *Leaving college: Rethinking the causes and cures of student attrition* (2nd ed.). University of Chicago Press.

Tomlinson-Clarke, S. M., & Hernández, E. (2019). Using culturally appropriate intervention strategies in practice. In M. Howard-Hamilton & J. Zhang (Eds.), *Multicultural and diversity issues in student affairs practice: A professional competency-based approach* (pp. 189–208). Charles C. Thomas Publisher.

Torres, V., & Hernández, E. (2007). The influence on ethnic identity on self authorship: A longitudinal study of Latino/a college students. *Journal of College Student Development, 48*(5), 558–573. https://doi.org/10.1353/csd.2007.0057

U.S. Census Bureau. (2015, March 3). *New Census Bureau report analyzes U.S. populations projections.* https://www.census.gov/newsroom/press-releases/2015/cb15-tps16.html

PART TWO

ALTERNATIVE FRAMEWORKS AND MODELS FOR AFRICAN AMERICAN COLLEGE STUDENT POPULATIONS

PART TWO

ALTERNATIVE FRAMEWORKS
AND MODELS FOR AFRICAN
AMERICAN COLLEGE
STUDENT POPULATIONS

3

FINDING MY WAY "BLACK"

Resilience Building Afrocentric Identity Theories

Chavez Phelps and Mary F. Howard-Hamilton

There has been a purposeful and systemic process of racial regression in this country. Specifically, there was a time when the country was overtly segregated, and Whites were clear in their disdain for individuals who did not look like them (Spring, 2013). From the 1800s until the late 1960s, the country supported the segregation of racial minorities through the enactment and enforcement of laws that kept them intellectually and economically bankrupt. We then moved into an era of compassionate conservatism, when President Ronald Reagan believed desegregation was a heavy burden on Whites and was a dismal failure (Altenbaugh, 2007). He vilified the poor, racial minorities, and women as unlawful citizens. In a number of his speeches, President Ronald Reagan provided narratives of these individuals who were violent or cheating the welfare system, thus justifying a need for racial discrimination under the guise of "law and order" (Dudas, 2009, p. 159). This verbal dehumanization by the oppressor, according to Freire (2018), is also a form of domination and manipulation which thrusts the oppressed into silence, mutism, and self-deprecation. Educations have systemically engaged in banking education (Freire, 2018) in order to deposit malicious and erroneous information about marginalized people, and students have received and internalized these messages.

Nearly a decade into the 21st century, the country began the Obama years when there was the assumption that the country had become a postracial society. However, Spencer and Swanson (2013) argued that President Obama's election provided a rationale to lessen the influence of color and race as an explanation for the challenges members of particular groups experience. In 2015, for instance, 860 criminal incidents classified as hate crimes occurred on college campuses, of which 40% were racially motivated (NCES, 2019). These data show that the country has reverted to previous patterns, and the current political climate has become a toxic one in which people are now forced into and defending their racial ethnic and cultural tribes against hate crimes. The oppressor is not seeing the oppressed as fully human and is "conquering them—increasingly and by every means, from the toughest to the most refined, from the most repressive to the most solicitous (paternalism)" (Freire, 2018, p. 138).

This *othering* can cause African American college students to feel inferior to their White peers. Therefore, it is crucial that higher education institutions create inclusive environments that value and nurture racial identity development for African Americans to mitigate the feelings of powerlessness (Lige et al., 2017). A continuation of the banking education concept "negates education and knowledge as processes of inquiry" (Freire, 2018, p. 72) and projects an absolute ignorance onto others. Racial identity models that transcend the negative narrative of the oppressor can be the impetus for intellectual and cultural liberation. Further, a positive Black racial identity is associated with greater resilience and better coping with discrimination (Zirkel & Johnson, 2016). Other studies revealed racial identity is also associated with a sense of belongingness with one's group (Ghavami et al., 2011; Hope et al., 2013). Because schools are a critical and unavoidable component of our society, which is rather polarizing at the moment, it is necessary for universities to consider Black identity models and oppression theory as a way to support their African American students. These models can help inoculate African American students against overt and covert forms of racism such as race-related trauma that they may experience on and off campus (Sue, 2010).

Oppression Theory

The framework that helps counselors, administrators, and faculty understand the deep-seated psychic power of oppression is Freire's (2018) *Pedagogy of the Oppressed*. Freire taught illiterate villagers how to read, understand, and challenge the political oppression and tyranny that were suppressing and repressing them. "Because his theory was radical and his methods were effective he was imprisoned then exiled from Brazil for nearly 20 years" (Alschuler, 1986, p. 492). Freire expounded upon the characteristics of the oppressor (i.e., necrophilic, manipulative, and cultural invaders/colonizers) and the structures around us that support their need to dominate and subjugate others (e.g., banking education). Even though there are some educators who believe that their good intentions are supporting oppressed students, they may actually "constitute active collusion in maintaining the oppressive situation" (Alschuler, 1986, p. 492). The oppressed must deconstruct the internalized wheels in the head or the self-deprecating ideals they have been taught and become responsible, loving human beings who can transform the world (Alschuler, 1986). Thus, if educators want to ensure their actions contribute to the liberation of their Black college students, it will require they engage in self-reflection and introspection, even if it is uncomfortable. Alschuler's (1986) three-stage developmental response to oppression might provide White educators with a lens to process their mindset and possible internal angst as the oppressor who wants to transcend such a position in this society. Individuals move through the developmental responses to an oppression model (Alschuler, 1986).

Black students have been developmentally challenged in each of the three stages presented by Alschuler because of systemic socialization, banking education, and conforming to norms that are biased and oppressive. Specifically, when playing host to the system in stages 1 and 2, the passive magical conforming individual arrives on campus and is comfortable with most students on campus who are similar in thought and beliefs. There is no need to "rock the boat" because you cannot change the system. "This inaction is a form of passive collusion to maintain oppressive situations" (Alschuler, 1986, p. 493). Playing host to the system continues in stage 2, naïve reforming, as the minoritized students are starting to engage in a reality check that something is wrong with themselves or with others. Students do not seek help with a difficult science course because they were successful in high school studying minimally. They tend to think along the following lines (Alschuler, 1986): "My first grade was a 'D,' and it must be the fault of the professor. So how can I improve myself or change others?" The third stage, critical transforming, finds the Black student attempting to change the system and exercising "their critical intellectual skills in naming the crucial rules and roles of the system that create unequal power, place people in conflict, and exploit, oppress, or hinder their responsible human development" (Alschuler, 1986, p. 493). It is in this state that the Black students become actively engaged in organizing others to change the policies, procedures, and systemic issues that impede the progress of minoritized students on campus. This may be in the form of a hunger strike, student protest, or petition that is presented to the academic leaders on campus. Understanding the developmental juncture of Black students from a Freireian lens can lead to problem-solving and growth within a culturally sensitive and supportive framework.

Racial Identity and Afrocentric Theories

Kambon and Bowen-Reid (2010) described Afrocentric theories as encompassing a proactive motivation style, strength based, and a positive adaptation of behavior and functioning standard of referent. One theory that needs to be revisited is Baldwin's Africentric model of Black personality. His theory suggests that a cultural misorientation could lead to racial disempowerment as well as mental health problems (Belgrave & Allison, 2006). The core system is named the African self-extension orientation and African self-consciousness with a number of basic traits such as collective survival thrust and self-reinforcing–enhancing beliefs, attitudes, values, and behaviors. A major tenet of the theory is that we strive for security and survival (Baldwin, 1984), so there is an acknowledgment of the harmful nature of racial oppression and a need to resist it actively (Constantine et al., 1998).

The African self-extension orientation is an innate, unconscious system that encapsulates spirituality, allowing one to have lived experiences; the African self-consciousness is the conscious manifestation of the African self-extension orientation (Baldwin, 1984). Baldwin proposed that African self-consciousness can be influenced by socialization experiences and institutional processes such as those purposed and upheld by universities can either promote or impede the Black personality system (Cokley & Garba, 2018). Thus, the Black personality can achieve full expression of basic traits such as attitudes, beliefs, and values when it is fully supported (Parham et al., 2000).

Linda Myers (1993) developed another relevant theory, optimal psychology, which suggests that self-knowledge is the root of all knowledge, and human and spiritual networks offer an avenue through which we can achieve our goals. A quote from President Obama's famous address after the Iowa Caucus embodies the essence of this theory, which is:

> Hope is not blind optimism. It's not ignoring the enormity of the task ahead or the roadblocks that stand in our path. It's not sitting on the sidelines or shirking from a fight. Hope is that thing inside us that insists, despite all evidence to the contrary, that something better awaits us if we have the courage to reach for it, and to work for it, and to fight for it. Hope is the belief that destiny will not be written for us, but by us, by the men and women who are not content to settle for the world as it is, who have the courage to remake the world as it should be. (Obama, 2008)

There is an account of the multigenerational psychological trauma and its effects on not only African Americans but also all of humanity (Myers & Speight, 2010). It is proposed that optimal functioning produces peace and harmony, but suboptimal functioning is grounded in competition, which produces racism, sexism, and classism. (Constantine et al., 1998). According to Myers (1993), a suboptimal conceptual system can double oppression for minorities because they are not only subjected to the various "isms" from the oppressor but also may buy into this worldview, creating a sense of inferiority. Myers's theory urges us to seek social justice for all oppressed groups and to value human diversity (Belgrave & Allison, 2006), which is a sentiment expressed in most universities' missions and visions. Researchers have reported that adding racial identity development to academic-based service learning can lead to a greater interest in working with culturally diverse students and an in-depth understanding of societal injustices (Simons et al., 2011). Thus, universities must be willing to examine how their written and unwritten policies and practices promote or impede equity for not only their African American students but also all of their marginalized students.

Furthering the Afrocentric paradigm discussion, there are two theories that could provide a foundation for a healthy Black self-image coupled with the components to develop resistance to toxic environments (Robinson & Howard-Hamilton, 1994). The Nguzo Saba value system (Karenga, 1980) and resistance modality model (Robinson & Ward, 1991) can be used to promote interpersonal growth. Direction and meaning could occur when using the seven Nguzo Saba principles of Umoja (unity), Kujichagulia (self-determination), Ujima (collective work and responsibility), Ujaama (cooperative economics), Nia (purpose), Kuumba (creativity), and Imani (faith) (Karenga, 1980; Robinson & Howard-Hamilton, 1994). These principles are further explored in Appendix 3A.

Resistance can be interpreted as negative or positive (Robinson & Howard-Hamilton, 1994). Specifically, negative resistance is exhibited behaviorally when an oppressive force is attempting to thwart the positive development of an individual, and that person must use an inordinate amount of emotional energy to survive the opposition.

> The unhealthy form of resistance represents dysfunctional and short-term adaptations to an oppressive environment, an environment that contributes to chronic feelings of powerlessness within the person, and this sense of powerlessness often permeates the entire community and is not the isolated experience of one person. In this case, self-determination is not a primary factor because the person's self-image is largely shaped and defined by external and economic forces that have their roots in racist ideology. (Robinson & Howard-Hamilton, 1994, p. 328)

Healthy resistance is "empowering and liberating" (Robinson & Howard-Hamilton, 1994, p. 327). Moreover, Robinson and Howard-Hamilton (1994) state that "it is characterized by an individual's ability to avoid internalizing negative and societal messages that can foster unhealthy self-images and self-depreciatory behaviors" (p. 328). The healthy self-image is nurtured and developed when Black individuals have been taught accurate historical, cultural, and racial connections to an Afrocentric perspective as opposed to a Eurocentric frame of reference (Robinson & Ward, 1991).

The Afrocentric perspectives of Nguzo Saba and the resistance model can intersect to "initiate and promote psychological health and satisfying interpersonal relationships within and between cultures for African Americans" (Robinson & Howard-Hamilton, 1994, p. 332). Umoja, or unity, emphasizes the importance of a close-knit community. "Conversely, based on the resistance modality schema, the unhealthy individual is isolated from other African Americans" (Robinson & Howard-Hamilton, 1994, p. 332). That is why it takes a village to support each other and be engaged with the sculpting of a healthy identity based on cultural norms.

Survival in today's society is contingent on resisting the negative and stereotypical images portrayed in the media, which is one of the great socializers (Robinson & Howard-Hamilton, 1994). Debunking these negative depictions of the Black community requires self-determination or Kujichagulia. "Persons who are self-determined define themselves in terms of their subjective knowledge base" (Robinson & Howard-Hamilton, 1994, p. 333). The third Nguzo Saba principle is Ujima or collective work and responsibility (Karenga, 1998). "To build and maintain our community together and make our brother's and sister's problems our problems and to solve them together" (Karenga, 1998, p. 7). The dominant society has indoctrinated individuals to be independent, self-sufficient, and self-centered. However, collective or community efforts move everyone forward and leave no one behind. This mindset requires that the Black community speaks from a "we" or "us" frame of reference and resists the individualistic narrative of the dominant culture.

If the community works together it must then pool the resources or engage in Ujaama or cooperative economics (Karenga, 1998). The Black community should support the stores, organizations, and other businesses owned by minoritized people. There is competition and there are challenges with this concept, because we live in a society that can find the best bargain online. Thus the Black retailer in the community cannot compete with the businesses that have millions of customers. The resiliency that must ensue is an understanding that successful business role models in the community can raise the self-efficacy of the individuals growing up in that neighborhood. Long-term gains could ensue if there is patience and willingness to pay a little more for the greater good. This concept leads into the principle of Nia which is purpose or "to make our vocation the building and developing of our community in order to restore our people to their original greatness" (Karenga,

1998, p. 7). The resistance modality connected to this principle is to learn from other resistors who engage in a delayed gratification process in order to uplift and support others.

Overall, having a creative and innovative mind is referred to as Kuumba (Karenga, 1998). It is the resilient person who seeks to transform the world and not conform to it. This creative spirit allows the individual to think outside of the box and enhance what has already been done (Robinson & Howard-Hamilton, 1994). Last, to move all of these principles in a positive direction the resistors must have faith or Imani (Karenga, 1998; Robinson & Howard-Hamilton, 1994). Having faith means embracing the past, present, and future because the Afrocentric resistor is cognizant of the sacrifices made by the ancestors in order to pave the way for future generations. An African symbol that models the principle of Imani is the sankofa bird. The sankofa bird, depicted as having its feet facing forward and the head looking to the rear, symbolizes the importance of never forgetting the past and retrieving that knowledge for personal and purposeful grounding (Karenga, 1998).

Implications for Higher Education

The mental health and wellness for African American students must be addressed due to the overwhelming social media overload of racial trauma and violence. Universities must be willing to acknowledge and validate that experiences of racism can be traumatizing for Black students. Carter (2007) reported that Black students are exposed to racial hostility at higher rates than any other ethnic minority group on college campuses, and there is strong evidence that racial discrimination is stressful and correlated with psychological disorders and poor psychosocial well-being. In particular, Black male students often feel overly policed in college campuses, which can lead to feelings of anger, disgust, distress, fear, and hopelessness (Smith et al., 2007). Often, the racial experiences that Black students endure manifest themselves in forms of microaggressions, which are subtle forms of racial discrimination that can negatively impact an individual's self-concept and mental well-being (Liu et al., 2019; Nadal et al., 2017; Sue et al., 2019).

Johnson (2001) proffered that "attempts to apply Afrocentricity to the development of African American college students will most likely meet the same type of opposition that has been met in applying it to other areas in higher education" (p. 420). The negative reaction to race-specific paradigms is that they are exclusionary and separatist and give rise to a racial binary that is Black or White. However, as Johnson states, "Afrocentrism is a means to include, and not continue to exclude, the values of other cultures from theory and practice in higher education administration" (p. 420). Higher education institutions must acknowledge racial identity development as a dynamic process that has long-lasting effects on African American college students' functioning across the lifespan (Yip et al., 2006). We must remember that dynamic process can be embedded in intersectionality for many students. For instance, the lived experiences of traumatic stress for a Black student who identifies as part of the LGBTQ+ community can be different than that of a cisgender heterosexual Black woman.

Herman (2008) indicated that when individuals who have endure trauma are silenced, it can worsen the manifestation of the traumatic stress. Thus, one way universities can support Black students who are organizing is to not prevent or oppress any of their attempts to challenge institutional and societal inequalities or inequities (Leath & Chavous, 2017). McGee and Stovall (2015) argued that Black students' civic engagement to address community or university problems is a part of radical healing that protects their self-concept and healthy development. There are a number of other microinterventions that colleges and universities can implement and support.

Whittaker and Neville (2010) recommended that university counseling centers and student affairs personnel advocate for a multiculturalist orientation and help resist racial self-hatred and rigid thinking about race through support groups for African American students. These support groups can help students develop a high sense of racial centrality, which can serve as a buffer against racial discrimination (Sellers et al., 2003). Further, researchers have indicated the following counseling recommendations relative to racial identity: (a) build African American students' self-esteem while diminishing a sense of the imposter syndrome, (b) challenge cognitive distortions about themselves or their abilities; and (c) utilize an identity measurement and culturally bounded interview protocols during the initial contact with African American students (McClain et al., 2016). It has been suggested that student affairs practitioners and mental health staff help ethnic minorities develop the coping skills to deal with discrimination such as microaggressions, which can negatively impair their identity and self-esteem (Nadal et al., 2017). In addition, Banks (2010) indicated that if student development personnel can help African American students adjust to typical college stressors it can help minimize the relationship between racial discrimination and depressive symptoms.

Finally, there is a resurgence of Afrocentric movies, clothing, hair styles, and mantras such as Black Lives Matter, I Can't Breathe, and Wakanda Forever that are positive indications of a demonstrated need to move away from a melting pot societal framework. These practices and mantras help

Black students regain a sense of humanity and reject the myth of Black inferiority (Barlow, 2018). In addition, for Black students these occurrences represent what their realities could and should look like in the 21st century. Kelley (2018) stated it best:

> These students are demonstrating how we might remake the world. They are ruthless in their criticism and fearless in the face of the powers that be. They model what it means to think through crisis, to fight for the eradication of oppression in all its forms, whether it directly affects us or not. They are *in* the university but not *of* the university. They work to understand and advance the movements in the streets, seeking to eliminate racism and state violence, preserve black life, defend the rights of the marginalized (from undocumented immigrants to transfolk), and challenge the current order that has brought us so much misery. And they do this work not without criticism and self-criticism, not by pandering to popular trends or powerful people, a cult of celebrity or Twitter, and not by telling lies, claiming easy answers, or avoiding the ideas that challenge us all. (p. 167)

Additional practices to enhance critical consciousness that could empower African American students who are traveling to an African country, learning an African language, reading Afrocentric literature, enrolling in an African diaspora studies course, and journaling or blogging the day-to-day experiences of becoming college educated for future publication.

Conclusion

Freire (2018) refers to the importance of developing a critical consciousness in order for the oppressed "to take action against the oppressive elements of reality" (p. 35). This intellectual exercise means that a transformation must take place to eject negative images of oneself and replace them with an empowering ideology. There can no longer be a "fear of freedom" (Freire, 2018, p. 36) in which the oppressed remain comfortable with what they have been taught about themselves, personally and culturally. "Black racial identity is pervasive and robust. Moreover, this has always been so and is not a recent development" (Zirkel & Johnson, 2016, p. 307). As administrators, educators, and counselors in higher education we must internalize, embrace, and implement the models delineated in this chapter so that the oppressed can be bound to an empowering reality (Freire, 2018). This reality could lead to boldness, cultural action, courage to love, and faith.

APPENDIX 3A
Resistance Modality: Two Orientations

Liberation/Empowerment	Survival/Oppression
Unity with African people that transcends age, socioeconomic status, geographic origin, and sexual orientation (Umoja)	Isolation, disconnectedness from the larger African American community
Self-determination through confrontation and repudiation of oppressive attempts to demean self; new models used to make active decisions that empower and affirm oneself and one's racial identity (Kujichagalia)	Self is defined by others (i.e., media, educational system) in a manner that oppresses and devalues "Blackness"
Collective work and responsibility where the self is seen in connection with the larger body of African people, sharing a common destiny of meaningful struggle (Ujima)	Excessive individualism and autonomy, racelessness
Cooperative economics advocates a sharing of resources through the convergence of the "I" and the "we" (Ujaama)	"I got mine, you get yours," attitude
Purpose in life that benefits the self and the collective, endorse delaying gratification as a tool in resistance (Nia)	Immediate gratification to escape life's harsh realities, the use of quick fixes to combat meaninglessness in life
Creativity through building new paradigms for the community, through dialogue with other resistors (Kuumba)	Maintaining the status quo, replicating existing models although they may be irrelevant
Faith through an intergenerational perspective in which knowledge of history of Africa and other resistors and care for future generations give meaning to struggle and continued resistance (Imani)	Emphasis on the here and now, not looking forward, myopic vision

Note. From Robinson, T. L., & Ward, J. V. (1991). A belief in self far greater than anyone's disbelief: Cultivating resistance among African American adolescents. *Women and Therapy, 11*, 87–103. https://doi.org/10.1300/J015V11N03_06. Reprinted with permission.

References

Alschuler, A. S. (1986). Creating a world where it is easier to love: Counseling applications of Paulo Freire's theory. *Journal of Counseling & Development, 64*(8), 492–496.

Altenbaugh, R. J. (2007). Liberation and frustration: Fifty years after *Brown*. *History of Education Quarterly, 44*(1), 1–9. https://doi.org/10.1111/j.1748-5959.2004.tb00142.x

Baldwin, J. A. (1984). African self-consciousness and the mental health of African-Americans. *Journal of Black Studies, 15*(2), 177–194.

Banks, K. H. (2010). African American college students' experience of racial discrimination and the role of college hassles. *Journal of College Student Development, 51*(1), 23–34. https://doi.org/10.1353/csd.0.0115

Barlow, J. N. (2018). Restoring optimal black mental health and reversing intergenerational trauma in an era of black lives matter. *Biography, 41*(4), 895–908. https://doi.org/10.1353/bio.2018.0084

Belgrave, F. Z., & Allison, K. W. (2006). *African American psychology: From Africa to America*. SAGE.

Carter, R. T. (2007). Racism and psychological and emotional injury: Recognizing and assessing race-based traumatic stress. *The Counseling Psychologist, 35*(1), 13–105. https://doi.org/10.1177/0011000006292033

Constantine, M. G., Richardson, T. Q., Benjamin, E. M., & Wilson, J. W. (1998). An overview of Black racial identity theories: Limitations and considerations for future theoretical conceptualizations. *Applied and Preventive Psychology, 7*(2), 95–99.

Cokley, K., & Garba, R. (2018). Speaking truth to power: How Black/African psychology changed the discipline of psychology. *Journal of Black Psychology, 44*(8), 695–721. https://doi.org/10.1177/0095798418810592

Dudas, J. R. (2009). Little monsters, wild animals, and welfare queens: Ronald Reagan and the legal constitution of American politics. In A. Sarat (Ed.), *Studies in law, politics, and society* (pp. 157–210). Emerald Publishing.

Ghavami, N., Fingerhut, A., Peplau, L. A., Grant, S. K., & Wittig, M. A. (2011). Testing a model of minority identity achievement, identity affirmation, and psychological well-being among ethnic minority and sexual minority individuals. *Cultural Diversity and Ethnic Minority Psychology, 17*(1), 79–88. https://doi.org/10.1037/a0022532

Freire, P. (2018). *Pedagogy of the oppressed: 50th anniversary edition*. Bloomsbury Academic.

Herman, J. (2008). Classics revisited, commentary. *Women's Studies Quarterly, 36*(1/2), 282–284. https://doi.org/10.1353/wsq.0.0030

Hope, E. C., Chavous, T. M., Jagers, R. J., & Sellers, R. M. (2013). Connecting self-esteem and achievement: Diversity in academic identification and disidentification patterns among Black college students. *American Educational Research Journal, 50*(5), 1122–1151. https://doi.org/10.3102/0002831213500333

Johnson, V. D. (2001). The Nguzo Saba as a foundation for African American college student development theory. *Journal of Black Studies, 31*(4), 406–422.

Karenga, M. (1980). *Kawaida theory: An introductory outline.* Kawaida Publications.

Karenga, M. (1998). *Kwanzaa: A celebration of family, community, and culture.* Sankore Press.

Kambon, K. K. K., & Bowen-Reid, T. (2010). Theories of African American personality classification, basic constructs and empirical predictions/assessment. *The Journal of Pan African Studies, 4*(8), 83–107.

Kelley, R. D. G. (2018). Black study, Black struggle. *Ufahamu: A Journal of African Studies, 40*(2), 153–167. https://escholarship.org/uc/item/8cj8q196.

Leath, S., & Chavous, T. (2017). "We really protested": The influence of sociopolitical beliefs, political self-efficacy, and campus racial climate on civic engagement among black college students attending predominantly white institutions. *The Journal of Negro Education, 86*(3), 220–237. https://doi.org/10.7709/jnegro education.86.3.0220

Lige, Q. M., Peteet, B. J., & Brown, C. M. (2017). Racial identity, self-esteem, and the imposter phenomenon among African American college students. *Journal of Black Psychology, 43*(4), 345–357. https://doi.org/10.1177/0095798416648787

Liu, W. M., Liu, R. Z., Garrison, Y. L., Kim, J. Y. C., Chan, L., Ho, Y. C. S., & Yeung, C. W. (2019). Racial trauma, microaggressions, and becoming racially innocuous: The role of acculturation and White supremacist ideology. *American Psychologist, 74*(1), 143–155. https://doi.org/10.1037/amp0000368

McClain, S., Beasley, S. T., Jones, B., Awosogba, O., Jackson, S., & Cokley, K. (2016). An examination of the impact of racial and ethnic identity, impostor feelings, and minority status stress on the mental health of Black college students. *Journal of Multicultural Counseling and Development, 44*(2), 101–117. https://doi.org/10.1002/jmcd.12040

McGee, E. O., & Stovall, D. (2015). Reimagining critical race theory in education: Mental health, healing, and the pathway to liberatory praxis. *Educational Theory, 65*(5), 491–511. https://doi.org/10.1111/edth.12129

Myers, L. J. (1993). *Understanding an Afrocentric world view: Introduction to an optimal psychology.* Kendall/Hunt Publishing Co.

Myers, L. J., & Speight, S. L. (2010). Reframing mental health and psychological well-being among persons of African descent: Africana/Black psychology meeting the challenges of fractured social and cultural realities. *The Journal of Pan African Studies, 3*(8), 66–82.

Nadal, K. L., Griffin, K. E., Wong, Y., Davidoff, K. C., & Davis, L. S. (2017). The injurious relationship between racial microaggressions and physical health: Implications for social work. *Journal of Ethnic & Cultural Diversity in Social Work, 26*(1-2), 6–17. https://doi.org/10.1080/15313204.2016.1263813

National Center for Education Statistics. (2019). *Indicator 22: hate crime incidents for postsecondary institutions.* https://nces.ed.gov/programs/crimeindicators/ind_22.asp

Obama, B. (2008, January 3). Barack Obama's caucus speech. *New York Times.* https://www.nytimes.com/2008/01/03/us/politics/03obama-transcript.html

Parham, T. A., White, J. L., & Ajamu, A. (2000). *The psychology of blacks: An African-centered perspective* (3rd ed.). Prentice Hall.

Robinson, T. L., & Howard-Hamilton, M. F. (1994). An Afrocentric paradigm: Foundation for a healthy self-image and healthy interpersonal relationships. *Journal of Mental Health Counseling, 16*(3), 327–339.

Robinson, T. L., & Ward, J. V. (1991). A belief in self far greater than anyone's disbelief: Cultivating resistance among African American adolescents. *Women and Therapy, 11*, 87–103. https://doi.org/10.1300/J015V11N03_06

Sellers, R. M., Caldwell, C. H., Schmeelk-Cone, K. H., & Zimmerman, M. A. (2003). Racial identity, racial discrimination, perceived stress, and psychological distress among African American young adults. *Journal of Health and Social Behavior, 44*(3), 302–317. https://doi.org/10.2307/1519781

Simons, L., Fehr, L., Black, N., Hogerwerff, F., Georganas, D., & Russell, B. (2011). The application of racial identity development in academic-based service learning. *International Journal of Teaching and Learning in Higher Education, 23*(1), 72–83.

Smith, W. A., Allen, W. R., & Danley, L. L. (2007). Assume the position . . . You fit the description: Psychosocial experiences and racial battle fatigue among African American male college students. *American Behavioral Scientist, 51*(4), 551–578. https://doi.org/10.1177/0002764207307742

Spencer, M. B., & Swanson, D. P. (2013). Opportunities and challenges to the development of healthy children and youth living in diverse communities. *Development and Psychopathology, 25*(4), 1551–1566. https://doi.org/10.1017/S095457941300076X

Spring, J. (2013). *Deculturalization and the struggle for equality: A brief history of the education of dominated cultures in the United States* (7th ed.). McGraw Hill.

Sue, D. W. (2010). *Microaggressions in everyday life: Race, gender, and sexual orientation.* John Wiley & Sons, Inc.

Sue, D. W., Alsaidi, S., Awad, M. N., Glaeser, E., Calle, C. Z., & Mendez, N. (2019). Disarming racial microaggressions: Microintervention strategies for targets, White allies, and bystanders. *American Psychologist, 74*(1), 128–142. https://doi.org/10.1037/amp0000296

Whittaker, V. A., & Neville, H. A. (2010). Examining the relation between racial identity attitude clusters and psychological health outcomes in African American college students. *Journal of Black Psychology, 36*(4), 383–409. https://doi.org/10.1177/0095798409353757

Yip, T., Seaton, E. K., & Sellers, R. M. (2006). African American racial identity across the lifespan: Identity status, identity content, and depressive symptoms. *Child Development, 77*(5), 1504–1517. https://doi.org/10.1111/j.1467-8624.2006.00950.x

Zirkel, S., & Johnson, T. (2016). Mirror, mirror on the wall: A critical examination of the conceptualization of the study of black racial identity in education. *Educational Researcher, 45*(5), 301–311. https://doi.org/10.3102/0013189X16656938

4

FINDING OUR WAY "BLACK" TO STUDENT DEVELOPMENT THEORY

Richard J. Reddick, Mariama N. Nagbe, Saralyn M. McKinnon-Crowley, G. Christopher Cutkelvin, and Howard A. Thrasher

Early scholars such as Chickering (1969) first conceptualized the area of student development theory in the late 1950s and 1960s, but scholars have pondered the college experience and its impact of students since the advent of higher education. These early conceptualizations, unsurprisingly, focused predominantly on young White men; indeed, Chickering's pioneering work appeared at the dawn of the integration of predominantly White institutions (PWIs). Hence, the development of Black students has come to the attention of researchers relatively recently, with researchers such as Tatum (2017), Cokley (2000), Harper and Quaye (2007), Harris (2010), Patton (2006), and Strayhorn (2015) investigating how Black students navigate postsecondary experiences.

In this chapter, we pose the question: How are student affairs professionals and faculty understanding the Black collegian's experience, specifically in the late 2010s? The question and timing are particularly significant, given the rapid demographic changes that have increased the college-aged population of people of color, including Black Americans, juxtaposed with a political and cultural climate that presents challenges and opportunities to Black collegians. A panoply of new considerations, specifically those focused on developmental models, mental health, contemporary issues, student organizing, and institutional support, will help us find our way "Black" to student development theory.

Then and Now: Analytical Comparisons of Black Student Development Models

In traditional research on college student development, scholars synthesized these models into five clusters of theoretical silos: psychosocial, cognitive developmental, maturity, typology, and person–environment interaction (Knefelkamp et al., 1978). Extending this critique on theoretical clustering, Baxter Magolda (2009) offered an integrative perspective "for student development theory based on contemporary research that takes a holistic approach" (p. 622). This proposed holistic approach to student development theory focuses on threads of college students' meaning-making across these clusters, arguing that while "research on particular dimensions of development is important, grounding it in a more holistic perspective that incorporates social context, epistemological, intrapersonal, and interpersonal developmental dimensions would contribute to creating more holistic theories" (Baxter Magolda, 2009, p. 633). While the point raised by these scholars about developing the whole student is notable, many traditional theories on student development are problematic in leaving out crucial elements such as race and ethnicity; gender; class; or, even more important, their intersections in shaping our understanding of college student experiences.

Just as these theories attempt to silo individual developmental dimensions of the whole student, student affairs professionals and faculty may apply these theories in similar monolithic, or one-size-fits-all, ways. Particularly among Black collegians, this monolithic application of student development theories is troublesome, as many of these models were constructed by studies based on a dominant prototype of White, traditional-aged, and middle-class college students. Additionally, Black collegians are often perceived solely within a vacuum encompassed by their college experience. In actuality, Black collegians are situated in a broader life experience that includes college. Our literature warrants a need to understand the uniqueness and complexity of finding our way "Black" to student development theory, and we also need to complicate how we position the college experience for Black collegians in an ecological context.

Bronfenbrenner (1979) proposed the ecological systems theory which identifies how a person's development is shaped by their social environment from five different levels: the microsystem, mesosystem, exosystem, macrosystem, and chronosystem. This ecological framework is a useful tool to make sense of college students' experiences and outcomes, especially given our focus on Black collegians and the sociopolitical environments they navigate at PWIs. In capturing this narrative, the following sections explore how student affairs professionals and faculty should approach understanding the

Black collegian's experience through three objectives: (a) analyzing theoretical models from the late 1990s, (b) comparing those models with more contemporary perspectives in the late 2010s, and (c) positioning Black student development as an institutional imperative.

Black Student Development in the 1990s

Two components of Black collegian experiences and development are characterized by students' race/ethnicity and academic ability. Dating back to the late 1990s, two foundational studies in the literature on Black student development explored this topic qualitatively using racial identity development (Tatum, 2017) and quantitatively using academic self-concept (Cokley, 2000). Each study's theoretical framework, findings, and implications are discussed next.

Tatum (2017) referenced William Cross's model of the "psychology of nigrescence" (p. 55) to codify the five stages of racial identity development for Black individuals in educational and noneducational settings, stemming from adolescence into adulthood. These five stages include "pre-encounter, encounter, immersion/emersion, internalization, and internalization-commitment" (Tatum, 2017, p. 55). Tatum (2017) used the stages of this framework to argue against the perception of self-segregation among Black students and adults as unproductive by offering up a counterperspective, viewing their assemblage as a "developmental process in response to an environmental stressor, racism" (p. 62). Racial grouping in educational contexts provides safe spaces for Black students to make meaning of, own, and operationalize their racial identity in a society that systemically devalues their Blackness. Cokley (2000) compared Black students attending historically Black colleges and universities (HBCUs) and their counterparts at PWIs to identify the best predictors of academic self-concept. Cokley defined *academic self-concept* as a process regarding "how a student views his or her academic ability when compared with other students" (p. 149). For Black students attending PWIs, Cokley found that the "quality of student-faculty relationships appears to be an important variable that affects a student's academic self-concept" (p. 163).

The interplay between these two studies is helpful for providing a perspective of the varying processes and key factors that shape how Black collegians understand their own racial identities and academic abilities. Comparing the timeframe when both studies were published to the advances in theorizing the complex and overlapping ways to examine Black student development in the 2010s era, we can build on the foundation set by Tatum (2017) and Cokley (2000). Several examples for doing so include fully addressing the

ecological contexts, holistic or intersectional identities, and numerous institutional stakeholders that shape the experiences and development of Black
collegians. Grappling with ecological realities of Black collegians at PWIs,
Tatum (2017) pinpointed how these students "must cope with ongoing
affronts to their racial identity" (p. 78). She also highlighted the reality that
White students and faculty tend to underestimate the overt and covert mani-
festations of racism that exist on their college campuses.

Alongside this recognition, Tatum (2017) noted some gender differences
concerning how young Black women are charged with "resisting . . . stereotypes and affirming other definitions of themselves . . . in both White and
Black communities" (p. 57), while global perceptions of young Black men are
depicted by "violen[ce] . . . suspic[ion] and fear" (p. 58). These gender differences indicate the need for student affairs professionals, faculty, researchers,
policy advocates, and other practitioners to further investigate the variability
of and intersectionality between aspects of Black identity development and
experiences beyond their race/ethnicity. Additionally, Tatum (2017) referred to
classrooms, dining halls, and student organizations as environmental sites that
foster Black collegians' developmental processes and experiences. Considering
how this environmental context extends beyond the confines of campus locations helps us recognize that Black collegians are in contact with broader systemic, social, and political realities within, and outside of, their institutions.

Cokley (2000) mentioned the low number of Black faculty at PWIs and
noted that Black students "need to have interpersonal skills to develop good
relationships with White and other non-Black faculty members" (p. 163).
This skill development around relationship-building is facilitated by several
influential stakeholders that Black collegians connect with during their time
on and off campus. To further Cokley's (2000) proposition that psychologists
should help develop and nurture these faculty–student relationships among
Black collegians, we must also consider the integral role student affairs, faculty, and other higher educational professionals play in this process. Building
on the important work of Tatum and Cokley more than 2 decades later, we
find an emergence of scholars reimagining theoretical concepts about the
development and experiences of Black collegians.

Black Student Development in the 2010s

Strayhorn (2015) posited that Bronfenbrenner's ecological systems theory
helps us grasp "the multiple external influences that shape students' social
interactions and responses to social stimuli" (p. 38). Reflecting on the cycli-
cal and developmental stages of defining her own Blackness throughout life,
Tatum (2017) conceded that despite generational differences between her

and current Black collegians "the process for racial identity development is the same" (p. 77). This demonstrates that as times change, so will the ecological context that Black collegians face. Consequently, student affairs professionals and faculty must also grow their understanding of and support around Black collegians' development and their experiences within the realities of today.

Within a study investigating the success of Black students at PWIs, Davis et al. (2004) challenged prior research on its failure to obtain the narratives from Black collegians themselves, relying instead on "structured questionnaires to measure variables preselected by researchers" (p. 423). This is an important perspective to utilize within quantitative approaches to this topic, as researchers must properly formulate questions that inform research and practice based on primary narratives from Black collegians. Additionally, listening to Black collegians' self-description of their experience positions student affairs professionals and faculty to be critical consumers and producers of knowledge surrounding Black student development theory in ways that closely align with the realities that Black collegians face.

Harper and Quaye (2007) found that Black male collegians involved in Black student organizations strengthened their skill acquisition in leadership and cross-cultural learning. Notably, these advantages spread across other intersectional identities such as gender, sexuality, and spirituality among the psychosocial development and achievement of Black collegians (Harris, 2010). This magnifies how Black student organizations facilitate the fifth stage of Cross's psychology of nigrescence, internalization-commitment, where an individual unapologetically embraces their Blackness and is engaged in meaningful cross-racial interactions (Tatum, 2017). Therefore, it would be advantageous for student affairs professionals, faculty, researchers, and policy advocates to familiarize themselves with various campus organizations with which to connect Black collegians, in addition to offering insight on how membership in these students groups will further Black collegians' development and campus integration. Listening to the concerns and needs expressed by Black collegians regarding their campus experiences will enhance the abilities of student affairs professionals and faculty to be intentional in knowing which type of student organizations to suggest.

Black Student Development as an Institutional Imperative

Meeting Black collegians at a deeper level of developmental and experiential understanding, per Strayhorn (2015), enables higher education institutions to learn students' context-specific experiences "to know them better, to forecast their responses, and predict their decisions under certain conditions, at certain times, and with certain currents pushing them in any number of directions" (Strayhorn, 2015, p. 37). In this respect, colleges and universities, particularly PWIs, must position the development and support of Black collegians as an institutional imperative. The onus of responsibility should not be placed solely on Black collegians to develop themselves, and neither should student affairs professionals and faculty approach these developmental efforts and support in monolithic ways.

A powerful tool for praxis entails grounding institutional efforts using Black student development theories while simultaneously becoming well-versed in the nuances within Black identities. Patton (2006) combined critical race theory, psychological nigrescence, and an interactionalist paradigm, to frame her study on Black collegian perspectives on Black cultural centers (BCCs) at PWIs. Black collegians in her study praised the usefulness of BCCs in meeting their needs academically, as a social safe haven, in providing resources, and as student-run organizational support. Patton (2006) concluded that "these factors provide a context for students to learn about themselves and feel appreciated and supported at PWIs" (p. 644). Despite the variability of institutional types and resources, Patton's work, along with the implications provided by other scholars, exemplies how student affairs professionals, faculty, policy advocates, and our higher education system writ large can successfully position finding our way "Black" to student development as an institutional imperative.

Mental Health of Black Collegians

Since the early 2000s, institutions of higher education have recognized a growing need for increased resources to treat the mental health needs of their students (McClain et al., 2016; Wilson, 2015). Student affairs professionals are also increasingly attuned to the mental as well as the intellectual and social needs of the students they serve. In addition, students have increased their use of mental health resources on college campuses. Though it is difficult to determine whether students are accessing mental health resources more frequently because of increased awareness or because there is in fact a greater frequency of mental health incidents, the *Chronicle of Higher Education* has described college campuses as experiencing a "mental health crisis" (Turnage, 2017). Black collegians are not immune to this perceived crisis. The research on the Black collegians' mental health does not tell a happy story.

Some Black collegians experience the *impostor phenomenon*, defined by Bernard et al. (2017) as the "feeling of intellectual incompetence experienced by some high achieving individuals" (p. 156) who, regardless of their educational attainment and success in other endeavors, do not attribute success to their own merits. Rather, despite evidence to the contrary, students experiencing the impostor phenomenon assume that they are not qualified or worthy to achieve success; any such success must be an accident or luck (Bernard et al., 2017; Cokley et al., 2013; Cokley et al., 2017; McClain et al., 2016). Psychological burdens from the impostor phenomenon and any form of discrimination are taxing both mentally and physically. As King (2005) writes, "Discrimination is bad for your health" (p. 202). In this section, we will explore aspects of Black collegians' mental health, focusing on racial battle fatigue and stereotype threat, and we will suggest possible interventions that institutions of higher education can implement to help.

Racial Battle Fatigue

Institutions of higher education are not often stress-free zones for Black collegians. Black collegians, especially those who attend PWIs, may suffer from "minority status stress" (McClain et al., 2016, p. 102) due to experiencing racism and a concomitant perception of nonbelonging on college campuses (Cokley et al., 2013; Cokley et al., 2017). Feelings of isolation are common for Black students attending PWIs (Brittian et al., 2009). One study found that Black collegians are more likely than their White peers to feel that their college experience is unsatisfactory and consider transferring to different institutions (JED Foundation & The Steve Fund, 2015).

In environments like PWIs, in which Black men collegians are under near-constant threat from microaggressions and assumptions that they are violent and do not belong in campus spaces, Smith et al.'s (2007) research found that Black men collegians could experience "racial battle fatigue" (p. 552) and opt out of constantly fighting stereotypes due to sheer exhaustion. Besides the mental health stressors, the "weathering" hypothesis posits that racism may also extract a physical toll on Black students, especially women (Geronimus et al., 2006, p. 826). Black women collegians may experience the "Strong Black Woman stereotype" (West et al., 2016, p. 391), which assumes that Black women are care-oriented and capable to a fault and will neglect their own needs in service of others. Like other stereotypes, the strong Black woman stereotype might be damaging to women's health.

Stereotype Threat

In addition to the physical and mental health experiences of Black collegians on college and university campuses, the psychological phenomenon of "stereotype threat" (Steele & Aronson, 1995, p. 797) may impact Black collegians' academic achievement. Stereotype threat refers to the intellectual stress experienced when a person engages in a task knowing that others assume someone with one of their identities will perform poorly at that task (Steele, 1997, 2003; Steele & Aronson, 1995). Cognizance of this assumption or stereotype occupies substantial mental energy and resources that would otherwise be devoted to completing the task at hand. Because mental energy is a scarce resource, knowledge of the stereotype may become a self-fulling prophecy: It requires mental energy to think about the stereotype and hard work to prove it wrong. Most commonly seen in standardized test results (Steele, 1997), stereotype threat may affect the academic performance of Black collegians.

Strategies to Improve the Mental Health of Black Collegians

Research indicates that institutions of higher education can take proactive steps to mitigate the negative mental health experiences described previously. Forming strong social networks with other Black collegians may help limit the detrimental impact of racism on students' mental health (Grier-Reed, 2013). Institutional encouragement of such networks may positively impact the psychology of Black collegians. Supportive religious and familial environments may also contribute to a better mental health environment for Black collegians (Fischer & Shaw, 1999; Kimbrough et al., 1996); thus, institutional acknowledgment that students do not suddenly cease to be members of other communities once they become collegians may create more beneficial student outcomes. To improve the mental health environment for Black collegians, student affairs professionals and faculty should continue encouraging antiracist institutional environments and work toward promoting mental wellness as a key part of the student development experience.

Contemporary Issues: Hostile Political Climate and Social Media

The environmental realities of mental health among Black collegians contextualize the heightened pressures they feel at American institutions of higher education in the 21st century. Increased racialized hostility from public officials like former Supreme Court Justice Antonin Scalia, U.S. Attorney General Jeff Sessions, and President Donald Trump have contributed to the pressure placed on Black collegians. Additionally, racialized micro- and macroaggressions by their White peers on social media have contributed to Black collegians' feelings of hostility on campus (Gin et al., 2017).

Trump Administration and Attacks on Affirmative Action

Institutions of higher education need to reach their Black collegians in the current political and social climate of the United States. Threats to their identities by public officials have the potential to create an unwanted hostile learning environment at American colleges and universities; this has also been accompanied by an increase in race-based hate crimes on college campuses since the November 2016 election (Bauman, 2018). The current era of hostility from government might have been heightened at the December 2015 hearing of the *Fisher v. University of Texas* affirmative action case, where Supreme Court Justice Antonin Scalia made comments suggesting Black collegians belong at "slower track" universities as opposed to elite colleges "where they do not do well" (as quoted in Jones & Reddick, 2017, p. 207), in support of Fisher's (unproven) claim that race-based admissions policies discriminate against White students (Hannah-Jones, 2016; Kopan, 2015). Scalia's comments were made despite existing evidence that students granted admission based on race are no less likely to succeed than their White peers (Ho, 2005). Furthermore, Scalia's comments preceded attacks by the Trump administration on race-based admissions policies, in particular, former Attorney General Jeff Sessions's attempts to confront race-based admissions policies at Harvard University (Wilson, 2017). Challenges to these policies can have a negative impact on Black collegians. The challenges call into question Black collegians' achievements; elimination of these policies also has a negative impact on the overall minority enrollment in top-tier universities (Alhaddab, 2015)—although Black collegians resisted and responded via social media via the hashtags #StayMadAbby and #BeckyWithTheBadGrades (Pettit, 2016).

In a study gauging the perception of race-based admission policies among Black collegians, Antwi-Boasiako and Asagba (2005) determined that a greater majority of the respondents to their survey felt race preference should be used to grant Black students access into predominantly White colleges and universities. Furthermore, all students surveyed either agreed or strongly agreed that affirmative action policies should continue as part of admissions decisions for Black students (Antwi-Boasiako & Asagba, 2005). Sessions's and the Department of Justice's efforts to challenge affirmative action policies, despite these numbers, show the Trump administration's complete disregard for Black collegians and devaluation of these students' opinions on their own education.

Results from a study by Hinrichs (2012) determined that banning race-based admissions policies at a university in the *U.S. News and World Report* top 50 rankings is directly associated with a decline in enrollment by Black collegians along with other populations of color. Moreover, bans of statewide affirmative action admissions policies have steered Black collegians away from applying to more selective universities and more toward less selective 2-year colleges, when they are equally qualified to succeed at top-tier universities (Backes, 2012). Therefore, challenges to these policies not only discourage Black collegians from attending more elite institutions but also reduce Black representation on elite campuses, contributing to the feelings of isolation, impostor syndrome, and possible tokenism experienced by admitted Black students. It is in the best interest of American higher education institutions to affirm the academic accomplishments of their admitted Black collegians in the face of hostile posturing by public officials and the Trump administration.

Social Media

One of the most significant developments in contemporary higher education is the advent of social media. This extension of campus life into the internet positively impacted student-peer interaction, as well as helped build connections among the students, the campus, and university communities (Rowan-Kenyon et al., 2016). However, despite the beneficial uses of social media in higher education, institutions face challenges concerning social media platforms, particularly the effects of anonymous and identified threats against the campus community (Reynolds et al., 2017). Black collegians at PWIs find themselves and their identities under attack on social media platforms through online racialized microaggressions expressed as microinsults (e.g., advocating sociopolitical dominance and alleging oversensitivity), microassaults (e.g., stereotype threat), and microinvalidations (e.g., denying racism) (Clark et al., 2011) or overt online racial discrimination.

Because of their presence on PWI campuses, Black collegians reported more diverse offline and online contact as well as more time spent on social media than their White counterparts, making them more susceptible to online racialized microaggressions (Tynes et al., 2013). Tynes et al. (2013) argued that online racial discrimination often transcends the label of microaggressions due to the overt nature of the racism depicted online, via images and videos of lynching, comparisons of Black people to animals, and disparaging posts about Barack Obama's racial makeup. Moreover, Tynes et al. (2013) noted the fact that these images can remain online in "perpetuity" (p. 111), allowing them to be easily accessed again. In a study conducted by Gin et al. (2017), Black collegians at a prominent PWI in the Midwest reported experiencing overt online racial discrimination through social media platforms. Students reported that these racialized statements were "decidedly threatening, unapologetic, and persistent" (Gin et al., 2017, p. 165). Additionally, students expressed several emotional responses consistent with the effects of racial battle fatigue (e.g., annoyance, anger, and paranoia), and the online racialized hostilities contributed to a sense of distrust toward their campus communities (Gin et al., 2017).

The responses of these Black collegians present a distressing trend in social media on PWI campuses. Institutions of higher education—PWIs in particular—need to disrupt the distribution of racially discriminatory content on social media. Gin et al. (2017) recommends antiracist peer education as a means of allowing White students to understand the hurtful nature of their posts and beliefs. However, if this approach is taken, institutions should be careful to avoid tokenizing Black collegians by making them responsible for educating their White peers, which contributes to the racial battle fatigue they already experience at PWIs (Smith et al., 2011). Fortunately, there are bulwarks protecting and supporting Black collegians with the political and social media climate—student organizations that have existed from more than a century ago to the present.

Black Student Organizations: Origins and Purposes

Black student organizations at PWIs likely find their genesis in the literary society movements of the early 20th century, which begat the "Divine Nine" National Pan-Hellenic Council (NPHC) sororities and fraternities (Ross, 2000). It is significant to note that these organizations placed peer support, scholarly engagement, and contributions to the community at their core during their formation and saw their greatest collective influence during the civil rights era of the 1950s and 1960s (Parks, 2008). While still impactful and relevant due to their established networks and collective political power, the late 1960s, 1970s, and 1980s ushered in the appearance of Black student unions (Williamson, 1999).

These organizations, initiated by the Black Student Union at San Francisco State University in 1968 (Rojas, 2010), brought a new consciousness forward. Open to all through coeducational means and invested in the principles of the Black Power Movement, Black student unions represented a new method of organizing students to improve conditions not only on college campuses but also in their surrounding communities (Williamson, 1999). Yet another progression in Black student organizations was the advent of professional organizations such as the National Society of Black Engineers (NSBE), established in 1975; the National Black MBA Association, established in 1970; and the National Association of Black Journalists (NABJ), established in 1975 (Foster, 2003; Pinkett & Robinson, 2010). These organizations linked Black collegians and professionals and ensured the establishment of a pipeline from college to career.

The Role of Grassroots Organizing

At the same time, grassroots activism created other organizational spaces relevant and important to Black students (Williamson, 1999). Prominent Black activist organizations came into being on college campuses, most notably at Merritt College in Oakland, where Bobby Seale and Huey P. Newton met in

1962 and eventually founded the Black Panthers (Brown, 2018). Other community, national, and international concerns have spurred Black students to organize with like-minded individuals on and off campus: Black feminism, anti-war, anti-poverty, literacy, and voter registration programs have often been the initiating concerns of these movements (Glasker, 2009; Greene, 2016; Horowitz, 2014). In the 1980s, grassroots organizing on campuses around the anti-apartheid movement demonstrated the power of community organizing (Soule, 1997). More recently, concerns about growing economic inequality and human rights inspired Black collegians to ally with and organize with the Occupy Wall Street movement in the early 2010s (Gay, 2015). Some of this organizing linked to the genesis of Black Lives Matter in 2013, which spanned the boundaries of college campuses—which were also proximal to violence toward Black people (e.g., Sandra Bland, near Prairie View A&M University, and Samuel DuBose near the University of Cincinnati, both in 2015) (DeBerry, 2015).

Black Student Organizations in the Modern Era

Perhaps the most visible and impactful example of Black student activism in the current era is the Concerned Student 1950 organization at the University of Missouri. Here, protests, demands, the actions of student leaders Peyton Head and Jonathan Butler, and the threat of the majority Black football team to boycott games led to the resignations of university chancellor Tim Wolfe and system president R. Bowen Loftin (Hartocollis, 2017). While the situation at the University of Missouri captured national media attention, a number of Black student movements have leveraged social media to amplify their voices and concerns: I, Too, Am Harvard; Being Black at the University of Michigan; the Black Bruins; and Black at SMU are just some of these movements (DeFrancesco, 2014; Lee, 2014). Technology, access to social media, and an increasingly coarse political discourse on race spurred renewed interest in affirmative action and have indicated to Black students that they must remain vigilant—and organized (Jones & Reddick, 2017). The aforementioned incidents suggest that there is a significant need for institutions to enhance and build support structures for Black students, which we discuss in the next section.

Institutional Support for Black Collegians

Colleges and universities must address issues of isolation and student engagement and commit to practices that enhance campus climate and experiences of Black students. If PWIs ignore Black collegians' racial and ethnic identities in programming and messaging toward this group, these institutions may communicate to Black collegians that they are invisible. Black collegians on PWI campuses are often isolated, leaving them without a person to whom or space in which to vent; students are unable to receive guidance or feel safe; and students often perceive that the academic environment complicates their sense of culture, potentially leading students to abandon their culture for the sake of assimilation (Aries & Seider, 2005; Jayakumar et al., 2013; Luna & Martinez, 2013). Likewise, the experiences of isolation suffered by Black collegians contribute to reduced academic performance (Davis et al., 2004; Hood, 1992; Parker et al., 2016). Student affairs professionals and faculty should take primary responsibility for connecting, maintaining, and developing Black collegians at their institution instead of expecting Black collegians to engage campus resources and opportunities on their own (Allen, 1992; Brooms et al., 2015; Parker et al., 2016). Placing the onus for finding and engaging with resources on the students absolves the institution of responsibility for Black collegians' potential isolation at PWIs.

Racially Conscious Engagement

Racially conscious engagement of Black collegians aids in dismantling structural barriers that may impede their success. Harper (2009) reasoned that "race-conscious student engagement is offered as a method likely to compel more racial minority students to reflect on powerful learning opportunities, institutional enablers of achievement, and outcomes-productive experiences" (p. 40). Therefore, institutional support for Black collegians via mentorship programs and connection to high-impact practices are optimal avenues for student affairs professionals and faculty to enhance the development and satisfaction of Black collegians.

Sinanan (2016) emphasized that academic and social integration are important aspects of student success facilitated by mentorship programs for Black collegians in higher education. Mentorship programs should be intentionally designed around the individual and collective needs of Black collegians to support their development, success, and connectedness to the larger campus community. High-impact practices provide Black collegians with opportunities to grow academically, professionally, and personally (Harper, 2009; Lu et al., 2015) and connect collegians with student affairs professionals who can impart navigational skills through a communitive approach (Davis et al., 2004; Harper, 2009; Sinanan, 2016). These high-impact practices include study abroad opportunities, service-learning projects, academic and social peer support groups, faculty- and staff-directed cocurricular activities, and faculty-led research projects. For mentorship and intentional engagement to work effectively, student affairs professionals and faculty must be conscious and committed in working across departmental silos to help Black collegians.

Institutional Improvements

To find our way "Black" to student development, student affairs professionals and faculty must improve their approaches to support Black collegians at their respective institutions. These approaches include adding mandatory cultural competency training and ensuring student affairs professionals and faculty are providing an environment of support instead of contributing to stressors and isolation of Black collegians. Additionally, cultural competency training for student affairs professionals and faculty cannot be the sole answer to addressing campus climate issues at PWIs. This effort should exist in conjunction with developing and hiring racially/ethnically diverse faculty and student affairs professionals with demonstrated commitments to equity and inclusion. As a result, these individuals will be positioned to provide mentorship and cultural support by fostering Black collegian development (Guiffrida, 2005). Sustaining these institutional improvements requires ensuring equitable task distribution, adequate compensation, and protection against overburdening or culturally taxing faculty and staff who assume these responsibilities (Miller et al., 2018).

Last, increasing resources for cocurricular programs tailored for Black collegians is a major factor in finding our way "Black" to student development. Although they operate outside the classroom context, cocurricular programs help make certain that Black collegians are not only persisting to graduation but also developing holistically through reflective components and measured learning outcomes, all of which lead to their growth (Athreya & Kalkhoff, 2010; Hood, 1992; Keen & Hall, 2009). Through the development of such cocurricular programs, along with meeting the needs of Black collegians appropriately, student affairs professionals and faculty can address issues such as accultural stress, isolation, and microaggressions.

Recommendations for Policy and Practice

In this chapter, we argued for a holistic, ecological analytical approach to understanding and improving the Black collegian experience. To that end, we recommend that institutions involve faculty, staff—including but not limited to student affairs professionals—and students in this enterprise. We suggest that institutions begin by creating a campus climate survey focusing on Black collegians, in which mentorship and mental wellness are specifically researched. Qualitative research should supplement any quantitative measures to ensure that the voices of Black collegians are heard. Data from existing campus climate surveys could be reviewed to see if the aspects of the Black collegian experience discussed in this chapter have been measured.

Next, with the data collected from that measure, institutions can take a close look at which of the best practices recommended in this chapter have been implemented at their campuses and set an action plan to meet their students' needs. Additional resources may be required to achieve these goals. As we have argued, it will take sustained efforts of everyone on the campus, beyond simple cultural competency training, to reach the goal of a welcoming environment for Black collegians. We include suggestions for theory and research in the conclusion.

Conclusion

Positioning Black student development as an institutional imperative allows us to reimagine how Black collegians navigate their experiences within a contemporary ecological context. Moving beyond monolithic understandings of the educational experiences and realities of Black collegians requires student affairs professionals and faculty to consider how the linkages among theoretical constructs, mental health, contemporary issues, student organizing, and institutional support shape a holistic approach to Black student development. Because this linkage depicts Black student development as a complex and intersectional construct, our approaches must be guided by realizing the experiential nuances we have presented in this chapter regarding Black collegians in the late 2010s.

While deepening our understanding of Black collegians' experiences in higher education is the focus of this chapter, we must also recognize that the developmental process does not end upon their completion of an undergraduate degree. Future researchers and practitioners can utilize the perspectives we highlighted to explore the developmental processes and outcomes of Black collegians in a postgraduate context. For example, this postgraduate context could include Black student development at the graduate school level. Additionally, scholars and practitioners could investigate how Black alumni, particularly from PWIs, make sense of their undergraduate experiences. To further complicate that investigation, one could identify how that sense-making shapes the life and career pathways of Black collegian alumni. In doing so, finding our way Black *to* student development theory is to also find our way *through* Black development across a lifespan that includes, but is not limited to, the entire educational pipeline.

Questions for the Reader

1. In what ways is my institution succeeding in creating a truly welcoming environment for Black collegians? How is my institution falling short?

2. What is one small step I can take today to create positive change at my institution for Black collegians?
3. How can I make positive change for the Black collegian experience last at the structural level?

References

Alhaddab, T. (2015). The consequences of eliminating affirmative action admission policies in minorities' college access. *Journal of the World Universities Forum, 8*(3), 1–8.

Allen, W. R. (1992). The color of success: African-American college student outcomes at predominantly White and historically Black public colleges and universities. *Harvard Educational Review, 62*(1), 26–45. https://doi.org/10.17763/haer.62.1.wv5627665007v701

Antwi-Boasiako, K. B., & Asagba, J. O. (2005). A preliminary analysis of African American college students' perceptions of racial preferences and affirmative action in making admissions decisions at a predominantly White university. *College Student Journal, 39*(4), 734–748.

Aries, E., & Seider, M. (2005). The interactive relationship between class identity and the college experience: The case of lower income students. *Qualitative Sociology, 28*(4), 419–443. https://doi.org/10.1007/s11133-005-8366-1

Athreya, K. S., & Kalkhoff, M. T. (2010). The engineering leadership program: A co-curricular learning environment by and for students. *Journal of STEM Education: Innovations and Research, 11*(3/4), 70.

Backes, B. (2012). Do affirmative action bans lower minority college enrollment and attainment? *Journal of Human Resources, 47*(2), 435–455. https://doi.org/10.3368/jhr.47.2.435

Bauman, D. (2018, February 16). After 2016 election, campus hate crimes seemed to jump. Here's what the data tell us. *Chronicle of Higher Education.* https://www.chronicle.com/article/After-2016-Election-Campus/242577

Baxter Magolda, M. B. (2009). The activity of meaning making: A holistic perspective on college student development. *Journal of College Student Development, 50*(6), 621–639. https://doi.org/10.1353/csd.0.0106

Bernard, D. D., Lige, Q. M., Willis, H. A., Sosoo, E. E., & Neblett, E. W. (2017). Impostor phenomenon and mental health: The influence of racial discrimination and gender. *Journal of Counseling Psychology, 64*(2), 155–156. https://doi.org/10.1037/cou0000197

Brittian, A. S., Sy, S. R., & Stokes, J. E. (2009). Mentoring: Implications for African American college students. *Western Journal of Black Studies, 33*(2), 87–97.

Bronfenbrenner, U. (1979). *The ecology of human development: Experiments by nature and design.* Harvard University Press.

Brooms, D. R., Goodman, J., & Clark, J. (2015). "We need more of this": Engaging Black men on college campuses. *College Student Affairs Journal, 33*(1), 105–123. https://doi.org/10.1353/csj.2015.0002

Brown, C. J. (2018). *Street stories: Oakland.* Street Stories. https://web.archive.org/web/20160221025932/http://www.streetstoriesoakland.com/

Chickering, A. W. (1969). *Education and identity.* Jossey-Bass.

Clark, D. A., Spanierman, L., Reed, T., Soble, J., & Cabana, S. (2011). Documenting web log expressions of racial microaggressions that target American Indians. *Journal of Diversity in Higher Education, 4,* 39–50. https://doi.org/10.1037/a0021762

Cokley, K. (2000). An investigation of academic self-concept and its relationship to academic achievement in African American college students. *Journal of Black Psychology, 26*(2), 148–164. https://doi.org/10.1177/0095798400026002002

Cokley, K., McClain, S., Enciso, A., & Martinez, M. (2013). An examination of the impact of minority status stress and impostor feelings on the mental health of diverse ethnic minority college students. *Journal of Multicultural Counseling & Development, 41*(2), 82–95. https://doi.org/10.1002/j.2161-1912.2013.00029.x

Cokley, K., Smith, L., Bernard, D., Hurst, A., Jackson, S., Stone, S., Awosogba, O., Saucer, C., Bailey, M., & Roberts, D. (2017). Impostor feelings as a moderator and mediator of the relationship between perceived discrimination and mental health among racial/ethnic minority college students. *Journal of Counseling Psychology, 64*(2), 141–154. https://doi.org/10.1037/cou0000198

Davis, M., Dias-Bowie, Y., Greenberg, K., Klukken, G., Pollio, H. R., Thomas, S. P., & Thompson, C. L. (2004). "A fly in the buttermilk": Descriptions of university life by successful black undergraduate students at a predominately white southeastern university. *The Journal of Higher Education, 75*(4), 420–445. https://doi.org/10.1353/jhe.2004.0018

DeBerry, J. (2015, July 31). Sandra Bland and Samuel DuBose talked back to police—and died. *New Orleans Times-Picayune.* https://www.nola.com/news/crime_police/article_fd1ba1ab-bf41-5570-ba61-b5319f5c3517.html

DeFrancesco, V. (2014, March 4). Black students at Harvard speak out through photo campaign. *Chronicle of Higher Education.* https://web.archive.org/web/20150923104055/http://chronicle.com/blogs/ticker/black-students-at-harvard-speak-out-through-photo-campaign/73787

Fischer, A. R., & Shaw, C. M. (1999). African Americans' mental health and perceptions of racist discrimination: The moderating effects of racial socialization experiences and self-esteem. *Journal of Counseling Psychology, 46*(3), 395–407. https://doi.org/10.1037/0022-0167.46.3.395

Foster, K. M. (2003). The contours of community: The formation and maintenance of a black student community on a predominantly white campus. *Race, Ethnicity and Education, 6*(3), 265–281. https://doi.org/10.1080/1361332032000109637

Gay, R. (2015, November 11). Student activism is serious business: The protesters at Mizzou and Yale need to be heard, not laughed off. *New Republic.* https://newrepublic.com/article/123431/student-activism-serious-business

Geronimus, A. T., Hicken, M., Keene, D., & Bound, J. (2006). "Weathering" and age patterns of allostatic load scores among blacks and whites in the United States. *American Journal of Public Health, 96*(5), 826–833. https://doi.org/10.2105/AJPH.2004.060749

Gin, K. J., Martínez-Alemán, A. M., Rowan-Kenyon, H. T., & Hottell, D. (2017). Racialized aggressions and social media on campus. *Journal of College Student Development, 58*(2), 159–174. https://doi.org/10.1353/csd.2017.0013

Glasker, W. C. (2009). *Black students in the ivory tower: African American student activism at the University of Pennsylvania, 1967–1990*. University of Massachusetts Press.

Greene, C. (2016). Women in the civil rights and Black power movements. *Oxford research encyclopedia: American history*. https://doi.org/10.1093/acrefore/9780199329175.013.212

Grier-Reed, T. (2013). The African American student network: An informal networking group as a therapeutic intervention for Black college students on a predominantly White campus. *Journal of Black Psychology, 39*(2), 169–184. https://doi.org/10.1177/0095798413478696

Guiffrida, D. (2005). Othermothering as a framework for understanding African American students' definitions of student-centered faculty. *The Journal of Higher Education, 76*(6), 701–723. https://doi.org/10.1353/jhe.2005.0041

Hannah-Jones, N. (2016, June 23). What Abigail Fisher's affirmative action case was really about. *Pro Publica*. https://www.propublica.org/article/a-colorblind-constitution-what-abigail-fishers-affirmative-action-case-is-r

Harper, S. R. (2009). Race-conscious student engagement practices and the equitable distribution of enriching educational experiences. *Liberal Education, 95*(4), 38–45. https://www.aacu.org/publications-research/periodicals/race-conscious-student-engagement-practices-and-equitable

Harper, S. R., & Quaye, S. J. (2007). Student organizations as venues for Black identity expression and development among African American male student leaders. *Journal of College Student Development, 48*(2), 127–144. https://repository.upenn.edu/gse_pubs/166/?utm_source=repository.upenn.edu%2Fgse_pubs%2F166&utm_medium=PDF&utm_campaign=PDFCoverPages

Harris III, F. (2010). College men's meanings of masculinities and contextual influences: Toward a conceptual model. *Journal of College Student Development, 51*(3), 297–318. https://doi.org/10.1353/csd.0.0132

Hartocollis, A. (2017, July 9). Long after protests, students shun the University of Missouri. *New York Times*. https://www.nytimes.com/2017/07/09/us/university-of-missouri-enrollment-protests-fallout.html

Hinrichs, P. (2012). The effects of affirmative action bans on college enrollment, educational attainment, and the demographic composition of universities. *Review of Economics and Statistics, 94*(3), 712–722. https://doi.org/10.1162/REST_a_00170

Ho, D. (2005). Affirmative action's affirmative actions: A reply to Sander. *The Yale Law Journal, 114*, 2011–2016.

Hood, D. W. (1992). Academic and noncognitive factors affecting the retention of Black men at a predominantly White university. *The Journal of Negro Education, 61*(1), 12–23. https://doi.org/10.2307/2295625

Horowitz, D. (2014). *It came from somewhere and it hasn't gone away: Black women's anti-poverty organizing in Atlanta, 1966–1996* [Unpublished thesis, Georgia State University]. ScholarWorks. https://scholarworks.gsu.edu/history_theses/83/

Jayakumar, U., Vue, R., & Allen, W. (2013). Pathways to college for young Black scholars: A community cultural wealth perspective. *Harvard Educational Review, 83*(4), 551–579. https://doi.org/10.17763/haer.83.4.4k1mq00162433l28

JED Foundation & The Steve Fund. (2015). *Students of color feel less academically and emotionally prepared for college (Infographic)*. http://www.settogo.org/wp-content/uploads/2017/01/SGNY_infogrphic2_v3-6-e1483736240520.jpg

Jones, V. A., & Reddick, R. J. (2017). The heterogeneity of resistance: How Black students utilize engagement and activism to challenge PWI inequalities. *The Journal of Negro Education, 86*(3), 204–219. https://doi.org/10.7709/jnegro education.86.3.0204

Keen, C., & Hall, K. (2009). Engaging with difference matters: Longitudinal student outcomes of co-curricular service-learning programs. *The Journal of Higher Education, 80*(1), 59–79. https://doi.org/10.1353/jhe.0.0037

Kimbrough, R. M., Molock, S. D., & Walton, K. (1996). Perception of social support, acculturation, depression, and suicidal ideation among African American college students at predominantly Black and predominantly White universities. *Journal of Negro Education, 65*(3), 295–307. https://doi.org/10.2307/2967346

King, K. R. (2005). Why is discrimination stressful? The mediating role of cognitive appraisal. *Cultural Diversity & Ethnic Minority Psychology, 11*(3), 202–212. https://doi.org/10.1037/1099-9809.11.3.202

Knefelkamp, L., Widick, C., & Parker, C. A. (Eds.). (1978). *Applying new developmental findings* (New Directions for Student Services, no. 4). Jossey-Bass.

Kopan, T. (2015, December 9). Scalia questions place of some black students in elite colleges. *CNN*. https://www.cnn.com/2015/12/09/politics/scalia-black-scientists -scotus/index.html

Lee, J. (2014, March 5). "I, Too, Am Harvard" photos tell Black students' stories. *USA Today.* https://www.usatoday.com/story/news/nation-now/2014/03/05/ black-students-harvard-tumblr/6013023/

Lu, C., Reddick, R. J., Dean, D., & Pecero, V. (2015). Coloring up study abroad: Exploring Black students' decision to study in China. *Journal of Student Affairs Research and Practice, 52*(4), 440–451. https://doi.org/10.1080/19496591.2015 .1050032

Luna, N. A., & Martinez, M. (2013). A qualitative study using community cultural wealth to understand the educational experiences of Latino college students. *Journal of Praxis in Multicultural Education, 7*(1), article 2. https://doi .org.10.9741/2161-2978.1045

McClain, S., Beasley, S. T., Jones, B., Awosogba, O., Jackson, S., & Cokley, K. (2016). An examination of the impact of racial and ethnic identity, impostor feelings, and minority status stress on the mental health of Black college students. *Journal of Multicultural Counseling and Development, 44*(2), 101–117. https:// doi.org/10.1002/jmcd.12040

Miller, R. A., Jones, V. A., Reddick, R. J., Lowe, T. A., Franks Flunder, B., Hogan, K., & Rosal, A. I. (2018). Educating through microaggressions: Self-care for diversity educators. *Journal of Student Affairs Research and Practice, 55*(1), 14–26. https://doi.org/10.1080/19496591.2017.1358634

Parker, W. M., Puig, A., Johnson, J., & Anthony, C. (2016). Black males on white campuses: Still invisible men? *College Student Affairs Journal, 34*(3), 76–92. https://doi.org/10.1353/csj.2016.0020

Parks, G. (Ed.). (2008). *Black Greek-letter organizations in the twenty-first century: Our fight has just begun.* University Press of Kentucky.

Patton, L. D. (2006). The voice of reason: A qualitative examination of Black student perceptions of Black culture centers. *Journal of College Student Development, 47*(6), 628–646. https://doi.org/10.1353/csd.2006.0068

Pettit, E. (2016, June 23). Why Twitter is calling Abigail Fisher "Becky With the Bad Grades": A brief explainer. *Chronicle of Higher Education.* https://web.archive.org/web/20191229111911/https://www.chronicle.com/blogs/ticker/why-twitter-is-calling-abigail-fisher-becky-with-the-bad-grades-a-brief-explainer/112384

Pinkett, R., & Robinson, J. (2010). *Black faces in white places: 10 game-changing strategies to achieve success and find greatness.* AMACOM.

Reynolds, C. L., Platt, R. E., Schaffer, L. M., & Foster, H. (2017). Social media and higher education: The problem of anonymous electronic threats to the campus community. *Journal of Cases in Educational Leadership, 20*(4), 58–71. https://doi.org/10.1177/1555458917711211

Rojas, F. (2010). Power through institutional work: Acquiring academic authority in the 1968 third world strike. *Academy of Management Journal, 53*(6), 1263–1280. https://doi.org/10.5465/amj.2010.57317832

Ross, L. C. (2000). *The divine nine: The history of African American fraternities and sororities.* Kensington Books.

Rowan-Kenyon, H. T., Martínez Alemán, A. M., Gin, K., Blakeley, B., Gismondi, A., Lewis, J., McCready, A., Zepp, D., & Knight, S. (2016). Social media in higher education. *ASHE Higher Education Report, 42*(5), 7–128. https://doi.org/10.1002/aehe.20103

Sinanan, A. (2016). The value and necessity of mentoring African American college students at PWI's. *The Journal of Pan African Studies (Online), 9*(8), 155–166.

Smith, W. A., Allen, W. R., & Danley, L. L. (2007). "Assume the position . . . You fit the description": Psychosocial experiences and racial battle fatigue among African American male college students. *American Behavioral Scientist, 51*(4), 551–578. https://doi.org/10.1177/0002764207307742

Smith, W. A., Hung, M., & Franklin, J. D. (2011). Racial battle fatigue and the miseducation of black men: Racial microaggressions, societal problems, and environmental stress. *The Journal of Negro Education, 80*(1), 63–82. http://www.jstor.org/stable/41341106

Soule, S. A. (1997). The student divestment movement in the United States and tactical diffusion: The shantytown protest. *Social Forces, 75*(3), 855–882. https://doi.org/10.1093/sf/75.3.855

Steele, C. M. (1997). A threat in the air: How stereotypes shape intellectual identity and performance. *American Psychologist, 52*(6), 613–629. https://doi.org/10.1037/0003-066X.52.6.613

Steele, C. M. (2003). Stereotype threat and Black student achievement. In T. Perry, C. M. Steele, & A. Hilliard (Eds.), *Young, gifted and black: Promoting high achievement among Black students* (pp. 109–130). Beacon Press.

Steele, C. M., & Aronson, J. (1995). Stereotype threat and the intellectual test performance of African Americans. *Journal of Personality and Social Psychology, 69*(5), 797–811. https://doi.org/10.1037/0022-3514.69.5.797

Strayhorn, T. L. (2015). *Student development theory in higher education: A social psychological approach.* Routledge.

Tatum, B. D. (2017). *Why are all the Black kids sitting together in the cafeteria? And other conversations about race.* Basic Books.

Turnage, C. (2017, August 9). In higher ed's mental-health crisis, an overlooked population: International students. *The Chronicle of Higher Education.* https://www.chronicle.com/article/In-Higher-Ed-s-Mental-Health/240891

Tynes, B. M., Rose, C. A., & Markoe, S. L. (2013). Extending campus life to the Internet: Social media, discrimination, and perceptions of racial climate. *Journal of Diversity in Higher Education, 6*(2), 102–114. https://doi.org/10.1037/a0033267

West, L. M., Donovan, R. A., & Daniel, A. R. (2016). The price of strength: Black college women's perspectives on the strong Black woman stereotype. *Women & Therapy, 39*(3/4), 390–412. https://doi.org/10.1080/02703149.2016.1116871

Williamson, J. A. (1999). In defense of themselves: The Black student struggle for success and recognition at predominantly White colleges and universities. *Journal of Negro Education, 68*(1), 92–105. https://doi.org/10.2307/2668212

Wilson, M. R. (2017, October 4). *DOJ investigating affirmative action at Harvard.* The Hill. http://thehill.com/business-a-lobbying/business-a-lobbying/353953-doj-investigating-affirmative-action-at-harvard

Wilson, R. (2015, August 31). An epidemic of anguish. *The Chronicle of Higher Education.* https://www.chronicle.com/article/An-Epidemic-of-Anguish/232721

ALTERNATIVE FRAMEWORKS AND MODELS FOR ASIAN AMERICAN COLLEGE STUDENT POPULATIONS

PART THREE

ALTERNATIVE FRAMEWORKS
AND MODELS FOR ASIAN
AMERICAN COLLEGE
STUDENT POPULATIONS

5

A CRITICAL PERSPECTIVE OF ASIAN AMERICAN IDENTITY

Creating Contexts to Cultivate Asian Americanness

Samuel D. Museus, Hannah Hyun White, and Vanessa S. Na

As an Asian American and a Khmer (Cambodian) American womxn,[1] I rarely receive messages that I am enough. Through constant questions about where I am from, I am being told that I cannot possibly be from "here." In my experiences with racial justice organizing, I have engaged in discussions with other people of color who tell me that they had never considered Asian Americans to be people of color. In these instances, I have felt invisible. Within Asian America, I feel exploited because Khmer Americans and other Southeast Asian Americans are often absent from community spaces and the dialogue. If we are included, it is never in holistic ways. Indeed, my Khmer American community has been racialized as inferior, dirty, untrustworthy, and inadequate. And so "not being good enough" is a state in which I constantly operate. I have also experienced objectification and hypersexualization as an Asian American womxn, both in my personal and professional lives. As an Asian American, I am not enough to be included in conversations about race and racism. As a Southeast Asian American, I am not enough for Asian America. As a womxn, my humanity is always an afterthought. (Vanessa S. Na)

I am balancing two worlds, as a transracial adoptee and Asian American. I am constantly told that I don't experience "real" racism or racism at all for that matter. I also never had a chance to write my own story or be empowered to share it when I was younger. Over the years, storytelling has become a powerful tool for me to express what it means to be an Asian American transracial adoptee. My experiences engaging in opportunities to fight for social justice in college, as well as personal narratives, continue to shape my identity as I navigate the system, continue my journey to cultivate greater resistance and agency, and learn to run my own race. (Hannah Hyun White)

Our opening contributor narratives provide a window into the complexity of Asian American identity. Our journeys highlight the often poorly understood mechanisms through which systems of oppression shape Asian American experiences and identities. They underscore the ways in which racial identities intersect with ethnic, gender, refugee, and transracial adoptee identities. Our stories also demonstrate how politics within the Asian American community shape perceptions of oneself in relation to this larger racial category. By reflecting on our trajectories, we can illuminate how context, community, and agency are woven into the ways in which people make sense of their Asian Americanness.

In this chapter, we leverage our stories to complicate conversations about Asian American identity by shifting the primary focus of identity discussions from individuals to their racial and cultural contexts. In the following section, we foreground our discussion with an overview of existing Asian American identity models. Next, we review Asian critical theory (AsianCrit) as a tool to advance more robust contextual and complex conversations about Asian American identity. Then, we present two more in-depth author narratives that demonstrate how AsianCrit might be useful in understanding and engaging in dialogue about Asian American identity. We use this discussion to offer a set of propositions about Asian American identity that can inform educators' work with Asian American students. Finally, we conclude with a set of specific recommendations for educators who work with and aim to promote identity development among Asian American students.

Existing Asian American Identity Models

In the United States, White supremacy is a critical factor shaping Asian American identity (J. Kim, 1981). Scholars explain that, in Western societies, race is a socially and politically constructed phenomenon used to classify and dehumanize non-White populations (Omi & Winant, 1994). They note that society lumps racially minoritized populations into monolithic categories and attaches racial meanings to them. Such racialization profoundly shapes the ways in which people of color see themselves in relation to larger society (Ibrahim et al., 1997; J. Kim, 1981; Nadal, 2004; Museus et al., 2013). In fact, it can be argued that all forms of Asian American identity are a reaction to systemic racial oppression.

Asian American identity development has been the focus of scholarly discourse for several decades. Since the 1980s, various Asian American identity development models have been proposed, with some of the earlier models being framed as sets of progressive stages. For example, J. Kim's

(1981) Asian American identity model (AAIM) was among the first proposed Asian American identity models and was based on the experiences of Japanese American women. In developing the model, J. Kim highlighted the social and psychological consequences of Asian Americans being racially marginalized in the United States and how their racial membership impacts their own racial identity and the process of working through racial identity conflict in a White society (J. Kim, 2012). J. Kim's model described the developmental process in five stages, and she noted that the stages are sequential but not intended to suggest a linear developmental process.

1. *Ethnic awareness* refers to the stage in which Asian Americans become increasingly aware of their ethnicity as a result of interactions with their families.
2. *White identification* occurs when individuals are exposed to racial prejudices, usually through school systems and peers, and consequently attempt to dissociate from their Asian American identity.
3. *Awakening to social political consciousness* refers to an increased awareness of racial oppression and political consciousness. The individual recognizes that they are a racial minority, and the view of being Asian American shifts to being more positive.
4. *Redirection to Asian American consciousness* signifies how individuals embrace their Asian American heritage and culture and view these aspects of their identity with pride. They may also develop anger toward the White population because of the realization that White supremacy was a cause of their negative experiences growing up.
5. *Incorporation* refers to individuals learning to balance their own identity with appreciating others. It also is a process through which Asian Americans blend their racial identity with other social identities they hold.

The AAIM is particularly useful for understanding how Asian American identities might evolve to become more complex over time.

While the AAIM is often viewed and discussed as an Asian American identity framework, it was heavily based on the voices of Japanese American women. Recognizing the need to acknowledge the greater diversity and complexity of Asian America, researchers have complicated the role of ethnicity in Asian American identity development processes and broadened understandings of how context shapes such identity (e.g., Ibrahim et al., 1997; Nadal, 2004; Museus et al., 2013). For example, Ibrahim et al. (1997) developed a model specific to South Asian immigrants. Ibrahim et al.'s (1997) developmental process is similar to J. Kim's (1981) model in many ways, but diverged from the latter in asserting that South Asian immigrants do not experience a White identification stage. Rather, they argued that histories of colonization of South Asian nations and the consequent incorporation of many different cultural influences into South Asian societies make accepting different cultures a normal way of life for South Asian immigrants.

In addition, Nadal (2004) underscored the significant social, cultural, economic, and psychological differences between Filipino and other Asian Americans.[2] He argued that these differences warranted an ethnic-specific Filipino identity model. Several of the phases in Nadal's Filipino identity model parallel J. Kim's (1981) stages, but panethnic Asian American consciousness and ethnocentric realization are two distinct concepts in the former. Nadal argued that Filipino Americans are often socialized to accept their Asian American identity and seek power in numbers through coalitions in the larger Asian American community. The model suggests that Filipino Americans subsequently realize that they have been unjustly categorized as Asian Americans, and there is an increased awareness of how they are marginalized within the Asian American community.

The stage models proposed by Ibrahim et al. (1997) and Nadal (2004) made significant contributions to discourse on Asian American identity development. First, they demonstrated how a more thorough consideration of culture and ethnicity in Asian American racial identity development conversations can offer a more nuanced perspective of identity formation processes (Museus, 2014a). In doing so, they suggest that Asian American identity development might be more complex than a one-size-fits-all model might suggest. Second, they reveal the importance of historical and social contexts of specific ethnic groups, such as the colonization of homelands and immigration to the United States, in shaping Asian American identity.

Over the last decade, researchers have proposed more fluid models that seek to explain Asian American identity development as a function of multiple and potentially ongoing interconnected processes that take place in complex contexts (e.g., Accapadi, 2012; Museus et al., 2013). For example, Museus et al. (2013) proposed a Southeast Asian American identity model that consists of multiple distinct and interconnected processes that can be active at any point during one's lifespan and influence Southeast Asian American identity formation:

- *Enculturation to ethnic cultures* indicates the process of Southeast Asian Americans' socialization and participation in their own community's cultural heritages.

- *Acculturation to the dominant culture* refers to the process of developing an understanding of how to navigate a predominantly White society and culture.
- *Awareness of oppression* refers to individuals developing increased awareness of oppression of the different groups with which they identify (e.g., Southeast Asian Americans, Asian Americans, people of color, and other marginalized populations).
- *Redirection of salience* indicates that various aspects of Southeast Asian Americans' identities—such as their identification with their ethnic, Asian American, and racially minoritized communities—assume varied and constantly shifting levels of salience depending on context (e.g., space and time).
- *Integration of dispositions* refers to the integration of these processes into a complex and holistic Southeast Asian American identity.

Museus et al.'s (2013) model offered a way of thinking about identity that explicitly deviated from the notion that a singular progression defines identity development. They underscored that identity is shaped by multiple processes that can mutually influence identity throughout the lifespan. In addition, Museus et al. reframed the relationship between race and ethnicity, as they deviated from other frameworks' suggestions that increased ethnic awareness and increased racial consciousness characterize separate stages in development. Instead, they posited that Southeast Asian Americans can simultaneously cultivate increased ethnic awareness and understanding of racial oppression, and these processes continuously shape their identity.

In addition, Accapadi (2012) centered her point of entry (POE) model on the intersection between environments and individuals to challenge scholars and practitioners to reconsider how they are conceptualizing identity development processes. She proposed that four environmental factors constitute points of entry into an Asian American identity journey that can spark further identity development: (a) the degree of an individual's connections to their ethnic community, (b) the impact of their families on their sense of self, (c) the historical immigration context that surrounds their racialization as Asian American, and (d) external influences (e.g., White perceptions and treatment of Asian Americans). She also explained how individuals are forced to work through the ways in which people categorize and otherize them based on their phenotypic features, and other social identities (e.g., class, gender, sexual orientation, ability) can provide a point of entry for Asian American consciousness (Kumashiro, 1999).

The POE model might be especially useful for educators working directly with Asian American students and seeking to foster their racial identity development. Unlike most other existing Asian American identity frameworks, the POE model focuses on factors that can be leveraged to catalyze Asian American identity development, instead of delineating a specific developmental path. In addition, the model more explicitly accounts for the contextual, complex, and multidimensional nature of Asian American identity processes. Moreover, the POE model brings other social identities into greater focus in efforts to understand identity formation.

Limitations of Asian American Identity Models

The aforementioned perspectives have made significant contributions to discourse on Asian American identity. This discourse, however, has limitations, and we discuss a few of them herein. First, early stage models can sometimes lead to assumptions that identity is characterized by a singular sequential process, and individuals are presumably situated within a particular point in their trajectories (Ibrahim et al., 1997; J. Kim, 1981; Nadal, 2004). Research on identity, however, highlights the reality that racial and ethnic identities are constantly changing, multifaceted, and multidirectional (Museus et al., 2013; Nagel, 1994; Wong, 2013).

Second, scholars have argued that stage models imply an evolutionary trajectory in which some Asian Americans have reached "higher" stages of identity development than others (Accapadi, 2012). They note that this type of framing can perpetuate hierarchical ways of thinking about Asian American identities and potentially perpetuate deficit perspectives toward those at "lower" stages. Moreover, given that key elements of multiple phases (e.g., developing knowledge of cultural communities and an awareness of oppression) can influence Asian American identity simultaneously, it is questionable whether most people can be easily and accurately situated within one stage of development at a given point in time.

Third, existing perspectives provide a limited understanding of how context shapes identity. Indeed, while existing stage models do recognize the significance of context, most of them do not center their focus on how varied contexts shape identity (e.g., Ibrahim et al., 1997; J. Kim, 1981; Nadal, 2004). Even when contextual factors (e.g., time, space, immigration histories) are noted as important (Accapadi, 2012; Museus et al., 2013), there is limited clarification regarding *how* they shape racial identification. For example, Accapadi (2012) explains that family shapes individuals' sense of self, which in turn influences whether they identify as Asian American, but existing models do not clarify *how* family interactions shape these processes. This limitation of existing models is understandable given that complex interactions between environments and identity are difficult to succinctly explain. Nevertheless, centering the role of contexts might lead to more holistic understandings of how they shape Asian American identity.

Fourth, early models often frame acquisition of knowledge about ethnic cultures and expanding racial awareness as two distinct and disconnected processes, with the former occurring in the early stages of identity formation (J. Kim, 1981; Nadal, 2004). More recent models argue that learning about the cultures of one's own communities and how they are distinct from White communities can happen continuously throughout one's life (Museus et al., 2013), and one's attachment to their ethnicity influences their degree of identification as Asian American (Accapadi, 2012). Yet, the nature of the interaction between ethnic and racial identities is not thoroughly explained by existing models.

There is some evidence that can be used to begin making sense of these interactions. For example, history suggests that processes of racial oppression and the culture of minoritized communities are not disconnected. One of the primary ways in which racism operates is via the eradication of the cultures of oppressed peoples (Acuña, 2015). Thus, the inability for some Asian Americans to learn about their own cultural communities is a consequence of systemic oppression and inhibits the cultivation of Asian American identity formation (Museus, 2014a). Moreover, Asian Americans' knowledge of how society marginalizes, invalidates, and erases the cultures of their own communities from mainstream discourse is an essential component of cultivating a greater awareness of the ways in which racial oppression enacts violence toward Asian American people. It could be argued, therefore, that race and culture should be viewed as continuously and inextricably intertwined.

In addition, researchers have demonstrated that systemic racial oppression shapes the ways in which Asian Americans identify with or otherize subgroups within the Asian American community (Pyke & Dang, 2003). They note, for example, that some Asian Americans might disengage from other members of the Asian American community who have a strong racial and ethnic identity in an attempt to distance themselves from Asian American stereotypes, perceived racial inferiority, and associated harm.

Finally, Asian American experiences are shaped by other social identities, including ability, adoption status, gender, immigration status, sexual orientation, religion, and socioeconomic status (Accapadi, 2012; J. Kim, 1981). Even when conversations around Asian American identity consider other social identities, the ways in which they intersect with each other are rarely meaningfully engaged in the discussion (Museus, 2014a). Yet, intersecting systems of oppression and associated identities mutually shape Asian Americans' complex experiences in profound ways (Buenavista et al., 2009; Museus & Truong, 2013). Thus, a greater engagement of intersecting systems and the multiple communities to which Asian Americans belong is warranted. In the remaining sections, we utilize AsianCrit to develop and offer a perspective that aims to address some of these limitations.

The Utility of AsianCrit in Complicating Asian American Identity Discourse

Building on the work of critical race theory and Asian American studies (Buenavista et al., 2009; Chew, 1994; Cho, 2003; Chon, 1995; Espiritu, 1993; Lowe, 1996; Museus & Kiang, 2009; Prasso, 2005), Museus and Iftikar (2013) proposed an AsianCrit framework composed of seven inter-related tenets that offer a lens to understand how race and racial oppression operate within societies that are built on foundations of White supremacy (Iftikar & Museus, 2019). Each of these tenets can be applied to understanding Asian Americanness:

First, *asianization* refers to the specific ways in which White supremacy, and the nativistic racism that emanates from it, racializes Asian Americans as perpetual and threatening foreigners, model minorities, and sexually deviant emasculated men and hypersexualized women (Chew, 1994; Cho, 2003; Chon, 1995; Espiritu, 1993; Lowe, 1996; Museus & Kiang, 2009; Prasso, 2005). It also recognizes that Asian American ethnic groups can be racialized in different ways, such as how Southeast Asian Americans are uniquely racialized as deviant, uneducated, welfare sponges in many localized contexts. These forms of racialization can lead to Asian Americans internalizing these socially constructed messages about them, developing negative views of themselves and the Asian American community, and rationalizing the oppression of their own communities and other communities of color (Pyke & Dang, 2003; Yoo et al., 2010).

Such racialization processes might impede one's ability to embrace and develop comfort with their Asian American identity. For example, the aforementioned racial tropes can lead Asian Americans to dissociate from their communities (J. Kim, 1981; Nadal, 2004). Moreover, the model minority myth can convince Asian Americans that they are not really racially minoritized and do not experience racism (Museus & Kiang, 2009), thereby hindering deep exploration into how these racial tropes might shape collective Asian American experiences (Yi et al., 2020). However, if Asian Americans develop an understanding of racial oppression and how it operates, they can become increasingly aware of the reality that the negative fictions of their racial groups are externally and socially constructed and forced upon them, rather than innate characteristics of their racial communities.

Second, *intersectionality* denotes the reality that White supremacy converges with other systems of oppression (e.g., sexism, heterosexism, ableism, etc.) to mutually shape the societal contexts within which Asian Americans exist and their lived experiences (Buenavista et al., 2009; Lee, 2006; Museus & Saelua, 2014). Of course, Asian Americans might also identify with historically oppressed ability, adoptee, gender, religious, class, and other groups that have shared struggles (Museus et al., 2016). Thus, it is important to consider the ways in which these other systems of oppression and identities that they shape might influence Asian Americanness. For example, heterosexism within Asian America could complicate the ways in which queer and trans* Asian Americans identify with it (Kumashiro, 2009; Pepin & Talbot, 2013). Similarly, the marginalization of particular ethnic subgroups within Asian America might complicate their group members' identification with Asian American communities (Ibrahim et al., 1997; Nadal, 2004).

Third, *transnational contexts* underscore the importance of understanding how imperialism, colonialism, racism, and other forms of oppression shape global political processes, as well as how these contexts continue to influence the lives of Asian Americans (Museus & Iftikar, 2013). Understanding these transnational contexts, above and beyond how racial oppression operates within U.S. borders, can provide a more holistic perspective regarding the factors that shape the identities of Asian Americans. For example, capitalism brought many relatively privileged East Asian Americans and South Asian Americans to the United States to fill job market demands, while U.S. imperialism and war led to the dislocation and immigration of many under-resourced Southeast Asian refugee communities that face some of the most significant systemic inequities (Iftikar & Museus, 2019). The latter group has often been utilized to highlight needs within Asian America, while their voices are typically marginalized in discourse related to this larger racial community (Yi et al., 2020).

Fourth, *(re)constructive history* highlights the reality of the pervasive exclusion of Asian Americans in U.S. history. It centers the need to transcend this invisibility and silence to develop a collective Asian American historical narrative and to (re)analyze existing discourses to highlight the voices and roles of Asian Americans in those histories (e.g., S. Chan, 1991; Takaki, 1998; Tamura, 2001, 2003; Umemoto, 1989). It could be argued that the exclusion of Asian Americans from the historical narrative is one primary mechanism by which systemic racism impedes the cultivation of collective consciousness. Thus, knowledge of Asian American history, including histories of racial oppression and this community's involvement in social justice advocacy, is essential for individuals to understand what it means to be Asian American within a U.S. context and foster the development of an Asian American identity.

Fifth, *strategic (anti)essentialism* refers to how Asian American communities acknowledge and resist the ways in which White supremacy racializes Asian Americans as a monolithic racial group while emphasizing that this community also has agency to shape such racialization processes. For example, this tenet underscores how Asian American scholars and activists engage in coalitions to embrace and (re)define essentialist racial categories as an act of political power (Coloma, 2006; Umemoto, 1989). It also underscores how Asian Americans engage in anti-essentialist efforts to deconstruct such categories and excavate intraracial diversity to advance racial justice (Yi et al., 2000). Thus, strategic (anti)essentialism highlights the complex, multifaceted, and fluid nature of Asian American identity and Asian Americanness.

Sixth, *story, theory, and praxis* recognizes that Asian American stories inform theory and practice, theory can shape practice, and practice can unearth stories and engage theory to facilitate positive individual and social transformation (Brayboy, 2005; Delgado, 1989; Ladson-Billings, 2000). In the current discussion, we argue that stories about how complex contexts shape identity can expand existing knowledge about Asian American identity. Specifically, they can center the complex contexts and nuances of identity formation. Moreover, personal narratives can be a useful tool for educators who seek to promote identity exploration.

Seventh, *commitment to social justice* highlights the assumption that AsianCrit is aimed at eradicating all forms of oppression, including racism, sexism, heterosexism, capitalist exploitation, and other systems of domination (Iftikar & Museus, 2019; Museus & Iftikar, 2013). As we discuss, it can be argued that a healthy Asian American identity is one that sees being Asian American as assuming a role in resisting systemic oppression and advocating for social justice (J. Kim, 1981; Nadal, 2004). Most identity theories imply that racial projects that dehumanize Asian Americans result in pressure for these individuals to assimilate into or be complacent in White society (J. Kim, 1981; Museus et al., 2013; Nadal, 2004), and knowledge of oppression can result in a heightened level of agency to resist it (Museus et al., 2012; Wang et al., in press). Such enhanced awareness can also contribute to an increased level of agency to contribute to the revival, nurturing, and maintenance of cultural communities.

Excavating the Complexity of Asian American Identity

In the previous section, we argue that an AsianCrit perspective can be utilized to better understand how systemic contexts might shape Asian American identities, the complexity of Asian Americanness, and the role that Asian American stories play in fostering Asian American identity. To further demonstrate this utility, we revisit Hannah and Vanessa's stories in greater depth. Their stories excavate how transnational contexts differentially shape their lives, how multiple streams of systemic violence shape their racial realities, the importance of Asian American histories and recognition of their invisibility in cultivating their racial consciousness, and the complexities of their commitments to social justice.

Hannah's Story

U.S. citizens' adoption of children born in Asia emerged as a result of U.S. imperialism and military intervention during the Cold War. At the end of the Korean Conflict, an operation to rescue Korean War orphans began, and the United States passed the Refugee Relief Act, which allowed Korean children of U.S. military men to migrate to the states (W. Kim, 1995). A transnational system of adoption was created and resulted in increased numbers of Korean adoptees coming to the United States long after the war and throughout the remainder of the 20th century. It is this transnational context that constitutes the backdrop for Hannah's story.

> According to my file, I was born on May 13 in a small town just outside Seoul, Korea. My birth mom came to the conclusion that it would be impossible to care for a baby by herself. Realizing that it would be better for me to grow up in an environment full of parental love and emotional, financial, and educational support, she gave me up for adoption. I grew up in Arizona with White cisgender, heterosexual parents. While I recognize the privilege that came with my adoption, it also came with a deeper level of trauma that nonadoptees will ever fully understand.
>
> On one hand, I am still marginalized, oppressed, and seen as inferior to the White people in society. On the other hand, I am often treated and perceived by my peers as being racially White. Because of these experiences, I have often felt pressure to racially assimilate into White culture, disregard my Asian American identity, and feel ashamed of being a transracial adoptee. Being a transracial adoptee, I am constantly working through a space that is somewhere in between how I identify myself and how others perceive and define me. I often crave a space where I can fit in and be surrounded by others that identify in similar ways. If I am being honest, I do not think that there will ever be a space for me to claim as my own and where I feel 100% authentically myself, but that is why I am here and that is why I continue to fight.

In high school, I had a difficult time reaching out and receiving support. My teachers and classmates often made me feel "stupid" or "incompetent" when I was not able to grasp a concept right away. As an Asian American, we are pressured to meet unrealistic standards of "perfection." As womxn, we are the "mothers" and "nurturers," who are seen as incompetent or incapable. As Asian American womxn, we're expected to be submissive, not encouraged to express and talk about our emotions. When I did make mistakes or didn't live up to people's excessive expectations of me, I silently suffered with depression but could not reach out for help.

When I entered college, I still felt the weight of living up to other people's expectations and their narratives dominated my life. After spending a year in therapy, I was able to overcome these feelings and begin to write my own story and define my own ideas of success. I ultimately found my heart and passion within the Asian Pacific American cultural center on campus. In this space, I met my undergraduate mentor who was the first person to empower me to shape my own identity, and I began to find my place in racial justice activism. I began to observe the ways in which Asian Pacific Islander Desi Americans are consistently excluded within institutions, and how White people and even other people of color do not believe we struggle or experience racism.

I worked with a group of student leaders from the various cultural centers to form a coalition of marginalized students. For many of the Asian American students, this was their first experience engaging in social and racial justice activism. Given the long-standing hxstory of Asian Americans being excluded and silenced, it was challenging for many students to engage in this type of work. For the first time, we stepped outside the lines and broke down barriers and stereotypes about the community. We were told that we were not doing "enough." When we did speak up, our input and experiences were often dismissed. I ultimately decided to disengage from the coalition, because I felt my and my community's voices and experiences did not matter.

As a result of my activism, I was seen as the loud, outspoken, and angry Asian. People did not like me expressing my voice, especially those within my own community. I was told time and time again that I was not a "true" Asian because I was raised by White people and will never fully understand what it means to be Asian American. So, what does it mean for me to be Asian American? I have struggled to answer this question for a long time, but storytelling has become a powerful tool for me. In having an invisible identity that is often overlooked or unrecognized, storytelling gives us a voice and space to have our narratives heard and valued. It also has supported me to understand the significance of identity, agency, and leadership. (Hannah)

Hannah's story provides a salient example of how society's racialization of Asian Americans as inferior and her experiences of marginalization within the Asian American community resulted in pressure to assimilate, making it difficult to identify as Asian American at certain points in her life. Also apparent in Hannah's story is how her multiple identities mutually shape her experiences. For example, it is clear that, as an Asian American woman, society constrains the ways in which she is able to resist racial oppression and identifying as a transracial adoptee profoundly shapes the ways which she experiences exclusion within the Asian American community. Her story also provides a powerful example of how Asian Americans engage in strategic coalition-building to advance justice, as well as how the silencing of Asian American voices within coalitions can diminish desire and agency to resist oppression.

Vanessa's Story

Similar to Hannah's narrative, Vanessa's story underscores how global contexts constitute an important backdrop of our journeys. Between 1975 and 1979, the communist party of Kampuchea, commonly known as the Khmer Rouge, engaged in a campaign of genocide (Chandler, 2000). It is estimated that over one million Cambodian people died, and millions more were forced into slavery during this period (Kiernan, 2002). Thus, many Khmer and other Southeast Asian refugees came to the United States to escape harsh conditions, political persecution, and genocide (Abueg & Chun, 1996; Boehnlein & Kinzie, 1997). They also settled into their new homes with few resources and encountered significant discrimination as they adjusted to the United States. As a result, many Khmer refugees experienced trauma before their arrival to the United States, which is often transmitted across generations. This transnational context is just one reality that distinguishes Vanessa's story from many other Asian Americans.

> On April 17, 1975, Phnom Penh, the capital of Cambodia, fell to the communist party of Kampuchea, the Khmer Rouge. Although I was not yet born, this date is etched into the fabric of my DNA because it heavily shapes my family's and community's hxstory. It was on this day that my family was forced to evacuate their homeland and relocate to refugee camps on the border of Thailand. Under the United States Refugee Act of 1980, my family was sponsored to migrate to the states. I was eventually born in Denver, Colorado, and lived in low-income housing (aka "the projects") for most of my childhood. The area I lived in was predominantly Latinx, but many of its inhabitants identified as Chicanx.

Eventually, my nuclear family moved to the wealthier, predominantly White suburbs of Denver. I stopped mentioning that my family were refugees. I stopped speaking Khmer to my grandparents. I stopped telling people that I was Khmer American. I did not seek out other Asian American students. I was guilty of burying my own hxstory and parts of myself. I had internalized my own oppression and only wanted to belong, but I was not doing it alone. School fueled the internalization.

The first time I saw Cambodia mentioned in school was when I read one small paragraph about the Vietnam War, and Cambodia was included in a list of countries that were involved in it. That was it. I assumed that additional details about Cambodia were not included because it was not relevant or important. I also remember reading a piece in a communications class about how culture can impact the ways in which people communicate. This article essentialized Asian Americans as being polite and passive, advising readers not to look them in the eye and to speak to them gently. It hurt to know that this was approved course material and that no one sensed that anything was wrong.

I eventually transferred to a new magnet school in Denver, a pivotal moment in my trajectory. My teachers infused their classrooms with social justice and ethnic studies literature and modeled activism by protesting for higher wages. One teacher in particular encouraged me to do a research project on the genocide in Cambodia, uncover my hxstory, and reconnect with my family because I had never read anything about Cambodia or the Khmer Rouge in my hxstory books. It was at this point that I developed a hunger to know and be a part of the Khmer American community. I began to finally embrace and honor my family's journey. I wanted to speak and practice Khmer. I understood that, as a daughter of Khmer refugees, the experience of genocide was deeply embedded into my body. I realized that the pressure to assimilate reflected a deliberate killing of my identity and community.

In college, I became involved in an Asian American student organization that made me feel as though my voice mattered. I first learned about Asian Pacific Islander and Desi American hxstory and movements through this organization. In response to the climate of the predominantly White institution, all of the student of color organizations before me had come together to embrace "alliance" as a political act—the Asian Student Alliance, Black Student Alliance, Latinx Student Alliance, Muslim Student Alliance, Queer Student Alliance, and others. It became clear to me that they understood that our liberation was truly intertwined.

Storytelling has kept my family's story alive. As refugees, they were forced to leave their lives behind. No documents, no photos, and no belongings. Yet, they carried their experiences in their bodies, and I am blessed to have those same experiences running through my veins. I share their stories whenever I share mine. Storytelling gives me an opportunity to bring truth to power. It ensures that others cannot claim my words and gives me agency to envision and determine my own narrative. (Vanessa)

Vanessa's narrative illuminates the ways in which her origins in a Khmer refugee community are deeply embedded in how she makes sense of her Asian Americanness. It also highlights how predominantly White contexts and the exclusion of Asian American voices from school curricula can partly impede the formation of Khmer and Asian American identities. However, both Hannah's and Vanessa's stories provide powerful examples of how curricula that centers Asian American voices can offer the promise of positive transformation, catapult students into a new recognition of the value of their Asian Americanness, and cultivate a renewed agency to shape their own destinies and the larger system that they resist.

Cultivating Environments to Nurture Asian Americanness

In this section, we utilize the AsianCrit framework, lessons learned from research with more than 100 Asian American students across five research projects, and the aforementioned narratives to delineate six propositions to describe how environmental conditions and processes shape Asian American identity. The propositions are grounded in the assumption that refocusing identity conversations on such contexts can spark questions and new conversations about how to cultivate optimal conditions for Asian American identity development.

Centering Asian American Histories Can
Foster Asian American Consciousness

As discussed, Asian American histories are often excluded from education curricula, and this exclusion can hinder identity exploration. In contrast, opportunities to acquire, exchange, and disseminate knowledge about Asian American community histories can increase the likelihood that Asian Americans will embrace, cultivate, and express their racial and ethnic identities (Accapadi, 2012; Kiang, 2002, 2009; Museus, 2008, 2014a, 2014b; Museus et al., 2012, 2013; Pendakur & Pendakur, 2016). Such experiences enhance one's understanding of how oppression erases their community histories and cultures from social, political, and educational systems. Indeed, knowledge that Asian Americans *have* histories in the United States enables one to understand the erasure of these histories from its society and education system. This awareness can also provide the foundation for Asian Americans to cultivate a commitment to resist the systemic oppression that contributes to the invisibility of their cultural communities.

Engaging Transnational Contexts Can Complicate Understandings of Asian America and Promote More Complex Asian American Identities

Opportunities to understand how global politics, including Western imperialism and war, shape Asian American communities' conditions, cultures, and perspectives can promote a more complex understanding of Asian America. Spaces that foster learning about these transnational processes can also help students comprehend the ways in which these systemic dynamics have led to persisting and drastic inequities *within* Asian American communities. Such learning can allow Asian Americans to understand why Southeast Asian Americans might be marginalized within Asian America, how their communities are racialized in unique ways, and reasons that they are relatively less privileged compared to East and South Asian American populations. For example, educators can use oral history projects to facilitate Asian American students' learning about these how transnational contexts differentially shape the trajectories of diverse communities and family members within this racial group. Grappling with such intraracial differences is vital to cultivating solidarity in social justice activism and advocacy across various groups within Asian America.

Storytelling and Reflection Can Cultivate Asian Americanness

Storytelling and reflection can facilitate the development of Asian American identity and agency. These experiences can positively impact identity formation in that they amplify and make relevant the voices of Asian Americans (Kiang, 2002, 2009; Museus, 2014a, 2014b; Tang, 2016; Vue, 2013; Wang et al., in press). For example, culturally relevant courses can incorporate assignments that allow students to interview members of their families and communities to excavate authentic Asian American narratives or encourage them to write their own stories. In addition to stories embedded in culturally relevant course material (e.g., literature and presentations), Asian American stories can be excavated through digital storytelling and visual and performing arts projects. Such stories can counter society's harmful racial constructions of them and challenge the internalization of negative views of Asian Americans.

Stories coupled with reflection can be especially valuable. Reflection ensures psychological space for students to make sense of their own experiences within larger cultural and racial contexts. For example, reflections can prompt critical thinking about how race shapes their peer group experiences, what factors led to them internalizing particular messages about what it means to be Asian American, ways in which their race and ethnicity shape their passions and educational goals, what it means to be Asian American on their college campus, and how they might engage in efforts to address problems that they encountered navigating school racial dynamics. Such reflection and sharing can easily be embedded into orientations, courses across disciplines, leadership development programs, mentoring programs, and capstone experiences.

Community Activism and Advocacy Can Solidify Commitments to Social Justice

Opportunities to give back to Asian American communities can increase students' attachment to them, expand their knowledge of problems that exist within Asian American communities, and enhance their appreciation of the meaningful investment in solutions to these challenges (Museus, 2008, 2014b; Museus et al., 2016; Wang et al., in press). Engagement in community activism and advocacy can also cultivate enhanced agency to resist oppression and commitments to social justice (Pendakur & Pendakur, 2016). Research and service projects, for example, can allow Asian American students to give back to their community and include those that aim to increase political participation of Asian American immigrant and refugee communities, disaggregate data to complicate stereotypes of Asian Americans, and understand and address racism that is targeted at Asian American communities in education, healthcare, and the media.

Intersectional Dialogues Can Complicate Understandings of Asian American Identity and Enhance Strategic Anti-Essentialism Capacities

Facilitating dialogues about diverse experiences within Asian America can increase understanding of systemic dehumanization, increase empathy, and contribute to agency to resist all forms of oppression as well. Asian Americans are often viewed as a monolithic community (Chang, 2011; Kiang, 2002; Museus & Kiang, 2009). When generalizations are made to all Asian Americans, it can marginalize some populations within this community and inhibit the exploration and development of their Asian American and other social identities. Groups whose realities are often ignored or misunderstood include South, Southeast, transracial adoptee, multiracial, queer and trans*, and undocumented Asian Americans. Practitioners must recognize and excavate these identities and their intersections with Asian America.

These conversations can incorporate dialogue on diversity within the Asian American community, the salience and complexity of multiple identities, the marginalization of subgroups within the Asian American community, and how the different Asian American communities are inherently and inevitably interconnected with each other. Continuing to complicate these conversations by acknowledging the diversity and multiple identities within Asian America is one salient condition in promoting holistic and complex identity development.

Critical Cross-Race Dialogues Can Promote Interracial Solidarity and Strengthen Commitments to Social Justice

Intentionally structured opportunities for Asian Americans to connect, engage in dialogue, and collaborate with other racially minoritized peers can allow them to develop a deeper and more complex understanding of the experiences of other racial groups and how systemic racial oppression differentially enacts violence on all communities of color (C. Kim, 1999; Wang et al., in press). Facilitating discussions and learning about struggles across racial groups can also empower students to build coalitions, share their experiences, and support each other. One approach educators can utilize to maximize engagement in these conversations is supporting student-led discussions around topics that are particularly significant to them. Such efforts center student voices at the core of conversations, validate the lived experiences of these students, and encourage collaboration, correspondence, and community among them.

It is important to note that Asian Americans are often marginalized or excluded from larger conversations about racial oppression and justice (Brown, 2005; Grim et al., 2019). Such marginalization and exclusion can lead Asian Americans to distance themselves from other communities of color and diminished recognition of both common and unique struggles. Therefore, if educators want Asian Americans to develop solidarities with other communities of color broadly and maximize their likelihood of engaging in racial justice work, they must ensure that Asian American voices and issues are meaningfully engaged in these conversations.

Conclusion

It is worth nothing that educational institutions often exclude, marginalize, invalidate, and dehumanize Asian Americans and other historically marginalized populations (Museus et al., 2015), and such environments can hinder identity development (J. Chan, 2017). In contrast, culturally responsive support can aid Asian Americans in navigating identity formation processes effectively. Because identity exploration and development can encompass many emotional processes and uncertainties, it is important for educators to consider how they can provide support that is holistic, humanized, and proactive throughout these processes (Museus, 2011; Museus & Neville, 2012). Specifically, students must be able to find support persons who they trust to help them navigate the complexities of learning about systems of oppression, coming to grips with internalized racism, unpacking emotional and difficult topics, and figuring out how to most constructively respond to racial challenges. These students might also need support persons who can proactively provide them with resources to help navigate these processes and role model how Asian Americans can cope with systemic racism in healthy ways. If such persons have strong Asian American identities themselves, they might be optimally equipped to provide Asian Americans with ongoing support as they develop their identities.

In the current chapter, we discuss supporting Asian Americans in their identity development journeys. However, for college educators to utilize the propositions and recommendations discussed herein effectively, they must understand their own biases about Asian American populations and anti-Asianness. For example, educators often assume that Asian American voices are irrelevant in conversations about social and political issues (Grim et al., 2019; Museus & Park, 2012). In addition, many educators who advocate for racial equity often assume that Asian American voices are only relevant when they help understand the challenges that other communities of color face (Yi et al., 2020). Such biases can hinder the ability of educators to holistically engage and effectively support Asian Americans throughout their developmental journeys. Therefore, it is also important for educators to deepen their knowledge of the transnational contexts, global contexts and histories, intersectional experiences, and advocacy dynamics of Asian American communities. If we, as educators, seek to positively transform those with whom we work, the transformation must begin with ourselves.

Notes

1. Throughout this chapter, our personal narratives employ feminist versions of words that traditionally privilege men within them—womxn instead of women and hxstory instead of history to denote gender inclusivity, shed light on patriarchal institutions and the resulting injustices faced by women, and symbolize resistance to patriarchal linguistic norms. Although our personal narratives employ feminist versions of particular words, identifiers utilized by cited authors are utilized to maintain consistency with the referenced article.

2. Although we use "race" to denote social constructed categories and identities imposed on communities of color (e.g., Asian), we use "ethnicity" to refer to collective identities typically tied to a particular local geographic region, culture, and language (e.g., Cambodian, Indian, Japanese, Vietnamese, etc.) (see Museus, 2014).

References

Abueg, F. R., & Chun, K. M. (1996). Traumatization stress among Asian and Asian Americans. In A. J. Marsella, M. J. Friedman, E. T. Gerrity, & R. M. Scurfield (Eds.), *Ethnocultural aspects of posttraumatic stress disorder: Issues, research, and clinical applications* (pp. 285–299). American Psychological Association.

Accapadi, M. M. (2012). Asian American identity consciousness: A polycultural model. In D. Ching & A. Agbayani (Eds.), *Asian Americans and Pacific Islanders in higher education: Research and perspectives on identity, leadership, and success* (pp. 57–94). NASPA Foundation.

Acuña, R. (2015). Occupied America. In R. Delgado & J. Stefancic (Eds.), *The Latino/a condition: A critical reader* (pp. 171–174). New York University Press.

Boehnlein, J. K., & Kinzie, J. D. (1997). Cultural perspectives on post-traumatic stress disorder. In T. W. Miller (Ed.), *Clinical disorders and stressful life events* (pp. 19–43). International Universities Press.

Brayboy, B. (2005). Toward a tribal critical race theory in education. *Urban Review, 37*(5), 425–446. https://doi.org/10.1007/s11256-005-0018-y

Brown, D. A. (2005). Moving beyond the Black/White paradigm: An introduction. *Washington and Lee Journal of Civil Rights and Social Justice, 12*(1), 1–4. https://scholarlycommons.law.wlu.edu/crsj/vol12/iss1/3/

Buenavista, T. L., Jayakumar, U. M., & Misa-Escalante, K. (2009). Contextualizing Asian American education through critical race theory: An example of U.S. Pilipino college student experiences. *New Directions for Institutional Research, 2009*(142), 69–81. https://doi.org/10.1002/ir.297

Chan, S. (1991). *Asian Americans: An interpretive history.* Twayne.

Chan, J. (2017). Complexities of racial identity development for Asian Pacific Islander Desi American (APIDA) college students. In D. C. Maramba & C. M. Kodama (Eds.), *Bridging research and practice to support Asian American students* [Special Issue] (New Directions for Student Services, no. 160, pp. 11–23). Wiley. https://doi.org/10.1002/ss.20240

Chandler, D. P. (2000). *A history of Cambodia.* (2nd ed.). Westview Press.

Chang, M. J. (2011). Battle hymn of the model minority myth. *Amerasia Journal, 37*(2), 137–143. https://doi.org/10.17953/amer.37.2.m1j0q8767202t21q

Chew, P. K. (1994). Asian Americans: The "reticent" minority and their paradoxes. *William and Mary Law Review, 36*(1), 1–94. https://scholarship.law.wm.edu/wmlr/vol36/iss1/2

Cho, S. K. (2003). Converging stereotypes in racialized sexual harassment: Where the model minority meets Suzie Wong. In A. K. Wing (Ed.), *Critical race feminism: A reader* (2nd ed., pp. 349–366). New York University Press.

Chon, M. (1995). On the need for Asian American narratives in law: Ethnic specimens, native informants, storytelling and silences. *UCLA Asian Pacific American Law Journal, 3–4*, 4–33. https://digitalcommons.law.seattleu.edu/cgi/view content.cgi?article=1331&context=faculty

Coloma, R. S. (2006). Disorienting race and education: Changing paradigms on the schooling of Asian Americans and Pacific Islanders. *Race, Ethnicity, and Education, 9*(1), 1–15. https://doi.org/10.1080/13613320500490606

Delgado, R. (1989). Storytelling for oppositionists and others: A plea for narrative. *Michigan Law Review, 87*(8), 2411–2441. https://doi.org/10.2307/1289308

Espiritu, Y. (1993). *Asian American panethnicity: Bridging institutions and identities.* Temple University Press.

Grim, J. K., Lee, N. L., Museus, S. D., Na, V. S., & Ting, M. P. (2019). Asian American college student activism and social justice in Midwest contexts. In S. D. Museus & M. P. Ting (Eds.), *Contemporary issues facing Asian Americans in higher education* (New Directions for Higher Education, no. 186, pp. 25–36). Jossey-Bass. https://doi.org/10.1002/he.20321

Ibrahim, F., Ohnishi, H., & Sandhu, D. S. (1997). Asian-American identity development: A culture specific model for South Asian-Americans. *Journal of Multicultural Counseling and Development, 25*(1), 34–50. https://doi .org/10.1002/j.2161-1912.1997.tb00314.x

Iftikar, J. S., & Museus, S. D. (2019). On the utility of Asian critical (AsianCrit) theory in the field of education. *International Journal of Qualitative Studies in Education, 31*(10), 935–949. https://doi.org/10.1080/09518398.2018 .1522008

Kiang, P. N. (2002). Stories and structures of persistence: Ethnographic learning through research and practice in Asian American Studies. In Y. Zou & E.T. Trueba (Eds.), *Ethnography and schools: Qualitative approaches to the study of education* (pp. 223–255). Rowman & Littlefield.

Kiang, P. N. (2009). A thematic analysis of persistence and long-term educational engagement with Southeast Asian American college students. In L. Zhan (Ed.), *Asian American vices: Engaging, empowering, enabling* (pp. 21–58). NLN Press.

Kiernan, B. (2002). *The Pol Pot regime: Race, power and genocide in Cambodia under the Khmer Rouge, 1975-79* (2nd ed.). Yale University Press.

Kim, C. J. (1999). The racial triangulation of Asian Americans. *Politics & Society, 27*(1), 105–138.

Kim, J. (1981). *Processes of Asian American identity development: A study of Japanese American women's perceptions of their struggle to achieve positive identities as Americans of Asian ancestry.* [Unpublished dissertation, University of Massachusetts Amherst]. Scholarworks. https://scholarworks.umass.edu/cgi/viewcontent.cgi?ar ticle=4686&context=dissertations_1

Kim, J. (2012). Asian American identity development theory. In C. L. Wijeyesinghe & B. W. Jackson III (Eds.), *New perspectives on racial identity development: Integrating emerging frameworks* (2nd ed., pp. 138–160). New York University Press.

Kim, W. J. (1995). International adoption: A case review of Korean children. *Child Psychiatry and Human Development, 25*(3), 141–154. https://doi.org/10.1007/BF02251299

Kumashiro, K. K. (1999). Supplementing normalcy and otherness: Queer Asian American men reflect on stereotypes, identity, and oppression. *Qualitative Studies in Education, 12*(5), 491–508. https://www.tandfonline.com/doi/abs/10.1080/095183999235917

Ladson-Billings, G. (2000). Racialized discourses and ethnic epistemologies. In N. Denzin & Y. Lincoln (Eds), *Handbook of qualitative research* (2nd ed., pp. 257–277). SAGE.

Lee, S. J. (2006). Additional complexities: social class, ethnicity, generation, and gender in Asian American student experiences. *Race, Ethnicity, and Education, 9*(1), 17–28. https://doi.org/10.1080/13613320500490630

Lowe, L. (1996). *Immigrant acts: On Asian American cultural politics.* Duke University Press.

Museus, S. D. (2008). The role of ethnic student organizations in fostering African American and Asian American students' cultural adjustment and membership at predominantly White institutions. *Journal of College Student Development, 46*(6), 568–586. https://doi.org/10.1353/csd.0.0039

Museus, S. D. (2011). Generating ethnic minority student success (GEMS): A qualitative analysis of high-performing institutions. *Journal of Diversity in Higher Education, 4*(3), 147–162. https://doi.org/10.1037/a0022355

Museus, S. D. (2014a). *Asian American students in higher education.* Routledge.

Museus, S. D. (2014b). The culturally engaging campus environments (CECE) model: A new theory of college success among racially diverse student populations. In M. B. Paulsen (Ed.), *Higher education: Handbook of theory and research* (pp. 189–227). Springer.

Museus, S. D., antonio, a. l., & Kiang, P. N. (2016). The state of scholarship on Asian Americans and Pacific Islanders in education: Anti-essentialism, inequality, context, and relevance. In S. D. Museus, A. Agbayani, & D. M. Ching (Eds.), *Focusing on the underserved: Immigrant, refugee, and indigenous Asian American and Pacific Islanders in higher education* (pp. 1–51). Information Age.

Museus, S. D., & Iftikar, J. (2013). An Asian critical race theory (AsianCrit) framework. In M. Y. Danico & J. G. Golson (Eds.), *Asian American society* (pp. 95–98). SAGE.

Museus, S. D., & Kiang, P. N. (2009). Deconstructing the model minority myth and how it contributes to the invisible minority reality in higher education research. In S. D. Museus (Ed.), *Conducting research on Asian Americans in higher education*

[Special Issue] (New Directions for Institutional Research, no. 142, 5–15). Wiley. https://doi.org/10.1002/ir.292

Museus, S. D., Lam, S., Huang, C., Kem, P., & Tan, K. (2012). Cultural integration in campus subcultures: Where the cultural, academic, and social spheres of college life collide. In S. D. Museus & U. M. Jayakumar (Eds.), *Creating campus cultures: Fostering success among racially diverse student populations* (pp. 106–129). Routledge.

Museus, S. D., Ledesma, M. C., & Parker, T. L. (2015). *Racism and racial equity in higher education.* Jossey-Bass.

Museus, S. D., & Neville, K. M. (2012). Delineating the ways that key institutional agents provide racial minority students with access to social capital in college. *Journal of College Student Development, 53*(3), 436–452. https://doi.org/10.1353/csd.2012.0042

Museus, S. D., Nguyen, T. K., Vue, R., & Yeung, F. (2013) A model of Southeast Asian American identity development: Merging theoretical perspectives. In S. D. Museus, D. C. Maramba, & R. T. Teranishi (Eds.), *The misrepresented minority: New insights on Asian Americans and Pacific Islanders, and the implications for higher education* (pp. 47–66). Stylus.

Museus, S. D., & Park, J. J. (2015). The continuing significance of racism in the lives of Asian American college students. *Journal of College Student Development, 56*(6), 551–569. https://doi.org/10.1353/csd.2015.0059

Museus, S. D., & Saelua, N. (2014). Realizing the power of intersectionality in higher education research: The case of Asian Americans and Pacific Islanders in higher education. In D. Mitchell Jr. (Ed.), *Intersectionality and higher education: Theory, research, and practice* (pp. 45–54). Peter Lang.

Museus, S. D., Shiroma, K., & Dizon, J. P. (2016). Cultural community connections and college success: An examination of Southeast Asian American college students. *Journal of College Student Development, 57*(5), 485–502. https://doi.org/10.1353/csd.2016.0064

Museus, S. D., & Truong, K. A. (2013). Racism and sexism in cyberspace: Engaging stereotypes of Asian American women and men to facilitate student learning and development. *About Campus, 18*(4), 14–21. https://doi.org/10.1002/abc.21126

Nadal, K. I. (2004). Pilipino American identity development model. *Multicultural Counseling and Development 32*, 45–62. https://doi.org/10.1002/j.2161-1912.2004.tb00360.x

Nagel, J. (1994). Constructing ethnicity: Creating and recreating ethnic identity and culture. *Social Problems, 41*(1), 152–176. https://doi.org/10.1525/sp.1994.41.1.03x0430n

Omi, M., & Winant, H. (1994). *Racial formation in the United States: From the 1960s to the 1990s* (2nd ed.). Routledge.

Pendakur, S. L., & Pendakur, V. (2016). Beyond boba tea and samosas: A call for Asian American race consciousness. In S. D. Museus, D. M. Ching, & A. Agbayani (Eds.), *Focusing on the underserved: Immigrant, refugee, and indigenous Asian American and Pacific Islanders in higher education* (pp. 55–72). Information Age.

Pepin, S., & Talbot, D. (2013). Negotiating the complexities of being Asian American and lesbian, gay, or bisexual. In S. D. Museus, D. C. Maramba, & R. T. Teranishi (Eds.), *The misrepresented minority: New insights on Asian Americans and Pacific Islanders, and the implications for higher education* (pp. 227–244). Stylus.

Prasso, S. (2005). *The Asian mystique: Dragon ladies, geisha girls, & our fantasies of the exotic Orient.* Public Affairs.

Pyke, K., & Dang, T. (2003). "FOB" and "Whitewashed": Identity and internalized racism among second generation Asian Americans. *Qualitative Sociology, 26*(2), 147–172. https://link.springer.com/article/10.1023/A:1022957011866

Takaki, R. (1998). *A history of Asian Americans: Strangers from a different shore.* Little, Brown & Company.

Tamura, E. H. (2001). Asian Americans in the history of education: An historiographical essay. *History of Education Quarterly, 41*(1), 58–71. https://doi.org/10.1111/j.1748-5959.2001.tb00074.x

Tamura, E. H. (2003). Asian Americans and educational history. *History of Education Quarterly, 43*(1), 1–9. https://doi.org/10.1111/j.1748-5959.2003.tb00112.x

Umemoto, K. (1989). "On Strike!" San Francisco State College strike, 1968-1969: The role of Asian American students. *Amerasia Journal, 15*(1), 3–41. https://doi.org/10.17953/amer.15.1.7213030j5644rx25

Vue, R. (2013). Campus contexts and Hmong students' experiences negotiating identity and higher education. In S. D. Museus, D. C. Maramba, & R. Teranishi (Eds.), *The misrepresented minority: New insights on Asian Americans and Pacific Islanders, and the implications for higher education* (pp. 182–197). Stylus.

Wang, A. C., Mac, J., & Museus, S. D. (in press). The power of ethnic studies at Asian American and Native American Pacific Islander serving institutions (AANAPISIs). *About Campus.*

Wong, A. (2013). Racial identity construction among Chinese American and Filipino American undergraduates. In S. D. Museus, D. C. Maramba, & R. T. Teranishi (Eds.), *The misrepresented minority: New insights on Asian Americans and Pacific Islanders, and the implications for higher education* (pp. 93–118). Stylus.

Yi, V., Mac, J., Na, V., Venturanza, R., Museus, S. D., Buenavista, T. L., & Pendakur, S. (2020). Toward an anti-imperialistic critical race analysis of the model minority myth. *The Review of Educational Research, 90*(4), 542–579. https://doi.org/10.3102/0034654320933532

Yoo, H. C., Burrola, K. S., & Steger, M. F. (2010). A preliminary report on a new measure: Internalization of the Model Minority Myth Measure (IM-4) and its psychological correlates among Asian American college students. *Journal of Counseling Psychology, 57*(1), 114–127. https://doi.org/10.1037/a0017871

6

UNBOXING ASIAN/
AMERICAN TRANSRACIAL
ADOPTEE COLLEGIAN
IDENTITIES

Nicholas D. Hartlep and Daniel K. Suda

This chapter examines a unique student population on college and university campuses: Asian/American transracial adoptees. Because a limited amount of research has been published on the experiences and racial identity development of this particular subset of the college student population, we offer a relevant student development model that extends our earlier work (see Suda & Hartlep, 2016) and builds upon the previous work of other scholars in different but overlapping fields of study (see Samura, 2016; Schlossberg, 1989; Ung et al., 2012). After examining the existing student development models, specifically Renn's (2004) ecological theory of mixed-race identity development, we offer a new, relevant model of racial identity development that is inclusive of the needs and experiences of transracial Asian/American adoptee students. Our racial identity development model seeks to inform college and university administrators, faculty, and practitioners.

What Is Meant by Transracial?

A *transracial adoptee* is defined simply as an individual who is adopted into a family with a race or multiple races different from the one(s) given from their birth parents. Rachel Dolezal made headlines when she claimed she was a transracial person. Born White, Dolezal claimed she felt her true race was African American. This phenomenon of Whites claiming a "transracial" identity is becoming more prevalent, a reality evidenced in mainstream news reporting on the scandalous claim that a person is transracial when one feels they were born the wrong race (Ianelli, 2020). For example, *USA Today* reported on a story about a White male (Adam) living in Florida, who goes by the Filipino name Ja Du (Flowers, 2017). Ja Du created a Facebook group, "Trans Racialism Support Group." According to the group's page, "The trans race support group or trsg is a group made to give TR [transracial] people closure and friendship through a tight knit community of cool loving people feel free to talk and strike up a conversation!" We argue in this chapter that the misuse of the term *transracial* undermines the very population we hope to move from the margins to the middle—Asian/American transracial adoptee collegians—because they matter.

Although transgender has become a commonly accepted identity in past years, there has not been much positive reception to the idea of transracialism. Tuvel (2017) wrote a philosophical article published in *Hypatia* that argued, "considerations that support transgenderism extend to transracialism" (p. 264). Her article received an overwhelming amount of backlash, including a petition for retraction from over 800 scholars, defense of the article from the editor of *Hypatia*, and then a formal apology from the *Hypatia* board of directors (Travis, 2017). The lay and scholarly worlds not being supportive of the idea of "transracial" being used in the manner Tuvel (2017) argued makes sense. This misuse of the term *transracial* has also been found problematic by those in the transracial adoptee community, which has championed the term since at least the 1970s, if not earlier (Simon & Alstein, 1977).

Transracial Asian/American Adoptees in U.S. Higher Education

To best understand the transracial Asian/American population it helps to research the number people that are adopted in the United States. According to the 2000 U.S. Census, "approximately 5 million Americans alive today are adoptees, 2–4 percent of all families have adopted, and 2.5 percent of all children under 18 are adopted" (Herman, n.d, para. 5). Going further,

> four out of ten adopted children are in transracial adoptions—that is, their parents reported that both adoptive parents are (or the single adoptive parent is) of a different race, culture, or ethnicity than their child. Transracial adoptions are most common for children whose families adopted internationally. (Vandivere et al., 2006)

Approximately 1% of the United States population is transracially adopted. With such a small number of people fitting into this demographic, why is it important to look at this population and their issues with racial identity development within colleges and universities?

According to National Center for Education Statistics (NCES, 2017) there are 6,000 colleges or universities in the United States. This statistic is the one we use because Title IV of the Higher Education Act of 1965 (HEA) covers the administration of the U.S. federal student financial aid programs, and this is a key indicator of quality. According to NCES (2019), "Females are expected to account for the majority of college and university students in fall 2019: about 11.3 million females will attend in fall 2019, compared with 8.6 million males" (para. 13). Also, according to NCES (2019), "Some 6.0 million students will attend 2-year institutions and 13.9 million will attend 4-year institutions in fall 2019. About 16.9 million students are expected to enroll in undergraduate programs and 3.0 million will enroll in post-baccalaureate programs" (para. 12). Since 1976 the racial diversity of students at colleges and universities has continued to trend upward. Enrollment of students of color was 15.7% in 1976 compared to 44% in 2017. Enrollment of students who were White was 84.3% in 1976 compared to 56% in 2017 (Figure 6.1) (NCES, n.d.).

College administrators and academic and student affairs practitioners responsible for diversity programming on college campuses are tasked with

Figure 6.1. Percentage distribution of university/college students by race, 1976–2017.

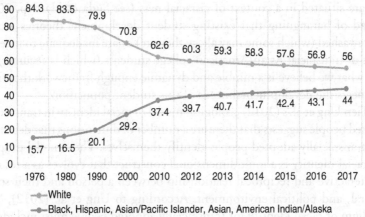

Source: NCES (n.d.).

considering how diverse students experience college. Asian/American adoptees are an often-overlooked population whose needs are not considered. According to Ung et al. (2012), "Incongruence between what an adopted person sees, feels and thinks about who they are racially is considered to be an outcome of their interactions with their environment" (p. 82). According to the 2010 U.S. Census, from 2009 through 2011 there were approximately 438,000 transracially adopted children under the age of 18, comprising 28% of all adopted children under 18. The largest proportion of transracially adopted children was Asian (2%) (Suda & Hartlep, 2016).[1]

Even though transracial Asian/American adoptees may only represent a small number of college students, their transracial adoptee status, is filtered through a "cisracial" lens, which ultimately leads them to be racialized as being culturally Asian/American and stereotyped through a "model minority" prism. Another reason this work is important, irrespective of being a small population is that according to Joy Hoffman and Edlyn Pena (2013) "few studies address how adoptees or transracial adoptees experience college" (p. 154).

Racial Identity Development and Sense of Belonging

While our chapter draws on the scholarly work of many diverse scholars, such as Kristen Renn's (2000) work on "situational identity," Amanda Baden's (2002) work on "cultural-racial identity," Grace Kim et al.'s (2010) work on "racial and ethnic identities," and Hoffman and Pena's (2013) work on "ethnic identity," we find the main limitation of these existing frameworks is that they are situated in a context of cisracial-ness (see Suda & Hartlep, 2016). Instead of haranguing that existing student development theories are too Whitewashed (which some may allege they are) or are inadequate to meet the needs of transracial Asian/American college students (which is accurate), we offer what we believe is a nimble and dynamic enough framework that traces and meets the developmental needs of this student population.

Tien Ung et al.'s (2012) ecological model of racial identity in transracially adopted people suggests that there are a number of dimensions that determine how transracially adopted people identify themselves. Their model proposes that racial identity is a multidimensional construct that evolves as a result of an interactive and reciprocal relationship between a person and their social, cultural, and political environment. According to Ung et al. (2012), "Any paradigm of racial identity for transracially adopted people must include the impact of racism" (p. 75). Racism in the United States is seen through a racial binary—Black or White—which translates into other dichotomies: racist or not racist, good or bad (McConahay, 1986). But where do transracial

Asian/American adoptees fit? Are they White (Zhou, 2004)? Are they Black (Kim, 1999)?

Stereotypes of Asian/Americans reveal racism, too. Asian/Americans are framed to be scholarly and exceptional students. Many do not consider this to be racist, asking, "How can a positive stereotype be racist?" We know the model minority stereotype to be racist toward Asian/Americans and non-Whites (Hartlep & Ozment, 2019). The difficulty of including the impact of racism in a racial identity paradigm, as implored by Ung et al. (2012), is that scholars have overlooked the institutional norm of cisracial-ness, something we have explored elsewhere (Suda & Hartlep, 2016).

Schlossberg (1989) looked at the terms *marginality* and *mattering* and examined how they played a role in people's lives, specifically in college students' lives. Schlossberg (1989) described marginality as not fitting in, as if a person does not matter to others, suggesting that marginality "can be a temporary condition during transition, a description of a personality type, or a way of life" (p. 8). A student will have a better chance to succeed in college if they feel as though they matter (Schlossberg, 1989). College students seeking a sense of belonging on campus often look to student groups, such as racial identity–based organizations (Asian/American Student Association, Latinx, Multiracial Greek Life, etc.). Students may be searching for a sense of mattering through membership in a group of peers who look similar or identify similarly to them. Schlossberg (1989) defined four aspects of mattering: *attention*, the feeling that one is noticed; *importance*, a belief that one is cared about; *ego-extension*, the feeling that someone else will be proud of what one does or will sympathize with one's failures; and *dependence*, a feeling of being needed. Student organizations can provide all four of Schlossberg's (1989) aspects to their student members, something we address later in this chapter.

An Adaption of Renn's (2004) Ecological Theory of Mixed-Race Identity Development

There has been a large amount of research done on mixed-race identity development in the past. However, we have discovered very little research on transracially adopted students and how they develop a racial identity. Through this chapter, we have sought to develop a theory to describe how transracially adopted individuals develop a mixed-race identity through nature and nurture influences. We believe that the present research relates very well when adapting Renn's (2004) ecological theory of mixed-race identity development. It is important to note from her original theory that a "single identity may be neither possible nor desirable for mixed-race students" (Evans et al., 2009, p. 297) and individuals can change how they identify depending on different experiences at various times in their life.

Renn's (2004) ecological theory described five identity patterns: *mono-racial*, where an individual identifies with one identity, typically their most salient, which is often congruent with their appearance; *multiple monoracial*, where an individual is conscious of more than one identity typically based on their parental heritage; *multiracial*, where an individual finds themselves outside of the mono paradigm and can integrate all of their identities into a positive self-concept; *extraracial*, where an individual chooses to identify with a race that is different than their mixed heritage (these students often viewed race as a social construct); and *situational*, where an individual chooses an identity based on their environment and current circumstances.

When considering how Renn's (2004) theory could be applied to adopted individuals, we noticed that her proposed identities really only worked for a nonadopted individual with influences from their birth parent(s). We have expanded upon Renn's (2004) five proposed identities and created seven identities for transracially adopted mixed-race individuals organized into four categories. Just as in Renn's (2004) model, these identities are meant to be fluid and nonexclusive, where an individual can change how they identify based on their different life experiences at any given time. Our research has led to the development of the transracially adopted mixed-race identity development model. The identity model we have developed is based on a continuum of nature versus nurture combined with the influences that both birth and adoptive parents can have on an individual's racial identity. As can be seen in Figure 6.2, there are two circles representing the influences from both birth parents and adoptive parents. Those circles create a Venn diagram along the nature versus nurture scale to show that the mixed influences from both facets can create new identities. Even though the seven identities are numbered, it is important to remember that this is not a unidirectional, linear model; rather, it is a fluid model, and identity processes can change at any given time. The categories and their respective identity patterns are shared in Figure 6.2 and in the following paragraphs.

Future research can test our belief that an individual will likely move from a nature-centric identity to a more nurture-centric identity. While we assert that identities can flow from one to another, we believe that an individual is more likely to identify with a biological feature and then understand an adoptive identity as they enter college and develop outside of their parents influence.

Biological Identities (Influenced by Nature)
Often, an adopted individual will know little to nothing about their birth family's history and may only know the ethnicity that is listed on their birth certificate. Research suggests that it is common for adopted individuals to question their roots. "The adoptees' 'dual identity' problem may prompt

Figure 6.2. Transracially adopted mixed-race identity development model for Asian/Americans.

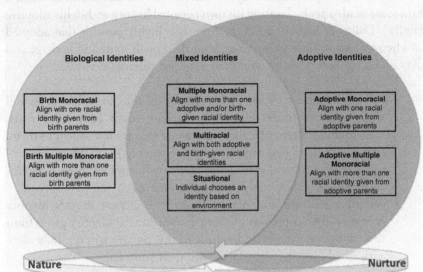

them to search out their past and pursue information about this unknown self in an effort to resolve the break in the continuity of their lives" (Hoopes, 1990, p. 160). Identifying with a biological identity may cause concern for adoptive parents, because "some adopted adolescents may feel that to identify very closely with the culture of their birthland is to 'dis-identify' with adoptive parents" (Smith, 2006, p. 254). However, at the same time a person in one of these identities may just be trying to understand more of their birth heritages:

- Birth monoracial identity: A person in this identity process will align with one racial identity given from their birth parents. Individuals will typically align with a race that is most salient to them, commonly associated with their appearance.
- Birth multiple monoracial identity: A person in this identity process will be conscious of more than one racial identity given from their birth parents. This process would be likely in the case that a transracial adoptee was born from birth parents that are interracial.

Adoptive Identities (Influenced by Nurture)
The environmental experiences that a child is placed in will play a large role in their development. The adoptive parents who raise a child are responsible

for instilling life values in children. "Without knowledge about and experience of biological parents, it may be difficult for the adolescent to build a firm sense of identity by locating his own personal history within his adoptive family" (Dalley & Kohon, 2008, p. 227). It is highly possible that adopted children will know little to nothing about their birth roots and heritage and may find it easier to identify with their adoptive parents' identities.

- Adoptive monoracial identity: A person in this identity process will align with one racial identity given from their adoptive parents. Individuals will typically align with a race that is most salient to them, commonly associated with the adoptive parent(s) with whom the person identifies most closely. This identity will come easily to individuals who look similar to their adoptive parents.
- Adoptive multiple monoracial identity: A person in this identity process will be conscious of more than one racial identity given from their adoptive parents. Individuals in this process will typically align with racial identities associated with their parent(s).

Mixed Identities (on Nature-Nurture Spectrum)
The following identities lie on the nature versus nurture spectrum. A person in one of these identities will be in a mixed-identity process due to influences from both birth and adoptive parent(s). All of these processes can lean more heavily to one side of the spectrum depending on an individual's current circumstances but will always have some amount of influence from both sides.

- Multiple monoracial: A person in this identity process will align with more than one racial identity. These identities are formed through a combination of influences from the individual's adoptive parents' identities and from their knowledge of birth-given heritages. A person in this process will likely identify with the races that they are most familiar with, possibly aligning with one that society has assigned them but will be salient of both the nature and nurture influences on their identity.
- Multiracial: A person with a multiracial identity will integrate both their nature and nurture influences into a positive self-concept. Similarly to Renn (2004), people in this identity process will see themselves as "existing outside of the monoracial paradigm" (Renn, 2004, p. 156). For adopted students, the ability to balance both influences may be difficult, as it could be difficult to understand their birth-given heritages without experiencing them during adolescence.

- Situational: In this identity process, an individual will choose an identity based on their environment and current circumstances. This identity would be possible for a person who has a friend group associated with others from their birth-given heritage or ethnicity. Perhaps this person would have an identity related to birth monoracial when with a peer group who looks like them and may identify more closely with their adoptive parents' racial identities when at home.

Transracial Asian/American Adoptees' Sense of Belonging in Higher Education

The most frequently cited framework for sense of belonging among college students in the literature is Tinto's (1994) model of integration. Tinto's classic *Leaving College: Rethinking the Causes and Cures of Student Attrition*, originally published in 1987 and updated in 1994, has been cited over 18,723 times, according to a Google search. Tinto's integration model has been critiqued by scholars for placing too much responsibility of integration on students themselves. What responsibility do colleges and universities have for ensuring that all of their students have a high sense of belonging, especially within the context of *in loco parentis*? Do college campuses fully adopt Asian/American transracial students or do Asian/American transracial adoptees have to adapt to college campuses?"

Scholars such as Samura (2016), Lee and Davis (2000), Museus and Maramba (2010), and Wells and Horn (2015) have studied Asian/Americans' sense of belonging in higher education. But while these studies are important, they do not address a subpopulation within the greater Asian/American transracial adoptees group.

Given what we know about college students' sense of belonging based on the literature, the needs and experiences of transracial Asian/American adoptee students continue to go unaddressed. For example, Samura (2016) found that when Asian/American undergraduate students have a decrease in sense of belonging in college, they remake themselves, reposition themselves, or remake space. Samura's study showed how Asian/American college students use their agency when they don't feel high levels of belonging on campus and informed the design of our framework for three main reasons. First, although Samura's participants were Asian/American, they were not Asian/American transracial adoptees. Second, while the setting for Samura's study was a large research institution on the west coast of the United States, we were interested in a model that applied to teaching-focused institutions as well. Third, the setting of Samura's study was the west coast of the United

States, which has a large Asian/American population. Could a model be developed that could translate to the midwest or other geographic locations?

Samura's (2016) study put into context many campus-specific nuances that our earlier model (Suda & Hartlep, 2016) didn't consider. For instance, smaller colleges and universities may not have fraternities or sororities. Moreover, they may or may not be residential. Consequently, any model of sense of belonging of transracial Asian/American adoptees must be nimble and considerate of the context of the institution of higher education (IHE). The reality is that while Samura's (2016) model may work for Asian/Americans in California at research-focused institutions of higher learning, transracial Asian/American adoptees may not be able to "remake" themselves by becoming involved socially on campus via Asian/American clubs—something pointed out by Suda and Hartlep (2016). Consequently, the sense of belonging of transracial Asian/American adoptees on our college campuses—be they research-focused or teaching-focused institutions—is an important contribution to the student and academic affairs literature. A framework that examines the responsibility of the institution of higher learning is of particular interest also because Asian/American should not be forced to adapt; rather, IHEs ought to embrace them as they are and meet their unique educational and developmental needs.

Toward a Transracial College Campus

In our previous work (Suda & Hartlep, 2016), we argued that IHEs can support transracially adopted Asian/American students on their campuses by creating safe spaces for this diverse student population:

> In our reconceptualized model, student affairs professionals are tasked with integrating the campus cultures to assist transracial students. Our data supports the notion that this population seeks to have opportunities to connect with other students who share similar identities, whether that means student who have similar racial heritage backgrounds, backgrounds like their adoptive parents, or just have an understanding of what living an adopted life is like. (p. 66)

The integrative model that we proposed in Suda and Hartlep (2016) is shown in Figure 6.3.

It is here that we offer a relevant student development model that builds on this earlier work and the previous work of other scholars, such as Samura's (2016) process of belonging model (see Figure 6.4), which illustrates the

Figure 6.3. The future transracial college campus.

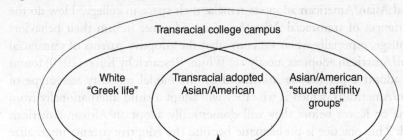

Source. Suda & Hartlep (2016).

three primary ways Asian/Americans show agency when (and if) their sense of belonging in college wanes. Asian/Americans whose sense of belonging dissipates remake themselves, reposition themselves, and/or remake their space. As we pointed out previously, Samura's model may not apply to Asian/American transracially adopted college students, because the culture and climate norm of IHEs is cisracial. Accordingly, remaking and repositioning themselves and their space may be harder for those Asian/American students who fall outside those ciscentric norms.

Figure 6.4. Samura's (2016) model of process and belonging.

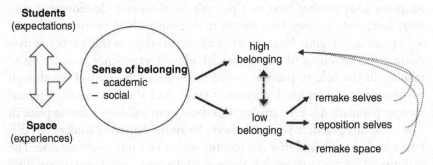

Source. Samura (2016).

Samura's work is all situated in a cisracial college milieu. How do transracial Asian/American adoptees remake their space in college? How do the experiences of transracial Asian/American adoptees inform their behaviors in college, especially when we know that the adoptive parents of transracial Asian/American adoptees mostly are White? Research by Kubo (2010) found that adoptive parents are influenced by the model minority stereotype of Asian/Americans, which is why they will adopt a child internationally from China or Korea before they will domestically adopt an African American child. This practice is problematic because the adoptive parents internalize a racial hierarchy into which they socialize their adoptive transracial child. Transracial Asian/American adoptees can internalize this myth as easily as their White adoptive parents (Fuchs, 2017).

In Suda and Hartlep (2016) we wrote:

> Student affairs professionals can assist transracial adoptees feel more comfortable on their campus by developing campus-wide mentoring programs. Perhaps adopted students can be paired with other adopted students to discuss the challenges and identity politics of being transracially adopted. The transracial adoptee population is small and, in most cases, invisible in the eyes of higher education administration and general student body. By highlighting to transracial adoptees that there are other students on campus with similar identities, connections can be made that would work to help students feel like they matter (Schlossberg, 1989). (p. 67)

Conclusion

When working with students in higher education, it is important to keep in mind the different influences that every student has had on their development. With our model, we have provided a way to consider both the nurture and nature influences on a student and their racial environment. Transracial adoption adds another layer to a person's racial identity development, and there is no clear set way for a person to develop with all of the possibilities for a given upbringing. Negative press on the ideology of transracialism may damper the argument of the transracial adoptee experience, and it's up to scholars in the field to prove the need to support this group. Even though the population of adopted students is small, and the transracially adopted student population is even smaller, this theory can still have a strong place in student affairs practice. We must always be aware that every student has different backgrounds and may not identify with a race one might assume. The majority of adoption research is done in adolescence, and there is very little research on how college impacts adopted individuals.

Note

1. At the time of writing this chapter the 2020 U.S. Census had not been completed. We hope that data/statistics on adopted people continue to be collected in subsequent decennial U.S. Censuses so that research can support this population.

References

Baden, A. L. (2002). The psychological adjustment of transracial adoptees: An application of the cultural-racial identity model. *Journal of Social Distress and the Homeless, 11*, 167–192. https://doi.org/10.1023/A:1014316018637

Dalley, T., & Kohon, V. (2008). Deprivation and development: The predicament of an adopted adolescent in search for identity. In D. Hindle & G. Shulman (Eds.), *The emotional experience of adoption: A psychoanalytic perspective* (pp. 225–236). Routledge.

Flowers, G. (2017, November 13). "Transracial" man, born white, says he feels Filipino. *USA Today*. https://www.usatoday.com/story/news/nation-now/2017/11/13/transracial-man-born-white-says-he-feels-filipino/858043001/

Fuchs, C. (2017, August 22). Behind the "model minority" myth: Why the "studious Asian" stereotype hurts. *NBC News*. https://www.nbcnews.com/news/asian-america/behind-model-minority-myth-why-studious-asian-stereotype-hurts-n792926

Hartlep, N. D., & Ozment, N. C. (2019). "Asians in the library": Sophistry and the conflation of affirmative action and negative action. In J. S. Brooks & G. Theoharis (Eds.), *Whiteucation: Privilege, power, and prejudice in school and society* (pp. 158–171). Routledge.

Herman, E. (n.d.). *Adoption statistics*. The Adoption History Project. https://pages.uoregon.edu/adoption/topics/adoptionstatistics.htm#:~:text=Approximately%205%205%20million%20Americans%20alive,affluent%20than%20families%20in%20general

Hoffman, J., & Pena, E. V. (2013). Too Korean to be White and too White to be Korean: Ethnic identity development among transracial Korean American adoptees. *Journal of Student Affairs Research and Practice, 50*(2), 152–170. https://doi.org/10.1515/jsarp-2013-0012

Hoopes, J. L. (1990). Adoption and identity formation. In D. M. Brodzinsky & M. D. Schechter (Eds.), *The psychology of adoption* (pp. 144–166). Oxford University Press.

Ianelli, J. (2020, January 17). Miami cop repeatedly accused of racism now claims he's Black on video. *The Miami New Times*. https://www.miaminewtimes.com/news/miami-cop-javier-ortiz-says-hes-black-11446181

Kim, G. S., Suyemoto, K., & Turner, C. (2010). Sense of belonging, sense of exclusion, and racial and ethnic identities in Korean transracial adoptees. *Cultural Diversity and Ethnic Minority Psychology, 16*(2), 179–190. https://doi.org/10.1037/a0015727

Kim, J. Y. (1999). Are Asians Black?: The Asian-American Civil Rights agenda and the contemporary significance of the Black/White paradigm. *The Yale Law Journal, 108*(8), 2385–2412. https://digitalcommons.law.yale.edu/cgi/viewcontent.cgi?article=7919&context=ylj

Kubo, K. (2010). Desirable difference: The shadow of racial stereotypes in creating transracial families through transnational adoption. *Sociology Compass, 4*(4), 263–282. https://doi.org/10.1111/j.1751-9020.2010.00274.x

Lee, R., & Davis, C. (2000). Cultural orientation, past multicultural experience, and a sense of belonging on campus for Asian American college students. *Journal of College Student Development, 41*, 110–115.

McConahay, J. B. (1986). Modern racism, ambivalence, and the modern racism scale. In J. F. Dovidio & S. L. Gaertner (Eds.), *Prejudice, discrimination, and racism* (pp. 91–125). Academic Press.

Museus, S. D., & Maramba, D. C. (2010). The impact of culture on Filipino American students' sense of belonging. *Review of Higher Education, 34*, 231–258. http://citeseerx.ist.psu.edu/viewdoc/download?doi=10.1.1.898.9168&rep=rep1&type=pdf

National Center for Education Statistics. (n.d.). Table 306.10: Total fall enrollment in degree-granting postsecondary institutions, by level of enrollment, sex, attendance status, and race/ethnicity or nonresident alien status of student: Selected years, 1976 through 2017. *Digest of Education Statistics.* https://nces.ed.gov/programs/digest/d18/tables/dt18_306.10.asp?current=yes

National Center for Education Statistics. (2017). *Back to school statistics.* https://nces.ed.gov/fastfacts/display.asp?id=372

National Center for Education Statistics. (2019). *Back to school statistics.* https://nces.ed.gov/fastfacts/display.asp?id=372

Pearson, K. H. (2013). Legal solutions for APA transracial adoptees. *UC Irvine Law Review, 3*, 1179–1220.http://www.law.uci.edu/lawreview/vol3/no4/Pearson.pdf

Renn, K. A. (2000). Patterns of situational identity among biracial and multiracial college students. *The Review of Higher Education, 23*(4), 399–420. https://doi.org/10.1353/rhe.2000.0019

Renn, K. A. (2004). *Mixed race students in college: The ecology of race, identity, and community on campus.* State University of New York Press.

Renn, K. A. (2008). Research on biracial and multiracial identity development: Overview and synthesis. (New Directions for Student Services, no. 123, pp. 13–21). http://citeseerx.ist.psu.edu/viewdoc/download?doi=10.1.1.545.5576&rep=rep1&type=pdf

Samura, M. (2016). Remaking selves, repositioning selves, or remaking space: An examination of Asian American college students' processes of "belonging." *Journal of College Student Development, 57*(2), 135–150. https://.doi.org/10.1353/csd.2016.0016

Schlossberg, N. K. (1989). Marginality and mattering: Key issues in building community. (New Directions for Student Services, no. 48, pp. 5–15.) http://citeseerx.ist.psu.edu/viewdoc/download?doi=10.1.1.842.3826&rep=rep1&type=pdf

Simon, R. J., & Alstein, H. (1977). *Transracial adoption*. Wiley.

Smith, J. F. (2006). Identity, race, and culture in adoption: Ethical values in the power of language. In K. Wegar (Ed.), *Adoptive families in a diverse society* (pp. 243–258). Rutgers University Press.

Suda, D. K., & Hartlep, N. D. (2016). "Balancing two worlds": Supporting transracially adopted Asian/American students on the college campus. *Journal of Educational Foundations, 29*, 55–72.

Tinto, V. (1994). *Leaving college: Rethinking the causes and cures of student attrition* (2nd ed.). University of Chicago Press.

Trans racialism support group. (n.d.). *Home* [Facebook]. https://www.facebook.com/Transracer

Travis, T. (2017, June 30). Teaching moments from the 'Hypatia' controversy. *Inside Higher Ed.* https://www.insidehighered.com/views/2017/06/30/instructor-analyzes-how-discuss-hypatia-controversy-her-grad-students-essay

Tuvel, R. (2017). In defense of transracialism. *Hypatia, 32*(2), 263–278. https://doi.org/10.1111/hypa.12327

Ung, T., O'Conner, S. H., & Pillidge, R. (2012). The development of racial identity in transracially adopted people: An ecological approach. *Adoption and Fostering, 36*(3/4), 73–84. https://etd.ohiolink.edu/!etd.send_file?accession=antioch150349 1768697273&disposition=inline

Vandivere, S., Hair, E. C., Theokas, C., Cleveland, K., McNamara, M., & Atienza, A. (2006). *How housing affects child well-being*. Funders' Network for Smart Growth and Livable Communities. https://citeseerx.ist.psu.edu/viewdoc/download?doi=10.1.1.526.4638&rep=rep1&type=pdf

Wells, A. V., & Horn, C. (2015). The Asian American college experience at a diverse institution: Campus climate as a predictor of sense of belonging. *Journal of Student Affairs Research and Practice, 52*(2), 149–163. https://doi.org/10.1080/19496591.2015.1041867

Zhou, M. (2004). Are Asian Americans becoming "white?" *Contexts, 3*(1), 29–37. https://doi.org/10.1525/ctx.2004.3.1.29

7

FORCED MIGRATION AND FORGED MEMORIES

Acts of Remembrance and Identity Development Among Southeast Asian American College Students

Jason Chan, Mike Hoa Nguyen, Latana Jennifer Thaviseth, and Mitchell J. Chang

It is the early evening of April 30. The sun is just beginning to set, and a group of students dressed in black gather around the fountain in the center of the campus quad. While there is some light chatter as students arrive and get settled, it is generally quiet; the mood is subdued, almost solemn. Linh begins to pass out candles to the students, quickly yet carefully lighting them one by one. She anxiously looks up every few seconds, scanning the quad to see if more students are on their way. Although the Vietnamese Student Association (VSA) holds this event every year, Linh, the organization's president, is hoping this year's remembrance of the Fall of Saigon is a more powerful experience for those who attend. Linh and her executive board have coordinated an evening of storytelling through poetry, music, and dance, and she is eager for the event to take place.

The parents and families of Linh and many of her Vietnamese peers were part of the mass and traumatic exodus of refugees out of Vietnam to the United States, which began after the Fall of Saigon on April 30, 1975. For weeks, the executive board of the VSA has been educating their peers about the Fall of Saigon by posting articles and videos on social media, hanging flyers and posters around the student union and the residence halls, and having conversations between classes and in the dining halls. This moment in history was pivotal in shaping the lives of many Vietnamese Americans, and Linh believes it is important for her peers to understand the significance of this event for their Vietnamese identity. After all, where and who would they be otherwise? As night falls on campus and with the glow of candlelight all around, Linh welcomes the dozens of students in attendance, and the event begins.

Many college students who identify as Cambodian, Hmong, Khmer, Lao, and Vietnamese, collectively known as Southeast Asian Americans (SEAAs),

114

are the children and grandchildren of refugees who fled their homelands due to conflict and genocide resulting from the Vietnam War. Although an increasing number of SEAA college students are not refugees themselves, year after year, they continue to perform acts of remembrance on their campuses. These acts of remembrance take a variety of forms, from cultural shows organized by student groups; to course assignments that include the creation of videos, art pieces, or research papers about their family's refugee experiences; to commemoration events like the one described in the opening vignette. These activities raise the following questions, articulated by Espiritu (2006): "How do [SEAA students] create their own memories of a war that took place before they were born? What is their relationship to the forged histories and memories of their families?" (p. 435). To these we add one more: What role do these acts of remembrance play in shaping SEAA students' sense of identity?

Despite not having been refugees themselves, many SEAA students are exposed to stories about war and the refugee experience from parents, extended family, and members of their ethnic community. Collectively, these narratives comprise what Hirsch (1996) called "postmemory" or the experience of remembering past traumatic events one did not live through or witness directly. Postmemory is created and passed down generationally, and while it can offer SEAA students a connection to their history, it can also challenge their sense of identity through "struggles between honoring [their family's] memory and constructing their own relation to this legacy" (Espiritu, 2006, p. 425). A SEAA student's identity is thus borne out of and inextricably linked to the shared history and experience of the broader SEAA community.

Among the ways in which postmemory manifests for SEAA students in a higher education context is through acts of remembrance. As undergraduates, SEAA students have the opportunity to participate and engage in activities designed to not only help them explore their connection to the past but also allow them to discern what it means to be SEAA today. This chapter examines these acts of remembrance to better understand identity development among SEAA students. By focusing on this student population, we also explore how their unique experiences may both challenge and enhance how higher education has traditionally conceptualized and approached college student identity development.

We first begin with a description of the SEAA student population and a brief overview of the forced migration and resettlement of SEAA communities. This is followed by a discussion of how forging collective memories associated with forced migration and performing acts of remembrance uniquely shape SEAA students' identities. In this discussion, we highlight distinct features of this developmental process that are not widely considered by student affairs practitioners and scholars and have implications for both theory and practice.

Who Are SEAA Students?

Although over 10 countries comprise Southeast Asia, we focus this chapter on students whose families hail from Cambodia, Laos, and Vietnam due to these countries' similar political and refugee history. Thus, our use of *Southeast Asian American* refers to those who identify as Cambodian, Hmong, Lao, and Vietnamese American. Although SEAA students may share common experiences connected to a history of forced migration, resettlement, trauma, and war, it is also important to acknowledge the diversity within the population and the multiple and intersecting identities that SEAA students possess. From numerous ethnic backgrounds and different gender identities to various religious faiths and a range of socioeconomic statuses, these identities can exert distinct influences on how SEAA students come to understand their racial identities. Identity development for this population is therefore a distinct phenomenon, one that warrants specific attention from higher education practitioners.

Identity Development Models for SEAA Students

Early models of Asian American identity development, such as Kim's (2001) Asian American racial identity development theory and Alvarez's (2002) adaptation of Helms's people of color racial identity model, have become standard references for student affairs professionals seeking to better understand their Asian American student populations. However, these models tend to discuss Asian American students as a monolithic group with a singular shared experience of racial identity, an assumption that more recent scholarship has critiqued (see Accapadi, 2012; Chan, 2017). Using these commonly cited models to understand SEAA students thus has the potential to yield inaccurate and misleading conclusions about their identity development experiences.

This chapter continues the evolution in thinking about Asian American students by offering a unique perspective for understanding SEAA students' experiences with racial identity. We acknowledge, however, that we are not the first to specifically examine the identity development of SEAA college students. Museus et al. (2013), for example, previously described a set of distinct yet interrelated processes through which SEAA students come to understand their SEAA, Asian American, immigrant and refugee, and racial minority identities. Students develop along these various identity dimensions as they become immersed in their ethnic culture and dominant U.S. culture, as they gain awareness of social and political issues affecting their communities, and as they work to integrate these multiple identities into a holistic sense of self.

Building on the work of Museus et al. (2013), we incorporate the concepts of forced migration and remembrance as critical components of SEAA students' identity development. We believe that how SEAA students come to understand who they are is inextricably linked to the remembrance of their family's experiences of relocation and transition to the U.S., as well as their sense of connection to the collective histories of their families and ethnic communities. It is to these unique experiences that we now turn.

Forced Migration and Resettlement

Although many Asian American groups voluntarily immigrated to the United States, SEAA populations experienced forced migration from their home countries. Experiences from French imperialism and colonization, as well as U.S. militarization and war, were key contributors to the mass exodus of refugees from Southeast Asia in the 1970s and 1980s (Chan, 1991; Um, 2015). The fact that SEAA populations arrived in the United States involuntarily and due to circumstances beyond their control has profound implications for the identity development of SEAA college students. We therefore provide a brief overview of the conditions that forced Southeast Asian refugees' migration as necessary background and context for understanding SEAA students' experiences. Because the conditions of migration differed across SEAA ethnic groups, we purposely discuss the experiences of each group separately.

Cambodian Americans

Cambodian refugees were victims of a mass genocide, in which some two million were killed after the Khmer Rouge overthrew the Cambodian government in 1975 (Chan & Kim, 2003). The Khmer Rouge instituted a savagely violent and ruthless campaign to eliminate Cambodians who had supported U.S. military forces in Southeast Asia, as well as those who were deemed educated or professional. Many others perished due to starvation, disease, and strenuous work conditions on Khmer Rouge farms and camps. In total, historians estimate one quarter to one third of the country's population was killed. In order to escape the "killing fields," more than half a million Cambodians fled by foot across the country into Thai border camps, though only a small percentage were eventually processed for resettlement.

Hmong Americans

During the wars in Southeast Asia, the Central Intelligence Agency (CIA) recruited members of the Hmong population, an ethnic group that resided in the highlands of North Vietnam and Laos, to fight against North Vietnamese forces (Takaki, 1998). This "secret war" was unknown to the American public at the time, and when Saigon fell, the situation became deadly for the Hmong. Fearing persecution for fighting alongside the CIA, Hmong refugees began their dangerous trek by foot through Laos and into Thailand. Many were killed or captured along the harrowing journey. By 1980, over 150,000 Hmong individuals found their way to refugee camps in Thailand, with hopes of being resettled in other countries (Robinson, 1998).

Lao Americans

Lao refugee migration was a direct result of colonization and war. After gaining independence from the French, Laos was thrust into the Vietnam War conflict as the Ho Chi Minh Trail, a resupply line for North Vietnamese forces, ran through the country. Procommunist forces, the Pathet Lao, were supported by the North Vietnamese, while the Royal Lao were recruited by U.S. forces (Takaki, 1998). By 1975, the Pathet Lao had taken power and began a violent repression of those who supported the United States. In order to escape the violence and seek sanctuary, Lao refugees fled across the border to camps in Thailand (Robinson, 1998). During this time of war, Laos became the most bombed country per capita in the world (Khamvongsa & Russell, 2009).

Vietnamese Americans

Vietnamese refugee migration began with the Fall of Saigon in 1975 after decades of war, sparking several waves of evacuees hoping to be resettled in a country without persecution. The first wave primarily consisted of those who were in the military and government or who had connections with the United States, and the subsequent and larger waves that fled Vietnam throughout the 1980s were members of the general population. Commonly referred to as *boat people* (Espiritu, 2014), these refugees set out into uncertain seas via small leaky boats, hoping to be rescued by other ships or fishing vessels. It is estimated that anywhere from 10% to 70% perished at sea

(Robinson, 1998), while pirates robbed, raped, and killed many others. Of those rescued, many were first placed in refugee camps throughout Southeast Asia before being processed and resettled in other countries.

Impact of Resettlement

Just as forced migration patterns have varied among SEAA populations, so have their patterns of resettlement to the United States. Because refugee relocation programs depended on the presence of sponsoring individuals and organizations or existing infrastructure and resources to support refugee communities (Hein, 1995), SEAA refugees were scattered across different parts of the United States. For example, SEAA communities emerged in places as geographically distant and demographically different as Minneapolis-St. Paul, Minnesota; New Orleans, Louisiana; Lowell, Massachusetts; and San Jose, California. In addition, many SEAA refugee populations were initially relocated to lower-income, urban, and working-class neighborhoods. This exposed them to challenges commonly present in these areas: poverty, overcrowding, school attrition, gang activity, and crime (Chhuon & Hudley, 2008; Lee, 1997; Um, 2003). Yet, the prevailing societal stereotypes of Asian Americans as model minorities rendered those challenges and hardships invisible (Ngo & Lee, 2007).

As a result of these experiences, many SEAA students may grow up with few opportunities to cultivate a strong SEAA identity that accounts for their unique collective backgrounds. The college environment may therefore be one of the first places where identity exploration becomes salient for SEAA students. A promising way for SEAA students to engage in this identity exploration process is through forged memories and acts of remembrance.

Forged Memories and Acts of Remembrance

Initially conceived as a way of understanding the experiences of second-generation Holocaust survivors, the concept of postmemory similarly applies to SEAA students who also "grow up dominated by narratives that preceded their birth . . . [and whose experiences are] shaped by traumatic events that can be neither fully understood nor recreated" (Hirsch, 1996, p. 662). For SEAA students, these traumatic experiences encompass not only the episodes of war, genocide, and forced migration from which their parents and families escaped and survived but also the struggles with post-traumatic stress disorder and other mental health challenges from which their family members have suffered as a result (Field et al., 2011).

The lingering effects of such trauma can have a profound impact on how memories are passed down intergenerationally. Whereas some parents and family may openly share stories of the refugee experience with their children, others may deliberately choose not to, resulting in a silence on the subject that SEAA youth may struggle to interpret. As such, many SEAA students are keenly aware of the refugee experience, even if their relationship to it is only indirect or abstract. Acts of remembrance performed on campus represent attempts to establish a connection to a history SEAA students did not directly experience but which has implications for their sense of identity, both individually and collectively.

On college campuses, SEAA students may demonstrate acts of remembrance through cultural shows and productions, their organizing and activism within student organizations, or the materials that they produce as part of class assignments and coursework. These efforts enable them to forge a collective memory of the SEAA experience and a shared understanding of SEAA identity. Together, the forced migration experiences of earlier generations and the forged memories of the current generation contribute uniquely to the identity development of SEAA college students.

Rethinking Identity Development: Acts of Remembrance

As SEAA students learn about and retell the history of their families and communities, they internalize these stories and memories as part of a cohesive narrative about who they are.

By retelling and reenacting these narratives through acts of remembrance on campus, students are thus simultaneously constructing an individual and a collective sense of themselves as SEAA individuals. Developing one's identity in this way runs counter to how student affairs professionals and scholars typically understand this process and forces us to rethink key features of such development. We highlight two key features associated with SEAA identity development that deserve greater attention in how we theorize and approach college student development.

Rethinking Scale: Individual and Collective Dimensions of Identity

By participating in acts of remembrance, SEAA students explore the question of not only "Who am I as a SEAA person?" but also "Who are we as a SEAA community?" By embracing notions of community, acts of remembrance extend the scale of association beyond the people within students' immediate environment to include SEAAs around the country, past and present. Notably, this larger-scale identification with both existing and historical communities transcends space and time, which parallels the experience of other diasporic populations (see Prashad, 2001). The process by which students actively forge a shared, collective understanding of SEAA identity thus occurs at multiple scales, constructed through a combination of memories of their own, their families', their ethnic communities', and the larger SEAA communities' experiences.

By performing acts of remembrance, SEAA students are learning about and developing a sense of racial identity through the dynamic interaction between individual and collective dimensions of identity. The individual dimension encompasses a student's relationship to their ethnic identity, their SEAA identity, and their identity as a refugee or the child of refugees (Museus et al., 2013). The collective dimension encompasses the degree to which a student feels a sense of connection to the broader ethnic, SEAA, and refugee communities, resulting from their relationship with immediate and extended family members, as well as their familiarity with the SEAA community's history of forced migration and resettlement.

The individual and collective dimensions, while distinct, are also intertwined. For example, as students learn more about the history of their families and their community, they construct narratives and forge memories that help them not only better understand where they fit within the larger narrative of the SEAA experience but also discover what it means for them to identify as a SEAA individual. Recognizing that identity development can operate at these multiple scales can enhance understanding of not only the SEAA student population but also college student development in general.

Rethinking Time: Individual and Generational Timelines

Another central and related feature of remembrance concerns the concept of time. Many racial identity development theories describe moments of dissonance in which students encounter situations that force them to critically reflect on or question their racial identity (Renn, 2012), with these episodes of dissonance occurring at various points throughout a student's life. Remembrance, however, does not share the notion of time as bounded by one's own life experiences. Although SEAA students may not have actually experienced the trauma of forced migration and resettlement, the community's collective memories of that experience can be passed down intergenerationally (Maffini & Pham, 2016) and still profoundly shape SEAA students' sense of identity.

Acts of remembrance therefore force us to rethink developmental timelines in ways that are not bounded by a student's own experiences but also include collective experiences across generations. While one's life experiences and memories are certainly important, forged memories drawn from the lives and memories of past generations may be just as compelling for how students develop their identities. If so, this suggests that both the past and present have and will continue to play important roles in shaping students' identities. This idea has implications for supporting and serving SEAA and other undergraduate students.

Implications for Higher Education Practice

The unique features of SEAA students' experiences with racial identity described in this chapter raise a number of implications for higher education and student affairs, particularly in supporting SEAA students. First, it uncovers conceptual and practical considerations for effectively serving SEAA students. For example, the history of forced migration and refugee settlement in the United States, combined with the current social and political issues facing refugee communities, can together influence SEAA students' identity development in ways that are not necessarily shared by other undergraduate populations. Likewise, these defining experiences for SEAA students do not universally apply to Asian American students of other ethnic backgrounds. Thus, a firm understanding of the distinct histories and experiences of SEAAs is critical for working successfully with students from different SEAA backgrounds.

Second, our discussion also points to the value that acts of remembrance hold in the identity development of SEAA students. Examples of such activities include those sponsored by SEAA student groups, including cultural shows, commemorations, and celebrations, as well as those sponsored by their institutions, including course offerings, ceremonial events, and high-profile guest speakers. Other opportunities for institutions to facilitate acts of remembrance include connecting students with the larger SEAA community by inviting SEAA authors, filmmakers, musicians, and other artists to campus and by developing partnerships with local community organizations, museums, and libraries to broaden educational outreach about the SEAA experience. Recognizing that these acts of remembrance are central to forging memories and constructing identities, faculty and staff may consider creating structured dialogue spaces during and after these activities for students to reflect upon and process questions related to their SEAA identities.

Last, the benefits associated with performing acts of remembrance may also apply to other college student populations. This is especially the case for those with shared refugee and intergenerational trauma experiences, such as students whose families were forced to escape places like Burma, Iraq,

Somalia, Bosnia, and Syria (Sangalang & Vang, 2017). Acts of remembrance may also be central to students from Native American, Indigenous, and other nonrefugee communities who have also endured intergenerational trauma (Bombay et al., 2009); the efforts of Native American and Indigenous students to recognize the tribal lands on which their institutions are built or host pow-wows and other cultural celebrations are just a few examples. Similarly, Black students who carry the traumatic postmemory of slavery and Jim Crow can benefit from institutional support of their acts of remembrance, which may range from Black History Month programming and Juneteenth commemorations to confronting their institution's history with racism and slavery.

Acts of remembrance are performed regularly by different groups of students on campus and may hold even more significance and value than we realize. It is thus imperative for higher education practitioners to make new meaning of these programs and events, many of which may appear to be merely educational, cultural, or social in nature, and reframe them as critical venues for identity development—and in doing so, also elevate the necessity to fund, support, and sustain these activities. Otherwise, students may well find themselves disconnected from their campuses, forcing them to seek other ways of connecting with a history that may be elusive or lost to them.

Conclusion

This chapter extends the current understanding of student affairs theory and practice by examining the roles that acts of remembrance based on forged memories play in the identity development of SEAA college students. Through acts of remembrance, SEAA students establish a connection to their roots by forging memories associated with a history of colonialism, genocide, and war that invariably resulted in distinct experiences of forced migration and resettlement in the United States. The intergenerational trauma passed down to SEAA students by their parents, families, and communities, which is central to defining the contemporary SEAA student experience, makes those distinct memories especially powerful in shaping their understanding of themselves and their bond to a larger community.

By illuminating how performing acts of remembrance facilitates the identity development of SEAA college students, we also uncover limitations with how student development is both theorized and practiced among student affairs scholars and practitioners. Key features associated with acts of remembrance and their contributions to the development of SEAA students challenge conventional notions of scale and time held by traditional student identity development theories. Rethinking our understanding of and approach to both scale and time when considering students' development has promising potential for developing alternative perspectives that can better serve not only SEAA students but also the larger college student population.

References

Accapadi, M. M. (2012). Asian American identity consciousness: A polycultural model. In D. Ching & A. Agbayani (Eds.), *Asian Americans and Pacific Islanders in higher education: Research and perspectives on identity, leadership, and success* (pp. 57–94). National Association of Student Personnel Administrators.

Alvarez, N. (2002). Racial identity and Asian Americans: Support and challenges. In M. K. McEwen, C. M. Kodama, A. N. Alvarez, S. Lee, & C. T. H. Liang (Eds.), *Working with Asian American college students* (New Directions for Student Services, no. 97, pp. 33–44). Jossey-Bass. https://doi.org/10.1002/ss.37

Bombay, A., Matheson, K., & Anisman, H. (2009). Intergenerational trauma: Convergence of multiple processes among First Nations peoples in Canada. *Journal of Aboriginal Health, 5*(3), 6–43. https://doi.org/10.3138/ijih.v5i3.28987

Chan, J. (2017). Asian Pacific Islander Desi American college students and the complexities of identity development. In D. C. Maramba & C. M. Kodama (Eds.), *Bridging research and practice to support Asian American students* (New Directions for Student Services, no. 160, pp. 11–24). Jossey-Bass. https://doi.org/10.1002/ss.20240

Chan, S. (1991). *Asian Americans: An interpretive history.* Twayne.

Chan, S., & Kim, A. U. (2003). *Not just victims: Conversations with Cambodian community leaders in the United States.* University of Illinois Press.

Chhuon, V., & Hudley, C. (2008). Factors supporting Cambodian American students' successful adjustment into the university. *Journal of College Student Development, 49*, 15–30. https://doi.org/10.1353/csd.2008.0005

Espiritu, Y. L. (2006). Toward a critical refugee study: The Vietnamese refugee subject in U.S. scholarship. *Journal of Vietnamese Studies, 49*(1), 410–433. https://doi.org/10.1525/vs.2006.1.1-2.410

Espiritu, Y. L. (2014). *Body counts: The Vietnam war and militarized refugees.* University of California Press.

Field, N. P., Om, C., Kim, T., & Vorn, S. (2011). Parental styles in second generation effects of genocide stemming from the Khmer Rouge regime in Cambodia. *Attachment & Human Development, 13*(6), 611–628. https://doi.org/10.1080/14616734.2011.609015

Hein, J. (1995). *From Vietnam, Laos, and Cambodia: A refugee experience in the United States.* Twayne.

Hirsch, M. (1996). Past lives: Postmemories in exile. *Poetics Today, 17*(4), 659–686. https://doi.org/10.2307/1773218

Khamvongsa, C., & Russell, E. (2009). Legacies of war: Cluster bombs in Laos. *Critical Asian Studies, 41*, 281–306. https://doi.org/10.1080/14672710902809401

Kim, J. (2001). Asian American identity development theory. In C. L. Wijeyesinghe & B. W. Jackson III (Eds.), *New perspectives on racial identity development: A theoretical and practical anthology* (pp. 67–90). New York University Press.

Lee, S. J. (1997). The road to college: Hmong American women's pursuit of higher education. *Harvard Educational Review, 67*(4), 803–827. https://doi.org/10.17763/haer.67.4.0296u12hu7r65562

Maffini, C. S., & Pham, A. N. (2016). Overcoming a legacy of conflict: The repercussive effects of stress and intergenerational transmission of trauma among Vietnamese Americans. *Journal of Aggression, Maltreatment & Trauma, 25*(6), 580–597. https://doi.org/10.1080/10926771.2016.1182955

Museus, S. D., Nguyen, T. K., Vue, R., & Yeung, F. (2013). A model of Southeast Asian American identity development: Merging theoretical perspectives. In S. D. Museus, D. C. Maramba, & R. T. Teranishi (Eds.), *The misrepresented minority: New insights on Asian Americans and Pacific Islanders, and the implications for higher education* (pp. 47–66). Stylus.

Ngo, B., & Lee, S. J. (2007). Complicating the image of model minority success: A review of Southeast Asian American education. *Review of Educational Research, 77*(4), 415–453. https://doi.org/10.3102/0034654307309918

Prashad, V. (2001). *The karma of brown folk.* University of Minnesota Press.

Renn, K. A. (2012). Creating and re-creating race: The emergence of racial identity as a critical element in psychological, sociological, and ecological perspectives on human development. In C. L. Wijeyesinghe & B. W. Jackson III (Eds.), *New perspectives on racial identity development: Integrating emerging frameworks* (2nd ed., pp. 11–32). New York University Press.

Robinson, W. C. (1998). *Terms of refuge: The Indochinese exodus and the international response.* Zed Books.

Sangalang, C. C., & Vang, C. (2017). Intergenerational trauma in refugee families: A systematic review. *Journal of Immigrant and Minority Health, 19*(3), 745–754. https://doi.org/10.1007/s10903-016-0499-7

Takaki, R. (1998). *Strangers from a different shore: A history of Asian Americans* (2nd ed.). Back Bay Books.

Um, K. (2003). *A dream denied: Educational experiences of Southeast Asian American youth.* Southeast Asia Resource Action Center (SEARAC).

Um, K. (2015). *From the land of shadows: War, revolution, and the making of the Cambodian diaspora.* New York University Press.

PART FOUR

ALTERNATIVE FRAMEWORKS AND MODELS FOR LATINX COLLEGE STUDENT POPULATIONS

8

FINDING MEANING IN THE MODELS AND FRAMEWORKS FOR LATINX COLLEGE STUDENTS

At the Intersection of Student Agency and Context

Zarrina Talan Azizova and Jesse P. Mendez

Like San Miguel and Donato (2009), we use *Latinx* as "an umbrella term that unites several groups with their cultural origins from several different Spanish-speaking countries" (Salinas & Lozano, 2019, p. 27). Today, higher education institutions enroll more Latinx students than a decade ago, and this trajectory has been steadily going up (de Brey et al., 2019). However, Latinx students' completion of a 4-year degree remains low (*Excelencia* in Education, 2018). To address the issues of low completion, higher education institutions have been taking more responsibility for diverse student experiences and success. The proliferation of student success centers, institutionalized academic advising and coaching models, and programs for first-year experiences is evidence of the growing institutional commitment to student success. To support these institutional efforts, however, innovative frameworks of diverse students' development need to emerge in order to inform and guide more nuanced program development and practices for student success (Patton et al., 2016).

First, we argue that innovative Latinx student development frameworks should be able to inform identity-conscious, ground-up program development in which educators' recognition of student agency and historical, policymaking, institutional, and community and family contexts is essential (Pendakur, 2017). In other words, these frameworks are built by intersecting

129

the student's self, as an active agent of their own experiences, with an external context, a social and cultural field in which a person develops agency. This argument is not new; it draws from Renn and Reason's (2013) presentation of a holistic approach to understanding student development, which conveys the shift from *what* in student development to *how* and *where* that development occurs.

Second, we argue that student development should go hand-in-hand with student success. Student success should not be reduced to academic achievement, persistence, and completion rates. Instead, student success should be viewed as a complex phenomenon where student development and desired goals of growth and completion of a college degree are interrelated. Therefore, new frameworks of Latinx student development should be explicitly value laden and goal oriented, and student agentic qualities and identity should play paramount roles.

The purpose of this chapter is to elaborate on these two arguments and propose recommendations for alternative Latinx college student development and success frameworks. To that end, we will

- review the traditional families of college development theories to reveal current limitations when attempting to showcase the intersection of student agency and student context(s),
- discuss two classical psychosocial student development theories that are aimed at racial and ethnic college students to reinforce our argument that context matters without necessarily being deterministic,
- provide an overview of the context in which Latinx students experience their educational journeys; and
- conclude with recommendations for alternative framework(s).

Take-Aways From the Traditional College Student Development Theories

Traditional college development theories range from cognitive-structural to psychosocial to sociological in their treatment of micro and macro units of analysis. On the face of it, key theoretical assumptions and foci of these theories can be placed along the continuum (Figure 8.1) with the emphasis on individuals on the left end and the emphasis on a context on the right end.

Figure 8.1. Continuum of student development and college impact theories.

Focus on Individuals ◄────────────────► Focus on a Context

Table 8.1 provides key theoretical concepts and assumptions that fall into each end of the continuum and into its middle point.

As Table 8.1 demonstrates, the left-end theories (e.g., Perry, 1970; Kohlberg, 1969; Torres & Magolda, 2004) are about individual learning and cognitive development, cognitive-structural shifts, and pure psychological development where students' change and growth happen internally without any consideration or problematization of a context. The right-end theories (Arbona & Nora, 2007; Astin, 1977, 1991; Nora et al., 1996; Terenzini & Reason, 2005; Tinto, 1987, 1993) provide a systematic way of looking at individual student characteristics and broad contextual factors that are either inputs or outputs of college experience and impact. Over time, this group of theories has helped explain, for example, race-based or class-based conditional effects. These theories have also, unintentionally, become responsible for characterizations of some student groups as *at-risk* (i.e., possessing sociocultural or socioeconomic characteristics that may predict college experiences and outcomes). Within this group of the structural sociological orientations, there are other theories (from the family of critical social theory) that problematize contexts (i.e., structures, systems, dominant cultures, and other macro-factors) of college experience and impact. In the middle of this continuum are traditional theories that target person-environment interactions and psychosocial development of students (see Chickering, 1969; Cross, 1971, 1978; Erikson, 1963; Ferdman & Gallegos, 2001; Kim, 2001). While context is absent in the left-end theories and acknowledged in the middle, it is critical in the right-end theories.

In order to more accurately study Latinx student development and more effectively design educational programs, researcher-practitioners need to recognize that there may be a risk in working with only the left-end or middle-point theories. In this approach, too much burden is placed on students themselves, as if they were the only ones responsible for their success in college (overly internal focus). However, there is also a limitation in relying too heavily on the right-end theories with a critical and deterministic view of the context. This approach may it difficult or impossible to recognize individual agency in students or find those self-empowering factors in the context(s) that facilitate student development and college success (overly external focus). This right-end critical focus may also push research agendas and practices to continue comparing minority racial and ethnic groups with majority groups, thus further shaping the deficit-oriented mindsets of researchers and practitioners. A better practice might be mixing cognitive-structural, psychosocial, and contextual factors into a holistic model to intersect the macro- and micro-perspectives. This approach may capture student development more

TABLE 8.1

Matrix of Key Concepts in the Traditional College Development Theories

	Focus on Individuals	*Middle Point*	*Focus on a Context*
Concept of Student Development as Change and Growth	Change as cognitive development, maturation; change in positive or negative directions; growth	Change as a cognitive and psychosocial/ affective/attitudinal developmental, maturation, self-awareness in a social world, change in positive or negative directions	Change as a repositioning within a broader socioeconomic system (e.g., access and graduation, socioeconomic mobility, uplift, occupational and educational attainment, improved lifestyle, to name a few)
Theories/ Research	Psychological and cognitive development theories	Psychosocial, person- environment models	Sociological, incorporating economic, legal, political, historical perspectives
How Student Development Change Is Triggered, Produced, or Achieved	Intrapersonal (ontogenetic) Cognitive- structural shifts over time and as a response to stimuli such as cognitive load (e.g., new content, new concepts, learning stimuli, etc.)	Interpersonal cognitive/ psychological, attitudinal development through social interactions and responses to influences of environmental factors (peers, cultural clubs, faculty-student interactions, organizational culture, etc.)	Change (along with all three points/levels on our continuum: cognitive and psychosocial as well as socioeconomic repositioning) is conditioned by contextual factors/ structural provisions (e.g., demographics, parents education, gender, socioeconomic status, etc.)
Context	Absent	Acknowledged; focused on organizational context (immediate interactional setting)	Always present and likely critical; focused on a broader context (even beyond an educational organization)

accurately, and the practitioners' role should be to monitor the context as an area of possible interventions for student success. The emerging higher education philosophy that recognizes educational practices, rather than students, as problematic should continue gaining its full recognition. In this philosophy, context matters in a more sophisticated way in Latinx student development.

Context in the Classical Student Develoment Theories

To illustrate our point about the role of context in racial and ethnic student development and that some traditional frameworks underestimate it in favor of race and ethnicity, we would like to briefly discuss two classical identity development theories: race identity (Cross & Phagen-Smith, 2001) and ethnic identity (Phinney, 2005).

Cross and Phagen-Smith (2001) introduced a complex theory that focuses specifically on the interplay between psychological and social nuances of the process of Black identity development across the lifespan. One of the primary concerns of the theory revolves around the idea that race and ethnicity should be placed at the center of the identity development theory. This model captures variations in defining Black identity and three various patterns of development. Individuals go through five stages in order to achieve identity development (pre-encounter, encounter, immersion-emersion, internalization, and internalization-commitment). At their internationalization stage, individuals emphasize race and Black culture in their everyday life. At the final stage, however, these individuals may differ in the degree of the emphasis that they place on the issues of race and culture. The authors stress that the variation in identity development can be accounted for by individual differences and contextual differences. According to this theory, factors such as family structure, socioeconomic status, and "neighborhood quality and dynamics" (p. 264) may contribute to variations among individuals.

Most importantly, however, this theory recognizes that achieved identity status reaches its culminating point when individuals' identities are shaped by an understanding of self-concepts and beliefs as well as the recognition of a possible impact of the beliefs and views of others. Thus, this theory suggests that to achieve a unique identity, one needs to be able to understand their position concerning others and society as a whole. Hence, the social-cultural context becomes an essential meaning-making platform in identity development. However, in this perspective the context (while critical) is static and unchanging; an individual eventually learns how to relate to it without a possibility of altering it.

A similar role of context is implied in Phinney's (2005) theory of ethnic identity development that provides concepts for understanding ethnic identity development in adolescents and adults. Her theory is based on research with racial/ethnic populations and conceptualized through pre-existing theories of ego or personal identity development (Erikson, 1968; Marcia, 1966). In her theorizing, Phinney (2005) emphasizes components and factors that are present in one's ethnic identity development. Like Cross and Phagen-Smith (2005), Phinney recognizes that the meaning of ethnic identity achievement varies for different individuals and groups. Such variation is possibly accounted for by their distinct historical and personal contexts. Phinney suggests that understanding "the state" (p. 302) of ethnic identity requires examining cases of "self-identification as a group member, a sense of belonging to the group, attitudes about one's membership, and ethnic involvement (social participation, cultural practices and attitudes)" (p. 302). She then offers the acculturation framework (i.e., one's socialization to dominant norms, values, practices) as a conceptual tool and suggests that there is a possibility of finding "strong ties to the dominant culture" (p. 309). Some qualitative findings informed by these theories, as Scheurich and Young (1997) assert, provide insights that "ethnic identity is not a linear construct" (Phinney, 2005, p. 309). Rather, it is a multidirectional and more complex concept that can vary, particularly from one group or individual to another, depending on the degree of involvement of these individuals in their own culture versus the mainstream culture.

These conceptualizations of identity development relative to mainstream or dominant cultures and contexts are precisely the targets of critical theorists. Nevertheless, critique and deconstruction are not enough as we move toward alternative frameworks of student development. We must realize that students have agency in their own racial and ethnic development. In addition, they may actively shape their own contexts, even as their contexts are shaping their individual agency. Thus, we want to emphasize that context is a significant, fluid element in Latinx student development in which these students take an active role. This emphasis warrants further discussions, to which we now turn.

Context Is Everything and Requires Student Agency

Latinx populations are not a monolith by any sense of the word, and they enroll in universities at different rates according to nationality and cultural backgrounds (de Brey et al., 2019). Figure 8.2 shows the percentages of students from different Central and South American countries in college.

Figure 8.2. Average college enrollment rates of 18- to 24-year-olds in degree-granting postsecondary institutions, by selected subgroups (2016).

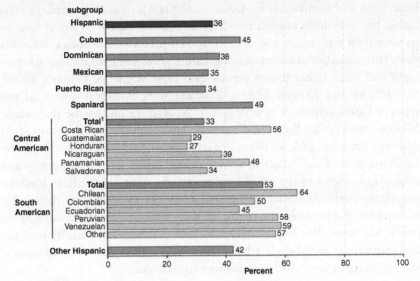

Source. Status and Trends in the Education of Racial Subgroups (2019)

As San Miguel and Donato (2009) observe, however, historically "these groups [Mexicans, Puerto Ricans, Cubans] . . . were politically powerless, economically impoverished, occupationally concentrated in unskilled and semi-skilled jobs, and socially alienated and discriminated by the dominant society" (p. 28). Latinx groups are very diverse in terms of their social, political, economic, and cultural characteristics (San Miguel & Donato, 2009), but the nature of their struggles and lack of opportunities for educational success are identical. Therefore, the principles of student development relative to how and where individual agency is active are consistent across all groups. However, how best to intervene to optimize individual agency development and student success may differ, which we address in the implications section.

History of Resilience and Achievement in Education

Historical context is a powerful meaning-making platform for students when storytelling puts stories of struggles and successes side-by-side. Critical approaches to student development and experiences tend to only problematize history/ies and focus on the system-level developments that caused oppression and marginalization of racial and ethnic people in society and education environments. Largely missing remain the educators' attention to the history/ies of success and their intentional integration of the powerful historical storytelling into college experiences. History can be a source of inspiration and motivation for Latinx students who aspire to a college education but may have limited resources or cultural capital to know how to go after their aspirations and dreams. In fact, numerous historical accounts show that educational success among Latinx groups is a communal achievement and value rather than a private gain (San Miguel & Donato, 2009). San Miguel and Donato (2009) conclude their historical review of the types of Latinx responses by saying that "we want to underscore that ethnic Mexicans and Puerto Ricans did not passively accept" (p. 32) the curriculum and organizational policies of social and economic subordination. A powerful illustration of the collective agency toward educational opportunity and success has origins in the small border town in West Texas where Mexican Americans established their own school district in 1929 to grow their cadre of teachers and administrators and to gain access to the policymaking in public education (San Miguel & Donato, 2009). Histories of Latinx students and community members in education reveal a very notable form of agency, such as contestation, which was community-driven.

> In the late 1960s and early 1970s, for instance, youth, community, and parent activists as well as community-based organizations challenged a host of exclusionary and discriminatory school practices at the local level. Some of the most important were inequitable and unequal treatment of Latino children in the public schools, Anglo control of schools, and an Anglo-centric curriculum, the suppression of their language and culture, and the exclusion of their community from the schools. In both Mexican American and Puerto Rican communities, a variety of tactics were used, including walkouts, boycotts, protests, and litigation to challenge school discrimination at the local level in this period. (San Miguel & Donato, 2009, p. 39)

Ignoring histories of educational success among Latinx groups in institutional discourses and sagas deprives Latinx students of a sense of ownership of, and a place in, the system of education, higher or otherwise. However, highlighting and celebrating the history of success is not enough; it helps students develop their self-efficacy (Torres & Solberg, 2001), but it does not necessarily help students transform their self-efficacy (i.e., belief in oneself) into their agency (i.e., the act of self-empowerment itself and the will to advocate for oneself). It is paramount to include the most immediate contexts as well, such as the ones shaped by families and communities, into Latinx student development.

Familial Context

Contemporary research does provide plenty of evidence of familial influences on the identity development of Latinx first-year students (Auerbach,

2006; Ramirez, 2003; Torres, 2003, 2004). Latinx parents' involvement in the academic journeys and lives of their children is profound, and their potential to empower their students to develop and strengthen agentic qualities is significant (Chrispeels & Rivero, 2001; Downs et al., 2008; Madrid, 2011). Latinx parents hold higher aspirations for their children's education compared to other racial and ethnic groups (Goldenberg et al., 2001). Beyond the affective roles, such as providing emotional and motivational support (Auerbach, 2006), Latinx parents exercise their parental agency to explore educational systems and funding opportunities on behalf of their children and help their children navigate college-going resources and activate other forms of capital (Azizova & Mendez, 2019; Ramirez, 2003). Family ties can also be game-changers in Latinx college student success as Latinx children are attuned to their family histories and struggles. As a result, they view their college education as a means for not only personal fulfillment but also improving their family's socioeconomic reality. We argue elsewhere that this self-expectation is an extra emotional burden for students (Azizova & Mendez, 2019), but we cannot ignore that helping their immediate families is a strong source of Latinx student development. Thus, families should be an inseparable part of the student development context.

Contextualized Experiences and Impact on Mental Health

Latinx students, as a whole, demonstrate a high level of agency through various means. A recent study found that Latinx students who are politically active enjoy some protection from racial discrimination in their environments (Hope et al., 2018). Other studies have found that Latinx students garner some protective benefits from other sources, such as family support (Baumann et al., 2010; Potochnick & Perreira, 2010), leadership experiences in student organizations (Garcia et al., 2017), or social and cultural capital (Pérez, 2017; Sanchez et al., 2019).

However, several other studies have also found a connection between psychological distress in Latinx students and exposure to discrimination and microaggressions (Arbona & Jimenez, 2014; DeFreitas et al., 2018; Sanchez et al., 2018). Badiee and Andrade (2019) examined family cohesion, social networks, acculturative stress, perceived discrimination, and foreigner objectification and found that perceived discrimination predicted anxiety and depression. Tasked with providing support to students, college counselors are at the forefront of intervention in terms of serving the emotional needs of Latinx students who are subjected to microaggressions on college campuses, particularly those students who are undocumented (Chang et al., 2017; Sanchez et al., 2019; Shi et al., 2018).

Implications for Latinx College Student Development Frameworks

Through hard work and activisim as part of a multilayered historical context that included different manifestions of discriminiation, Latinx students have earned hard-won social opportunities; however, underrepresentation in college and other vehicles of social mobility and dependency on the K–12 curriculum and education quality remain a significant barrier for Latinx communities. However, because "Latinx" is also quite a diverse descriptor, it bears repeating that different segments of Latinx people operate in different political contexts, whether due to nationality, immigration status, or cultural or linguistic nuances. For example, immigration as a policy issue affects the general Latinx community but does not apply to Puerto Ricans. For those Latinx individuals who do not enjoy the relationship that Puerto Rico maintains with the U.S. government, there are a variety of political attitudes that cannot be easily summarized (Lopez et al., 2016). For those without U.S. citizenship, the issue of immigration adds another layer of complexity, particularly for those who are first-generation students and first-generation citizens. These complexities drive us to take a closer look at the driving forces of agency, particularly, what generates high aspirations for higher education— and how student affairs professionals fit within these frameworks.

Student affairs professionals are at the forefront of assisting students' growth throughout their collegiate experiences as agents of their college success. Therefore, to serve Latinx students' growth, student affairs staff should have not only a full appreciation of the Latinx culture but also an understanding of their experience in college (Rodriguez et al., 2015; Tello & Lonn, 2017). Studies suggest that Latinx students grow their agentic qualities under thoughtful mentorship or advisement (Torres & Hernandez, 2010; Torres et al., 2009), but unfortunately, some studies also report that educators perceive Latinx families and parents as not valuing education (Madrid, 2011; Vega, 2010) despite well-documented evidence that shows the opposite. The presence and engagement of staff of color provide the opportunity for students of color, including Latinx students, to garner some cultural capital from these relationships (Luedke, 2017), but not all institutions are blessed with high levels of diversity among the staff. Until institutions reach such diversity and inclusion benchmarks, student affairs professionals must make a concerted effort to understand the lived experiences and perspectives of their Latinx student populations. In particular, training for working with diverse student population is key. Tierney (2000) framed the need for this type of understanding to serve students better and interweave them into the fabric of the university. Institutions, particularly Hispanic-serving institutions (HSIs), may need to reevaluate the training needs of their faculty and staff so they can adequately serve the Latinx population. Pope et al. (2004) found that student affairs professionals may not have adequate training and knowledge to serve the needs of their respective Latinx populations, making these institutions inert as vehicles of social mobility.

Recommendations for Alternative Frameworks

Finally, we conclude with the following recommendations for alternative frameworks with the emphasis on *how* and *where* the development occurs. Higher education institutions need to recognize that the *how* element of development is closely connected to the *where* element. In other words, Latinx student development is a complex psychosocial process that operates at the intersection of a cognitive drive for self-actualization and a contextual determinism. Neither may take precedence over the other because the role of each is profound and codependent. This codependence constitutes the essence and phenomenology of Latinx student agency. To assist students' activation of their agency, institutions should be in the position of enlarging their context by relying on the families and communities (i.e., the direct sources of empowerment) as well as the racial and ethnic histories of educational success. Institutional missions and visions that integrate cultural ethos and manifest aspirations may become significant contextual variables in individuals' agency development. Institutions that have a history of exclusion may look for the histories of the cultural communities to weave the stories of success into the new collective narratives to signify new commitment to opportunities, social justice, and diversity on their campuses. Moreover, intentional educational programming and curricular revisions that reflect Latinx realities and positive images can activate one's agency, in turn (re)shaping these programming initiatives and curricular offerings through an ongoing feedback loop. Charging students to be more responsible for molding their environments, equipping them with the tools for change and contestation, and facilitating their active contribution to their educational success are the essential elements of how student development occurs.

All in all, no longer *in loco parentis* or bystanders, colleges and universities need to embrace a completely new role in Latinx student development—a role of a narrator, a partner, and an advocate with and for a Latinx student. The institutions need to realize that the new relationship with their students is no longer authoritative, bureaucratic, and top-down (or mitigatory of so-called risk factors). Instead, this new relationship is cultural and coconstructive. Latinx students do not have deficiencies that the instutions need to look for to correct. Instead, Latinx students are active stakeholders who bring their cultural wealth and agentic drive for educational success and uplifting life opportunities. That is the core for alternative student development frameworks for Latinx student success.

References

Arbona, C., & Jimenez, C. (2014). Minority stress, ethnic identity, and depression among Latino/a college students. *Journal of Counseling Psychology*, *61*(1), 162–168. https://doi.org/10.1037/a0034914

Arbona, C., & Nora, A. (2007). The influence of academic and environmental factors on Hispanic college degree attainment. *The Review of Higher Education*, *30*(3), 247–269. https://doi.org/10.1353/rhe.2007.0001

Astin, A. W. (1977). *Four critical years*. Jossey-Bass.

Astin, A. W. (1991). *Assessment for excellence: The philosophy and practice of assessment and evaluation in higher education*. American Council on Education and Macmillan Publishing Co.

Auerbach, S. (2006). "If the student is good, let him fly": Moral support for college among Latino immigrant parents. *Journal of Latinos and Education*, *5*(4), 275–292. http://dx.doi.org/10.1207/s1532771xjle0504_4

Azizova, Z. T., & Mendez, J. P. (2019). Understanding *Promise*: Impact of state support on Latino high school student habitus. *Journal of Latinos and Education*. https://doi.org/10.1080/15348431.2019.1590203

Badiee, M., & Andrade, E. (2019). Microsystem and macrosystem predictors of Latinx college students' depression and anxiety. *Journal of Hispanic Higher Education*, *18*(4), 422–434. https://doi.org/10.1177/1538192718765077

Baumann, A. A., Kuhlberg, J. A., & Zayas, L. H. (2010). Familism, mother-daughter mutuality, and suicide attempts of adolescent Latinas. *Journal of Family Psychology*, *24*, 616–624. https://doi.org/10.1037/a0020584

Chang, A., Torrez, M. A., Ferguson, K. N., & Sagar, A. (2017). Figured worlds and American dreams: An exploration of agency and identity among Latinx undocumented students. *The Urban Review*, *49*, 189–216. https://doi.org/10.1007/s11256-017-0397-x

Chickering, A. W. (1969) *Education and identity*. Jossey-Bass.

Chrispeels, J. H., & Rivero, E. (2001). Engaging Latino families for student success: How parent education can reshape parents' sense of place in the education of their children. *Peabody Journal of Education*, *76*(2), 119–169. https://doi.org/10.1207/S15327930pje7602_7

Cross, W. E., Jr. (1971). The Negro-to-Black conversion experience. *Black World*, *20*(9), 13–27.

Cross, W. E., Jr. (1978). The Thomas and Cross models of psychological nigrescence: A review. *Journal of Black Psychology*, *5*, 13–31. https://doi.org/10.1177/009579847800500102

Cross, W. E., & Phagen-Smith, P. (2001). Patterns of African American identity development: A life span perspective. In C. L. Wijeyesinghe, & Jackson III, B.W. (Eds.), *New perspectives on racial identity development: A theoretical and practical anthology* (pp. 243–270). New York University Press.

de Brey, C., Musu, L., McFarland, J., Wilkinson-Flicker, S., Diliberti, M., Zhang, A., Branstetter, C., & Wang, X. (2019). *Status and trends in the education of racial and ethnic groups 2018* (NCES 2019-038). U.S. Department of Education. National Center for Education Statistics. https://nces.ed.gov/pubs2019/2019038.pdf

DeFreitas, S. C., Crone, T., DeLeon, M., & Ajayi, A. (2018). Perceived and personal mental health stigma in Latino and African American college students. *Frontiers in Public Health, 6*(49). https://doi.org/10.3389/fpubh.2018.00049

Downs, A., Martin, J., Fossum, M., Martinez, S., Solorio, M., & Martinez, H. (2008). Parents teaching parents: A career and college knowledge program for Latino families. *Journal of Latinos and Education, 7*(3), 227–240. https://doi.org/10.1080/15348430802100295

Erikson, E. H. (1963). *Childhood and society*. Norton.

Erikson, E. H. (1968). *Identity, youth, and crisis*. Norton

Excelencia in Education. (2018). *Latino college completion: United States*. https://www.edexcelencia.org/sites/default/files/LCCStateStats/Exc-2018-50StateFS-USA-04_0_0.pdf

Ferdman, B., & Gallegos, P. (2001). Racial identity development and Latinos in the United States. In C. Wijeyesinghe & B. J. Jackson III (Eds.), *New perspectives on racial identity development: A theoretical and practical anthology* (pp. 32–66). New York University Press

Garcia, G. A., Huerta, A. H., Ramirez, J. J., & Patrón, O. E. (2017). Contexts that matter to the leadership development of Latino male college students: A mixed methods perspective. *Journal of College Student Development 58*(1), 1–18. https://doi.org/10.1353/csd.2017.0000

Goldenberg, C., Gallimore, R., Reese, L., & Garnier, H. (2001). Cause or effect? A longitudinal study of immigrant Latino parents' aspirations and expectations, and their children's school performance. *American Educational Research Journal, 38*(3), 547–582. https://doi.org/10.3102/00028312038003547

Hope, E. C., Velez, G., Offidani-Bertrand, C., Keels, M., & Durkee, M. I. (2018). Political activism and mental health among Black and Latinx college students. *Cultural Diversity and Ethnic Minority Psychology, 24*(1), 26–39. https://doi.org/10.1037/cdp0000144

Kim, M. M. (2001). Institutional effectiveness of women-only colleges: Cultivating students' desire to influence social conditions. *The Journal of Higher Education, 72*(3), 287–321. https://doi.org/10.1080/00221546.2001.11777096

Kohlberg, L. (1969). Stage and sequence: The cognitive-developmental approach to socialization. In D. Goslin (Ed.), *Handbook of socialization theory and research* (pp. 347–480). Rand McNally.

Lopez, M. G., Gonzalez-Barrera, A., Krogstad, J. M., &Lopez, G. (2016, October 21). *Democrats maintain edge as party 'more concerned' for Latinos, but views similar to 2012.* Pew Research Institute. https://www.pewresearch.org/hispanic/2016/10/11/democrats-maintain-edge-as-party-more-concerned-for-latinos-but-views-similar-to-2012/

Luedke, C. L. (2017). Person first, student second: Staff and administrators of color supporting students of color authentically in higher education. *Journal of College Student Development, 58*(1), 37–52. https://doi.org/10.1353/csd.2017.0002

Madrid, E. M. (2011). The Latino achievement gap. *Multicultural Education, 19*(3), 7–12.

Marcia, J. E. (1966). Development and validation of ego-identity status. *Journal of personality and social psychology, 3*(5), 551. https://doi.org/10.1037/h0023281

Nora, A., Cabrera, A. F., Hagedon, L. S., & Pascarella, E. T. (1996). Differential impacts of academic and social experiences on college-related behavioral outcomes across different ethnic and gender groups at four-year institutions. *Research in Higher Education, 37*, 427–451. https://doi.org/10.1007/BF01730109

Patton, L. D., Renn, K. A., Guido, F. M., & Quaye, S. J. (2016). *Student development in college: Theory, research, and practice* (3rd ed.). Jossey-Bass.

Pendakur, V. (2017). *Closing the opportunity gap: Identity-conscious strategies for retention and student success.* Stylus.

Pérez, D. II (2017). In pursuit of success: Latino male college students exercising academic determination and community cultural wealth. *Journal of College Student Development 58*(2), 123–140. https://doi.org/10.1353/csd.2017.0011

Perry, W. G. (1970). *Forms of intellectual and ethical development in the college years: A scheme.* Holt, Rinehart and Winston.

Phinney, J. S. (2005). Ethnic identity in adolescents and adults: Review of research. In Wilson, M., & Wolf-Wendel, L. (Eds.), *ASHE reader on college student development theory* (pp. 295–318). Pearson Custom Publishing.

Pope, R. L., Reynolds, A. L., & Mueller, J. A. (2004). *Multicultural competence in student affairs.* Jossey-Bass.

Potochnick, S. R., & Perreira, K. M. (2010). Depression and anxiety among first-generation immigrant Latino youth: Key correlates and implications for future research. *The Journal of Nervous and Mental Disease, 198*, 470–477. https://doi.org/10.1097/NMD.0b013e3181e4ce24

Ramirez, A. F. (2003). Dismay and disappointment: Parental involvement of Latino immigrant parents. *The Urban Review, 35*(2), 93–110. https://doi.org/10.1023/A:1023705511946

Renn, K. A., & Reason, R. D. (2013). *College students in the United States: Characteristics, experiences, and outcomes.* Jossey-Bass.

Rodriguez, E., Rhodes, K., & Aguirre, G. (2015). Intervention for high school Latino students in preparing for college: Steps for consideration. *Journal of Hispanic Higher Education, 14*(3), 207–222. https://doi.org/10.1177/1538192714551369

Salinas Jr., C., & Lozano, A. (2019) Mapping and recontextualizing the evolution of the term *Latinx*: An environmental scanning in higher education. *Journal of Latinos and Education, 18*(4), 302–315. https://doi.org/10.1080/15348431.201 7.1390464

San Miguel, G., Jr., & Donato, R. (2009). Latino education in twentieth-century America: A brief history. In E. G. Murillo Jr, S. Valenas, R. T. Galván, J. Sánchez Munoz, C. Martinez, and M. Muchado-Casas (Eds.), *Handbook of Latinos and education* (pp. 27–62). Routledge.

Sanchez, D., Adams, W. N., Arango, S. C., & Flannigan, A. E. (2018). Racial-ethnic microaggressions, coping strategies, and mental health in Asian American and Latinx American college students: A mediation model. *Journal of Counseling Psychology, 65*(2), 214–225. https://doi.org/10.1037/cou0000249

Sanchez, M., Diez, S., Fava, N. M., Cyrus, E., Ravelo, G., Rojas, P., Li, T., Cano, M. A., & De La Rosa, M. (2019) Immigration stress among recent Latino immigrants: The protective role of social support and religious social capital, *Social Work in Public Health, 34*(4), 279–292. https://doi.org/10.1080/19371918.2019.1606749

Scheurich, J., & Young, M. (1997). Coloring epistemologies: Are our research epistemologies racially biased? *Educational Researcher, 26*, 4–16. https://doi .org/10.3102/0013189X026004004

Shi, Y., Jimenez-Arista, L. E., Cruz, J., McTier, T. S., & Koro-Ljungberg, M. (2018). Multilayered analyses of the experiences of undocumented latinx college students. *The Qualitative Report, 23*(11), 2603–2621. https://nsuworks.nova.edu/ tqr/vol23/iss11/1

Status and Trends in the Education of Racial Subgroups. (2019). *Indicator 19 snapshot: College participation rates for racial/ethnic subgroups.* National Center for Education Statistics. https://nces.ed.gov/programs/raceindicators/indicator_reas. asp

Tello, A. M., & Lonn, M. R. (2017). The role of high school and college counselors in supporting the psychosocial and emotional needs of Latinx first-generation college students. *Professional Counselor, 7*(4), 349–359.

Terenzini, P. T., & Reason, R. D. (2005, November). *Parsing the first year of college: Rethinking the effects of college on students.* [Paper presentation]. Association for the Study of Higher Education, Philadelphia, PA.

Tierney, W. G. (2000). Power, identity, and the dilemma of college student departure. In J. M. Braxton (Ed.), *Reworking the student departure puzzle* (pp. 213–234). Vanderbilt University Press.

Tinto, V. (1987) *Leaving college: Rethinking the causes and cures for student attrition.* University of Chicago Press.

Tinto, V. (1993) *Leaving college: Rethinking the causes and cures of student attrition,* (2nd ed.). University of Chicago Press.

Torres, J. B., & Solberg, V. S. (2001). Role of self-efficacy, stress, social integration, and family support in Latino college student persistence and health. *Journal of Vocational Behavior, 59*(1), 53–63. https://doi.org/10.1006/jvbe.2000.1785

Torres, V. (2003). Influences on ethnic identity development of Latino college students in the first two years of college. *Journal of College Student Development,* *44*(4), 532–547. https://doi.org/10.1353/csd.2003.0044

Torres, V. (2004). Familial influences on the identity development of Latino first-year students. *Journal of College Student Development, 45*(4), 457–469. https://doi.org/10.1353/csd.2004.0054

Torres, V., Campos, Cidhinnia, M., Phinney, J., Perez-Brena, N., Kim, C., Ornelas, B., Nemanim, L., Kallemeyn, D., Mihecoby, A., & Ramirez, C. (2009). A mentor-based targeted intervention for high-risk Latino college freshmen: A pilot study. *Journal of Hispanic Higher Education, 8*(2), 158–178. https://doi.org/10.1177/1538192708317621

Torres, V., & Hernandez, E. (2007). The influence of ethnic identity on self-authorship: A longitudinal study of Latino/a college students. *Journal of College Student Development, 48*(5), 558–573. https://doi.org/10.1353/csd.2007.0057

Torres, V., & Magolda, M. B. (2004). Reconstructing Latino identity: The influence of cognitive development on the ethnic identity process of Latino students. *Journal of College Student Development, 45*(3), 333–347. https://doi.org/10.1353/csd.2004.0043

Vega, D. (2010). Increasing Latino parent involvement in urban schools. *School Psychology: From Science to Practice, 2*(1), 20–25.

9

LATINX STUDENT DEVELOPMENT THROUGH *FAMILISMO* AND *CONOCIMIENTO*

Karina Chantal Canaba

Traditional student development theory is considered to be a useful tool that helps student affairs practitioners better understand changes their college students may be experiencing. Practitioners use student development theory as a guide to shape campus policies that put students' needs at the forefront of programming decisions to help foster positive growth as they matriculate through college (Evans et al., 2010). These theories seek to cultivate students' notions of competence, autonomy, and independence (Astin, 1977; Chickering, 1969; Kuh & Pike, 2005) and develop the whole student.

Special emphasis is placed on extracurricular activities, indicating that positive outcomes are correlated with extended participation in student organizations and events taking place on campus and in residence halls (Astin, 1977). Traditional perspectives of student development view the college environment as a training ground for students. It is within the confines of the university that students will learn the cultural and societal expectations for ensuring success upon graduation (Chickering, 1969). Although it is important that students' emotional needs are met while on campus, administrators need to be willing to question what "rules" or "real world" students are being prepared for (Patton et al., 2007).

Conventional student development theory is based on European psychology and serves to reinforce Euro-American customs that are not reflective of or responsive to the needs of students of color (Johnson, 2001;

McEwen et al., 1996; Patton et al., 2007). Demographic shifts require that student affairs practitioners reevaluate their programming to see that experiences are meaningful to students of different racial and ethnic backgrounds. Theories based on racial and ethnic identity are vital in helping students of color become aware of who they are and build self-esteem (Johnson, 2001) to allow them to create their own meanings of the world around them (Torres & Baxter Magolda, 2004). A deeper understanding of identities and diverse perspectives also has the potential to allow individuals to engage in critical discussion and exchange that lead toward political and social transformation (hooks, 1990; Patton et al., 2007). Reimagining student development from a cultural foundation helps make a richer and more profound college-going experience for minoritized students who have traditionally been relegated to the margins of mainstream educational systems. Failure to do so limits the psychosocial growth of minoritized students that administrators seek to serve (Cheatham & Berg-Cross, 1992; Patton et al., 2007).

Latinx Demographic Profile

The Latinx student experience is not very well reflected in established theories of student development, which requires new perspectives to better serve these students' needs. As the Latinx population grows and reaches college-going age, it will become more important to establish racial and ethnic identity theories for this population that needs on-campus support. In 2017, the median age of Latinos was 29, compared to 41 for non-Hispanic White males (U.S. Census Bureau, 2017a), and from 2000 to 2017 the number of Latinx adults increased 72% (Schak & Howard-Nichols, 2017). Latinx students are also the second largest group enrolled in higher education. In 2015–2016, Latinx students represented 19% of all undergraduate students, compared to White students (56%), African American students (14%), and Asian students (6%) (National Center for Education Statistics, 2017).

While the Latinx population in postsecondary education is larger than other groups, only 3% of first-year undergraduate students at 4-year institutions were Latinx in 2017 (U.S. Census Bureau, 2017b). This suggests that although there is a push for Latinx students to pursue postsecondary education, most students will be attending community colleges at some point in their academic careers. Latinos are much more likely to be first-generation college students than other racial/ethnic groups, with nearly half of Latinos (44%) indicating they were the first in their family to attend college (*Excelencia* in Education, 2019). Acceptance to any postsecondary institution is only part of the challenge Latinx students face; they must manage a number of responsibilities in and out of the classroom. Nationwide,

Latinx students complete college at public 4-year institutions at a lower rate than their peers across the country and have the highest rates of reverse-transfer, transferring from a 4-year college to a 2-year college, of all groups (Acevedo-Gil, 2017). Latinx students are more likely enroll part-time or go back and forth between part-time and full-time enrollment on a semester basis (*Excelencia* in Education, 2019).

The overwhelming majority (77%) of Latinx students work a minimum of 20 hours a week to finance their education and live off-campus or with their parents, more so than any other ethnic group (*Excelencia* in Education, 2019), and half care for dependent children. These experiences make a traditional development theory difficult to relate to, as students do not have the luxury of free time to participate in extracurricular activities because of work or caring for dependents. Interdisciplinary frameworks are necessary to be able to create experiences that are relevant and resonate with Latinx students and their realities. Student affairs administrators and policymakers need to recognize the different experiences these students have related to language, culture, gender, class, and immigration status that are overlooked in universally accepted notions of student development (Bennett & Bennett, 2004; Gallegos & Ferdman, 2007; Harris, 1994).

Using the frameworks of *familismo* and *conocimiento* allows practitioners to reflect on how they can create community among their Latinx students and encourage them to stay and graduate. *Familismo* is a means to understand why Latinx students choose college and how it fits into their long-term goals in life (Acevedo-Gil, 2017; Martinez, 2013). Often Latinx students carry the hopes of their parents and family who view education as part of the greater good (Martinez, 2013). *Conocimiento* is the process through which students will better understand their identity and interrogate the world from new directions (Anzaldúa, 2002).

Familismo

Familismo (familism) is one of the most significant cultural values among Latinx people (Martinez, 2013). Familismo is a reflection of the beliefs Latinx share in relation to extended families. Solidarity, loyalty, and reciprocity are heavily valued, and it requires that an individual submit to a collective form of decision-making. Through familismo, there is an added sense of responsibility and obligation to see that extended and nuclear family members are cared for (Martinez, 2013; Marín & Marín, 1991). From this perspective, students see their futures in postsecondary education as a way to contribute to their extended families and communities, a stark contrast to the individualistic pursuits of the U.S. educational system (Martinez, 2013; Rosas & Hamrick, 2002).

Familismo is important for Latinx students as the family unit is often a source of invaluable support. Parents may not always be familiar with what the college-going process entails, so they are more likely to provide financial and emotional encouragement while their children attend college (Ceja, 2006). Older siblings who have already attended college serve as guides for younger relatives who are starting college (Acevedo-Gil, 2017; Martinez, 2013). Attending college is a long-term goal for not only the students who are enrolled but also the larger extended family. Incorporating the family unit is vital for Latinx students and also serves as part of their development, which is antithetical to traditional models of student development theory.

As previously mentioned, Latinx students work while attending college; some workloads are the equivalent of full-time jobs. Though traditional student development theories suggest that students invest large quantities of time in cocurricular activities to spur personal growth (Astin, 1977; Chickering, 1969), that is sometimes not feasible for Latinx students. From a practical perspective, if students are forced to choose to spend time away from their family (especially young children) or work to attend extracurricular activities or meetings, Latinx students will more often than not choose their responsibilities over school interests. Communalism serves as a touchstone for many Latinx students, allowing for cooperation and belonging to arise from a group's common interests and goals (Pálsson,1996). Those ambitions are shared through intimate, personal relationships to create an atmosphere of general reciprocity among members of that group. Through the path of conocimiento, students are able to take the tenets of communalism to share their experiences and help those in their extended family that come after them.

Conocimiento

Conocimiento is a theory of individual development that challenges oppressive and conventional ways of knowing the world by creating individual consciousness and social justice actions (Anzaldúa, 2002). Conocimiento challenges "official and conventional ways of looking at the world, ways set up by those benefitting from such constructions" (Anzaldúa, 2002, p. 542). Comprising seven stages or steps, the entire process of conocimiento allows individuals to convert their most painful experiences into gifts that may be used to liberate and empower others as they learn to understand and love themselves.

The Seven Stages/Spaces of Conocimiento

Each of the seven stages of conocimiento is distinct; however, the process of going from desconocimiento (ignorance) to conocimiento (awareness) is nonlinear and ongoing (Figure 9.1). Skills and coping mechanisms learned through this process help the students manage future disruptions and difficulties but also help others within the community who may be experiencing similar circumstances. The process cultivates confidence in students to navigate adversity and lead others through obstacles on and off campus. The entire process starts with a shocking event.

El Arrebato (The Earthquake)

As Anzaldúa (2002) describes the first stage of conocimiento, *el arrebato* is an impactful event that forces an individual out of their sense of comfort and reality. It is here where one begins their journey toward change, as they can no longer return to how things were before the earthquake. Questions begin to be asked about who they are and everything that they thought they knew of the world. This stage awakens *la facultad*, or one's ability to see things on a much deeper level, and challenges their previously held assumptions and beliefs.

Latinx students can experience these earthquakes when they first arrive on campus. They may be unsure of where to go if they have specific questions. The campus environment can be difficult to traverse when they do not have networks of support available to them. If they are the first in their families to attend college, they have family members at home who are supportive of them attending college but may not be able to offer much advice

Figure 9.1. The seven stages of conocimiento.

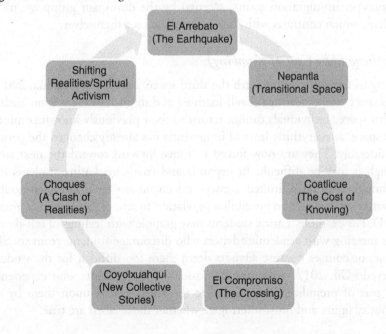

on how the system works. They may encounter conflicts with other students or support staff. They may also be registered in courses that no longer reflect a hegemonic body of knowledge, like Chicano Studies, or that open them up to histories that were never previously taught to them (Johnson, 2001). All of these experiences have the potential for students to feel isolated both at home and at school. Students are exposed to a new reality that is different from anything they have previously known.

Nepantla (Transitional Space)

Nepantla is the transitional space where one is overwhelmed with new perspectives and information. Different viewpoints become overwhelming, and Latinx students are forced to manage contradictory identities. In seeing oneself through restrictive societal restrictions, "you don't know whether to assimilate, separate, or isolate" (Anzaldúa, 2002, p. 548). In nepantla, one is forced to navigate and negotiate multiple worlds at any given time and make a commitment toward something new—to reconcile the image created by others with one they want to forge for themselves.

Students in this space can be managing preconceived low academic expectations from other college students, faculty, and staff that are different from their personal postsecondary aspirations (Immerwahr, 2003). Universities privilege a Eurocentric view that others marginalized groups and renders Latinx students invisible on a Black-White binary (Solórzano & Yosso, 2001). It is here where the labels and borders placed upon them (e.g., phenotype, immigration status, accents) by the dominant group are more evident, which contrasts with the ways students see themselves.

Coatlicue (The Cost of Knowing)

Living in nepantla brings forth the third space, *coatlicue* (Anzaldúa, 2002). This space evokes feelings of self-loathing and disgust, as there is no anchor in this space. Individuals cannot return to their previously known comfortable space, as everything learned in nepantla has already changed the person considerably. They are now forced to move forward toward the next step, though it may be difficult. In nepantla and coatlicue, Latinx students feel as though they have limited agency and encounter feelings of self-doubt, imposter syndrome, and invisibility in relation to school (Solórzano & Yosso, 2001). For example, Latinx students may grapple with feelings of self-doubt after meeting with academic advisers who discourage students from specific majors or courses because advisers deem them too difficult for the student (Acevedo-Gil, 2017; Solórzano & Yosso, 2001). Students who experience this sort of prejudice may internalize the labels placed upon them by an authority figure and must interrogate whether those labels are true.

El Compromiso (The Compromise)

During the fourth stage, *el compromiso*, individuals have a desire to evaluate and sort their previous experiences—to organize and to recreate an identity that aligns with their new reality (Anzaldúa, 2002). New communities are created, where one is led to a sense of higher purpose. In this stage, one leaves outdated parts of their identity behind in order to create new ones. Being exposed to new ideas and knowledge begins the emergence of a new epistemology. They realize that their struggles are part of a more universal experience that is meant to be shared with others. For instance, Latinx students share on-campus racist encounters with other Latinx students and realize that they are not alone (Flores & Garcia, 2009). Conversations such as these allow Latinx students a space to heal, as well as share ideas and suggestions with other Latinx students as they embark on similar paths. Though the journey is difficult, Latinx students realize that these lessons learned can be useful to themselves, their families, and their communities.

Coyolxauhqui (New Collective Stories)

Though students actively construct their identity through the seven stages, in *coyolxauhqui*, they actively recall previous experiences and place them within the larger collective story. This stage demands alternative ways of knowing, seeing, and thinking of the world (Anzaldúa, 2002). Here is where one can view fragments of their life from a completely new perspective, outside of the ideas of the ruling system, and they can evaluate past narratives that have kept them in tension between feelings of assimilation and isolation.

This new synthesized reality becomes a bridge that allows Latinx students to write their own stories beyond the confines of borders and labels. Latinx students begin to feel liberated from the limits placed on them by counselors, advisers, and other educators who may think Latinx students cannot succeed in postsecondary education (Acevedo-Gil, 2017). Where they previously would have been burdened with self-doubt if an adviser questioned the courses they were planning to take, at this stage students are able to advocate for themselves and their academic needs. Latinx students in this stage begin to feel comfortable with who they are and what they want out of their postsecondary career.

Choques (A Clash of Realities)

When entering the world with a new identity, inevitably conflict will arise. In the sixth stage of conocimiento, students are forced to deal with disappointments that arise when confronting old structures with their new way of knowing (Anzaldúa, 2002). These *choques*, or collisions (Rendón et al., 2014), happen on college campuses. These incidents can be academic, financial, or social and may force students to reevaluate their identities and place on their campuses.

Microaggressions can be a form of these collisions, in which Latinx students are made to feel unwelcome on their college campuses (Flores & Garcia, 2009; Lozano Rodriguez et al., 2000; Rendón et al., 2014; Solórzano & Yosso, 2001). For example, asking students where they are from or if they speak English are subtle ways to make Latinx students feel like outsiders on college campuses (Solórzano & Yosso, 2001). These situations can also cause stress when Latinx students fear that their reactions may reinforce the assumption that they do not belong on campus. University structures and practices, through unspoken rules and implicit expectations, can create a campus that is hostile toward Latinx students (Yosso et al., 2009). These feelings of hostility can cause Latinx students to feel so unwelcome that they may want to leave their college entirely and seek out a more hospitable place. Student affairs practitioners must manage these *choques* to ensure that Latinx students feel part of the campus and persist in their undergraduate journey.

Shifting Realities and Spiritual Activism

Once Latinx students are equipped with the tools of self-advocacy, they will be able to manage choques as they come up. Students develop approaches and utilize spiritual activism to manage conflicts that they will encounter in their daily lives both on campus and in the future. Anzaldúa (2002) describes spiritual activism as the ability to nurture the empowerment of the individual as well as the collective, with the hope of resolving the issue and bringing forth transformational change. This stage is not limited to the end of the process—students are able to learn to advocate for themselves at any point along the path.

Spiritual activism encourages those who develop it to include outward actions in their lives (Anzaldúa, 2002). As students learn to navigate the campus and become aware of available resources, they are able to advocate for themselves and other students (Martinez, 2013). Filled with a sense of responsibility and community, students are able to create and foster networks of support, especially in spaces where resources may be limited (Nuñez et al., 2007). Latinx students cultivate their campus communities by helping each other and advocating for one another to encourage success for all. As newer students come to campus, the community grows; more senior students guide the newer students as they experience college. Aligning with familismo, those support networks serve as an extended family unit of students who are able to encourage and look after one another while they are on campus and fulfill the call to serve others.

Implications for Policy

University policy must be interrogated to create an accurate picture of the campus culture and how it has the potential for Latinx students to feel excluded. From a critical race theory (CRT) and Latino/a critical race theory (Lat/Crit) perspective, racism is embedded in the fabric of America and is manifested and reproduced through institutions like education (Delgado, 1995; Solórzano & Yosso, 2001). Campus policymakers need to critically examine the unspoken rules of their campuses and evaluate the messages that are being sent to Latinx students and students of color.

Discouraging students from speaking Spanish, not having Latinx faculty on campus, and not recognizing that Latinx students come from different backgrounds all deliver the message that these students are not meant to be in higher education in general and on that campus in particular (Flores & Garcia, 2009; Lozano Rodriguez et al., 2000; Solórzano & Yosso, 2001). It is also important to recognize that Latinx students' journeys toward a degree are not always linear. Latinx student enrollment can vary from one term to another, with some students seesawing from full-time to part-time status based on a variety of economic and familial reasons (*Excelencia* in Education, 2019). These enrollment changes can be frustrating to administrators who deal with very specific definitions of enrollment and retention for the purposes of financial aid, institutional reporting, and funding (National Center for Education Statistics, 2019). Students who do not maintain full-time status are viewed as reaffirming negative stereotypes for Latinx students, completely devoid of the realities that Latinx students deal with (*Excelencia* in Education, 2019). Changes in enrollment should not be viewed as lack of academic interest on the student's part but instead should be viewed as a reflection of the balancing act many students manage on a day-to-day basis. Anything to the contrary only reinforces negative perceptions and ideologies that Latinx students have heard repeatedly throughout their educational careers and serves as another explicit microaggression toward Latinx students.

Implications for Practitioners

Incorporating familismo and conocimiento into extracurricular and cocurricular programming can positively impact Latinx beginning and experiencing college. Programming must be intentional to allow Latinx students to feel validated and part of the larger college context (Powell et al., 2013; Rolón-Dow, 2019; Rowe, 2008). When planning student events, administrators and student affairs practitioners should strongly consider allowing students to bring their families (e.g., parents, siblings, children, grandparents) as this is beneficial on numerous fronts (Acevedo-Gil, 2017; Martinez, 2013). Inviting families reinforces the notion that everyone has a role to play in seeing Latinx students succeed. Though families may not know to navigate the university, they are able to provide emotional and other support for Latinx students (Ceja, 2006; Martinez, 2013). Families are able to encourage students, particularly when students experience choques at school, to continue and persist (Acevedo-Gil, 2017; Martinez, 2013). The Latinx family can thus become familiar with the campus environment and feel as though they are a part of the collegiate journey with their student. They, in turn, are vested in seeing their students persevere and succeed. A family's positive on-campus experience can also encourage future generations of family members to attend that university, as research suggest that family's college choice preferences are influenced by meeting college counselors and representatives (Martinez, 2013). Students feel a sense of comfort knowing that they do not have to choose between their families and their education. This has the potential to limit the feeling of isolation that Latinx students sometimes experience while in college. Opportunities for creating community can also be done in the classroom. Examples include creating learning communities, creating class study groups or allowing students to speak Spanish more freely in class and on campus. These activities allow students to develop social capital and create networks, while at the same time identify spaces where they feel validated and supported (Rendón et al., 2014).

Learning communities are especially valuable for Latinx students, as they are able to find community in their classes where it may normally be lacking. In allowing Latinx students to enroll in certain course sequences together, students get to know one another and form supportive relationships within a classroom setting. Latinx students should also be proactively encouraged to enroll in Chicano or other ethnic studies courses as well as visit ethnic cultural centers, which can only help them better understand their racial and ethnic identities and allow them to learn other ways of knowing that can spark nepantla for students. Cultural centers and ethnic cultural centers also serve as counterspaces for students where they can escape the sometimes harsh racial college environments (Patton, 2006; Patton et al., 2007). These spaces also give Latinx students the opportunity to share strategies with other students who may be going through similar circumstances (Rendón et al., 2004).

Older students and students in higher years can serve as mentors or peer leaders to incoming first-years as they begin their collegiate careers (Acevedo-Gil, 2017; Martinez, 2013). This mentoring allows students to find a larger collective and participate in the spiritual activism that is the bedrock of conocimiento. The mentors are able to share their stories with the collective community and serve the greater good. Students who are newer to the college environment are given important advising and help at critical moments in their academic careers and know that whatever their struggles, they are not alone. This relationship is conocimiento and familismo in action, where Latinx students are able to contribute to the larger collective through acts of solidarity, loyalty, and reciprocity that Latinx students are already familiar with (Anzaldúa, 2002; Marín & Marín, 1991; Martinez, 2013; Pálsson,1996).

Culturally speaking, the benefit of the individual for Latinx students is typically secondary to that of the larger family unit, and the reasons have to be extremely compelling to ask students to miss out on what is expected of them at home. This calls for creativity on the part of practitioners who must identify purposeful modes of engagement that are not an additional burden on Latinx students who manage other commitments outside of school, financial or otherwise (Powell et al., 2013; Rolón-Dow, 2019). Federal work study can be leveraged to run programs that would allow Latinx students the opportunity to partake in a number of on-campus activities and alleviate the burden of having to work so many hours to support themselves and their families. While that may not be feasible on all campuses, it is an important consideration to encourage Latinx engagement on campus to reaffirm the college's commitment to Latinx students and let them know they belong (Lozano Rodriguez et al., 2000; Powell et al., 2013; Rendón et al., 2004; Rowe, 2008; Solórzano & Yosso, 2001). A reimagining of these types of programs benefits not only Latinx students but also other groups of students who may have similar off-campus responsibilities.

Conclusion

Creating an atmosphere for Latinx students to thrive on college campuses requires a commitment from administrators, student affairs practitioners, and faculty to restructure activities, programs, and courses in new ways. Latinx students manage a number of circumstances on and off campus that require flexibility and creativity on behalf of universities to see to it that these students feel welcomed and thrive on campus. As student populations become more diverse, the need for student affairs administrators to rethink traditional notions of development will only become more pressing. That can only benefit all minoritized students.

References

Acevedo-Gil, N. (2017) College-conocimiento: Toward an interdisciplinary college choice framework for Latinx students. *Race Ethnicity and Education, 20*(6), 829–850. https://doi.org/10.1080/13613324.2017.1343294

Anzaldúa, G. (2002). Now let us shift: Conocimiento . . . the path of inner work, public acts. In G. Anzaldúa & A. Keating (Eds.), *This bridge we call home: Radical visions for transformation* (pp. 540–578). Routledge.

Astin, A.W. (1977). *Four critical years: Effects of college on beliefs, attitudes, and knowledge.* Jossey-Bass.

Bennett, J. M., & Bennett, M. J. (2004). Developing intercultural sensitivity: An integrative approach to global and domestic diversity. In D. Landis, J. M. Bennett, & M. J. Bennett (Eds.), *Handbook of intercultural training* (3rd ed., pp. 147–165). SAGE.

Ceja, M. (2006). Understanding the role of parents and siblings as information sources in the college choice process of Chicana students. *Journal of College Student Development, 47*(1), 87–104. https://doi.org/10.1353/csd.2006.0003

Cheatham, H. E., & Berg-Cross, L. (1992). College student development: African Americans reconsidered. In L. C. Whitaker & R. E. Slimak (Eds.), *College student development* (pp. 196–192). Haworth.

Chickering, A. (1969). *Education and identity.* Jossey-Bass.

Delgado, R. (1995). *Critical race theory: The cutting edge* (2nd ed.).Temple University Press.

Evans, N. J., Forney, D. S., Guido, F. M., Patton, L. D., & Renn, K. A. (2010). *Student development in college: Theory, research, and practice* (2nd ed.). Jossey-Bass.

Excelencia in Education. (2019, April.) Latinos in higher education: Compilation of fast facts. Author. https://www.edexcelencia.org/research/publications/latinos-higher-education-compilation-fast-facts

Flores, J., & Garcia, S. (2009). Latina 'testimonios': A reflexive, critical analysis of a 'Latina space' at a predominantly white campus. *Race, Ethnicity and Education, 12*(2), 155–172. https://doi.org/10.1080/13613320902995434

Gallegos, P. V., & Ferdman, B. (2007). Identity orientations of Latinos in the United States: Implications for leaders and organizations. *The Business Journal of Hispanic Research, 1*(1), 26–41. http://bernardoferdman.org/Articles/GallegosFerdman IdentityOrientationsBJHR2007.pdf

Harris, A. (1994). Forward: The jurisprudence of reconstruction. *California Law Review, 82*(4), 741–785. https://www.jstor.org/stable/23478088

hooks, b. (1990) *Yearning: Race, gender, and cultural politics.* South End Press.

Immerwahr, J. (2003). *With diploma in hand: Hispanic high school seniors talk about their future.* National Center for Public Policy and Higher Education. http://www.highereducation.org /reports/hispanic/hispanic.shtml

Johnson, V. D. (2001). The Nguzo Saba as a foundation for African American college student development theory. *Journal of Black Studies, 31*(4), 406–422. https://doi.org/10.1177/002193470103100402

Kuh, G. D., & Pike, G. R. (2005). A typology of student engagement for American colleges and universities. *Research in Higher Education, 46*(2), 185–209. https://doi.org/10.1007/s11162-004-1599-0

Lozano Rodriguez, A., Guido-DiBrito, F., Torres, V., & Talbot, D. (2000). Latina college students: Issues and challenges for the 21st century. *NASPA Journal*, *37*(3), 511–527. https://doi.org/10.2202/1949-6605.1111

Marín, G., & Marín, B. V. (1991). *Research with Hispanic populations (applied social research methods)* (1st ed.). SAGE.

Martinez, M. A. (2013). (Re)considering the role familismo plays in Latina/o high school students' college choices. *The High School Journal*, *97*(1), 21–40. https://doi.org/10.1353/hsj.2013.0019

McEwen, M. K., Roper, L. D., Bryant, D. R., & Langa M. J. (1996). Incorporating the development of African American students into psycho social theories of student development. In F. D. Stage, G. L. Anaya, J. P. Bean, D. Hossler, & G. D. Kuh (Eds.), *College students: The evolving nature of research* (pp. 217–226). Simon & Schuster.

National Center for Education Statistics. (2017). *Digest of education statistics, 2017.* U.S. Department of Education. https://nces.ed.gov/pubs2018/2018070.pdf

National Center for Education Statistics. (2019). *2019-20 survey materials: Glossary.* https://surveys.nces.ed.gov/ipeds/Downloads/Forms/IPEDSGlossary.pdf

Nuñez, A., McDonough, P., Ceja, M., & Solórzano, D. (2007). Diversity within: Latino college choice and ethnic comparisons. *Social Forces*, 86, 561–575. https://doi.org/10.1093/sf/86.2.553

Pálsson, G. (1996). Human-environmental relations: Orientalism, paternalism and communalism. In P. Descola & G. Pálsson (Eds.), *Nature and society: Anthropological perspectives* (pp. 63–81). Routledge.

Patton, L. D. (2006). The voice of reason: A qualitative examination of black student perceptions of black culture centers. *Journal of College Student Development*, *47*(6), 628–646. https://doi.org/10.1353/csd.2006.0068

Patton, L. D., McEwen, M., Rendón, L., & Howard-Hamilton, M. F. (2007). Critical race perspectives on theory in student affairs (New Directions for Student Services, no. 120, pp. 39–53). https://doi.org/10.1002/ss.256

Powell, C., Demetriou, C., & Fisher, A. (2013, October 31). Micro-affirmations in academic advising: Small acts, big impact. *The Mentor: An Academic Advising Journal*, 15. https://doi.org/10.26209/MJ1561286

Rendón, L. I., Garcia, M., & Person, D. (2004). *Transforming the first year of college for students of color.* National Center on the First Year Experience and Students in Transition.

Rendón, L. I., Nora, A., & Kanagala, V. (2014). *Ventajas/assets y Conocimientos/knowledge: Leveraging Latin@ strengths to foster student success.* Center for Research and Policy in Education, The University of Texas at San Antonio. https://www.utsa.edu/strategicplan/documents/2017_12%20Student%20Success%20_Ventajas_Assets_2014.pdf

Rolón-Dow, R. (2019). Stories of microaggressions and microaffirmation: A framework for understanding campus racial climate. *NCID Currents*, *1*(1), 64–78. http://dx.doi.org/10.3998/currents.17387731.0001.106

Rosas, M., & Hamrick, F. (2002). Postsecondary enrollment and academic decision making: Family influences on women college students of Mexican descent. *Equity & Excellence in Education, 35*(1), 59–69. https://doi.org/10.1080/713845240

Rowe, M. (2008). Micro-affirmations and micro-inequities. *Journal of the International Ombudsman Association, 1*(1), 45–48. https://ioa.memberclicks.net/assets/docs/Volume1Journal.pdf

Schak, J. O., & Howard-Nichols, A. (2017). *Degree attainment for Latino adults: National and state trends.* The Education Trust. https://edtrust.org/wp-content/uploads/2014/09/Latino-Degree-Attainment_FINAL_4-1.pdf

Solórzano, D. G., & Yosso, T. J. (2001) Critical race and LatCrit theory and method: Counter-storytelling. *International Journal of Qualitative Studies in Education, 14*(4), 471–495. https://www.doi.org/10.1080/09518390110063365

Torres, V., & Baxter Magolda, M. (2004). Reconstructing Latino identity: The influence of cognitive development on the ethnic identity process of Latino students. *Journal of College Student Development, 45,* 333–347. https://doi.org/10.1353/csd.2004.0043

U.S. Census Bureau. (2017a). *Table B01002: Median age by sex (American community survey).* https://data.census.gov/cedsci/table?q=B01002&g=1600000US0908000_0100000US&tid=ACSDT5Y2017.B01002H&vintage=2017

U.S. Census Bureau (2017b). *Table 5: Type of college and year enrolled for college students 15 years old and over, by age, sex, race, attendance status, control of school, and enrollment status: October 2017.* https://www.census.gov/data/tables/2017/demo/school-enrollment/2017-cps.html

Yosso, T. J., Smith, W., Ceja, M., & Solórzano, D. (2009). Critical race theory, racial microaggressions, and campus racial climate for Latina/o undergraduates. *Harvard Educational Review, 79*(4), 659–691. https://doi.org/10.17763/haer.79.4.m6867014157m707l

¿*QUIÉN ERES*?

Identity Development of Latinx Student-Athletes

Nikola Grafnetterova and Rosa M. Banda

The United States is the only nation in the world where athletic programs are an integral part of higher education (Coakley, 2008). Just like all other divisions of student affairs, intercollegiate athletics and its staff have the duty to promote holistic development of their student-athletes (Reason & Broido, 2017). Indisputably, college years mark an important era of transition from adolescence to early adulthood for traditional-age students. It is a time of discovery, attainment of an advanced knowledge, and mastery of skills by students with the purpose of higher education to prepare them for their professional careers (Spring, 2011). Yet, one of the most important outcomes of college is for students to understand their own selves and become comfortable with their identities in a community of others (Chickering & Reisser, 1993; Erikson, 1959; Torres et al., 2009).

The U.S. college student body has diversified extensively since the term *identity development* was first coined by Erikson (1959) and initially applied to college student population by Chickering (1979). In particular, the college enrollment of Latinx students increased by 240% from 1996 to 2012 (Krogstad & Fry, 2014).[1] Further, various student subpopulations (e.g., immigrants; those identifying as lesbian, gay, bisexual, transgender, or questioning [LGBTQ]; and students with disabilities) have become more visible on college campuses. By the same token, the National Collegiate Athletic Association (NCAA) student-athlete body has gradually diversified in the past decades. Student-athletes from a myriad of cultural backgrounds, races, ethnicities, and nationalities participate in 24 sports currently governed by the NCAA (n.d.).

One of the guiding principles of the student affairs profession is to make decisions based on empirically grounded research (Reason & Broido, 2017).

Therefore, it is essential that the body of scholarly literature on student identity development expands and diversifies at the same pace as today's students. Unfortunately, many of the presently applied theoretical models, including Erikson's (1959) pioneering work, are outdated and thus do not sufficiently explain identity development of today's diverse student populations primarily because norm-referenced populations for such models are based on White males (see Côté & Levine, 1987 to read a critique of Erikson's theory, which was developed on the study). Moreover, as Abes (2009) asserts, all theoretical perspectives that undergird research are incomplete and require expansion.

The U.S. Latinx population has been growing rapidly, which has, in turn, spurred growth in studies exploring identity development of students of this ethnic background. Yet, the subpopulation of Latinx student-athletes remains vastly underexplored. Indisputably, a complex interlocking social system of power, privilege, and oppression has been at play (Johnson, 2018), resulting in a small representation of Latinxs competing in the NCAA and subsequent low level of interest from researchers. Nevertheless, the time has come to devote attention to this subpopulation, especially since in the student affairs profession, the success of every student matters.

Subsequently, the purpose of this chapter is to introduce a conceptual identity development framework for Latinx student-athletes. While separate theoretical models pertaining to identity development of the student-athlete and Latinx populations exist, as of this writing, a framework combining these intersecting identities is yet to be developed. First, this chapter provides background information on the Latinx population within the United States, higher education, and the NCAA. Second, a description of the traditional student-athlete experience is provided, and, third, a more in-depth discussion and description of how it varies from that of Latinx student-athletes is examined. Fourth, an overview of the traditional frameworks pertaining to student-athletes and Latinxs is provided in order to lay out the necessary foundations for our Latinx student-athlete identity development theory. Fifth, the details of the proposed theory along with practical recommendations for its application within the student affairs profession is offered.

Who Are Latinxs?

To fully understand the experiences of Latinx student-athletes, it is important to provide some basic information about the Latinx population that will serve as a foundation for our Latinx student-athlete identity development theory. According to the U.S. Census Bureau as of 2019, it is estimated that nearly 61 million of Latinxs reside in the United States; they are already the largest ethnic group and continue to grow steadily (Flores et al., 2019). Broadly defined, *Latinx* refers to any person of Latin American descent living in the United States (Garcia-Navarro, 2015) but is frequently substituted with the term *Hispanic*, which is a racial/ethnic category created by the U.S. government (Alcoff, 2005).

Many scholars emphasize that the Latinx designation is just a proxy variable since Latinxs are a diverse group of individuals with different cultural backgrounds (Gonzalez & Morrison, 2016; Núñez, 2014; Rodriguez et al., 2017). For example, unique to all other panethnic groups, racial identification and skin color differences span within and across the different Latinx groups (Fergus, 2016). As a result, most Latinxs do not identify with the standard racial and ethnic categories utilized by the U.S. Census Bureau's surveys (Parker et al., 2015); for example, in one survey, half of Latinx self-identified as some other race, 36% as White, and 3% as Black (Taylor et al., 2012).

Unmistakably, finding a common label for this diverse population is challenging. According to the surveys by the Pew Research Center (Taylor et al., 2012), Latinxs prefer using their family's country of origin over the terms *Latinx/Hispanic* to describe their identity. In 2016, 63.2% of Latinx were of Mexican origin, 9.5% were Puerto Rican, 3.9% were Cuban, 3.8% were Salvadoran, 3.3% were Dominican, and 2.5% were Guatemalan (U.S. Census Bureau, 2017). Further, Latinxs differ by their generational status within the United States, which is a key factor for understanding Latinx students' identity development in college (Torres, 2003). Today, 65.6% of Latinxs were born in the United States while 34.4% are immigrants (Flores, 2017). Those who immigrated are also recognized by scholars as first-generation Latinxs. Second-generation Latinxs are those born in the United States to immigrant parents, while Latinxs from the third-generation and higher are those born in the United States to U.S.-born parents (Pew Research Center, 2004).

Latinx Student-Athletes

Latinxs account for 18.3% of the U.S. population (U.S. Census Bureau, 2019); this percentage resembles closely the overall representation of Latinx within the full-time undergraduate student body, 17.4% (National Center for Education Statistics [NCES], 2019). However, in the group of approximately 490,000 NCAA student-athletes (NCAA, 2018b), only 5.7%, or 28,587 athletes, are Latinxs in comparison to 64.5% Whites and 16.3% Blacks (NCAA, 2018c). Unlike African American student-athletes, who comprise the majority of rosters in the revenue-generating sports of men's basketball, women's basketball, and football, Latinxs have not found their niche sport(s). They are present in most of the NCAA athletic programs but generally within nonrevenue sports, such as soccer, softball, and baseball (Lapchick, 2019; NCAA, 2018c). Further, no large discrepancies exist in the distribution of Latinxs across the three NCAA Divisions—I, II, III—or men's and women's sports (Lapchick, 2019) (see Table 10.1). To summarize, Latinx representation is disappointingly low across the board.

Overall, Latinx participation in college athletics has been gradually expanding. See Figure 10.1 for a visual representation of the growth of Latinx within the NCAA Student-Athlete Body from 1999 to 2017. Specifically, the

TABLE 10.1

Distribution of Latinx Student-Athletes Among the NCAA Divisions by Gender, 2017–2018

NCAA Division I (Latinx Representation)		NCAA Division II (Latinx Representation)		NCAA Division III (Latinx Representation)	
Men	Women	Men	Women	Men	Women
5.1%	5.1%	7.0%	7.0%	6.2%	5.0%

Note. Only athletes receiving financial aid are included in this table. Data were compiled from Lapchick (2019).

Figure 10.1. Percentage of Latinx student-athletes within the NCAA student-athlete body from 1999 to 2017, all NCAA divisions.

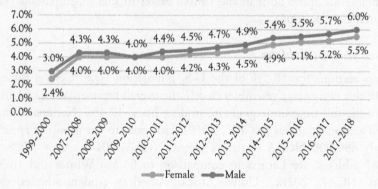

Percentage of Latinx within NCAA Student-Athlete Body, 1999-2007

Note. Adapted from Lapchick (2019) and NCAA (2018c).

number of Latinx student-athletes increased by 294% from 1999 to 2017 (NCAA, 2018c). Part of this growth is a result of increased participation opportunities in college sports as the NCAA student-athlete body grew by 140% from 1999 to 2017 (NCAA, 2018c).

Institutional Type and Setting

Overall, it is well-established by researchers that students' identity development and overall experiences vary across different institutional settings (e.g., Cuellar, 2014; Griffin & Hurtado, 2011; Pascarella & Terenzini, 2005). Sixty-six percent of today's Latinx students (Hispanic Association of Colleges and Universities [HACU], 2019) enroll at Hispanic-serving institutions (HSIs), defined by the federal government as U.S. colleges and universities with at least 25% equivalent full-time enrollment of students who are Latinxs (HACU, n.d.). Further, approximately 46% of all Latinx undergraduates, the highest share of any race or ethnicity, enroll at 2-year institutions (HACU, 2019).

In contrast, all of the 1,113 member institutions of the NCAA are 4-year colleges and universities (NCAA, 2017b, 2020). Further, 8% of the NCAA Division I, 13% of Division II, and 5% of Division III institutions are designated as HSIs; the majority of NCAA universities fall under the category of a predominantly White institution (PWI) (NCAA, 2017b). However, as asserted by Bourke (2016), PWI designation signals far more than just a large proportion of Whites in the overall student body. Rather, it reflects how the institution operates with embedded institutional practices based on White ideology (Bourke, 2016). Subsequently, Latinx students, along with others from traditionally marginalized groups, often perceive PWI campuses as unwelcoming and at times even hostile (Rankin & Reason, 2005; Von Robertson et al., 2016; Yosso et al., 2009).

However, as an aggregate, HSIs face similar criticisms. Scholars accuse HSIs of also promoting White norms and further perpetuating societal inequity, given that the majority of HSIs were founded as PWIs. The designation of HSI was an afterthought and only a result of the shifts in the U.S. population and the increase of Latinxs within certain geographical locations (Contreras & Contreras, 2015; Garcia, 2019; Laden, 2004; Núñez, 2015). Thus, scholars assert that the espoused missions to serve Latinxs do not match the enacted missions of many HSIs (Calderon, 2015; Contreras & Contreras, 2015; Fosnacht & Nailos, 2016).

Nevertheless, the campus racial climate varies from institution to institution. If Latinxs perceive it as unwelcoming, or even hostile, research shows that it will negatively impact their sense of belonging, which in turn, is linked to student attrition (e.g., Hurtado & Carter, 1997; Hurtado & Ponjuan, 2005; Locks et al., 2008; Rodriguez et al., 2017). However, the environments of HSIs, if developed and utilized properly, are well-positioned to allow Latinx students to assert a sense of belonging due to a high proportion of students with similar cultural identity (Arana et al., 2011). As voiced by Quaye et al. (2009), all institutions, no matter their institutional type and setting, need to create initiatives and programming that place students' racial and ethnic identities at the forefront of the learning process in order to meet their unique needs.

Latinx student-athletes tend to attend different types of institutions than most of their nonathlete Latinx peers. Nevertheless, based on their ethnic and racial group identity, they are likely to experience similar issues in terms of discrimination and subsequent lack of sense of belonging on many of today's campuses. In addition, as the sections that follow will describe in detail, Latinx student-athletes face additional challenges stemming from their participation in intercollegiate athletics, whose culture is also perceived as incongruent with the current majority culture of the academia. We start by turning the discussion to what constitutes a traditional student-athlete experience and how it varies from that of the general student body.

Student-Athlete Experience

In many aspects, student-athletes are just like all other students. When they first arrive on campus, they face various social and academic transition challenges. They must pass courses in order to meet degree requirements, attend class lectures, and study. Developmentally, they have the same needs as their nonathlete peers as they need to form their identity, become independent critical thinkers, and establish meaningful relationships within the campus community. However, student-athletes face additional challenges stemming from their sport participation and subsequent attempts at balancing the dual roles of both student *and* athlete.

Time Constraints

Participation in intercollegiate sports imposes large time demands on student-athletes. Per the NCAA requirements, student-athletes must be enrolled in at least 12 credit hours as full-time students. In addition, athletes spend time in practice, weight-training sessions, and mandatory team meetings. When in season, the demands intensify with additional time dedicated to travel and competition. According to the NCAA (2016), Division I student-athletes, the most competitive level, spend on average 32 hours per week on athletically related activities while in-season. The off-season demands are no less stringent. Two thirds of Divisions I student-athletes report as much or more time spent on athletics as in-season (NCAA, 2016).

Reasonably, concerns prevail over the academic and personal development of student-athletes given their limited amount of unstructured time (Comeaux & Harrison, 2011; Jolly, 2008). Additionally, many institutions provide athlete-only facilities and services, which may further limit opportunities for athletes to engage with the rest of the campus community (Huml et al., 2014; Otto et al., 2019; Rubin & Moses, 2017). However, research finds mixed results in regard to student-athletes' level of campus involvement and interactions with nonathlete peers. Some studies associate athletic involvement with possible isolation from the rest of the student body and subsequent low participation in on-campus events and activities (e.g., Adler & Adler, 1985; Astin, 1977; Huml et al., 2014; Rubin & Moses, 2017). Other scholars do not find significant differences in student engagement between athletes and nonathletes (e.g., Aries et al., 2004; Crawford, 2007; Gaston-Gayles & Hu, 2009; Potuto & O'Hanlon, 2007; Rettig & Hu, 2016; Umbach et al., 2006). Nonetheless, the majority of student-athletes from all NCAA divisions report wishing for more time to focus on academics, visit home or family, socialize with friends, and relax (NCAA, 2016). Thus, time constraints certainly provide unique dynamics to college athletes' identity development.

Stereotypes

Time constraints are not the only challenge facing athletes. Various high-profile scandals have resulted in an ongoing tarnished public perception of intercollegiate athletics. The enduring commercialization of college sports and drive for revenue are credited for the upsurge in misconduct cases ranging from recruiting violations to academic fraud (e.g., Adamek, 2017; Clotfelter, 2019; Gurney et al., 2017; New, 2016; Smith & Willingham, 2015; Yost, 2010). Subsequently, critics raise concerns over the presumably incompatible cultures of intercollegiate athletics and academia (e.g., Bowen & Levin, 2003; Feezell, 2015; Harrison & Bukstein, 2014; Jayakumar & Comeaux, 2016; Shulman & Bowen, 2001).

As a result, student-athletes frequently experience an unwelcoming campus environment where faculty, staff, and students negatively stereotype athletes in regard to their academic abilities and place within higher education institutions, viewing them as so-called dumb jocks (Eggleston & Mitchell, 2005; Paule & Gilson, 2010; Simons et al., 2007; Wininger & White, 2015; Yopyk & Prentice, 2005). Yet, while athletic participation erects obstacles, it also simultaneously presents opportunities for academic success (Gaston-Gayles & Baker, 2015). Specifically, based on empirical findings, involvement in college sports is linked to heightened sense of belonging, persistence intentions, and academic performance of student-athletes (Fearon et al., 2013; NCAA, 2016; Sung et al., 2015). Notably, this double-edged relationship is one of the key elements of the Latinx student-athlete identity development theory.

Athletic Identity

Balance is essential for healthy development of college student-athletes. Yet, critics assert that the culture of many college athletic programs encourages prioritization of athletics at the expense of academics (e.g., Bowen & Levin, 2003; Flowers, 2009; Gurney et al., 2017; Jayakumar & Comeaux, 2016; Saffici & Pellegrino, 2012; Shulman & Bowen, 2001). Expectedly, a number of student-athletes view themselves more as athletes than students, with their identities intertwined with athletic talent and achievements (Potuto & O'Hanlon, 2007; Rubin, 2015). This construct is known as *athletic identity*, defined as the degree of identification with the role of athlete (Brewer et al., 1993).

Student-athletes possess various degrees of athletic identity as well as student identity. In fact, the majority of NCAA student-athlete body reports having strong identities as students as well as athletes (NCAA, 2013). It is important to note that empirical findings do not link high athletic identity to low levels of academic performance (NCAA, 2013). Rather, a low student identity is to blame as it predicts future academic problems (NCAA, 2013).

High athletic identity is linked to various positive outcomes, such as life satisfaction and overall well-being (Williams, 2007). The negative consequences usually stem from exclusive athletic identity, which interferes with the development of other occupational and/or ideological identity alternatives (Brewer & Petitpas, 2017). Additionally, when foreclosing their athletic identity, student-athletes with salient athletic identity are likely to experience various issues, such as psychological problems, an increased risk of substance abuse, lack of interest in exploration of career options, and various other transition issues (Brewer & Petitpas, 2017; Menke, 2015; Miller & Kerr, 2003). Subsequently, student affairs professionals working with student-athletes must provide opportunities to explore and further commit to other roles in addition to that of an athlete.

As such, student-athletes face additional challenges stemming from their athletic participation that include hurdling the added time constraints, dealing with stereotypes concerning their fit within the domain of academia, and balancing the development of their athletic identity along with other role aspirations. Latinx student-athletes also face these challenges but they take on a slightly different form given their unique cultural backgrounds. The next section highlights these variations.

Latinx Student-Athlete Experience

Students do not experience college in the same way. Intersecting social identities influence students' notion of who they are, how they see themselves, and how they relate to others (Torres & McGowan, 2017). Therefore, identity does not embody one's personality but rather amounts to one's reflective self-concept within a particular culture in reference to others (Côté & Levine, 2002; Torres & McGowan, 2017). The literature on the student-athlete population typically simplifies the concept of identity by solely featuring the student and athlete roles. For Latinx student-athletes, however, the experiences are far more complex given that they operate within a majority culture that seeks to assimilate them rather than embrace the aspects of their own culture (Jamieson, 2003; Yosso, 2005). Therefore, student affairs professionals working with this population must first understand how the experiences differ in order to assist Latinx student-athletes through the task of creating a balanced, healthy identity (Torres & McGowan, 2017).

Latinx Culture

The scholarly literature on what Latinx student-athletes experience is incomplete. Most of the available studies focus on reasons for the low representation of Latinxs within intercollegiate athletics, which include a broken pipeline from youth sports, lack of familiarity with the athletic recruitment system, and cultural differences (Alamillo, 2013; Cameron, 2012; Jamieson, 2005). Specifically, despite its diversity, scholars describe Latinx culture as prioritizing familial relationships and valuing hard labor (Arana et al., 2011; Cameron, 2012; Gloria & Castellanos, 2012; Jamieson, 2005; Kouyoumdjian et al., 2017). Subsequently, many Latinxs decide to stay close to their families, attend local community colleges, and/or work full-time after high school while attending college part-time (Santiago, 2011). Latinx student-athletes do not fit this pattern as they must venture out of their communities in order to play college sports (Jamieson, 2005).

In order to participate in the NCAA, Latinxs must overcome systemic barriers (Alamillo, 2013; Hextrum 2018; Jamieson, 2005; McGovern, 2018), which are amplified for those who are *first-generation college students*, defined as first in the family to pursue college education (Pike & Kuh, 2005). Generally, Latinxs, athletes and nonathletes, comprise a high proportion of first-generation students (NCAA, 2016; NCES, 2015). However, instead of attributing their success to the process of assimilation to the dominant culture, Latinxs rely on their cultural capital (Darvin et al., 2017; Jamieson, 2003, 2005; Yosso, 2005). As Jamieson (2005) asserts, Latinx student-athletes must simultaneously separate from their cultures while staying connected to this important network of resources.

Only approximately 6% of all high school athletes make it to the NCAA, and only a portion of those, 2%, earn an athletic scholarship (NCAA, 2017a, 2018b). Thus, as Jamieson (2005) posits, Latinxs turn their athletic ability into cultural capital when they earn full or partial athletic scholarship to attend college. Still, navigating and adjusting to a new culture of their campuses and the university's region can prove challenging. However, Latinxs stay connected to their families and communities, using their cultural and social capital to persist as athletes and students (Jamieson, 2005; Yosso, 2005). As Jamieson (2005) posits, Latinx student-athletes are not only products of their communities but also change agents within them.

Overall, the experiences of Latinxs vary depending on their sport as differences prevail between athletes from revenue and nonrevenue teams (Gaston-Gayles & Hu, 2009; Osborne, 2014; Paule & Gilson, 2010). In spite of time constraints of balancing athletics and academics, some student-athletes also have part-time employment (NCAA, 2016). Among the general student population, Latinx students are more likely to work while in college in comparison to their peers from other racial/ethnic groups (Santiago, 2011). As such, many Latinx student-athletes likely work part-time, especially since Latinxs want to make their families proud and give back to their communities (Jamieson, 2005; Kouyoumdjian et al., 2017). Overall, while some Latinxs may feel conflicted for leaving their communities to pursue intercollegiate athletics, they use their cultural traditions, families, and communities as motivation and a source of empowerment on their journey to a college degree.

Racism

As Jamieson (2003) posits, sports encompass a cultural space upholding the ideologies in regard to race, social class, gender, and sexuality. Specifically, sports transmit values and beliefs associated with the dominant White culture (Jamieson, 2003, 2005), which is one of the primary reasons why Latinxs remain underrepresented within intercollegiate athletics. Subsequently, Latinxs who gain access to the NCAA may perceive feeling "inside in an outside way" (Cuádraz, 1992, p. 32) because of their intersecting identities of student, athlete, and Latinx, among others.

As student-athletes, Latinxs face an inescapable double-bind in regard to fitting in the student and athlete domains. Just like other athletes, Latinxs may perceive being negatively stereotyped for their academic abilities and belonging in academia due to the aforementioned *dumb jock* assumption. In addition, given their ethnic backgrounds, Latinxs may further encounter negative stereotypes about their athletic prowess (Alamillo, 2013). Notably, these experiences may vary depending on the perceptions of Latinxs' nuanced race and ethnicity in the population.

It is also important to keep in mind that Latinxs encounter systemic racism within higher education through unwelcoming campus environments and various forms of discrimination, such as microaggressions (Ballinas, 2017; Ortega, 2019; Von Robertson et al., 2016; Yosso et al., 2009). With the current political context triggering a backlash against immigrants, these negative experiences extend to Latinxs' interactions outside of campuses (Renn & Reason, 2013). Therefore, Latinxs face the additional developmental task of dealing with racism (Torres, 2009; Torres & Hernandez, 2007). Ultimately, the way students make meaning of experiences that are racist, sexist, and homophobic will influence their persistence intentions, holistic development, and overall well-being (Torres & McGowan, 2017). Students who possess a secure sense of their identity can withstand these negative experiences (Porter & Washington, 1993).

Ethnic Identity

For many Latinxs, *ethnic identity,* defined as one's self as part of an ethnic group (Bernal et al., 1993), can thwart the negative effects of prejudice, stereotypes, and racism as it increases students' sense of belonging on campus (Syed et al., 2007; Torres & McGowan, 2017). Overall, the systems of power, privilege, and oppression influence Latinx identity development as the majority culture can project unfavorable images on this ethnic group, which may result in an internalized negative sense of self and/or desire to fit in with the majority (Torres et al., 2009). As such, Latinx students deal with stress as they reflect on who they are in relation to others on their campuses, home communities, and society as a whole (Torres, 2003).

In essence, ethnic identity forms inside, outside, and in relation to groups to which one perceives belonging as well as to groups of which one is not a member (Renn & Reason, 2013). As Weinreich (2003) explains, Latinx ethnic identity has overlapping and common elements but is never completely homogenous. Thus, description of Latinx identity development proves challenging for researchers (Miville, 2010).

Overall, positive ethnic identity promotes student learning, sense of belonging, and enhanced self-esteem (Richardson et al., 2010; Syed et al., 2007; Torres et al., 2009; Umaña-Taylor, 2004, 2011). In contrast, identity conflict is linked to student attrition (Evans et al., 1998). Unfortunately, the culture of intercollegiate athletics may hinder one's identity development beyond that of an athlete due to overemphasis on sports (Bowen & Levin, 2003; Shulman & Bowen, 2001).

As aforementioned, sports encompass a cultural space where different identities form, become reproduced, but also may encounter resistance (Jamieson, 2003). Overall, identity formation is a complex process, with students inhabiting a range of identities that may fall into privileged but also oppressed categories (Collins, 2000; Johnson, 2018). As Torres et al. (2009) posit, the current scholarship uses an *additive approach* when looking at identity development. Under this perspective, scholars examine social identities independently (e.g., racial identity and sexual identity) and presume that the resultant experiences can be comprehended singularly (Bowleg, 2008; Torres et al., 2009). Instead, scholars call for utilization of *intersectionality* as an analytical lens to develop new theories (Bowleg, 2008; Torres et al., 2009). Such a lens accounts for the within-group differences as well as recognizes the different interdependent, intersecting, and mutually constitutive parts of one's identity (Bowleg, 2008; Dill & Zambrana, 2009; Torres et al., 2009). As Bowleg (2008) notes, "When Black + Lesbian + Woman ≠ Black Lesbian Woman" (p. 312). In other words, "Being Black and lesbian confers a unique experience, above and beyond being Black or lesbian" (Bowleg, 2008, p. 319). Our Latinx student-athlete identity development theory follows the recommendation of utilizing intersectionality as analytical lens. However, prior to its introduction, it is paramount to highlight the existing, but separate, traditional identity development models for Latinxs and student-athletes.

Traditional Identity Development Models

Student affairs professionals rely on identity theories to understand their students' complex experiences (Torres & McGowan, 2017). With the increasing diversity of college populations, scholars have expanded the assortment of identity development models. As such, Phinney's (1993) model of ethnic identity development and Torres's (1999, 2003) bicultural orientation model (BOM) are useful for personnel working with Latinx students. While not well-established, some theoretical frameworks also exist about student-athlete identity formation. Thus, this section evaluates these models' applicability to Latinx student-athletes. Further, the subsequent paragraphs provide foundations of our Latinx student-athlete theory framed by concepts of intersectionality (Crenshaw, 1989), *mestizaje* (Anzaldúa, 1987), and coalescence (Lugones, 1994).

Phinney's Model of Ethnic Identity Development

Phinney (1993) was among the first scholars to develop an ethnic identity development framework. Importantly, this three-stage linear model is not centered only on Latinx identity; rather, it applies across all ethnic groups (Patton et al., 2016). In this model, individuals progress through stages of (a) unexamined ethnic identity, (b) ethnic identity search/moratorium, and (c) ethnic identity achievement. Specifically, individuals begin at a point of complete unawareness of their ethnic identity during which they accept the values and attitudes of the majority culture. After experiencing some sort of oppressive incident, however, they begin a quest for further exploration of their ethnicity. This search culminates in the final stage where the individuals achieve a confident sense of their ethnic identity (Phinney, 1993).

Torres's BOM

Utilizing Phinney's (1993) model as its framework, Torres (1999) introduced a model specific to the Latinx population known as the BOM. Torres (1999) validated this model by demonstrating a correlation between acculturation and ethnic identity. The BOM consists of four cultural orientation quadrants. Latinx students who demonstrate high levels of acculturation and ethnic identity are *bicultural,* which indicates comfort with both Latinx and Anglo cultures. In contrast, low levels on both constructs point to a *marginal orientation* where Latinxs struggle to function in either of the two cultures. Latinx students who display high levels of acculturation feel more comfortable with the majority culture, known as *Anglo orientation,* while those with high levels of ethnic identity feel less comfortable with the majority culture, known as *Latinx orientation* (Patton et al., 2016; Torres, 1999).

In a follow-up study, Torres (2003) further expanded on the BOM and conceptualized ethnic identity development for Latinxs during first 2 years of college. Torres (2003) found that students' identity varies at the start of college years, depending on the environment where they grew up as well as the family's generational status and family's ethnic identification (e.g., country of origin). Specifically, Latinxs who grew up in diverse environments have a strong sense of ethnicity in comparison to those who grew up in regions with a White majority and thus exhibit the Anglo orientation. Further, students from first-generation families experience cultural conflict when they enter college. Second- and third-generation Latinxs come from more acculturated families and thus experience less stress as they are able to function well in cultures of their home communities as well as their university's campuses (Torres, 2003).

Ethnic identity is a dynamic construct. Therefore, Latinx ethnic identity develops continuously, with Torres (2003) attributing this change in students to the conflict with college culture and shift in relationships with the environment. Specifically, Latinx identity evolves as students interact with their peers, navigate the campus environments, and compare their sense of culture with the expectations of others. In other words, Torres (2003) described the complexity of Latinx identity development. Unlike Phinney (1993), Torres (2003) demonstrated that every Latinx journey in terms of ethnic identity formation is unique as numerous elements shape it.

Student-Athlete Identity

Similar to Latinxs, NCAA student-athletes are a heterogeneous population (Comeaux & Harrison, 2011). Therefore, attempts to develop conceptual identity models applicable to all subsets of this population prove difficult. Overall, Brewer and Cornelius (2001) introduced the athletic identity measurement scale (AIMS) to measure the level of one's athletic identity. Scholars recognize this instrument, along with its expanded version of AIMS-plus, as effective tools for research and intervention for athletic identity (Cabrita et al., 2014; Cieslak, 2004). However, as of 2020, the quest for a holistic student-athlete identity development model continues.

Overall, limited findings indicate that student-athletes begin college with more salient athletic identities but they progressively change to more salient student identities (Lally & Kerr, 2005; Miller & Kerr, 2003). However, in the seminal work by Adler and Adler (1991), athlete identity strengthened as student-athletes progressed through their college careers. As such, the different research conclusions indicate that student-athlete identity is a complex, nonparallel construct. The environment and culture of intercollegiate athletics impact its formation (Adler & Adler, 1991; Miller & Kerr, 2003). Notably, as a result of the commercialization of athletics, the level of athletic and academic identities varies between athletes from revenue and nonrevenue teams (Comeaux et al., 2011; Harrison & Bukstein, 2014; Potuto & O'Hanlon, 2007). However, one must be careful when generalizing, as the research conclusions are still mixed.

Intersectionality, Mestizaje, and Coalescence

The aforementioned models briefly examine ethnic and athletic identity independently. However, Latinx student-athletes possess multiple, intersecting social identities that comprise a more holistic identity. Described as *intersectionality* by Crenshaw (1989), this lens recognizes that one's identity is multidimensional and exists within the context of larger social structures of power, privilege, and oppression. Therefore, scholars cannot understand one's experiences by looking at each identity dimension, such as race, social class, gender, and sexuality, singularly (Crenshaw, 1989; Torres et al., 2009). As such, even if some characteristics are shared among individuals (e.g., ethnicity, race, or gender), the identity development process is not the same.

Unfortunately, traditional identity models utilize binary dualism, with students either fitting into one category *or* the other. Anzaldúa (1987) challenges this notion when describing the concept of *mestizaje* where Latinxs occupy a metaphorical middle space. They traverse boundaries of different social categories (the borders) and resist classification under one dimension, thus inhabiting the borderlands. In other words, Anzaldúa (1987) views identity as a fluid concept rather than a single, fixed position. Therefore, Latinx identity is a hybrid as it transcends binaries.

Lugones (1994) expands on the concept of mestizaje by introducing the concept of coalescence and uses the metaphor of emulsifying mayonnaise to explain it. Specifically, when mayonnaise separates, it is never again egg and oil. Rather, a yolky egg and an oily yolk remain as egg coalesces toward oil or toward water (Lugones, 1994). In other words, identity never consists of stable, concrete categories (Anderson, 2010). Rather, one identity percolates into another identity just like mayonnaise when it emulsifies (Garry, 2011; Lugones, 1994). The idea that mayonnaise might separate focuses on purity and is a metaphor for dominance and control over marginalized groups. In contrast, emulsifying refers to impurity, which symbolizes resistance to intersected oppressions (Friedman, 1998; Garry, 2011). Overall, Lugones (2014) views categories and categorical thinking as tools of oppression by those in power (Lugones, 2014). Therefore, hybrid identity encompasses a privileged space for Latinxs where they get to embrace and express their plural, multiple selves (Friedman, 1998; Sheth, 2014). As Anderson (2010) asserts, Lugones blurs edges of hard distinctions between people and celebrates human complexity.

As of the publication of this book, a gap exists in regard to theoretical models applicable to the diverse Latinx student-athlete population. As noted throughout this section, identity is complex, multidimensional, fluid, and context-specific. The aforementioned concepts of intersectionality, mestizaje, and coalescence serve as the fundamentals for our Latinx student-athlete theory that expands on the traditional models of ethnic and athletic identity development. The next section builds on all of this background and reveals the details of our framework.

Model of Identity Development of Latinx Student-Athletes

Latinx student-athletes possess multiple intersecting identities when they begin their college studies. The context determines which identity, or combination of identities, is most salient in the moment. Latinx student-athletes move among the identities of Latinx, student, and athlete in response to the given environment, a practice also known as code switching. As such, our model of identity development of Latinx student-athletes (MIDLSA) consists of three basic domains: cultural, intellectual, and athletic (Table 10.2).

Cultural Domain

The cultural domain refers to various components that other scholars group under the umbrella term of *ethnic identity*. Specifically, Latinxs vary in their family's country of origin and generational status in the United States, socioeconomic demographics (e.g., gender, race, and socioeconomic status), culture (e.g., language, religion, customs, etc.), the environment of their hometown community, and overall family expectations. In other words, no two Latinx student-athletes are the same in their ethnic identity, as implied by Lugones (1994). However, using the intersectional lens (Crenshaw, 1989), the combination of all of these elements determines Latinxs' level of adjustment to and overall experience of college.

Intellectual Domain

The intellectual domain refers to various components that comprise Latinxs' student identity. When Latinxs arrive on college campuses, they have already

TABLE 10.2
Primary Domains of the MIDLSA

Cultural Domain	Intellectual Domain	Athletic Domain
Ethnic Identity	Student Identity	Athletic Identity
Country of origin	Federal, state, and institutional policies	NCAA rules and regulations
Generational status in the United States	Institutional type, setting, and overall culture	Culture of the athletic department
Culture (language, religion, customs, etc.)	Campus climate	Team's culture and overall sport dynamics
Environment of hometown community	Interactions with students, faculty, and staff	Interactions with teammates, coaches, and athletic staff
Family's expectations	Precollege educational experiences	Precollege athletic experiences

endured 12 years in primary and secondary schools that largely intellectually shaped who they are as students. Because of socioeconomic status, these schools vary in the level of resources such as qualified teachers and curriculum offerings (Almy & Theokas, 2010; Darling-Hammond, 2001; U.S. Commission on Civil Rights, 2018) as well as student and teacher diversity. Therefore, the intellectual domain largely consists of precollege educational experiences, which can negatively or positively affect success in college. Moreover, the elements of the college/university also form Latinxs' student identity. Specifically, the institutional type, setting, and overall culture; campus climate; and interactions with students, faculty, and staff all combine to play an important role in the development of student identity of Latinx student-athletes. The NCAA's (2013) findings that low levels of student identity are linked to negative academic performance and persistence of student-athletes further highlight the importance of student identity development in Latinxs.

Athletic Domain

The third domain is the athletic domain and consists of elements that comprise athletic identity. Unique among other identities, some athletes identify with their sport early in life and thus cultivate their athletic identity since childhood (Webb et al., 1998). As such, Latinx athlete identity consists of precollege athletic experiences. Moreover, the culture of the intercollegiate athletic department; the team's culture and overall sport dynamics; and interactions with teammates, coaches, and other athletic staff further evolve this identity component. As aforementioned, the culture of college athletics tends to overpromote this identity while potentially hindering development in other identity domains. In addition, some research suggests that variations in the level of athletic identity exist between athletes in high-profile revenue sports of football and basketball in comparison to athletes from nonrevenue sports (Comeaux et al., 2011; Harrison & Bukstein, 2014; Potuto & O'Hanlon, 2007). Therefore, the level of athletic identity varies immensely among Latinxs since they participate in the NCAA revenue and nonrevenue sports (NCAA, 2018c).

MIDLSA

Unlike other models on identity development of students that examine domains in isolation, Latinx student-athletes simultaneously intersect and interact with the three domains in the MIDLSA. Most importantly, the MIDLSA consciously accounts for the societal systems of power, privilege, and oppression that influence Latinx student-athletes' identity development in an institutional setting (see Figure 10.2 for a visual representation of the MIDLSA). What follows is a description of (a) institutional setting as well as (b) the structural systems of power, privilege, and oppression on the intersecting and multidimensional ethnic, student, and athletic identities of Latinx student-athletes.

Institutional Setting
Latinx student-athletes attend colleges and universities that differ in their type, setting, and overall culture. As aforementioned, the majority of the NCAA institutions are PWIs and doctorate-granting institutions with large student bodies (NCAA, 2017b). Some of these colleges and universities are HSIs where Latinxs are able to interact with a greater proportion of peers, faculty, and staff of the same ethnic background (Arana et al., 2011; Núñez, 2014). However, as criticized, the majority of HSIs still operate with institutional practices based on White ideology (Calderon, 2015; Contreras & Contreras, 2015; Fosnacht & Nailos, 2016; Garcia, 2019). Overall, HSI and PWI designations are just categories. As Núñez (2015) asserts, it is important to look at institutional context rather than group colleges and universities by their type.

Figure 10.2. MIDLSA.

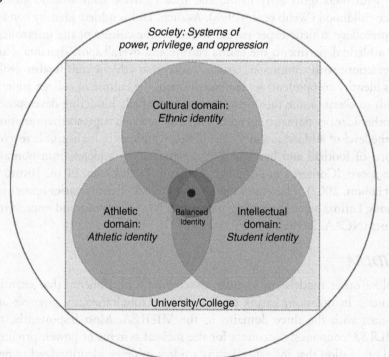

Given that Latinxs possess different ethnic identities, or *orientations* in Torres's (1999, 2003) terms, students' reactions to these environments and the unique institutional settings vary. For instance, Latinxs with Anglo orientations may feel more comfortable at PWI campuses than their peers with Latinx orientations. In contrast, Latinxs who grew up in communities with a large proportion of Latinxs and/or who come from first-generation families in the United States are more likely to experience a conflict in adjusting to the PWI campus environments while also staying connected to their home communities. The combinations of aspects from the three domains are endless. Thus, these parts coalesce into a unique experience for every Latinx student-athlete that influences and shapes their identity development.

One's identity is not a static construct. As Anzaldúa (1987) asserts, Latinxs possess fluid identities. As such, ethnic, student, or athletic identities become more dominant in certain university/college contexts and situations than others. The institutional context, in other words, plays an integral role in the development of intersecting student identities. Specifically, when Latinxs attend PWIs and become token Latinxs within their athletic teams, their athletic identities become more important for them in order to assert a sense of belonging on their campuses. In contrast, when the campus constituents embrace negative attitudes toward student-athlete population, Latinxs may overplay their student identity and/or ethnic identity. The dynamics are complex as in some cases the campus community incorrectly conflates Latinxs with African American or White populations. As a result, Latinxs have vastly different experiences and identity development needs in those settings than they would in other environments.

As Lugones (2014) posits, categorical thinking is a tool of oppression. Ideally then, Latinxs student-athletes resist classification and occupy the proverbial borderlands, or middle space, by being comfortable with their hybrid identities (Anzaldúa, 1987; Lugones, 1994). Still, Latinxs rely on institutional agents to validate their belonging, competence, and abilities and to also affirm their identities, not trying to assimilate them to the dominant culture (Arana et al., 2011; Gloria & Castellanos, 2012). The aforementioned aids in their sense of belonging which can positively impact student persistence.

Importantly, Latinxs more often than not rely on their culture and home communities to persist (Yosso, 2005). Thus, while athletic or student identities may become salient in some situations to assert belonging and thwart negative effects of discrimination and stereotyping as result of their intersectionality, the influence of the components of their ethnic identity is still present in some form or shape. Generally, student affairs professionals working with student-athletes do not acknowledge the importance of ethnic identity for this population's healthy development and well-being in their college journeys. This, of course, jeopardizes the true holistic identity development of Latinx student-athletes.

Systems of Power, Privilege, and Oppression

As Freire (1970) asserts, educational institutions have the power to oppress. These systems of power, privilege, and oppression remain present within U.S. society and in all aspects of people's lives (Johnson, 2018). Thus, educational institutions perpetuate inequities as well (Núñez, 2014; Yosso, 2005). The patterns of inequality are evident throughout the pipeline from youth sports to intercollegiate athletics as talent and hard work are just two small ingredients leading to athletic glory. Those born with economic, social, and educational privilege reap the benefits of early specialized training, club and/or travel teams, and knowledge of the complex recruiting process that substantially increase one's odds of becoming an NCAA athlete (Hextrum, 2018; McGovern, 2018).

Latinx student-athletes who make it to the NCAA continue to encounter systemic racism in the cultural, intellectual, and athletic domains, which influences the way they experience college and develop their identities. For example, various federal, state, and institutional policies stimulate Latinxs' student identities (e.g., admissions policies utilizing standardized test scores). In the athletic domain, it is the NCAA rules and regulations that determine who can and cannot participate in college athletics (NCAA, 2019a, 2019b, 2019c). Overall, leaders create these policies with students from the majority culture in mind. Therefore, Latinxs may experience cultural conflict in order to overcome the various systemic barriers. As various scholars posit, Latinx college students face the additional developmental task of dealing with racism (Ortega, 2019; Phinney, 1993; Torres, 2009; Torres & Hernandez, 2007).

Balanced Identity

The goal for student affairs professionals is to understand and assist Latinx student-athletes to grow holistically in all identity domains, which include ethnic, student, and athletic identity. When Latinx student-athletes feel comfortable and confident with who they are, they achieve a healthy, balanced identity. We do not suggest that domains must be ideal and utopian in nature; rather, we argue that these domains—often cumbersome in systemic privilege and oppression—will result in uncomfortable experiences for Latinx student-athletes and will shape the manner in which they negotiate and develop their intersecting identities. The successful negotiation of domains is what leads to a balanced identity. However, it is important to note that balanced identity is not a constant construct; it is continuously revisited and negotiated by each individual. While the diagram of our MIDLSA, a static snapshot, may suggest that this balance consists of an identity equally divided among the three components, this is not the case. We consider a healthy identity for Latinx student-athletes to occupying a middle space, or borderlands, as described by Anzaldúa (1987). In other words, Latinxs are self-aware of who they are and are comfortable with not fitting in just one social category or with being viewed by others in the society as *other* or *different*. In other words, Latinxs with balanced identity resist the various forms of oppression within the societal systems and carve out a place of their own.

The MIDLSA can be compared to sailing on a boat while withstanding different elements in the environment. Latinxs traverse borders of different social classifications in order to instill a sense of belonging and persevere in a given space. At times, Latinxs may rely on a singular domain to sail smoothly. At other times, parts of two or all three domains coalesce to keep the proverbial boat afloat. When Latinx student-athletes occupy borderlands, they are well-positioned to learn as students, compete as athletes, and develop as individuals who make their Latinx communities proud. The next section provides student affairs professionals with practical recommendations of how to apply the MIDLSA within their institutional context to allow Latinx student-athletes to achieve a healthy, balanced identity within the borderlands.

Recommendations for Student Affairs Practitioners

Like many student development theories, the proposed MIDLSA seeks to capture the complexities associated with Latinx student-athletes who must negotiate and develop intersecting identities while simultaneously operating in multiple domains. To be sure, we recognize that there are numerous agents in each domain that can inadvertently aid or hinder the development of a balanced identity for Latinx student-athletes. What follows is a set of recommendations specifically for student affairs professionals (inclusive of athletic staff) who work with Latinx student-athletes at universities.

1. *Check your privilege.* Regardless of institutional type, ample data illustrate that most of the athletic staff who work with Latinx student-athletes are not Latinx (Lapchick, 2019; NCAA, 2018a). In order to genuinely aid the multiple and intersecting identities of Latinx student-athletes, we argue that student affairs professionals must embrace critical epistemological views that force them to check their privilege in regard to race, gender, socioeconomic status, and sexual orientation, to name a

few. Cognizance of such privileges will lay the foundation for empathy warranted to understand the myriad of experiences that Latinx student-athletes encounter on a daily basis. Recognizing one's own privilege will build an authentic dialogue about how to best aid the holistic identity development of Latinx student-athletes.

2. *Stop perpetuating the systemic inequities.* Student affairs professionals can make a difference by not further perpetuating the systemic inequities. As part of this approach, staff members must affirm students' sense of belonging and validate them. They take into consideration Latinxs' unique backgrounds and experiences. Further, student affairs professionals do not try to box Latinx student-athletes into certain social categories but support them unconditionally for who they are based on what aspect of their multiple identities may be salient or code-switched at a given time. Student affairs professionals must recognize that Latinx student-athletes have encountered different levels of systemic racism and may at times need extra support when in college to assert a sense of belonging, feel competent, and persist to degree attainment. These interactions should be authentic, intentional, and not an act of serendipity.

3. *Embrace an asset-based lens.* Student affairs professionals working with Latinx student-athletes must recognize that Latinxs are products of their communities and one day will be change agents within them (Jamieson, 2005). Therefore, athletic staff cannot locate their respective sport as the primary and singular influence in Latinx student-athletes' lives. Rather, the success of Latinx student-athletes is a result of contributions from parents, families, communities, and cultural traditions (Jamieson, 2003). Student affairs professionals can become an important source of support as well if only they recognize the importance of providing learning environments where Latinxs can develop and express their identities fully without inhibiting their ethnic, student, and/or athletic identities in any way. In other words, a balanced identity is possible when Latinx student-athletes—inclusive of their experiences and communities—are validated from an asset-based lens.

Conclusion

Traditional identity development models have historically been norm-referenced on White males. Such theoretical constructs, unfortunately, continue to be applied unilaterally to all student populations. If agents of universities authentically wish to cultivate balanced identities, theoretical constructs must be devised with the specific student population in mind to guide the identity development process. The MIDLSA is a theoretical model that captures a snapshot of the complexities associated with the development of the multiple and intersecting identities that Latinx student-athletes negotiate through their tenure and journey to degree attainment. We caution that the MIDLSA should not be applied uniformly to all Latinx student-athletes. Rather, we propose a model that leaves ample room to address the nuances within the vast heterogeneity found within the experiences of Latinx, students, and athletes. The model provides a framework for a student population that is widely seen on university campuses but rarely ever heard. The MIDLSA offers an alternative framework of *¿Quién eres?*, or in English *Who are you?*, to encapsulate a richer and more accurate reflection of the complexity associated with identity development of Latinx student-athletes.

Note

1. The term *Latinx* is intentionally used in lieu of Latina/o to avoid gender binaries and promote inclusiveness of the intersecting identities of Latin Americans who identity as agender, queer, trans, nonbinary, gender nonconforming, or gender fluid.

References

Abes, E. S. (2009). Theoretical borderlands: Using multiple theoretical perspectives to challenge inequitable power structures in student development theory. *Journal of College Student Development, 50*(2), 141–156. https://doi.org/10.1353/csd.0.0059

Adamek, J. (2017). Academic fraud in revenue and non-revenue sports. *The Sport Journal*, 1–10. https://thesportjournal.org/article/academic-fraud-in-revenue-and-nonrevenue-sports/

Adler, P., & Adler, P. A. (1985). From idealism to pragmatic detachment: The academic performance of college athletes. *Sociology of Education, 58*(4), 241–250. https://www.jstor.org/stable/2112226

Adler, P., & Adler, P. A. (1991). *Backboards and blackboards: College athletes and role engulfment.* Columbia University Press.

Alamillo, J. M. (2013). *American Latino theme study: Beyond the Latino sports hero: The role of sports in creating communities, networks, and identities.* National Park Service. https://www.nps.gov/heritageinitiatives/latino/latinothemestudy/sports.htm

Alcoff, L. M. (2005). Latino vs. Hispanic: The politics of ethnic names. *Philosophy & Social Criticism, 31*(4), 395–407. https://doi.org/10.1177/0191453705052972

Almy, S., & Theokas, C. (2010). *Not prepared for class: High-poverty schools continue to have fewer in-field teachers.* The Education Trust. https://edtrust.org/wp-content/uploads/2013/10/Not-Prepared-for-Class.pdf

Anderson, E. (2010). *The imperative of integration.* Princeton University Press.

Anzaldúa, G. (1987). *Borderlands/la frontera: The new mestiza.* Spinsters/Aunt Lute Books.

Arana, R., Castañeda-Sound, C., Blanchard, S., & Aguilar, T. E. (2011). Indicators of persistence for Hispanic undergraduate achievement: Toward an ecological model. *Journal of Hispanic Higher Education, 10*(3), 237–251. https://doi.org/10.1177/1538192711405058

Aries, E., McCarthy, D., Salovey, P., & Banaji, M. R. (2004). A comparison of athletes and nonathletes at highly selective colleges: Academic performance and personal development. *Research in Higher Education, 45*(6), 577–602. https://doi.org/10.1023/B:RIHE.0000040264.76846.e9

Astin, A. W. (1977). *Four critical years.* Jossey-Bass.

Ballinas, J. (2017). Where are you from and why are you here? Microaggressions, racialization, and Mexican college students in a new destination. *Sociological Inquiry, 87*(2), 385–410. https://doi.org/10.1111/soin.12181

Bernal, M. E., Knight, G. P., Ocampo, K. A., Garza, C. A., & Cota, M. K. (1993). Development of Mexican American identity. In M. E. Bernal & G. P. Knight (Eds.), *Ethnic identity: Formation and transmission among Hispanics and other minorities* (pp. 31–46). State University of New York Press.

Bourke, B. (2016). Meaning and implications of being labeled a predominantly White institution. *College and University, 91*(3), 20–21. http://www.aacrao.org/resources/publications/college-university-journal-(c-u)

Bowen, W. G., & Levin, S. A. (2003). *Reclaiming the game: College sports and educational values.* Princeton University Press.

Bowleg, L. (2008). When Black + lesbian + woman ≠ Black lesbian woman: The methodological challenges of qualitative and quantitative intersectionality research. *Sex Roles, 59*, 312–325. https://doi.org/10.1007/s11199-008-9400-z

Brewer, B. W., & Cornelius, A. E. (2001). Norms and factorial invariance of the Athletic Identity Measurement Scale. *Academic Athletic Journal, 16*, 103–113. https://www.researchgate.net/publication/263734479_Norms_and_factorial_invariance_of_the_Athletic_Identity_Measurement_Scale

Brewer, B. W., & Petitpas, A. J. (2017). Athletic identity foreclosure. *Current Opinion in Psychology, 16*, 118–122. https://doi.org/10.1016/j.copsyc.2017.05.004

Brewer, B. W., Van Raalte, J. L., & Linder, D. E. (1993). Athletic identity: Hercules' muscles or Achilles heel? *International Journal of Sport Psychology, 24*, 237–254. http://www.ijsp-online.com/

Cabrita, T. M., Rosado, A. B., Leite, T. O., Serpa, S. O., & Sousa, P. M. (2014). The relationship between athletic identity and career decisions in athletes. *Journal of Applied Sport Psychology, 26*, 471–481. https://doi.org/10.1080/10413200.2014.931312

Calderon, B. (2015). Achieving "first in the world:" Hispanic Serving Institutions and closing the attainment gap. *Harvard Journal of Hispanic Policy, 27*, 60–64. https://www.questia.com/library/journal/1G1-413337475/achieving-first-in-the-world-hispanic-serving-institutions

Cameron, C. D. (2012). You can't win if you don't play: The surprising absence of Latino athletes from college sports. *Wake Forest Journal of Law & Policy, 2*(1), 227–246. https://wfulawpolicyjournaldotcom.files.wordpress.com/2016/05/vol-2-1-article-cameron.pdf

Chickering, A. W. (1979). *Education and identity.* Jossey-Bass.

Chickering, A. W., & Reisser, L. (1993). *Education and identity* (2nd ed.). Jossey-Bass.

Cieslak, T. J. II. (2004). *Describing and measuring the athletic identity construct: Scale development and validation* (UMI No. 3144860) [Doctoral dissertation, The Ohio State University]. ProQuest Dissertations and Theses database.

Clotfelter, C. T. (2019). *Big-time sports in American Universities* (2nd ed.). Cambridge University Press.

Coakley, J. (2008). *Sports and society.* McGraw-Hill.

Collins, P. H. (2000). *Black feminist thought: Knowledge, consciousness, and the politics of empowerment.* Routledge.

Comeaux, E., & Harrison, K. C. (2011). A conceptual model of academic success for student-athletes. *Educational Researcher, 40*, 235–245. https://doi.org/10.3102/0013189X11415260

Comeaux, E., Speer, L., Taustine, M., & Harrison, K. C. (2011). Purposeful engagement of first-year Division I student-athletes. *Journal of the First-Year Experience & Students in Transition, 23*, 35–52. https://eric.ed.gov/?id=EJ952032

Contreras, F., & Contreras, G. J. (2015). Raising the bar for Hispanic Serving Institutions: An analysis of college completion and success rates. *Journal of Hispanic Higher Education, 14*(2), 151–170. https://doi.org/10.1177/1538192715572892

Côté, J. E., & Levine, C. G. (1987). A formulation of Erikson's theory of ego identity formation. *Developmental Review, 7*(4), 273–325. https://doi.org/10.1016/0273-2297(87)90015-3

Côté, J. E., & Levine, C. G. (2002). *Identity formation, agency, and culture: A social psychological synthesis.* Lawrence Erlbaum Associates.

Crawford, T. K. (2007). *Intercollegiate athletic participation and undergraduate student engagement* (UMI No. 3268766) [Doctoral dissertation, Washington State University]. ProQuest Dissertations and Theses database.

Crenshaw, K. (1989). Demarginalizing the intersection of race and sex: A Black feminist critique of antidiscrimination doctrine, feminist theory and anti-racist politics. *University of Chicago Legal Forum, 1989*, 139–167. http://chicagounbound.uchicago.edu/uclf/vol1989/iss1/8/

Cuádraz, G. H. (1992). Experiences of multiple marginality: A case study of Chicana 'scholarship women.' *Association of Mexican American Educators Journal, 12*, 31–43. https://files.eric.ed.gov/fulltext/ED355064.pdf

Cuellar, M. (2014). The impact of Hispanic-Serving Institutions (HSIs), emerging HSIs, and non-HSIs on Latina/o academic self-concept. *The Review of Higher Education, 37*(4), 499–530. https://doi.org/10.1353/rhe.2014.0032

Darling-Hammond, L. (2001). Inequality in teaching and schooling: How opportunity is rationed to students of color. In B. D. Smedley, A. Y. Stith, L. Colburn, & C. H. Evans, *The right thing to do, the smart thing to do* (pp. 208–233). National Academies Press.

Darvin, L., Cintron, A., & Hancock, M. (2017). *¿Por qué jugar?* Sport socialization among Hispanic/Latina female NCAA division I student-athletes. *Journal of Amateur Sport, 3*(2), 27–54. https://journals.ku.edu/jams/article/view/6460

Dill, B. T., & Zambrana, R. E. (2009). *Emerging intersections: Race, class, and gender in theory, policy, and practice.* Rutgers University Press.

Eggleston, T., & Mitchell, J. (2005). Addressing student-athlete issues in a first-year seminar. *E-Source for College Transitions, 2*(4), 6–7. https://sc.edu/nrc/system/pub_files/ES_2-4_Feb05.pdf

Erikson, E. H. (1959). *Identity and the life cycle: Selected papers.* International University Press.

Evans, N. J., Forney, D. S., & Guido-DiBrito, F. (1998). *Student development in college: Theory, research, and practice.* Jossey-Bass.

Fearon, D., Barnard-Brak, L., Robinson, E., & Harris, F. (2013). Sense of belonging and burnout among first-year student-athletes. *Journal for the Study of Sports and Athletes in Education, 5*(2), 139–156. https://doi.org/10.1179/ssa.2011.5.2.139

Feezell, R. (2015). Branding the role and value of intercollegiate athletics. *Journal of the Philosophy of Sport, 42*(2), 185–207. https://doi.org/10.1080/00948705.2014.911098

Fergus, E. (2016). Understanding Latino student racial and ethnic identification: Theories of race and ethnicity. *Theory Into Practice, 55*, 20–27. https://doi.org/10.1080/00405841.2016.1116861

Flores, A. (2017). *How the U.S. Hispanic population is changing.* Pew Research Center. http://www.pewresearch.org/fact-tank/2017/09/18/how-the-u-s-hispanic-population-is-changing/

Flores, A., Lopez, M. H., & Krogstad, J. M. (2019). *U.S. Hispanic population reached new high in 2018, but growth has slowed.* Pew Research Center. https://www.pewresearch.org/fact-tank/2019/07/08/u-s-hispanic-population-reached-new-high-in-2018-but-growth-has-slowed/

Flowers, R. D. (2009). Institutionalized hypocrisy: The myth of intercollegiate athletics. *American Educational History Journal, 36*(2), 343–360. https://eric.ed.gov/?id=EJ863698

Fosnacht, K., & Nailos, J. N. (2016). Impact of the environment: How does attending a Hispanic-Serving Institution influence the engagement of baccalaureate-seeking Latina/o students? *Journal of Hispanic Higher Education, 15*(3), 187–204. https://doi.org/10.1177/1538192715597739

Freire, P. (1970). *Pedagogy of the oppressed.* Continuum.

Friedman, S. S. (1998). *Mappings: Feminism and the cultural geographies of encounter.* Princeton University Press.

Garcia, G. A. (2019). *Becoming Hispanic-serving institutions: Opportunities for colleges & universities.* Johns Hopkins University Press.

Garcia-Navarro, L. (2015, August 27). *Hispanic or Latino? A guide for the U.S. presidential campaign.* NPR. http://www.npr.org/sections/parallels/2015/08/27/434584260/hispanic-or-latino-a-guide-for-the-u-s-presidential-campaign

Garry, A. (2011). Intersectionality, metaphors, and the multiplicity of gender. *Hypatia: A Journal of Feminist Philosophy, 26*(4), 826–850. https://doi.org/10.1111/j.1527-2001.2011.01194.x

Gaston-Gayles, J. G., & Baker, A. R. (2015). Opportunities and challenges for first-year student-athletes transitioning from high school to college. In D. A. Stenta, & C. W. McFadden (Eds.), *Student leadership development through recreation and athletics* (New Directions for Student Leadership, no. 147, pp. 43–51). Wiley. https://doi.org/10.1002/yd.20142

Gaston-Gayles, J. L., & Hu, S. (2009, May/June). The influence of student engagement and sport participation on college outcomes among Division I student athletes. *The Journal of Higher Education, 80*(3), 315–333. https://doi.org/10.1353/jhe.0.0051

Gloria, A., & Castellanos, J. (2012). *Desafíos y bendiciones*: A multiperspective examination of the educational experiences and coping responses of first-generation college Latina students. *Journal of Hispanic Higher Education, 11*(1), 82–99. https://doi.org/10.1177/1538192711430382

Gonzalez, R. G., & Morrison, J. (2016). Culture or no culture? A Latino critical research analysis of Latino persistence research. *Journal of Hispanic Higher Education, 15,* 87–108. https://doi.org/10.1177/1538192715579460

Griffin, K. A., & Hurtado, S. (2011). Institutional variety in American higher education. In J. H. Schuh, S. R. Jones, S. R. Harper, & Associates (Eds.), *Student services: A handbook for the profession* (5th ed., pp. 24–42). Jossey-Bass.

Gurney, G., Lopiano, D. A., & Zimbalist, A. (2017). *Unwinding madness: What went wrong with college sports—and how to fix it.* Brookings Institution Press.

Harrison, C. K., & Bukstein, S. (2014). Canaries in the goal mines: A timely analysis of college athletics and the role of student-athlete. *Journal of Intercollegiate Athletics, 7,* 109–119. https://doi.org/10.1123/jis.2014-0133

Hextrum, K. (2018). Amateurism revisited: How U.S. college athletic recruitment favors middle-class athletes. *Sport, Education, and Society, November 2018,* 1–13. https://doi.org/10.1080/13573322.2018.1547962

Hispanic Association of Colleges & Universities. (n.d.). *Hispanic-Serving Institution definitions.* http://www.hacu.net/hacu/HSI_Definition1.asp

Hispanic Association of Colleges & Universities. (2019). *2019 fact sheet: Hispanic higher education and HSIs.* https://www.hacu.net/hacu/HSI_Fact_Sheet.asp

Huml, M. R., Hancock, M. R., & Bergman, M. J. (2014). Additional support or extravagant cost? Student-athletes' perceptions on athletic academic centers. *Journal of Issues in Intercollegiate Athletics, 7*, 410–430. https://ir.library.louisville.edu/faculty/141/

Hurtado, S., & Carter, D. F. (1997). Effects of college transition and perceptions of campus racial climate on Latinos' sense of belonging. *Sociology of Education, 70*(4), 324–345. https://doi.org/10.2307/2673270

Hurtado, S., & Ponjuan, L. (2005). Latino educational outcomes and the campus climate. *Journal of Hispanic Higher Education, 4*, 235–251. https://doi.org/10.1177/1538192705276548

Jamieson, K. M. (2003). Occupying a middle space: Toward a mestiza sport studies. *Sociology of Sport Journal, 20*, 1–16. https://doi.org/10.1123/ssj.20.1.1

Jamieson, K. M. (2005). 'All my hopes and dreams': Families, schools, and subjectivities in collegiate softball. *Journal of Sport & Social Issues, 29*(2), 133–147. https://doi.org/10.1177/0193723504269889

Jayakumar, U. M., & Comeaux, E. (2016). The cultural cover-up of college athletics: How organizational culture perpetuates an unrealistic and idealized balancing act. *The Journal of Higher Education, 87*, 488–515. https://doi.org/10.1080/00221546.2016.11777411

Johnson, A. G. (2018). *Privilege, power, and difference* (3rd ed.). McGraw-Hill Education.

Jolly, C. J. (2008). Raising the question #9: Is the student-athlete population unique? And why should we care? *Communication Education, 57*(1), 145–151. https://doi.org/10.1080/03634520701613676

Kouyoumdjian, C., Guzmán, B. L., Garcia, N. M., & Talavera-Bustillos, V. (2017). A community cultural wealth examination of sources of support and challenges among Latino first- and second-generation college students at a Hispanic Serving Institution. *Journal of Hispanic Higher Education, 16*(1), 61–76. https://doi.org/10.1177/1538192715619995

Krogstad, J. M., & Fry, R. (2014, April 24). *More Hispanics, Blacks enrolling in college, but lag in bachelor's degrees.* Pew Research Center. http://www.pewresearch.org/fact-tank/2014/04/24/more-hispanics-blacks-enrolling-in-college-but-lag-in-bachelors-degrees/

Laden, B. V. (2004). Hispanic-serving institutions: What are they? Where are they? *Community College Journal of Research and Practice, 28*, 181–198. https://doi.org/10.1080/10668920490256381

Lally, P. S., & Kerr, G. A. (2005). The career planning, athletic identity, and student role identity of intercollegiate student athletes. *Research Quarterly for Exercise and Sport, 76*, 275–285. https://doi.org/10.1080/02701367.2005.10599299

Lapchick, R. (2019, February 27). *The 2018 racial and gender report card: College sport.* The Institute for Diversity and Ethics in Sport. https://docs.wixstatic.com/ugd/7d86e5_c8e69a54d92b4c35a94a5e399e7fe167.pdf

Locks, A. M., Hurtado, S., Bowman, N., & Oseguera, L. (2008). Extending notions of campus climate and diversity to students' transition to college. *Review of Higher Education, 31*(3), 257–285. https://doi.org/10.1353/rhe.2008.0011

Lugones, M. (1994). Purity, impurity, and separation. *Signs, 19*(2), 458–479. https://doi.org/10.1086/494893

Lugones, M. (2014). Radical multiculturalism and women of color feminisms. *Journal for Cultural and Religious Theory, 13*(1), 68–80. http://www.jcrt.org/archives/13.1/lugones.pdf

McGovern, J. (2018). "You have to have money to be good": How capital accumulation shapes Latinas' pathways to college sports. *Journal of Intercollegiate Sport, 11*, 149–171. https://doi.org/10.1123/jis.2018-0038

Menke, D. J. (2015). The 3-I career advising process and athletes with foreclosed identity. The *Journal of the National Academic Advising Association, 35*(1), 22–28. https://files.eric.ed.gov/fulltext/EJ1069270.pdf

Miller, P. S., & Kerr, G. A. (2003). The role experimentation of intercollegiate student athletes. *The Sport Psychologist, 17*, 196–219. https://doi.org/10.1123/tsp.17.2.196

Miville, M. L. (2010). Latina/o identity development: Updates on theory, measurement, and counseling implications. In J. G. Ponterotto, J. M. Casas, L. A. Suzuki, & C. M. Alexander (Eds.), *Handbook of multicultural counseling* (3rd ed., pp. 241–282). SAGE.

National Center for Education Statistics. (2015). *Profile of undergraduate students: 2011-12.* https://nces.ed.gov/pubs2015/2015167.pdf

National Center for Education Statistics. (2019, January). *Profile of undergraduate students: Attendance, distance and remedial education, degree program and field of study, demographics, financial aid, financial literacy, employment, and military status: 2015-2016.* https://nces.ed.gov/pubs2019/2019467.pdf

National Collegiate Athletic Association. (n.d.). *Frequently asked questions about the NCAA: What is the NCAA?* http://www.ncaa.org/about/frequently-asked-questions-about-ncaa

National Collegiate Athletic Association. (2013). *Do NCAA student-athletes view themselves as students or athletes?* http://www.ncaa.org/sites/default/files/Identity.pdf

National Collegiate Athletic Association. (2016). *NCAA convention: Results from the 2015 GOALS study of the student-athlete experience.* https://www.ncaa.org/sites/default/files/GOALS_convention_slidebank_jan2016_public.pdf

National Collegiate Athletic Association. (2017a). *Estimated probability of competing in college athletics.* http://www.ncaa.org/about/resources/research/estimated-probability-competing-college-athletics

National Collegiate Athletic Association. (2017b). *Institutional characteristics of NCAA member schools: Institutional characteristics study findings.* http://www.ncaa.org/sites/default/files/2017RES_institutional_characteristics_edited_20180119.pdf

National Collegiate Athletic Association. (2018a). *NCAA demographics database.* http://www.ncaa.org/about/resources/research/ncaa-demographics-database

National Collegiate Athletic Association. (2018b). *NCAA recruiting facts.* https:// www.ncaa.org/sites/default/files/Recruiting%20Fact%20Sheet%20WEB .pdf

National Collegiate Athletic Association. (2018c). *Sport sponsorship, participation and demographics search.* http://web1.ncaa.org/rgdSearch/exec/main

National Collegiate Athletic Association. (2019a). 2019-2020 *NCAA Division I manual.* http://www.ncaapublications.com/productdownloads/D120.pdf

National Collegiate Athletic Association. (2019b). 2019-2020 *NCAA Division II manual.* http://www.ncaapublications.com/productdownloads/D220.pdf

National Collegiate Athletic Association. (2019c). 2019-2020 *NCAA Division III manual.* http://www.ncaapublications.com/productdownloads/D320.pdf

National Collegiate Athletic Association. (2020). *NCAA member schools.* http:// www.ncaa.org/about/resources/research/ncaa-member-schools

New, J. (2016, July 8). An 'epidemic' of academic fraud. *Inside Higher Ed.* https:// www.insidehighered.com/news/2016/07/08/more-dozen-athletic-programs- have-committed-academic-fraud-last-decade-more-likely

Núñez, A. M. (2014). Advancing an intersectionality framework in higher education: Power and Latino postsecondary opportunity. *Handbook of Theory and Research in Higher Education, 29*, 33–92. https://doi.org/10.1007/978-94-017- 8005-6

Núñez, A. M. (2015). *Hispanic-Serving Institutions: Where are they now? Excelencia* in Education. http://www.edexcelencia.org/sites/default/files/Current-HSIs- Nunez_April2015.pdf

Ortega, G. (2019, September 15). Examining the intersection of race and athletics for Latino male student-athletes. *Journal of Hispanic Higher Education*, 1–14. https://doi.org/10.1177/1538192719876091

Osborne, B. (2014). The myth of exploited student-athlete. *Journal of Intercollegiate Sport, 7*, 143–152. https://doi.org/10.1123/jis.2014-0136

Otto, M. G., Martinez, J. M., & Barnhill, C. R. (2019). How the perception of athletic academic services affects the overall college experience of freshmen student-athletes. *Journal of Athlete Development and Experience, 1*, 40–52. https:// doi.org/10.25035/jade.01.01.05

Parker, K., Horowitz, J. M., Morin, R., & Lopez, M. H. (2015, June 11). *Chapter 7: The many dimensions of Hispanic racial identity.* Pew Research Center. https:// www.pewsocialtrends.org/2015/06/11/chapter-7-the-many-dimensions-of- hispanic-racial-identity/

Pascarella, E. T., & Terenzini, P. T. (2005). *How college affects students: A decade of research* (Vol. 2). John Wiley & Sons, Inc.

Patton, L. D., Renn, K. A., Guido, F. M., Quaye, S. J., Evans, N. J., & Forney, D. S. (2016). *Student development in college: Theory, research, and practice.* John Wiley & Sons, Inc.

Paule, A. L., & Gilson, T. A. (2010). Current collegiate experiences of big-time, non-revenue, NCAA athletes. *Journal of Intercollegiate Sport, 3*, 333–347. https://doi.org/10.1123/jis.3.2.333

Pew Research Center. (2004). *Generational differences: Fact sheet.* http://www.pewhispanic.org/2004/03/19/generational-differences/

Phinney, J. S. (1993). A three-stage model of ethnic identity development in adolescence. In M. E. Bernal & G. P. Knight (Eds.), *Ethnic identity formation and transmission among Hispanic and other minorities* (pp. 61–79). SUNY Press.

Pike, G. R., & Kuh, G. D. (2005). First- and second-generation college students: A comparison of their engagement and intellectual development. *Journal of Higher Education, 76*(3), 276–300. https://doi.org/10.1080/00221546.2005.11772283

Porter, J. R., & Washington, R. E. (1993). Minority identity and self-esteem. *Annual Review of Sociology, 19*, 139–161. https://doi.org/10.1146/annurev.so.19.080193.001035

Potuto, J. R., & O'Hanlon, J. (2007). National study of student-athletes regarding their experiences as college students. *College Student Journal, 41*(4), 947–966. https://eric.ed.gov/?id=EJ816818

Quaye, S. J., Tambascia, T. P., & Talesh, A. (2009). Engaging racial/ethnic minority students in predominantly White classroom environments. In S. R. Harper & S. J. Quaye (Eds.), *Student engagement in higher education: Theoretical perspectives and practical approaches for diverse populations* (pp. 157–178). Routledge.

Rankin, S. R., & Reason, R. D. (2005). Differing perceptions: How students of color and White students perceive campus climate for underrepresented groups. *Journal of College Student Development, 46*, 43–61. https://doi.org/10.1353/csd.2005.0008

Reason, R. D., & Broido, E. M. (2017). Philosophies and values. In J. H. Schuh, S. R. Jones, S. R. Harper, & Associates (Eds.), *Student services: A handbook for the profession* (6th ed., pp. 39–55). Jossey-Bass.

Renn, K. A., & Reason, R. D. (2013). *College students in the United States: Characteristics, experiences, and outcomes.* Jossey-Bass.

Rettig, J., & Hu, S. (2016). College sport participation and student educational experiences and selected college outcomes. *Journal of College Student Development, 57*(4), 428–446. https://doi.org/10.1353/csd.2016.0054

Richardson, T. Q., Bethea, A. R., Hayling, C. C., & Williamson-Taylor, C. (2010). African and Afro-Caribbean American identity development: Theory and practice implications. In J. G. Ponterotto, J. M. Casas, L. A. Suzuki, & C. M. Alexander (Eds.), *Handbook of multicultural counseling* (3rd ed., pp. 227–239). SAGE.

Rodriguez, C., Parrish, J., & Parks, R. (2017, Summer). Unseen differences: Cultural diversity among Hispanic and Latino students. *College and University, 92*(3), 14–26. http://www.aacrao.org/resources/publications/college-university-journal-(c-u)

Rubin, L. M. (2015). Advising student-athletes. *NACADA Journal.* http://www.nacada.ksu.edu/Resources/Clearinghouse/View-Articles/Advising-Student-Athletes.aspx

Rubin, L. M., & Moses, R. A. (2017). Athletic subculture within student-athlete academic centers. *Sociology of Sport Journal, 47*(1), 1–36. https://doi.org/10.1177/0013124512468006

Saffici, C., & Pellegrino, R. (2012). Intercollegiate athletics vs. academics: The student-athlete or the athlete-student. *The Sport Journal.* http://thesportjournal.org/article/intercollegiate-athletics-vs-academics-the-student-athlete-or-the-athlete-student/

Santiago, D. (2011). *Roadmap for ensuring America's future by increasing* Latino *college completion. Excelencia in Education.* http://files.eric.ed.gov/fulltext/ED517165.pdf

Sheth, F. A. (2014). Interstitiality: Making space for migration, diaspora, and racial complexity. *Hypatia: A Journal of Feminist Philosophy, 29*, 75–93. https://doi.org/10.1111/hypa.12075

Shulman, J. L., & Bowen, W. G. (2001). *The game of life: College sports and educational values.* Princeton University Press.

Simons, H. D., Bosworth, C., Fujita, S., & Jensen, M. (2007). The athlete stigma in higher education. *College Student Journal, 41*, 251–273. https://eric.ed.gov/?id=EJ777933

Smith, J. M., & Willingham, M. (2015). *Cheated: The UNC scandal, the education of athletes, and the future of big-time college sports.* Potomac Books.

Spring, J. (2011). *The politics of American education: Sociocultural, political, and historical studies in education.* Routledge.

Sung, J., Gi-Yong, K., Kim, S., & Dittmore, S. W. (2015). Enhancement of non-academic environment by intercollegiate athletics and its intangible benefit in higher education. *Journal of Physical Education and Sport, 15*(1), 47–52. https://doi.org/10.7752/jpes.2015.01008

Syed, M., Azmitia, M., & Phinney, J. S. (2007). Stability and change in ethnic identity among Latino emerging adults in two contexts. *Identity: An International Journal of Theory and Research, 7*(2), 155–178. https://doi.org/10.1080/15283480701326117

Taylor, P., Lopez, M. H., Martínez, J., & Velasco, G. (2012, April 4). *When labels don't fit: Hispanics and their views of identity.* Pew Research Center. https://www.pewresearch.org/hispanic/2012/04/04/when-labels-dont-fit-hispanics-and-their-views-of-identity/

Torres, V. (1999). Validation of bicultural orientation model for Hispanic college students. *Journal of College Student Development, 40*(3), 285–298. https://eric.ed.gov/?id=EJ596708

Torres, V. (2003). Influences on ethnic identity development of Latino college students in the first two years of college. *Journal of College Student Development, 44*(4), 532–547. https://doi.org/10.1353/csd.2003.0044

Torres, V. (2009). The developmental dimensions of recognizing racism. *Journal of College Student Development, 50*(5), 504–520. https://doi.org/10.1353/csd.0.0088

Torres, V., & Hernandez, E. (2007). The influence of ethnic identity on self-authorship: A longitudinal study of Latino/a college students. *Journal of College Student Development, 48*(5), 558–573. https://doi.org/10.1353/csd.2007.0057

Torres, V., Jones, S. R., & Renn, K. A. (2009). Identity development theories in student affairs: Origins, current status, and new approaches. *Journal of College Student Development, 50*(6), 577–596. https://doi.org/10.1353/csd.0.0102

Torres, V., & McGowan, B. L. (2017). Psychosocial and identity development. In J. H. Schuh, S. R. Jones, S. R. Harper, & Associates. (Eds.), *Student services: A handbook for the profession* (6th ed., pp. 185–204). Jossey-Bass.

Umaña-Taylor, A. J. (2004). Ethnic identity and self-esteem: Examining the role of social context. *Journal of Adolescence, 27*(2), 139–146. https://doi.org/10.1016/j.adolescence.2003.11.006

Umaña-Taylor, A. J. (2011). Ethnic identity. In S. J. Schwartz, K. Luyckx, & V. L. Vignoles (Eds.), *Handbook of identity theory and research* (pp. 791–810). Springer.

Umbach, P. D., Palmer, M. M., Kuh, G. D., & Hannah, S. J. (2006). Intercollegiate athletes and effective educational practices: Winning combination or losing effort? *Research in Higher Education, 47*(6), 709–733. https://doi.org/10.1007/s11162-006-9012-9

U.S. Census Bureau. (2017). *Hispanic heritage month 2017.* https://www.census.gov/content/dam/Census/newsroom/facts-for-features/2017/cb17-ff17.pdf

U.S. Census of Bureau. (2019). *Quick facts: United States.* https://www.census.gov/quickfacts/fact/table/US/RHI725218

U.S. Commission on Civil Rights. (2018). *Public education funding inequity: In an era of increasing concentration of poverty and resegregation.* http://www.usccr.gov/pubs/2018-01-10-Education-Inequity.pdf

Von Robertson, R., Bravo, A., & Chaney, C. (2016). Racism and the experiences of Latina/o college students at a PWI (predominantly White institution). *Critical Sociology, 42*(4–5), 715–735. https://doi.org/10.1177/0896920514532664

Webb, W. M., Nasco, S., A., Riley, S., & Headrick, B. (1998). Athlete identity and reactions to retirement from sports. *Journal of Sport Behavior, 21*(3), 338–362. https://www.cabdirect.org/cabdirect/abstract/19981810694

Weinreich, P. (2003). Identity structure analysis. In P. Weinreich & W. Saunderson (Eds.), *Analysing identity: Cross-cultural, societal and clinical contexts* (pp. 7–76). Routledge.

Williams, D. J. (2007). *An examination of athletic identity, sport commitment, time in sport, social support, life satisfaction, and holistic wellness in college student-athletes* (UMI No. 3273333) [Doctoral dissertation, University of North Carolina–Greensboro]. ProQuest Dissertations and Theses database.

Wininger, S. R., & White, T. A. (2015). An examination of the dumb jock stereotype in collegiate student-athletes: A comparison of student versus student-athlete perceptions. *Journal for the Study of Sports and Athletes in Education, 9,* 75–85. https://doi.org/10.1179/1935739715Z.00000000036

Yopyk, D. J., & Prentice, D. A. (2005). Am I an athlete or a student? Identity salience and stereotype threat in student–athletes. *Basic and Applied Social Psychology, 27*(4), 329–336. https://doi.org/10.1207/s15324834basp2704_5

Yosso, T. J. (2005). Whose cultural capital? A critical race theory discussion of community cultural wealth. *Race, Ethnicity, and Education, 8*(1), 69–91. https://doi.org/10.1080/1361332052000341006

Yosso, T. J., Smith, W. A., Ceja, M., & Solórzano, D. G. (2009). Critical race theory, racial microaggressions, and campus racial climate for Latina/o undergraduates. *Harvard Educational Review, 79*, 659–690. https://doi.org/10.17763/haer.79.4.m6867014157m707l

Yost, M. (2010). *Varsity green: A behind the scenes look at culture and corruption in college athletics.* Stanford University Press.

PART FIVE

ALTERNATIVE FRAMEWORKS AND MODELS FOR LGBTQIA COLLEGE STUDENT POPULATIONS

II

FRAMING AND REFRAMING THE LGBTQ COLLEGE STUDENT DEVELOPMENT EXPERIENCE

Kristen A. Renn

Lesbian, gay, bisexual, transgender, and queer (LGBTQ) students are increasingly visible at all but the most conservative postsecondary institutions. Students who hold minoritized sexual orientation (e.g., lesbian, gay, bisexual, asexual, queer) and/or gender (e.g., transgender, gender nonconforming, nonbinary, genderqueer) identities experience college in many of the same ways as their majoritized peers but with some notable differences in student development and experiences. There are few reliable statistics about how many college students identify as LGBTQ, though 5% of respondents to the American College Health Association's National College Health Assessment did not identify as cisgender and 21% did not identify as straight/heterosexual (Bourdon et al., 2018).

In the first decades of the 21st century, higher education has generally improved the campus climate for LGBTQ college students (Garvey et al., 2017). LGBTQ visibility on campus has increased as more students form social and political advocacy groups, more campuses house LGBTQ resource centers, and more LGBTQ curriculum has moved into the mainstream. Changes in U.S. law and policy (e.g., LGBQ people serving openly in the military, marriage equality) and state/local nondiscrimination laws accompany these campus-based improvements. Progress toward increasing acceptance of LGBTQ people in society has not been universal, however, and after several years of improvement K–12 school climate for LGBTQ youth has stalled (Kosciw et al., 2018).

A number of recent large regional and national studies have included sexual orientation and gender identity as demographic variables in ways that make it possible to know something about trends among LGBTQ college students and about campus climate. LGBTQ students engage in high-impact practices such as undergraduate research and service-learning (Garvey et al., 2018; Kilgo et al., 2019) and benefit from additional in-class positive interactions with faculty and instructors (Linley et al., 2016). They engage in LGBTQ-specific activities and in general campus contexts in ways that support leadership and identity development (Bazarsky et al., 2015) and form kinship networks that create spaces of belonging and support on campus (Nicolazzo, 2016; Nicolazzo et al., 2017). In addition, LGBTQ students of color negotiate the intersections of racism, sexism, homophobia, and transphobia (Duran, 2019; Duran & Pérez, 2017; Garvey et al., 2019; Means, 2017).

In terms of campus climate overall, as a social media campaign (It Gets Better Project, 2010–2018) proclaimed, "It Gets Better": Successive generations of LGBTQ students have found the climate decreasingly hostile (Garvey et al., 2017). Yet, Greathouse et al. (2018) combined findings from multiple surveys (American College Healthy Association-National College Health Assessment, 2016; National Survey of Student Engagement, 2017; Undergraduate Student Experience at the Research University Survey, 2016) and four surveys from the Higher Education Research Institute (HERI) and found higher education "is failing to provide an equitable learning environment for queer-spectrum and trans-spectrum students, along with troubling disparities across academic engagement and student health" (p. 3). An increase in research on LGBTQ climate at community colleges shows that classroom climate contributes significantly to overall perception of campus climate (Garvey et al., 2015), and there is much progress to be made in improving the digital campus climate (Taylor et al., 2018), the climate for first-generation students (Garvey et al., 2015), and the availability of campus resources that are known to contribute to LGBTQ student success (Nguyen et al., 2018). In the context of improving but still suboptimal climate and with increasing knowledge about the experiences of LGBTQ students, understanding identity development can be useful to educators and policymakers.

Traditional Frameworks for Understanding Development of LGBQ and Trans Identities

For decades the dominant theories for understanding college student sexual orientation and gender identity ignored the development of majoritized identities (heterosexual, cisgender) and focused on LGBQ and trans identities. They tended to reflect psychological approaches to identity development, proceeding through stages or positions from realization of minoritized identity through "coming out" to increasingly broader groups and joining an LGBT community (Bilodeau, 2005; Bilodeau & Renn, 2005; Cass, 1979; D'Augelli, 1994). The reliance on coming out as a marker of identity development does not translate well across cultures and creates an overly simplistic criterion; it also fails to acknowledge the realities that identities are fluid and coconstructed and that "outness" may vary from context to context, even in an individual who has a fully developed LGBQ or trans identity. These theories proved useful for introducing the study of LGBTQ identity development into the field but ultimately are not robust and inclusive enough to describe the processes and outcomes of LGBTQ identity development.

More recently, models have emerged that accommodate developmental fluidity and context. A social-cognitive theory of gender identity development like the one created by Bussey (2011; Bussey & Bandura, 1999) can be used to understand the development of any gender (e.g., cisgender woman, cisgender man, transgender, transwoman, transman, genderqueer, nonbinary, fluid). The theory considers interactions among three components: personal, behavioral, and environmental. Personal factors include biological characteristics, self-concept, self-perception, and regulation. Behavorial factors are gender-related activity patterns. Environmental factors include families, peers, schools, media, and digital contexts. Interactions among these elements occur as college students present their understanding of their gender identity, or perhaps one they are exploring; receive feedback from the environment; and react to deepen, question, or continue to explore gender identity. This theory works to explain the development and expression of cisgender, transgender, and nonbinary identities in college students.

Dillon et al. (2011) presented what they called a "unifying model of sexual identity development" (p. 649) that, like the social-cognitive theory of gender identity development just described, can be used to understand majoritized and minoritized students. Dillon et al. (2011) posited that biopsychosocial processes contribute to individual sexual identities and social identities, which in turn interact with one another and contribute to sexual identity development. This model accounts for sexual orientation identity, dimensions of human sexuality, group membership identity, and attitudes toward sexual identity groups. These psychological, social, and biological factors interact in the context of exploration and commitment as described more generally by Marcia (1966, 1980) in relation to identity development. In Marcia's (1966, 1980) conception, individuals engage in a matrix of identity explorations and commitments, with four main statuses: foreclosure (commitment with no exploration), diffusion (no exploration, no commitment), moratorium (exploration with no commitment), and achievement (commitment with exploration). Dillon et al. (2011) applied these processes to the development of sexual orientation identities. An individual begins in compulsory heterosexuality (the common default assumption for all people); they may accept this commitment with no exploration and move to a lifetime of heterosexual identity and synthesis. Alternatively, they may leave compulsory heterosexuality to enter active exploration (exploration, no commitment) or diffusion (unexplored identity with no commitment). From either of these processes they might move to a deepening and commitment status (either after exploration or directly from compulsory heterosexuality). From deepening and commitment, the individual may move to synthesis, which brings together all of the biopsychosocial processes described. Individuals of any sexual orientation can reach synthesis, but according to Dillon et al. (2011), those who have explored their own identity before deepening commitment to it are more likely to be open in their thinking about people of other sexual identities.

Psychological models provide important insight into the development of sexual orientation and gender identities, but they lack key elements of context that are captured in a model that also incorporates an ecological perspective. Woodford et al. (2016) offered a conceptual model to understand LGBTQ college students' health and academic success; this model included LGBTQ identity, the college context, and identity development as key components. The model includes socioecological theory (Bronfenbrenner, 1994) and Astin's (1977) familiar inputs-environment-outcomes (I-E-O) framework. Also evident in this model are research on campus climate (e.g., Hurtado et al., 2012; Milem et al., 2005), institutional departure (Tinto, 1988, 1993), and minority stress (Meyer, 2003). Woodford et al.'s model provides a way to look at academic, identity, and health and well-being outcomes for LGBTQ college students. Precollege factors related to identity, academic preparation, community, and wellness feed into academic and social experiences in college, which are influenced by campus, state, local, and national climate and policies. Precollege and in-college experiences of identity, climate, and engagement lead to postcollege outcomes.

Introducing an Ecological Systems Cycle of LGBTQ Identity Exploration and Commitment

Adopting the exploration and commitment processes central to the unifying model of sexual identity development (Dillon et al., 2001) and the ecological context of the LGBTQ student success model (Woodford et al., 2016), I propose understanding LGBTQ identity development in a cycle embedded in an ecological system (Figure 11.1). In this model, LGBTQ identities are constantly created and recreated as a function of exploration of and momentary commitment to sexual orientation and gender identities. These explorations happen in the context of the college environment, broadly construed to include in-person, online, and social media interactions; academic and nonacademic engagements; work; family; and other identities. The college system is embedded in community, state, and national settings that present development opportunities and challenges. Wider sociohistorical and cultural factors surround the individuals' developmental ecosystem, further influencing LGBTQ identity exploration and momentary commitment. Precollege ecosystems and identities influence what happens in college, which in turn influences postcollege LGBTQ identity development (in Figure 11.1, the college system is larger for purposes of illustration; the model does not imply that LGBTQ identity is necessarily smaller or less salient before or after college).

Within this nested system, the individual undertakes processes of exploration and momentary commitment to LGBQ and/or trans identities. As in the unifying model (Dillon et al., 2011), an individual may explore without commitment, commit without exploration, or cycle through various explorations and commitments to sexual orientation and gender identities. I use the

Figure 11.1. Ecological systems cycle of LGBTQ identity exploration and commitment.

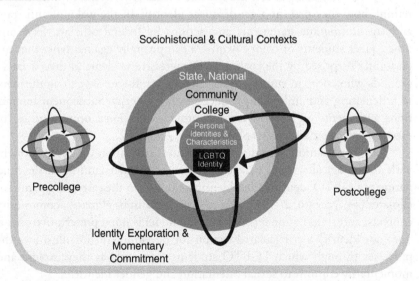

term *momentary commitment* to indicate that commitment to identity is an ongoing, fluid, ever-under-construction idea. Identities exist in context and may be expressed differently in different contexts.

Fictional student Skye illustrates the ecological systems cycle. Skye comes to college with a sense of sexual orientation identity and a gender identity. Skye experiences attractions to people of the same gender and explores what this might mean (a nonheterosexual identity). Going to a meeting at the LGBTQ campus resource center Skye encounters other Latinx students who find themselves not fully at home in the predominantly White LGBTQ student organizations. At the same time, Skye observes homophobia in the Latinx student community, causing them to moderate their behavior and discussions of personal life. Skye appreciates supportive policies and resources on campus, and one of their faculty members invites them to serve on a research team studying international perspectives on transgender people and immigration policy; these positive interactions create a wider space in which Skye can consider ethnic, sexual orientation, and gender identities.

In Skye's second year, they move off campus to live with other queer students of color in an apartment in a student rentals neighborhood. The apartment becomes a focal point for queer students, creating a supportive microsystem for Skye to consider gender identity in addition to sexual orientation and to commit to a queer identity through social life and peer engagement. A bias incident in the neighborhood (students, apparently White men, living in another house shout slurs and throw empty bottles at Skye and friends as they return to their house one weekend night) interrupts this sense of supportive off-campus community and makes Skye wonder if they should rethink how they present a genderqueer identity. In the wake of anti-trans and anti-immigrant statements and actions by federal officials, Skye and other queer students of color organize a campus rally against hate; they are pleasantly surprised by the coalition of progressive students of diverse backgrounds who come in support. This support reinforces Skye's commitment to articulating and embodying a queer Latinx identity. Subsequent interactions and events on and off campus provide additional opportunities for exploring and committing to Skye's LGBTQ identity.

The combination of individual identity exploration and commitment with an ecological systems perspective allows an understanding of the fluid nature of LGBTQ identities and identification. As in the case of Skye, microclimates (see Vaccaro, 2012) play a role, as do campus climates, community contexts, and state/national contexts. The model is not a prescriptive one; it does not identify a particular direction for development but illustrates the processes through which LGBTQ students may cycle as they explore and momentarily commit to sexual orientation and gender identities.

Insight and Recommendations From the Ecological Systems Cycle of LGBTQ Identity Exploration and Commitment

The ecological systems cycle of LGBTQ identity exploration and commitment offers insight to and recommendations for higher education professionals, instructors, faculty in higher education/student affairs programs, and policymakers. The people responsible for creating and maintaining post-secondary environments have a role to play in creating optimal spaces for students to explore sexual orientation and gender identities. Knowing something about the students coming to the college environment is important. Have they had opportunities to explore their identities in secondary settings (e.g., through a Gay Straight Alliance in high school) or home communities, or are they likely to be having their first opportunity to explore in college? If a majority of an institution's students come directly from high school, what are those home communities and schools like? Students from regions that feature, for example, "no promo homo" (p. 1) laws that are designed to prohibit the "promotion of homosexuality" (p. 1) are less likely to have been exposed to positive portrayals of LGBQ people (GLSEN, 2018). College may be the first chance for students of any sexual orientation to learn about positive queer identities. Adult learners may have had wider exposure to the world and explored their own sexual identity through relationships and possibly partnering and parenting. Understanding the students coming to college lays a foundation for good practice.

Higher education professionals should also engage in ongoing professional development for themselves and their staff, to stay current in research and best practices. The 2010s have seen a surge of scholarship on LGBTQ college students, with particular emphasis on intersecting identities and trans students (e.g., Garvey et al., 2019; Marine & Nicolazzo, 2014; Taylor et al., 2018; Tillapaugh, 2015; Woodford et al., 2018). Undertaking periodic climate surveys and audits to understand how LGBTQ students experience campus today supplements what is known of climate research historically (Garvey, Flint, & Sanders, 2018). New tools, such as an LGBQ microaggressions scale (Woodford et al., 2015), provide additional perspectives to well-developed campus climate scales in wide use (see Rankin et al., 2010).

Faculty and instructors have a role to play in contributing to an environment in which students can explore their sexual and gender identities and make commitments to them. Linley et al. (2016) found that instructors who include LGBTQ topics in curriculum create space for exploration, but so too do instructors who are simply open to conversations with students and to supporting students in their independent research related to sexuality and gender. Given that Rankin et al. (2010) found that a high percentage of anti-LGBT hostility occurred in classroom settings, instructors have a particular role to play in creating educational environments that are free from overt and microaggressive discrimination and threat.

Faculty teaching in graduate programs in higher education and student affairs have opportunities to use the ecological cycle model to lead graduate students in the study of a model that integrates key ideas from multiple theories (i.e., developmental ecology, Marcia's identity statuses, sexual and gender identity development). Similar models could likely be developed for other aspects of identity, and graduate students can use this example as a way to think about theory development. What are the advantages and drawbacks of combining theories in this way? What is gained? What is lost? Are there other ways to combine ecological approaches with the exploration/commitment framework?

Finally, policymakers could benefit from considering an ecological cycle model operating within postsecondary settings. If they took seriously that identity is not fixed, policymakers would need to think about how, when, and whether students could self-identify as being in need of services for LGBTQ students. For example, marking identities on a college application—and there are a small number of institutions that do collect, on a voluntary basis, data about sexual orientation and/or gender identities—fixes this information in a student record. Can students update or correct the record? If a student does not self-identify on application, how could they later access services? Conducting a full audit of all campus policies (housing, names, health care, enrollment/registration, etc.) for instances of bias against LGBTQ people is a good first step, ideally conducted with an eye toward students who identify as LGBTQ before entry and those who may change their identity along the way. How would a student change their name in the registration system, request gender inclusive housing, or change sports teams to align with their gender identity? Any of these policies could be addressed in ways that would make identity exploration and commitment more likely and more positive for LGBTQ students.

Conclusion

LGBTQ identities are dynamic before, during, and after college. Considering them through an ecological cycle model provides a way to understand interactions between process and context. The processes of exploring and committing to identities, in the context of nested ecosystems, result in opportunities for students to understand themselves and their sexual orientation and gender identities. Campus actors—professionals, instructors, policymakers—have opportunities to provide supportive and challenging environments for this exploration.

References

Astin, A, W. (1977). *Four critical years*. Jossey-Bass.

Bazarsky, D., Morrow, L. K., & Javier, G. C. (2015). Cocurricular and campus contexts. In D. L. Stewart, G. B. Brazelton, & K. A. Renn (Eds.), *LGBTQ college student success* (New Directions for Student Services, no. 152, pp. 55–71). Jossey-Bass. https://doi.org/10.1002/ss.20145

Bilodeau, B. L. (2005). Beyond the gender binary: A case study of two transgender students at a Midwestern university. *Journal of Gay and Lesbian Issues in Education, 3*(1), 29–46. https://doi.org/10.1300/J367v03n01_05

Bilodeau, B. L., & Renn, K. A. (2005). Analysis of LGBT identity development models and implications for practice. In R. L. Sanlo (Ed.), *Gender identity and sexual orientation: Research, policy, and personal perspectives*. (New Directions for Student Services, no. 111, pp. 25–40). Jossey-Bass. https://doi.org/10.1002/ss.171

Bourdon, J. L., Saunders, T. R., & Hancock, L. C. (2018). Acknowledgement and support matter: A brief report on gender identity and sexual orientation at a large, urban university. *Journal of American College Health, 66*(8), 809–812. https://doi.org/10.1080/07448481.2018.1432627

Bronfenbrenner, U. (1994). Ecological models of human development. In T. Husen & T. N. Postlethwaite (Eds.), *International encyclopedia of education* (2nd ed.), Vol. 3, pp. 1643–1647). Pergamon Press.

Bussey, K. (2011). Gender identity development. In S. J. Schwartz, K. Luyckx, & V. L. Vignoles (Eds.), *Handbook of identity theory and research* (pp. 603–628). Springer. https://doi.org/10.1007/978-1-4419-7988-9_25

Bussey, K., & Bandura, A. (1999). Social cognitive theory of gender development and differentiation. *Psychological Review, 106*(4), 676–713. https://doi.org/10.1037/0033-295X.106.4.676

Cass, V. C. (1979). Homosexual identity formation: A theoretical model. *Journal of Homosexuality, 4*(3), 219–235. https://doi.org/10.1300/J082v04n03_01

D'Augelli, A. R. (1994). Identity development and sexual orientation: Toward a model of lesbian, gay, and bisexual identity development. In E. J. Trickett, R. J. Watts, & D. Birman (Eds.), *Human diversity: Perspectives on people in context* (pp. 312–333). Jossey-Bass.

Dillon, F. R., Worthington, R. L., & Moradi, B. (2011). Sexual identity as a universal process. In S. J. Schwartz, K. Luyckx, & V. L. Vignoles (Eds.), *Handbook of identity theory and research* (pp. 649–670). Springer.

Duran, A. (2019). Queer and of color: A systematic literature review on queer students of color in higher education scholarship. *Journal of Diversity in Higher Education, 12*(4), 390–400. https://doi.org/10.1037/dhe0000084

Duran, A., & Pérez II, D. (2017). Queering la familia: A phenomenological study reconceptualizing familial capital for queer Latino men. *Journal of College Student Development, 58*(8), 1149–1165. https://doi.org/10.1353/csd.2017.0091

Garvey, J. C., BrckaLorenz, A., Latopolski, K., & Hurtado, S. S. (2018). High-impact practices and student–faculty interactions for students across sexual orientations. *Journal of College Student Development, 59*(2), 210–226. https://doi.org/10.1353/csd.2018.0018

Garvey, J. C., Flint, M. A., & Sanders, L. A. (2018). Perceptions of campus climate among LGBTQ alumnx. *Philanthropy & Education, 2*(1), 97–124. https://doi.org/10.2979/phileduc.2.1.05

Garvey, J. C., Mobley Jr., S. D., Summerville, K. S., & Moore, G. T. (2019). Queer and trans* students of color: Navigating identity disclosure and college contexts. *The Journal of Higher Education, 90*(1), 150–178. https://doi.org/10.1080/0022 1546.2018.1449081

Garvey, J. C., Sanders, L. A., & Flint, M. A. (2017). Generational perceptions of campus climate among LGBTQ undergraduates. *Journal of College Student Development, 58*(6), 795–817. https://doi.org/10.1353/csd.2017.0065.

Garvey, J. C., Taylor, J. L., & Rankin, S. (2015). An examination of campus climate for LGBTQ community college students. *Community College Journal of Research and Practice, 39*(6), 527–541. https://doi.org/10.1080/10668926.2013.861374

GLSEN. (2018). Laws prohibiting "promotion of homosexuality" in schools: Impacts and implications (Research brief). GLSEN. https://www.glsen.org/sites/default/files/2019-10/GLSEN-Research-Laws-that-Prohibit-Promotion-of-Homosexuality-Implications.pdf

Greathouse, M., BrckaLorenz, A., Hoban, M., Huesman, Jr., R., Rankin, S., & Stolzenberg, E. B. (2018). *Queer-spectrum and trans-spectrum student experiences in American higher education: The analyses of national survey findings.* Tyler Clementi Center, Rutgers University. https://tcc-j2made.s3.amazonaws.com/uploads/2018/09/White-Paper-Final.pdf

Hurtado, S., Alvarez, C., Guillermo-Wann, C., Cuellar, M., & Arellano, L. (2012). A model for diverse learning environments. In J. C. Smart & M. B. Paulsen (Eds.), *Higher education: Handbook of theory and research* (vol. 27, pp. 41–122). Springer.

It Gets Better Project. (2010-2018). *Welcome to the It Gets Better Project.* https://itgetsbetter.org/

Kilgo, C. A., Linley, J. L., Renn, K. A., & Woodford, M. R. (2019). High impact for whom? The influence of environment and identity on lesbian, gay, bisexual, and queer college students' participation in high-impact activities. *Journal of College Student Development. 60*(4), 421–436. https://doi.org/10.1353/csd.2019.0038

Kosciw, J. G., Greytak, E. A., Zongrone, A. D., Clark, C. M., & Truong, N. L. (2018). *The 2017 National School Climate Survey: The experiences of lesbian, gay, bisexual, transgender, and queer youth in our nation's schools.* GLSEN. https://www.glsen.org/sites/default/files/2019-10/GLSEN-2017-National-School-Climate-Survey-NSCS-Full-Report.pdf

Linley, J. L., Nguyen, D., Brazelton, G. B., Becker, B., Renn, K., & Woodford, M. (2016). Faculty as sources of support for LGBTQ college students. *College Teaching, 64*(2), 55–63. https://doi.org/10.1080/87567555.2015.1078275

Marcia, J. E. (1966). Development and validation of ego-identity status. *Journal of Personality and Social Psychology, 3*, 551–558. https://doi.org/10.1037/h0023281

Marcia, J. E. (1980). Identity in adolescence. In J. Adelson (Ed.), *Handbook of adolescent psychology* (pp. 159–187). Wiley.

Marine, S. B., & Nicolazzo, Z. (2014). Names that matter: Exploring the tensions of campus LGBTQ centers and trans* inclusion. *Journal of Diversity in Higher Education, 7*(4), 265–281. http://dx.doi.org.proxy2.cl.msu.edu/10.1037/a0037990

Means, D. R. (2017). "Quaring" spirituality: The spiritual counterstories and spaces of Black gay and bisexual male college students. *Journal of College Student Development, 58*(2), 229–246. https://doi.org/10.1353/csd.2017.0017

Meyer, I. H. (2003). Prejudice, social stress, and mental health in lesbian, gay, and bisexual populations. *Psychological Bulletin, 129*, 674–697. https://doi.org/10.1037/0033-2909.129.5.674

Milem, J. F., Chang, M. J., & Antonio, A. L. (2005). *Making diversity work on campus: A research-based perspective.* Association of American Colleges & Universities.

Nguyen, D. J., Brazelton, G. B., Renn, K. A., & Woodford, M. R. (2018). Exploring the availability and influence of LGBTQ+ student services resources on student success at community colleges: A mixed methods analysis. *Community College Journal of Research and Practice, 42*(11), 783–796. https://doi.org/10.1080/10668926.2018.1444522

Nicolazzo, Z. (2016). "Just go in looking good": The resilience, resistance, and kinship-building of trans* college students. *Journal of College Student Development, 57*(5), 538–556. https://doi.org/10.1353/csd.2016.0057

Nicolazzo, Z., Pitcher, E. N., Renn, K. A., & Woodford, M. (2017). An exploration of trans* kinship as a strategy for student success. *International Journal of Qualitative Studies in Education, 30*(3), 305–319. https://doi.org/10.1080/09518398.2016.1254300

Rankin, S., Weber, G., Blumenfeld, W., & Frazer, S (2010). *2010 state of higher education for lesbian, gay, bisexual & transgender people.* Campus Pride.

Taylor, J. L., Dockendorff, K. J., & Inselman, K. (2018). Decoding the digital campus climate for prospective LGBTQ+ community colleges students. *Community College Journal of Research and Practice, 42*(3), 155–170. https://doi.org/10.1080/10668926.2017.1281177

Tillapaugh, D. (2015). Critical influences on sexual minority college males' meaning-making of their multiple identities. *Journal of Student Affairs Research and Practice, 52*(1), 64–75. https://doi.org/10.1080/19496591.2015.996059

Tinto, V. (1988). Stages of student departure: Reflections on the longitudinal character of student living. *The Journal of Higher Education, 59*, 438–455. https://doi.org/ 10.1080/00221546.1988.11780199

Tinto, V. (1993). *Leaving college: Rethinking the causes and cures of student attrition* (2nd ed.). University of Chicago Press.

Vaccaro, A. (2012). Campus microclimates for LGBT faculty, staff, and students: An exploration of the intersections of social identity and campus roles. *Journal of Student Affairs Research and Practice, 49*(4), 429–446. https://doi.org/10.1515/jsarp-2012-6473

Woodford, M. R., Chonody, J., Kulick, A., Brennan, D. J., & Renn, K. A. (2015). The LGBQ microaggressions on campus scale: A scale development and validation study. *Journal of Homosexuality, 62*(12), 1660–1687. https://doi.org/10.108 0/00918369.2015.1078205

Woodford, M. R., Joslin, J. Y., & Renn, K. A. (2016). LGBTQ students on campus: Fostering inclusion through research, policy, and practice. In P. A. Pasque, N. Ortega, & J. C. Burkhardt, & M. P. Ting. (Eds.), *Transforming understandings of diversity in higher education: Demography, democracy and discourse* (pp. 57–80). Stylus.

Woodford, M. R., Weber, G., Nicolazzo, Z., Hunt, R., Kulick, A., Coleman, T., Coulombe, S., & Renn, K. A. (2018). Depression and attempted suicide among LGBTQ college students: Fostering resilience to the effects of heterosexism and cisgenderism on campus. *Journal of College Student Development, 59*(4), 421–438. https://doi.org/10.1353/csd.2018.0040

12

RACING THE RAINBOW

Applying Critical Race Theory to LGB(TQ²) Ethnic Minority College Students' Development

Terrell L. Strayhorn

The most recent *Digest of Education Statistics* published by the U.S. Department of Education (DOE) indicates that there are over 21 million college students enrolled in the nation's more than 4,300 colleges and universities (U.S. Department of Education, 2019). Over half of all U.S. college students identify as women; approximately one third identify as first in their immediate family to attend college (hereafter termed *first-generation*); and over a quarter are underrepresented or underserved racial/ethnic minorities (REMs) such as African Americans, Latino Americans, Native Americans, and in some cases, subgroups of Asian Americans such as Hmong and Thai. Although national estimates are not available through DOE, research reports based on large-scale survey studies (Rankin, 2003) suggest that 10% to 13%, or more, of all college students may identify as lesbian, gay, bisexual, transgender, or queer/questioning, abbreviated here as LGB(TQ²). Of course, it is important to note that any published statistic likely underestimates the true size of the LGB(TQ²) student population due to the fact that many people do not disclose their identity to others or they view sexual orientation as a private matter (Renn, 2010). Be that as it may, current estimates would make LGB(TQ²) college students a very sizable group, larger in proportion than most REM populations. Indeed, some LGB(TQ²) youth also identify as REMs, and much more information is needed about their collegiate experiences.

Insights From Existing Literature

Prior higher education research on college students focused almost exclusively on heterosexual individuals or ignored any explicit mention of sexual orientation, presuming it to be irrelevant, impolite, or insignificant. Canonical studies of this kind make a number of erroneous assumptions, presuming most *traditional* students to be straight and *nontraditional* students, whatever that means nowadays, more likely to be gay than their counterparts. There have been notable exceptions, however, and recent years have brought much-needed attention to the collegiate experiences of LGB(TQ²) students in terms of campus climate (Rankin, 2006), gender identity (Bilodeau, 2005), leadership development (Renn, 2007), harassment (D'Augelli, 1992), and even Black gay males' experiences in campus residence halls (Strayhorn & Mullins, 2012), to name a few. For instance, Renn (2007) analyzed qualitative data from 15 students leading LGBT campus groups and uncovered that their campus involvement experiences reinforced their public LGBT identity on campus. Within this, she discovered evidence supporting three distinct identities: LGBT leader, LGBT activist, and queer activist.

Much of what is known from research about LGB(TQ²) populations has focused heavily on sexual identity development and the process through which individuals come to assume and accept their gay identity (e.g., Chan, 1989; Renn, 2007) using a number of prevailing theoretical models. For example, Cass (1979) hypothesized a model describing the "process by which a person comes first to consider and later to acquire the identity of homosexual as a relevant aspect of self" (p. 219). Her model consists of six stages representing gay identity development as growth from identity confusion to identity synthesis through four other temporally ordered, sequential phases of identity comparison, identity tolerance, identity acceptance, and identity pride.

Another principal model of gay identity development was advanced by D'Augelli (1991). As shown in Figure 12.1, his model posits gay identity development as a six-stage process that unfolds hierarchically over time, starting with "exiting heterosexual identity," then "becoming an LGB(TQ) offspring," and ultimately "enter[ing] a LGB(TQ) community." While there are a number of strengths to the model, there are several major challenges or limitations associated with its applicability to REMs who also identify as LGB(TQ²) college students (Fassinger, 1991; Strayhorn et al., 2010). First, virtually all widely cited gay identity models were formulated based on results from early research studies based almost exclusively on White gay male samples, men whose privileged experiences do not generally reflect those of LGB(TQ²) students of color. Second, predominant gay identity models were published in the early 1990s or even earlier. Consequently, they reflect the sociopolitical environments of the 1960s, 1970s, and 1980s when public policies and individual civil liberties were more restricted and qualitatively different than they are now for both REMs and LGB(TQ²) persons. Modern-day civil rights campaigns, the gay rights movement, and marriage equality protections have advanced quality of life personally and politically. Traditional, normative models suffer from another limitation—they lack elasticity to accommodate the complex ways in which the influence of race and racism intersects on the experiences of minoritized individuals moving through the rigid phases outlined in the model. For instance, D'Augelli's (1991) model is virtually silent in trying to explain how race and religion affect *how, if,* and *when* Black gay men choose to become gay offspring by disclosing their sexual identity to family members.

Neoanalytic Critique: A Fresh Perspective

For these reasons and more, dominant gay identity development models deserve contemporary critique—what I call *neoanalysis*. Neoanalysis refers to an up-to-date evaluation of the veracity of such models that is socially conscious, sympathetically liberating, and courageously critical.

In this chapter, I advance a neoanalysis of D'Augelli's (1991) gay identity development model (see Figure 12.1) that is socially conscious in its responsiveness and sensitivity to the present conditions, dreams, miseries, needs, and realities of people for whom such models were not designed originally, namely LGB(TQ²) students of color. I put forth a neoanalytic critique that is sympathetically liberating; its epistemic framing reflects authentic, intimate contact with the people who stand to benefit from the fresh perspective. Liberating neoanalytic critique awakens the evaluator from intellectual slumber to a level of critical consciousness—or, "scholarly wokeness"—that produces penetrating insights, new directions, and worldly wisdom. Deep insights and culturally congruent wisdom provide the power that can emancipate imprisoned identities (e.g., being young, gifted, Black, and gay) from the oppression of finite boxes and overly simplistic directional arrows that characterize most traditional models in the academic canon. In doing so, neoanalytic critique challenges unexamined assumptions and interrogates false dichotomies so that individuals might grow, move, and breathe (even live) freely outside the box, beyond the margin, or just as they are.

Lastly, in the spirit of scholarly activism, I am arguing for and proposing a neoanalysis that is courageously critical in its unapologetic unveiling of the ways in which power plays out (obviously and tacitly) in processes, people, places, and philosophies that masquerade as objective (especially in the

Figure 12.1. D'Augelli's (1991) gay identity development model.

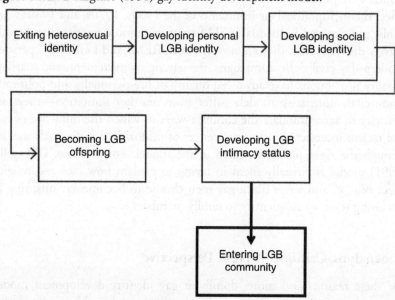

Note. "LGB" means lesbian, gay, or bisexual, in keeping with the original model.

academy) while surreptitiously oppressing marginalized voices, demonizing diverse experiences, and reducing the complexities of heroic humanity (e.g., negotiating identity as a gay man of color in a "White man's world") to nothing more than arrested development, covert *passing*, or *living on the down low*, borrowing a term from J. L. King's (2004) incendiary book on the topic.

This is the expressed purpose of the present chapter—to critique an existing model that has been used extensively to understand LGB(TQ²) students and to offer an alternative framework for LGB(TQ²) students of color, in keeping with this book's overall aim. Specifically, the next sections present a critical race neoanalysis of D'Augelli's (1991) model, highlighting key strengths of the theory, any limits, and its epistemic underpinnings that relate to race and racism. Then, given the important roles that campus climate, peer relations, and faculty/staff support play in the educational success of LGB(TQ²) students of color (e.g., Strayhorn & Mullins, 2012), I offer a race-conscious perspective on sense of belonging as an alternative framework for educators working with queer students of color.

Critical Race Theory and Neoanalysis

There should be no question that D'Augelli's (1991) six-phase gay identity development lifespan model has a number of virtues. First, it exists; has been published in the academic literature; and continues to be circulated broadly in canonical textbooks on student development theory, gender studies, and related topics. One metric for judging the worth of a theory is counted in the number of studies that flow from its development, and D'Augelli's model has been cited in hundreds of theses, dissertations, and published works.

Second, unlike other traditional identity models that presume development unfolds evenly and gradually over time in linear fashion, D'Augelli admitted that the process is interactive—factors external to the model influence what happens to the individual *during* the process. Unfortunately, the original conceptualization did not address these factors directly. Parenthetical references to things like personal subjectivities and sociohistorical connections were alluded to in some treatments of the topic but often given short shrift.

Third, the model does well to admit that identity is socially constructed and shaped by different degrees of social situations. For instance, gay identity is not based solely on what one does (e.g., sleeping with same-sex partners), but also on the meaning that individuals make of themselves and how they come to understand their sexual attractions. What's more, the model posits sexual orientation development as a lifelong process and acknowledges that environmental changes can impact developmental plasticity.

Critical Race Theory: A "Woke" Framework

While certainly useful, there are several major limits of the model that reduce its applicability to ethnic minority LGB(TQ[2]) people who lead complex lives, further complicated by other social identities like age, gender, social class, race—any and all of these. Critical race theory (CRT) provides a framework for addressing these complexities, contradictions, and intersections as it draws from an expansive literature on race and ethnic relations, history, sociology, and law (Solórzano & Villalpando, 1998). Consequently, CRT is perfectly suited for conducting a neoanalysis of D'Augelli's (1991) model, since CRT seeks to identify, unearth, resist, and transform structural and cultural aspects of society—and, yes, education—that perpetuate inequities, maintain hierarchies, and deny the centricity of race.

CRT serves as a "woke" framework that emphasizes the importance of dismantling oppressive structures (and beliefs) through a dynamic process of unlearning and relearning. CRT provides language for talking about race and racism as social constructions and its core tenets can be used to deconstruct each stage of D'Augelli's original model, consequently raising important race-conscious questions that deserve future consideration and sympathetic introspection. The following core tenets form the basis of CRT's model, as published elsewhere (Strayhorn, 2013):

- centrality and intersectionality of race and racism,
- challenge(s) to dominant ideologies (e.g., democracy, meritocracy),
- commitment to social justice,
- importance of experiential knowledge, and
- use of an inter- or transdisciplinary perspective.

CRT also serves as glue to rebuild and reconstitute the prevailing model in a way that better accommodates the racialized realities of LGB(TQ²) ethnic minorities. It enables the neoanalysis by centering race, critiquing dominant ideologies, acknowledging counterstories, and casting the experiential knowledge of LGB(TQ²) students of color as legitimate claims for advancing what we know about these students, even *all other* students. Indeed, CRT proves to be a useful heuristic in this critical analysis, just one tool for "racing the rainbow" or positioning race and racism as central to understanding LGB(TQ²) college students' experiences.

A Critical Race Neoanalysis of D'Augelli's Model

One of the basic premises of CRT is the notion that race and racism are permanent fixtures in American life. They play and continue to play a dominant role in American society, both consciously and unconsciously. Therefore, it is reasonable and realistic to conclude (and accept) that "racist hierarchical structures govern all political, economic, and social domains," even our most liberal social institutions like schools, colleges, and universities (DeCuir & Dixson, 2004, p. 27). For instance, many readers will easily acknowledge how race is classified on government forms to categorize, compartmentalize, and organize people into groups based on whether they identify as White, Black, Hispanic, Asian, and so on. However, it may be less obvious to some readers that public schools are still raced (and classed) in patterned hierarchies that provide some students (mostly White) with qualified teachers, immaculate buildings, rigorous advanced placement courses, and ever-flowing opportunities to prepare for college and career, while others (mostly minority) are left behind with teachers working outside their field, raggedy structures, dated materials, and free or reduced lunch vouchers. In keeping with this logic, D'Augelli's model makes a number of fallacious assumptions that fail to account for the role of race and the permanence of racism. For instance, the model posits that the process begins by exiting heterosexual identity or what is presumed as normative, general, and "natural" to assume a gay identity, intimacy status, and community. But the model fails to appreciate whether and how this stage is shaped by the realities of race, racism, and what it means to be in the numerical minority as an LGB(TQ²) college student of color, yearning for social acceptance and belonging, yet feeling the need to leave that which you've known to take on that which is unknown. And what about gay people of color who intentionally (and knowingly) lead public lives as heterosexuals but engage privately in same-sex relations—do they ever *really* exit heterosexual identity? Is that essential? One student described it this way in one of my interview studies:

> Like, I really don't know how to explain for real. I mean, yes, I'm gay and I'm Black in terms of my sexuality and stuff. But that's just one part of me and I don't really identify like that to everybody. A lot of my male friends are straight and they're Black, but my gay friends in college tend to be White [laughing] . . . so I spend a lot more time with my Black straight friends, doing stuff with them like PS4 [Play Station 4], shooting [basket] ball, or talking about girls. I mean, I don't want them but it's just what dudes do when they hang out together. (Anonymous, personal communication, November 3, 2018)

The original model presumes that gay men must exit heterosexual identity as one step in healthy development, even though such an exit may be isolating, alienating, threatening, or unnecessary for some gay people of color. Without "exiting," however, gay people of color are doomed to be judged as underdeveloped, premature, or developmentally delayed according to the model, which only serves to reify racialized stereotypes about ethnic minorities generally. Stories from LGB(TQ^2) college students of color suggest that it may not be necessary to "exit" heterosexual identity per se and students of color may engage in a far more complicated set of identity negotiation tactics than previously understood.

The second and third phases of D'Augelli's model involve figuring out what it means to be gay—largely assessed via cues, messages, and signals learned from other LGBT individuals—which, in turn, facilitates development of one's personal and social gay identity. While internally consistent with dominant assumptions of the hypothesized theory, these phases fail to recognize the pervasiveness of race and racism in both American society and the gay community. Many scholars have noted the strong divide that exists between Black and gay communities—Black is often assumed to be heterosexual and White to be gay (Boykin, 1997). In fact, essayists have pointed out that much of the gay rights movement reflects the concerns and political wishes of the White gay community without meaningful inclusion of gay communities of color. Even in online dating environments (e.g., gay.com), ethnic minorities report intentionally concealing their racial identity to avoid discrimination, rejection, or verbal harassment from others (Callander et al.,

2016). For instance, in one of my interview studies, a student expressed his frustration with online personal profiles where presumably White gay men would racialize their sexual interests as "Whites only" or "No Blacks," reminiscent of racist signage that characterized the Jim Crow era (Anonymous, personal communication, December 9, 2017). For these reasons and more, developing a personal and social gay identity is not necessarily automatic and it can be very difficult for gay students of color who rarely see people like themselves on campus or even online. As illustrated, race and racism significantly limit the partners and role models available to gay college students of color. Race and racism also shape the type of cues sent or received about whether LGB(TQ²) college students of color belong in the community and constrict the possibilities that gay people of color see in their initial exploration of this personal status. Several students explained it this way in my research:

> I came to college to come out because it was too hard to do it when I was in high school, back home. But even after coming out—if that's what you call it—to some of my close friends, I still don't have many gay friends who are my same race. Most of them are White . . . I mean, it's easier for White people to be out. There's so many of them that even if they lose a few friends, they still got [sic] a whole lot more. For us [Black men], it's harder because if you're rejected by some, you feel rejected by all. (Anonymous, personal communication, October 11, 2010)

> Dating is the hard part (laughing). I used to say that I only date White guys because I'm used to them more. Like where I lived was mostly White, even though I'm Black. . . . I'm like the Whitest Black boy you'll ever meet, you know. I'm preppy and I talk proper [sic]. But when I got called the N-word by one of my boyfriend's friends and he didn't speak up or anything, I was so fu*king pissed. It's like I don't need to deal with racism in the real world and in the gay world . . . but it's there. That sh*t is always there. (Anonymous, personal communication, October 19, 2010)

Thus, as all of these quotes illustrate, developing a personal and social gay identity is far more complicated and nuanced than explained in D'Augelli's original model, and the experience can be powerfully shaped by race and racism for LGB(TQ²) college students of color. Much more information is needed to fully understand how this process unfolds over time for this precarious group of students.

Counterstorytelling is an essential feature of CRT (Matsuda, 1995). It is defined as a method of storytelling that "aims to cast doubt on the validity of accepted premises or myths, especially ones held by the majority" (Delgado & Stefancic, 2001, p. 144). I believe it is a necessary tool for neoanalysis, a means for exposing, uncovering, and *consciously* critiquing routinized, *privileged* discourses—that is, discourses of the majority or those in power—that perpetuate inequities, stereotypes, and marginalization. Counterstories "give voice" to those who speak with soft voices out of respect for Eastern cultural norms; those whose voices are weak from protesting and rallying; or those whose voices are hardly ever heard in board rooms, state houses, laboratories, or classrooms in the ivory tower. In many ways, the quotes presented previously are excerpts of counterstories that challenge commonly held assumptions about how gay identity develops over the lifespan. Counterstories can also be helpful in challenging—perhaps even resisting—the mindset undergirding the third stage of D'Augelli's model that requires individuals to become gay offspring by disclosing their sexual orientation to their parents. The developmental significance of this phase rests on a set of liberal assumptions that true acceptance of one's self as LGB necessitates a degree of public transparency and disclosure of one's affectional status to those who are closest to them. It is clear that the model positions parents at the very top of that social hierarchy such that one cannot be fully developed or mature without breaking the silence about their sexual orientation to their parents. CRT, however, calls attention to a number of racial realities and cultural beliefs that reveal significant flaws with this logic:

- Sexuality is taboo in many communities of color, and that alone may complicate if, when, and to whom gay youth of color disclose their identity.
- Youth who disclose often suffer serious psychological, familial, and spiritual consequences, and these can be exacerbated for youth of color who might come to see their sexual orientation as less important than the love and affection of family in a world that still judges them by the color of their skin.
- Many youth of color are raised by surrogate parents, fictive kin,[1] in foster care, constructed/chosen family, or other arrangements that may alter the meaning that they attach to certain relationships with adults, peers, or case workers. What does "becoming a gay offspring" *really mean* to a gay Black male formerly in foster care? Or a pushed-out youth of color whose relationship with their dad terminated years ago when they moved-in with their "gay daddy" (fictive kin) who is in no way biologically related but their sole provider? The prevailing model is remarkably silent on this matter, yet insists on this student "coming out" to their birth parents who, as one put it in an interview with me, "probably wouldn't give a damn anyway" (Anonymous, personal communication, August 12, 2019).

As D'Augelli (1991) explained in his original article in the *Journal of College Student Development,*

> Revealing lesbian or gay identity to others [Stages 5 and 6] initiates another set of developmental processes—relating to lesbian and gay people, socializing in lesbian and gay settings, becoming involved in lesbian and gay communities, and integrating lesbian and gay status into all domains of personal life. (p. 140)

So much of what has been shared to this point in the chapter reveals how overly simplistic all of this seems, especially for people of color when race and racism are taken into account. Even the term *integration* has a storied (and racialized) history with people of color, especially Blacks in America, and CRT provides the scaffolding needed to interrogate use of this word that often equates mere presence with full participation. And since integration did not work very well for Blacks in American social life—as Blacks still struggle with unfair housing policies, inadequate schools, and mass incarceration—it is unlikely to serve us well as a theory explaining the developmental needs of Black and other ethnic minority gay people.

Coming to terms with one's sexual orientation as a person of color is far more complicated than any stage-wise processional that strives toward integration of multiple identities. Counterstories that I have heard from my interviewees over the years reveal an unpredictable process punctuated by moments of silence, disclosure, hiding (sometimes for safety reasons), inclusion, and even reconciliation. As one Black gay male, Jamel, majoring in engineering put it:

> I don't need to tell everybody my business. I'm in engineering, we need to talk about design elements, thermodynamics, not who I'm fu*king. I'm not trying to tell my business to everyone everywhere, with every Tom, Dick, and Harry, you know (laughing). . . . I'm just trying to find a place where I belong.

His sentiments echo the general chorus sounded by so many in my studies on gay students of color (e.g., Strayhorn et al., 2010; Strayhorn & Mullins, 2012)—more than "coming out" they want to "fit in" and find a sense of belonging in college. Indeed, sense of belonging matters to everyone, especially college students (Strayhorn, 2012, 2019), and may represent a useful alternative model for examining the lives of LGB(TQ^2) students of color.

Sense of Belonging as Critical Theory

The need to belong is among the most basic and essential of all human needs and motivations. Definitions abound but generally converge on the idea that *sense of belonging* refers to "a feeling that members matter to one another and to the group, and a shared faith that members' needs will be met through their commitment to be together" (McMillan & Chavis, 1986, p. 9). It is largely assessed through perceived social support, feelings of connectedness, or the degree to which one seems to matter to others. Belonging is part of a larger motivational matrix, and it drives human behaviors (Strayhorn, 2012).

Not only are humans motivated to "do things" to satisfy their need to belong, but there is reason to believe that they *cannot* do some things until they fulfill this basic, fundamental need. For instance, consider Maslow's (1954) theory of personality that led to the production of his infamous "hierarchy of needs" illustration that depicts higher order human functioning (e.g., creativity, integrity) as a consequence of satisfying more basic needs like air, water, food, shelter, safety, and belongingness. In fact, its location directly in the middle of the pyramid suggests that sense of belonging is central to optimal human functioning. One simply cannot reach their full potential without finding a sense of belonging first. To illustrate my point, a critical adaptation of belonging theory might uncover how power and privilege conspire with race to position some people in the world (or college) in ways that deny them access to basic needs or threaten their socioemotional safety, which renders them lonely and unfulfilled. Figure 12.2 presents a summary of Maslow's model, as conceptualized by Strayhorn (2012).

A healthy sense of belonging is an important contributor to one's overall psychological health and well-being (McBeath et al., 2018), especially for LGB(TQ²) students of color. Numerous studies have shown that social isolation, loneliness, or threatened (thwarted) sense of belonging are consistently associated with anxiety, depression, grief, suicidal ideation, psychiatric disorders, substance abuse, and even a weakened immune system (Baumeister & Leary, 1995; Joiner, 2009; Thoits, 2011). Data from the National Institutes of Health and Centers for Disease Control also clearly indicate that loneliness rates are soaring in the United States as the number of Americans who report feeling lonely has tripled since the 1980s, and rates are higher among stigmatized populations like LGBT people of color. What's more is that the impact of loneliness (versus belonging) on one's body is equivalent to smoking 15 cigarettes a day, according to federal agencies. These effects are felt by gay students of color, too—in one study, my colleagues and I found that

Figure 12.2. Maslow's hierarchy of needs.

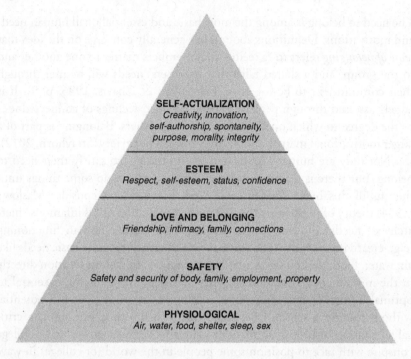

SELF-ACTUALIZATION
*Creativity, innovation,
self-authorship, spontaneity,
purpose, morality, integrity*

ESTEEM
Respect, self-esteem, status, confidence

LOVE AND BELONGING
Friendship, intimacy, family, connections

SAFETY
Safety and security of body, family, employment, property

PHYSIOLOGICAL
Air, water, food, shelter, sleep, sex

100% of Black gay college men in our sample had contemplated suicide at least once due to issues related to their race and/or sexual orientation (Strayhorn et al., 2010).

The influence of sense of belonging on health, well-being, and human functioning is more pronounced during adolescence, emerging adulthood, or in times and places when one is most vulnerable to feeling alienated, isolated, lonely, or *out of place* (Drolet & Arcand, 2013; Strayhorn, 2019). I have argued that college is a time when a strong sense of belonging is crucial for positive cognitive, social, and emotional development; positive sense of belonging leads to students' educational success, while social isolation or rejection can compromise one's academic plans (Strayhorn, 2012). A critically conscious deployment of sense of belonging theory would expose how existing power structures provide majority students, on the one hand, with access to valuable networks that offer the social connections needed to feel as if they belong, while denying access to minorities on the other hand.

College is also a time characterized by major life stressors like moving away from home, separating from one's family and close friends, transitioning to a physical campus, or making significant decisions like choosing an academic major (Brunwasser, 2012; Hunt & Eisenberg, 2010). It is also during this stage of life that individuals are sorting through important identity questions about who they are, why they exist (i.e., purpose), and how they will coexist with others (i.e., community), so issues like self-esteem, mattering, peer acceptance, and friendship are crucial. It's also important to note that individuals work through these issues in varying patterns of order and timing. All of this can take on heightened importance for gay college students of color who may be inclined to feel lonely or "out of place" at predominantly White institutions (PWIs); in conservative Black colleges (Harper & Gasman, 2008); or when struggling to reconcile who they *really are* while developing racial pride, comfort with one's sexuality, and/or other core dimensions of self.

Generally speaking, sense of belonging in education has been interpreted as a sense of community, connectedness, membership, or a "students' sense of being accepted, valued, included, and encouraged by others (teachers and peers) in the academic classroom setting . . . feeling oneself to be an important part of the life and activity of the class" (Goodenow, 1993, p. 25). Others have argued, like I once did, that sense of belonging is based on the perception of fitting in with one's peers (Pittman & Richmond, 2008; Strayhorn, 2008), although I have since changed my belief based on my more recent research discoveries (Strayhorn, 2019). Sense of belonging is not about "fitting in" per se, especially not when circumstances and existing power structures may require one to conceal or deny core aspects like race to gain the acceptance of others. On the contrary, true sense of belonging is about creating, finding, or joining communities where one is *truly* accepted, affirmed, included, validated, and valued as they are, for who they are, scars and all.

The weight of empirical evidence suggests that higher levels of belongingness are associated with more positive academic, social, and mental health outcomes including academic motivation, self-efficacy, higher grades, lower attrition rates, greater emotional intelligence, and satisfaction with college, to name a few (Goodenow & Grady, 1993; Strayhorn, 2008). For example, I analyzed survey data from Black, Latino, and Native American college students responding to the College Student Experiences Questionnaire (CSEQ) and found that frequent, positive peer interactions and strong supportive relationships with campus staff and faculty positively predicted ethnic minority students' sense of belonging (Strayhorn, 2008). Students who felt a strong sense of belonging in college earned better grades and were more satisfied with their undergraduate experience. Beyond grades and satisfaction, sense of belonging may also buffer against depression and the psychological stress associated with the transition to college, especially for first-year students (Brunwasser, 2012) or the stressors that LGB(TQ²) college students of color face due to racism, discrimination, and conservatism, to name a few.

Although the vast majority of research on students' sense of belonging has focused on K–12 school contexts (e.g., Goodenow, 1993) and research on college students' sense of belonging has been preoccupied with heterosexual students or ignored sexual orientation altogether (e.g., Pittman & Richmond, 2008), there is clear evidence to support my argument that the construct has especially important implications for ethnic minority LGB(TQ^2) college students who have received growing attention in recent years (Duran, 2019; Renn, 2010). Beyond the ideas offered here, I encourage future researchers to continue to mine this largely uncharted terrain for new ideas, fresh perspectives, and critical ways to *race the rainbow.*

Conclusion

Left as they are, dominant gay identity development models like D'Augelli's render most LGB(TQ^2) college students of color as developmentally delayed, underdeveloped, or arrested in their development by interpreting their behaviors through a lens set on dominant beliefs and values that pay little to no attention to different worldviews. This is a massive problem as they simply reinforce a discursive narrative that portrays people of color as broken, deficient, retarded (in a literal sense), or subordinate to those who move in an orderly fashion through stages derived from 61 White men surveyed by a White man back in the late 1980s. To fix this problem, we need more compelling evidence that flows from neoanalyses of this kind, alternative frames, and critically conscious scholarship, especially work produced by woke women, people of color, LGB(TQ^2) scholars, or those who are blessed to live at the intersection of several of these. After all, CRT holds that the aim of critical work is never merely to sound deep, to win awards, or build monuments to ourselves. No, it is to achieve social justice, to change the material conditions of those negatively impacted by race, power, and privilege, and to leave the world—or at least the literature, in the case of scholars—better than we found it.

Note

1. *Fictive kin* refers to individuals who are not related biologically but share an emotionally significant relationship, or chosen family.

References

Baumeister, R. F., & Leary, M. R. (1995). The need to belong: Desire for interpersonal attachment as a fundamental human motivation. *Psychological Bulletin, 117,* 497–529. https://doi.org/10.1037/0033-2909.117.3.497

Bilodeau, B. L. (2005). Beyond the gender binary: A case study of two transgender college students at a Midwestern research university. *Journal of Gay and Lesbian Issues in Education, 3*(1), 29–44. https://doi.org/10.1300/J367v03n01_05

Boykin, K. (1997). *One more river to cross: Black and gay in America.* Anchor.

Brunwasser, S. (2012). *Depressive symptoms during the transition to college: Evaluating trajectories and predictors among freshmen and transfer students* [Unpublished doctoral dissertation]. University of Michigan. http://citeseerx.ist.psu.edu/viewdoc/download?doi=10.1.1.862.160&rep=rep1&type=pdf

Callander, D., Holt, M., & Newman, C. E. (2016). 'Not everyone's gonna like me': Accounting for race and racism in sex and dating web services for gay and bisexual men. *Ethnicities, 16*(1), 3–21. https://doi.org/10.1177/1468796815581428

Chan, C. S. (1989). Issues of identity development among Asian American lesbians and gay men. *Journal of Counseling and Development, 68,* 16–20. https://doi.org/10.1002/j.1556-6676.1989.tb02485.x

D'Augelli, A. R. (1991). Gay men in college: Identity processes and adaptations. *Journal of College Student Development, 32,* 140–146.

D'Augelli, A. R. (1992). Lesbian and gay male undergraduates' experiences of harassment and fear on campus. *Journal of Interpersonal Violence, 7,* 383–395. https://doi.org/10.1177/088626092007003007

DeCuir, J. T., & Dixson, A. D. (2004). "So when it comes out, they aren't that surprised that it is there": Using critical race theory as a tool of analysis of race and racism in education. *Educational Researcher, 33*(5), 26–31. https://doi.org/10.3102/0013189X033005026

Delgado, R., & Stefancic, J. (2001). *Critical race theory: An introduction.* New York University Press.

Drolet, M., & Arcand, I. (2013). Positive development, sense of belonging, and support of peers among early adolescents: Perspectives of different actors. *International Education Studies, 6*(4), 29–38. https://doi.org/10.5539/ies.v6n4p29

Duran, A. (2019). Queer and of color: A systematic literature review on queer students of color in higher education scholarship. *Journal of Diversity in Higher Education, 12*(4), 390–400. https://doi.org/10.1037/dhe0000084

Goodenow, C. (1993). Classroom belonging among early adolescent students: Relationships to motivation and achievement. *Journal of Early Adolescents, 13,* 21–43. https://doi.org/10.1177/0272431693013001002

Goodenow, C., & Grady, K. E. (1993). The relationship of school belonging and friends' values to academic motivation among urban adolescent students. *Journal of Experimental Education, 62,* 60–71. https://doi.org/10.1080/00220973.1993.9943831

Harper, S. R., & Gasman, M. B. (2008). Black male undergraduates and the politics of historically Black colleges and universities. *Journal of Negro Education, 77*(4), 336–351. https://repository.upenn.edu/cgi/viewcontent.cgi?article=1204&context=gse_pubs

Hunt, J., & Eisenberg, D. (2010). Mental health problems and help-seeking behavior among college students. *Journal of Adolescent Health, 46*(1), 3–10. https://doi.org/10.1016/j.jadohealth.2009.08.008

Joiner, T. E. (2009). Suicide prevention in schools as viewed through the interpersonal-psychological theory of suicidal behavior. *School Psychology Review, 38*(2), 244–248. https://www.tandfonline.com/doi/abs/10.1080/02796015.2009.1208 7835

King, J. L. (2004). *On the down low: A journey into the lives of "straight" Black men who sleep with men.* Harlem Moon.

Maslow, A. H. (1954). *Motivation and personality.* Harper & Row.

Matsuda, M. (1995). Looking to the bottom: Critical legal studies and reparations. In K. Crenshaw, N. Gotanda, G. Peller, & K. Thomas (Eds.), *Critical race theory: The key writings that formed the movement* (pp. 63–79). The New Press.

McBeath, M., Drysdale, M. T. B., & Bohn, N. (2018). Work-integrated learning and the importance of peer support and sense of belonging. *Education + Training, 60*(1), 39–53. https://doi.org/10.1108/ET-05-2017-0070

McMillan, D. W., & Chavis, D. M. (1986). Sense of community: A definition and theory. *Journal of Community Psychology, 14*(January), 6–23. https://doi .org/10.1002/1520-6629(198601)14:1<6::AID-JCOP2290140103>3.0.CO;2-I

Pittman, L. D., & Richmond, A. (2008). University belonging, friendship quality, and adjustment during the transition to college. *The Journal of Experimental Education, 76*(4), 343–361. https://doi.org/10.3200/JEXE.76.4.343-362

Rankin, S. R. (2003). Campus climate for LGBT people: A national perspective. National Gay and Lesbian Taskforce Policy Institute. https://doi.org/10.1300/ J367v03n02_11

Rankin, S. R. (2006). LGBTA students on campus: Is higher education making the grade? *Journal of Gay and Lesbian Issues in Education, 3*(2/3), 111–117. https:// doi.org/10.1300/J367v03n02_11

Renn, K. A. (2007). LGBT student leaders and queer activists: Identities of lesbian, gay, bisexual, transgender, and queer-identified college student leaders and activists. *Journal of College Student Development, 48*(3), 311–330. https://doi .org/10.1353/csd.2007.0029

Renn, K. A. (2010). LGBT and queer research in higher education: The state and status of the field. *Educational Researcher, 39*(2), 132–141. https://doi .org/10.3102/0013189X10362579

Solórzano, D. G., & Villalpando, O. (1998). Critical race theory: Marginality and the experience of students of color in higher education. In C. A. Torres & T. R. Mitchell (Eds.), *Sociology of education: Emerging perspectives* (pp. 211–224). SUNY Press.

Strayhorn, T. L. (2008). Fittin' in: Do diverse interactions with peers affect sense of belonging for Black men at predominantly White institutions? *The NASPA Journal, 45*(4), 501–527. https://doi.org/10.2202/1949-6605.2009

Strayhorn, T. L. (2012). *College students' sense of belonging: A key to educational success.* Routledge.

Strayhorn, T. L. (2013). *Theoretical frameworks in college impact research.* University Press of America, Inc.

Strayhorn, T. L. (2019). *College students' sense of belonging: A key to educational success for all students* (2nd ed.). Routledge.

Strayhorn, T. L., Blakewood, A. M., & DeVita, J. M. (2010). Triple threat: Challenges and supports of Black gay men at predominantly White campuses. In T. L. Strayhorn & M. C. Terrell (Eds.), *The evolving challenges of Black college students: New insights for policy, practice and research* (pp. 85–104). Stylus.

Strayhorn, T. L., & Mullins, T. G. (2012). Investigating Black gay male undergraduates' experiences in campus residence halls. *The Journal of College and University Student Housing, 39*(1), 140–161.

Thoits, P. A. (2011). Mechanisms linking social ties and support to physical and mental health. *Journal of Health and Social Behavior, 52*(2), 145–161. https://journals.sagepub.com/doi/10.1177/0022146510395592

U.S. Department of Education, National Center for Education Statistics. (2016). *The condition of education 2016.* U.S. Government Printing Office.

13

BREAKING THROUGH BARRIERS

Examining the Stresses That Impact Transgender Students' Collegiate Transitions

Christy Heaton and Alonzo M. Flowers III

ccording to the Campus Pride 2010 National College Climate Survey, "The overwhelming majority of Lesbian, Gay, Bisexual, Transgender, Queer, Questioning and Intersex (LGBTQI) students, of every race, color and ethnicity, report harassment, isolation and fear on their college campuses" (Rankin et al., 2010, p. 6). Transmasculine respondents (87%) and transfeminine respondents (82%) indicated that their gender expression was the basis for harassment, compared to 20% of men and 24% of women (Rankin et al., 2010). This is crucial in recognizing that transgender students face harassment based on their gender identity and expression, and institutions should be asking the question, "What can we do to educate our communities?" Further, Dugan et al. (2012) found that "transgender students reported more frequent encounters with harassment and discrimination as well as a significantly lower sense of belonging within the campus community" (p. 732). The most significant factor in changing notions of belonging within the campus community for transgender students is the establishment of inclusive policies and procedures (Goldberg et al., 2018; Goldberg & Kuvalanka, 2018). As such, if transgender students are reporting high levels of harassment based on gender expression on college campuses and do not feel as though they belong, then it is clear that institutions of higher education are not fulfilling their responsibility to create inclusive and supportive environments for transgender populations. This chapter uses research-based data to discuss the experiences of transgender college students and their ongoing challenges with Breaking Through Barriers within institutions of higher education. Rankin et al. (2010) found that transgender people felt oppressed on campuses through "harassment, violence, marginalization, tokenization, and exploitation" (p. 12). These findings indicate that transgender students are affected by distal (or external) stressors that could be impacting their integration into their campus communities. These fears and feelings can lead to a sense of exclusion among transgender individuals. Colleges and universities make it clear to transgender populations (students, staff, and faculty) with their policies, or lack thereof, whether they are valued and recognized (Nicolazzo, 2015).

As students navigate their gender identity and continue "coming out" as transgender on college campuses, it is beneficial to incorporate alternative transitional theories that can assist in framing the stories and experiences of these students. This chapter examines how transgender students navigated their college experiences, especially their first year or their first year out as a transgender student, and how gender identity played a role in their college transition to the campus community. Thus, this chapter seeks to examine the lived experiences of transgender college students and how breaking through barriers was an essential part of their collegiate experience. In this chapter, transition theory, minority stress theory, and academic and social integration theory provide a foundation from which to view the experiences of transgender college students. Schlossberg (1981) defined *transition* as an event or a nonevent that can result in a change regarding roles, relationships, and/or a routine (Anderson et al., 2012). Schlossberg's (1981) transition theory focuses on the four S's: situation, self, support, and strategies. It served as a valuable resource in conjunction with minority stress theory and academic and social integration theory, and also served as a reference for how transgender students coped with their transition to college and how higher education professionals could create support and strategies to assist in this process. Additionally, it assisted in outlining the transgender students' experiences by exploring how each participant utilized situation, self, support, and strategies in their transition to university life. This chapter concludes with student support strategies and institutional policies that provide student affairs and higher educational leaders with practical guidelines for working with transgender college students and help facilitate healthy transitional experiences for transgender college students.

Conceptual Framework

As students navigate their gender identity and continue "coming out" as transgender on college campuses, it is beneficial to incorporate theories to assist in framing the stories and experiences of these students. This emerging conceptual framework of utilizing multiple theories to understand lived experiences can help those working with transgender college students develop a greater understanding of their experiences in academe, particularly as they relate to overcoming barriers. This conceptual framework, composed of transition theory, minority stress theory, and academic and social integration theory, examined all three theories in depth to assist in our understanding of how transgender students experience their college transition. Together, these theories provided a framework for the experiences of the transgender student participants.

Transition Theory

When students are making the transition to college, several factors can influence their success. Schlossberg (1981) defined *transition* as an event or a nonevent that can result in a change regarding roles, relationships, and/or a routine (Anderson et al., 2012). Schlossberg's (1981) transition theory focuses on the four S's: situation, self, support, and strategies. Situation focuses on who or what caused the transition and whether the transition is within the control of the person experiencing it. Self focuses on the characteristics of the person in transition, for example, socioeconomic status, gender, and sexual orientation. Support refers to how individuals obtain assistance as they navigate periods of transition. Strategies are the skills and coping mechanisms the individual develops to assist in transition (Anderson et al., 2012). In the study reported in this chapter, the authors used transition theory as a foundation from which to view transgender college students and ascertained how study participants utilized and created strategies to assist them in their college transition and integration processes.

Minority Stress Theory

Meyer (2003) originally proposed ideas regarding minority stress as it pertained to lesbian, gay, and bisexual individuals. As an alternative framework, the contributors of this chapter applied minority stress theory (Meyer, 2003) as an element of studying transgender college students, as it assisted in identifying stressors experienced by the participants within their campus communities. Minority stress occurs when stigmatized and marginalized populations, like LGBT populations, experience high levels of stress (Meyer, 2003). Stress can be divided into distal stressors (external factors, e.g., discrimination or prejudice) and proximal stressors (internal factors, e.g., self-concept) (Meyer, 2003), and Meyer focused on distal and proximal stressors in the marginalized LGBT population. Breslow et al. (2015) adapted this theory specifically for transgender individuals. Transgender individuals can be exposed to harassment and discrimination (distal stressors), and those experiences can negatively impact their self-concept (a proximal stressor) (Breslow et al., 2015). Antitransgender discrimination can lead to psychological distress among transgender individuals (Breslow et al., 2015). Similarly, many transgender individuals experience minority stress, which is socially based, and the individuals experiencing it have no control over it (Meyer, 2003).

Minority stress theory was beneficial in studying transgender college students as it assisted in identifying stressors experienced by the participants within their campus communities. When transgender students experience distal and proximal stressors, it has the potential to affect their college transition and integration into campus life. Meyer (2003) also pointed out that individuals can experience unique additional stress by being a part of a sexual minority population. When people who are within a minority population continue to have experiences that reinforce their minority status, it can spark initial stress and can lead to further psychological distress (Meyer, 2003).

Academic and Social Integration Theory
Several factors can affect a student's integration into campus life. Additionally, according to Tinto (1975) academic and social integration can influence a student's persistence. Academic integration involves structural dimensions (the standards of the institution) and normative dimensions (a student's identification within the academic system). Social integration involves how the student and the social system, both college level and subcultures of the institution, are congruent (Tinto, 1975). Tinto's interactionalist theory states that a student's initial commitment to their institution will affect their degree of academic and social integration and that their initial commitment is influenced by the student's characteristics. Once past the initial commitment, the greater the student's level of academic and social integration, the greater their continued commitment to the university (Tinto, 1975). For transgender students particularly, looking at characteristics they had at entry into their institution can assist in understanding how their initial experiences affected their integration into campus life.

Braxton et al. (2004) added that the commitment of the institution to student welfare, communal potential, institutional integrity, proactive social adjustment, psychosocial adjustment, and ability to pay are all factors that affect a student's social integration. For transgender students, academic and social integration may be affected by whether or not they see themselves represented in the university's social and academic systems. This representation can be seen in policy, opportunities for engagement, and recognition by institutions.

Transition theory, minority stress theory, and academic and social integration theory assisted in framing the stories and experiences of transgender students. Transition theory guided stories of students in transition, and the systems of support and strategies set in motion the ability to help students with their college transition. Minority stress theory aided in identifying distal and proximal stressors that influenced a participants' experience and affected how well they were able to academically and socially integrate into their institutions.

Research Design and Methods

This study was qualitative with a narrative research focus. Qualitative research allows researchers to understand the experiences of individuals and how people construct and interpret their worlds (Merriam, 2009). Narrative research tells individuals' stories, explores the life of an individual, involves the researcher through observations and interviews, and allows the researcher to interpret the meaning of the stories the subject tells (Creswell, 2013). Stories are a way for us to make meaning of the human experience (Merriam, 2009). In this study, the narrative approach allowed transgender participants to make meaning of their college transition process and their academic and social integration, and it also gave a voice to their stories. Sharing personal stories is key in narrative research (Holstein & Gubrium, 2012). Utilizing various techniques to allow participants to share their stories assists the researcher in understanding the narratives of how participants construct their experiences (Keats, 2009).

Participants

Participants for this research study identified as transgender, gender non-conforming, or gender queer, and they currently or had previously attended a 4-year college or university in the southern United States. Based on the limited access to the transgender student population, some participants were recruited through snowball sampling (i.e., participants identified additional participants who might meet the criteria for the study [Merriam, 2009]). Following are the participant's profiles for the study.

Ayla

Ayla was a 25-year-old junior in college. She was a first-semester transfer student who recently transferred from a local 2-year community college to a 4-year public institution in the South. Ayla lived off campus and was a commuter student. She identified as a transgender woman and used female pronouns (she/her/hers). She was Native American and Hispanic. The intersection of these identities created an interesting dilemma for Ayla. Her Native American culture was open to and accepting of transgender individuals, while her Hispanic identity was situated in a culture where masculinity and femininity are defined so clearly that even words are either masculine or feminine. She identified her sexual orientation as asexual. At the time of data collection, though Ayla identified as a transgender woman, she was not out to her entire family. She was out to her grandfather but only regarding her asexual identity. She was also only out to close friends, many of whom were part of her online community. Though she encountered challenges along her academic journey, she was persistent in her endeavors. She was smart and funny and genuinely wanted to connect with people.

Andrew

Andrew was a 19-year-old traditional first-year student. Andrew identified as a transgender man and used male pronouns (he/him/his). Andrew was White and identified as gay. He attended a 4-year private institution in the South. Andrew was from another southern state and lived on campus at his institution in a single room. Andrew studied music. He was out to his family and close friends. Andrew was quiet at times and often pensive before responding to questions. He wanted to talk about his identity with others but was not always sure how to navigate those conversations. Andrew was funny and honest. He shared his experiences pertaining to his first year of college and coming out to peers and his family with a fair and thoughtful voice. Andrew was able to see from others' perspectives even when that meant challenging moments for himself.

Danielle

Danielle was a 21-year-old transgender woman who also identified as pansexual. She was in her fourth year of her undergraduate experience at the time of data collection; however, it was her first year out as a transgender woman. Danielle came out during the fall semester. She attended a 4-year, public institution in the South and was majoring in political science. Danielle was White and mixed race. She had lived on campus since beginning college. She was knowledgeable about the world around her and was perhaps the most socially engaged on her campus of all the participants. Her engagement helped her to navigate her coming out process as a transgender woman. Danielle thought critically about her surroundings and the information presented to her.

Griffin

Griffin was an 18-year-old traditional first-year student at a 4-year public institution in the South. Griffin identified as gender fluid at the initial participant/researcher meeting, using gender neutral pronouns such as they and them. However, at our first interview, Griffin shared that he now identified as a man and used male pronouns (he/him/his). Griffin identified his sexual orientation as pan/demisexual. He was an art major and lived on campus. Griffin was kind and thoughtful. He was forthcoming with divulging experiences, stories, interactions, thoughts, and feelings. His honesty and vulnerability allowed him to express himself both openly and authentically. Griffin was a gifted individual who spoke openly about his challenges in presenting as male. His gender identity development had been fluid throughout high school and into his first year of college.

Discussion of Findings

Findings outlined in this chapter connected closely with the theories previously mentioned.

Transition Theory

Participant findings divided into the four S's are outlined in the following sections.

Situation

Situation focuses on who or what caused the transition and whether the transition is within the control of the person experiencing it (Anderson et al., 2012). When students start college they encounter a variety of changes, from people to academic settings to housing accommodations (Pittman & Richmond, 2008). In this study, the situation causing transition and changes to the environment was different for each participant. For Ayla, Andrew, and Griffin, the transition was experienced through the lens of being a transgender student at a new institution. Andrew and Griffin were traditional first-year students navigating their transgender identities as they also explored their new environments as first-year college students. Ayla was a first-year student at her institution as well; however, she was a first-year transfer student, meaning it was her first year and first semester at a new institution but not her first time in a college setting. Though a little bit older than a traditional first-year college student, she still found herself in a new setting with new systems and policies to navigate. Experiencing life at a 4-year institution was also new for Ayla, as she had transferred from a 2-year institution. Danielle was not a first-year student; however, it was her first semester being out as a transgender woman. While Danielle had previous experiences at her institution and the benefit of institutional knowledge, she found herself with new opportunities, challenges, and experiences centered on her transgender identity.

Self

Self focuses on the characteristics of the person in transition (Anderson et al., 2012). Each participant had their own unique characteristics and experiences that assisted them as they journeyed through their first semesters of college as transgender individuals. For example, Ayla, who was both Native American and Hispanic, relied on her strength in storytelling. Leaning on her Native American heritage and her skills in creative writing, she was able to shape her story as she transitioned to a new institution. Danielle had been at her institution for 3 years before coming out. As an involved student, she had developed as a student leader, and this position arguably served her well as she began navigating a new chapter in her college career. Griffin relied on previous experiences of being out as a transgender individual in high school to assist navigating college transition.

Support

Support refers to how individuals obtain assistance as they navigate periods of transition. Notions of support often refer to family members, friends, relationships, and other networks or communities that help with the transition process (Anderson et al., 2012). Danielle had already been at her institution for 3 years; therefore, she had created several systems of support for herself through her involvement in organizations and campus employment. When Danielle came out as a transgender woman, even though she was met with a mixture of responses, it was, for the most part, a positive experience. She had peers and staff on campus who were supportive, and she noted that her supervisor had been especially supportive throughout this process. For Griffin and Andrew, this piece of their transition was a bit more difficult at first because they were new to their respective institutions. Andrew had not yet cultivated systems of support at his institution. However, Griffin was able to connect to support networks through his involvement in a presemester college transition program for first-year students. Griffin also felt that public university was a place where he could make friends. Andrew was new to both his campus and the community surrounding the institution.

Ayla was cautious when sharing her identities. When she shared her asexual identity with family she was met with resistance, with the exception of her grandfather. Ayla tried reaching out to classmates, but she stated that she had not found support outside of her participation in an LGBTQ organization. Andrew also noted an overwhelming lack of support from his family at first and admitted that his mother was handling his identity better than his father. Participants also relied on support from online communities and forums. Ayla was quite active in Second Life while Andrew relied on online support systems for advice on what to do at his new institution. Online communities were positive resources for Griffin and Ayla as well.

Strategies

Strategies are the skills and coping mechanisms the individuals develop to assist in times of transition (Anderson et al., 2012). Several participants emailed their professors before the semester started. Andrew was able to reach out to professors via email before classes began to introduce himself and share his preferred name and pronouns. For Danielle, coming out in the middle of the semester as a transgender woman meant that she had to contact professors well into the academic year. Danielle intentionally came out on a Friday afternoon on social media, allowing herself and others the weekend to process the information. In the following semester, Danielle contacted professors ahead of time and was met with acceptance. She also added that she only came out to one person the previous year, and that was another transgender person. Andrew was not quite sure how to share his identity with others, so his strategy was to casually bring it up in conversation with others.

Minority Stress Theory

Recall that minority stress occurs when minority populations experience high levels of stress related to stigmatization or marginalization based on their minority identity (Meyer, 2003). Mounts et al. (2006) found that first-year students who had developed friendships or felt they had support had lower levels of anxiety and depression. This suggests that having support systems (transition theory) leads to lower levels of proximal stress (minority stress theory) experienced by transgender students, an important connection.

Participants' distal stressors varied from not being able to use their preferred name on college applications; to being misgendered by peers, faculty, and staff; to overhearing other students talk disparagingly about marginalized populations. Griffin described being misgendered as "devastating." The distal stressor of not being accepted as male affected him internally, a proximal stressor. Danielle internalized the idea of acceptance from others. Friendships can be an important factor in college student belonging (Fass & Tubman, 2002). One of Ayla's worst experiences in a classroom occurred during her first semester. Prior to the professor arriving in the classroom, students were making jokes and disparaging remarks about transgender and gay individuals. In short, distal stressors, such as hearing insults from other students, affected how participants felt internally about their identities. Those insults also affected how and to whom participants disclosed their identities, even causing fear for physical safety, as reported by Ayla. Even when peers, staff, and faculty unintentionally misgendered participants, it caused feelings ranging from devastation and demoralization to vulnerability.

Academic and Social Integration Theory

Academic and social integration can influence a student's persistence (Tinto, 1975). Students who feel like they "belong" at their institutions are more likely to experience positive adjustment (Pittman & Richmond, 2008). In addition, increased academic and social integration can contribute to students' persistence (Tinto, 1975).

Academic Integration

Each participant reported different classroom experiences related to their gender identity. Although the participants who disclosed their identities prior to the start of the semester received no pushback from professors, there were instances where they felt excluded in the classroom. Ayla was called out by a professor for wearing a safety pin, which represented that she identified as an ally for marginalized populations. The safety pin became popular during the immigration ban discussions in early 2017. Though the faculty member was not exposing Ayla as a transgender woman, it did indicate, perhaps, a lack of understanding of the challenges some marginalized populations face. Andrew shared examples of being misgendered in the classroom as well, but he also shared that some of those professors followed up after class to apologize. He also shared that after starting hormone treatment which changed his voice, his music faculty were supportive and worked with him so that he was able to persist academically as a music student. Danielle and Griffin each reported acceptance from faculty when they disclosed their identities.

Social Integration

It is an important part of the college transition process for students to engage in college life outside of the classroom (Kuh et al., 2005). Social integration started early for a couple of participants. Griffin's participation in a presemester transition program for first-year students helped him connect with other students and campus resources. He also joined an LGBTQ Facebook group that helped him to feel confident in being out on his campus. All of the participants were able to connect to LGBTQ student groups on their campuses, although involvement in other social groups varied for each participant. Danielle had been involved in a fraternity prior to being out as a transgender woman. However, noninclusive commentary from a particular member made her feel that the group was not the place for her. Overall, Andrew, Danielle, and Griffin found positive connections through social integration, while Ayla struggled to make those connections. Andrew, Danielle, and Griffin reported that living on campus contributed to their social integration experiences.

Recommendations

After data collection and analysis, ideas surfaced from participant experiences which could serve as a basis for creating more inclusive and accepting places and spaces on college campuses. Recommendations for student affairs and educational leaders are inclusion of gender identity, preferred names, and preferred pronouns on college applications; exploration of institutional online platforms as a resource for transgender students; and increased campus awareness and trainings for faculty, staff, and administrators regarding transgender populations.

College Applications and Class Rosters

The first recommendation for inclusion comes early in a college student's experience: the application. One of the biggest challenges institutions are facing is how to be more inclusive to transgender populations (Tilsley, 2010). Asking for gender identity during the application process has the potential to lessen the number of times a student has to self-disclose that piece of their identity each semester. Furthermore, this information could be used to inform institutional decisions and assist institutions in best understanding the needs of transgender students. Beemyn et al. (2014) suggested guidelines for documenting a student's gender identity through the entire college experience. Following are some examples of suggested guidelines:

- Change software to enable students to use a name other than their legal first name on campus records, including course and grade rosters, directory listings, unofficial transcripts, advisee lists, and other documents.
- Where not specifically prevented by law, allow students to use a name other than their legal first name on campus ID cards and diplomas.
- Enable students to change the gender marker on their campus records upon their request (i.e., without a letter from a therapist or doctor and without the need to change other documents).
- Change software to enable students to indicate the pronouns they use for themselves that would appear on course and grade rosters and advisor lists. Suggested options: she, he, ze, and they.

- Have an easily accessible web page that details the policies and procedures related to changing names and gender markers and indicating pronouns on campus records.
- Enable students to self-identify their gender on forms. (p. 3)

With the addition of Beemyn et al.'s (2014) suggested practices, institutions have the opportunity to obtain the number of transgender students on college campuses (or at least those who choose to self-identify). This information can be used to inform institutional decisions, policies, and practices pertaining to transgender populations, such as housing policies and health services.

The University of Vermont developed a method in which students were able to disclose pronouns and preferred names that appeared on class rosters (Tilsley, 2010). Inclusion of such information also sends the message that institutions recognize transgender students and are working to maintain and improve inclusive practices.

Online Forums

The second method is to utilize online spaces for student inclusion. Online forums, online groups, and online spaces like Second Life provide space for participants to share their identities, connect to others, and feel safe while doing so. Kasch (2013) conducted a qualitative study of 35 undergraduate students, exploring their presentation on the social media platform Facebook. He discovered that those students had what he called a "curated self" (p. 90), which was a digital version of themselves separate from their physical self. If transgender students are already using online forums to share a version of themselves and find resources, then creating online forums moderated by the student's institution allows the students direct access to institutional resources and people.

In addition, the participants in this study discussed that they would like to have opportunities to talk about their identities. Often though, they are not quite sure how to engage in those conversations, and they do not always feel safe in those conversations. Higher education professionals must rethink how to use online platforms to engage transgender students to continue to learn about themselves but also learn about their new college community (Nicolazzo, 2016). Online forums have the potential to help transgender students and higher education professionals to start and continue those conversations.

Increased Awareness

Participants also discussed the need for cross-campus awareness and support. Each participant could identify persons at an individual level who

assisted them in their college transition and were supportive as they journeyed through their first semesters as out transgender students. However,
there was still a need for support from the administration. More often than
not, institutions do not act unless a student speaks out (Tilsley, 2010). This
is called *reactionary support*. In contrast, there is a need for institution-wide
proactive support of transgender students. Institutions can show commitment to transgender populations and an increased awareness to the campus
community by creating support groups specifically for transgender students
(Seelman, 2014).

Support, in this context, means that the university administration needs
to recognize how binary gender norms can make it difficult for transgender
students as they integrate into campus life (Beemyn et al., 2005). Support
and awareness can be shown in a variety of ways, such as clearly including
gender identity in antidiscrimination and harassment statements and creating
more inclusive physical spaces. If institutions are unable to create transgender
specific support groups or more inclusive physical spaces, there are additional ways in which they can create awareness and support. Institutions can
also implement trainings, campus conversations, and workshops that address
transgender populations and their needs (Seelman, 2014). However, when
institutions offer programs such as orientations and workshops, there is often
a lack of information specific to transgender populations (Seelman, 2014).
Showing transgender students engaged in all aspects of campus life can highlight opportunities available to transgender students. Illustrating transgender
student engagement and opportunities on websites allows other transgender
students to see someone who is representative of a population to which they
belong.

Recommendations for Higher Education Leaders

Following are recommendations based on the collected data from student
interviews.

1. Include transgender college students as active change agents on campus
   to ensure inclusivity. Institutions need to incorporate policies that specifically include transgender students as part of the process in creating
   more awareness and inclusion on campus. Nicolazzo (2016) discussed a
   "trickle up approach" (p. 138), to diversity and inclusion, drawing from
   Spade's (2015) research, recognizing that marginalized populations are
   often left out of the conversation or are not included if they are not visible on their campuses. When institutions do use transgender inclusive

policies, transgender students want to be part of the policymaking and see what accountability looks like for individuals who trespass such policies (Seelman, 2014).

2. Create inclusive physical and virtual spaces for transgender college students. Institutions who claim to be inclusive spaces that recognize diversity can do more than simply say so. Institutions can validate transgender students' experiences by enacting policies that have clear statements regarding transgender students, showing students like them as participants in advertising materials and websites, and promoting that they are as much a part of the campus community as their cisgender counterparts. Taking it one step further, Spade (2011) argued that such policies do not always bring transgender people the outcome they need; instead, what is needed is a continual process where everything's effectiveness is always questioned.

Conclusion

Having a voice and being included in all spaces are important factors for transgender college students who are attempting to break through institutional barriers. Renn and Patton (2011) stated that environments influence people and can be key for student learning and student development. Institutions of higher education must recognize the ever-growing presence of transgender students on their campuses. Moreover, institutions have the ability and responsibility to create policies, spaces, and opportunities that allow transgender college students to have a supportive academic and social integration process. There is much still to be discovered about transgender college students and how their perceptions of gender identity affect their integration into college life. Participants in this study were part of a growing community that seeks to continue the conversation on how we create inclusive spaces for transgender students, how we assist them in their academic and social integration, and how institutions' actions can match their words. Beyond this book chapter, this conversation must continue, and the lived experiences of transgender students like Ayla, Andrew, Danielle, and Griffin can be a means of offering a critical perspective on how higher education institutions can incorporate transgender college student's stories into the overall campus narrative.

References

Anderson, M, Goodman, J., & Schlossberg, N. (2012). *Counseling adults in transition: Linking Schlossberg's theory with practice in a diverse world* (4th ed.). Springer.

Beemyn, B., Curtis, B., Davis, M., & Tubbs, N. (2005). Transgender issues on college campuses. In R. L. Sanlo (Ed.), *Gender, identity, and sexual orientation: Research, policy, and personal* (New Directions for Student Services, no. 111, pp. 49–60). Wiley. https://doi.org/10.1002/ss.173

Beemyn, G., Jones, A. J., Hinesley, C. H., Martin, C., Dirks, D. A., Bazarsky, B., Javier, G., & Robinson, L. (2014). *Suggested best practices for supporting trans* students*. LGBT Resource Professionals. https://lgbtcampus.memberclicks.net/assets/consortium%20suggested%20trans%20policy%20recommendations-compressed.pdf

Braxton, J., Hirschy, A., & McClendon, S. (2004). *Understanding and reducing college student departure*. Wiley.

Breslow, A. S., Brewster, M. E., Velez, B. L., Wong, S., Geiger, E., & Soderstrom, B. (2015). Resilience and collective action: Exploring buffers against minority stress for transgender individuals. *Psychology of Sexual Orientation and Gender Diversity, 2*(3), 253–265. https://doi.org/10.1037/sgd0000117

Creswell, J. W. (2013). *Qualitative inquiry and research design: Choosing among five approaches* (3rd ed.). SAGE.

Dugan, J. P., Kusel, M. L., & Simounet, D. M. (2012). Transgender college students: An exploratory study of perceptions, engagement, and educational outcomes. *Journal of College Student Development, 53*(5), 719–736. https://doi.org/10.1353/csd.2012.0067

Fass, M. E., & Tubman, J. G. (2002). The influence of parental and peer attachment on college students' academic achievement. *Psychology in the Schools, 39*, 561–573. https://doi.org/10.1002/pits.10050

Goldberg, A. E., Beemyn, G., & Smith, J. Z. (2018). What is needed, what is valued: Trans' students' perspectives on trans-inclusive policies and practices in higher education. *Journal of Educational & Psychological Consultation, 29*(1), 27–67. https://www.doi.org/10.1080/10474412.2018.1480376

Goldberg, A. E., & Kuvalanka, K. A. (2018). Navigating identity development and community belonging when "there are only two boxes to check": An exploratory study of trans nonbinary college students. *Journal of LGBT Youth, 15*, 106–131. https://doi.org/10.1080/19361653.2018.1429979

Holstein, J. A., & Gubrium, J. F. (2012). *Varieties of narrative analysis*. SAGE.

Kasch, D. M. (2013). *Social media selves: College students' curation of self and others through Facebook* [Doctoral dissertation]. University of California, Los Angeles eScholarship. https://escholarship.org/uc/item/04259791

Keats, P. A. (2009). Multiple text analysis in narrative research: Visual, written, and spoken stories of experience. *Qualitative Research, 9*(2), 181–195. https://doi.org/10.1177/1468794108099320

Kuh, G. D., Kinzie, J., Schuh, J. H., & Whitt, E. J. (2005). *Assessing conditions to enhance educational effectiveness: The inventory for student engagement and success*. Jossey-Bass.

Merriam, S. B. (2009). *Qualitative research: A guide to design and implementation*. Jossey-Bass.

Meyer, I. H. (2003). Prejudice, social stress, and mental health in lesbian, gay, and bisexual populations: Conceptual issues and research evidence. *Psychological Bulletin, 129,* 674–697. https://doi.apa.org/doiLanding?doi=10.1037%2F0033-2909.129.5.674

Mounts, N. S., Valentiner, D. P., Anderson, K. L., & Boswell, M. K. (2006). Shyness, sociability, and parental support for the college transition: Relation to adolescents' adjustment. *Journal of Youth and Adolescence, 35,* 71–80. https://doi.org/10.1007/s10964-005-9002-9

Nicolazzo, Z. (2015). *"Just go in looking good": The resilience, resistance, and kinship-building of trans* college students* (Doctoral dissertation). Miami University. http://orcid.org/0000-0002-6470-5080

Nicolazzo, Z. (2016). *Trans* in college: Transgender students' strategies for navigating campus life and the institutional politics of inclusion.* Stylus.

Pittman, L. D., & Richmond, A. (2008). University belonging, friendship quality, and psychological adjustment during the transition to college. *The Journal of Experimental Education, 76*(4), 343–362. https://doi.org/10.3200/JEXE.76.4.343-362

Rankin, S., Weber, G., Blumenfeld, W., & Frazer, S. (2010). National college climate survey. *Campus Pride.* https://www.campuspride.org/wp-content/uploads/campuspride2010lgbtreportssummary.pdf

Renn, K. A., & Patton, L. D. (2011). Campus ecology and environments. In J. H. Schuh, S. R. Jones, & S. R. Harper, *Student services: A handbook for the profession.* (5th ed., pp. 242–256). Jossey-Bass.

Schlossberg, N. K. (1981). A model for analyzing human adaptation to transition. *The Counseling Psychologist, 9*(2), 2–18. https://doi.org/10.1177/001100008100900202

Schlossberg, N. K., Waters, E. B., & Goodman, J. (1995). *Counseling adults in transition: Linking practice with theory* (2nd ed.). Springer.

Seelman, K. L. (2014). Recommendations of transgender students, staff, and faculty in the USA for improving college campuses. *Gender and Education, 26*(6), 618–635. https://doi.org/10.1080/09540253.2014.935300

Spade, D. (2011). Some very basic tips for making higher education more accessible to trans students and rethinking how we talk about gendered bodies. *Radical Teacher, 92*(1), 57–62. https://diversityandinclusion.lehigh.edu/sites/diversityandinclusion.lehigh.edu/files/center-pride/Dean_Spades_tips_for_higher_ed_regarding_trans.pdf

Spade, D. (2015). *Normal life: Administrative violence, critical trans politics, and the limitations of the law* (2nd ed.). Duke University Press.

Tilsley, A. (2010). New policies accommodate transgender students. *Chronicle of Higher Education, 56*(39), A19–A20. https://www.studentaffairs.com/CustomerContent/www/CMS/files/VCS/2016/UniversityOfDayton_corner.pptx

Tinto, V. (1975). Dropout from higher education: A theoretical synthesis of recent research. *Review of Educational Research, 45,* 89–125. https://doi.org/10.3102/00346543045001089

ALTERNATIVE FRAMEWORKS AND MODELS FOR BI- AND MULTIRACIAL AND NATIVE AMERICAN COLLEGE STUDENT POPULATIONS

14

TURNING POINTS

Imagining and Designing Place and Belonging for Native Students

Amanda R. Tachine, Taylor Notah, Brian Skeet, Sequoia Lynn Dance, and Bryan McKinley Jones Brayboy (Lumbee)

Native college students' lives,[1] time and time again, are in constant tension with federal policies and sociopolitical forces that influence a sense of belonging in society and colleges.[2] Many of the conversations surrounding Native rights are rarely mentioned in or on mainstream media. There may be some commentary, but too often the general public is unaware and uninformed of the ways that Native communities and peoples are being affected, neglected, and abused throughout the United States. "Invisibility Is the Modern Form of Racism Against Native Americans" was the headline of a *Teen Vogue* article (Nagle, 2018). This article brings to life a national research study, *Reclaiming Native Truth*, a first of its kind in investigating national public opinion about how non-Natives perceive Native peoples (First Nations Development Institute & Echo Hawk Consulting, 2018). Findings revealed that a majority of respondents believe that the Native population is declining (which is empirically false; Native populations are actually increasing) and that many do not think about Native people (further exacerbating invisibility and sense of belonging). *Reclaiming Native Truth* provides data to support what countless Native people already know to be true: Misrepresentation, perceived nonexistence, and a fractured sense of belonging to a society that was built upon Indigenous lands has a profound impact on the daily lives of Native peoples. These realities run parallel to conversations in higher education. If mentioned at all, Natives in higher education research are often relegated to a mere asterisk indicating that they are statistically "insignificant." Indigenous scholars are challenging the field to move "beyond the asterisk" by seeking ways to include Native perspectives in higher educational research thereby asserting visibility and belonging (Shotton et al., 2013).

The lack of statistical significance and sense of belonging is magnified when sociopolitical conditions have a hold on your existence. For example, in 2016 Native peoples and allies alike gathered and opposed the drilling and transport of oil near the Standing Rock Sioux Tribe's lands. Many of us watched and cried with disgust and sorrow as federal and state officers attacked our relatives and friends with dogs, pepper spray, and freezing water during the bitter cold North Dakota winter months. An outpouring of support and disillusionment showered Facebook and Twitter feeds as many Native college students across the country viewed, in real time, these actions online. Weeks passed until national media finally caught up with what was unfolding. Some refer to this experience as a "media blackout" (Kostelecky, 2020, para. 2). Several hundred Native college students from across the nation made the long journey to Cannonball, North Dakota, to help in any way possible, and countless Native college students were unable to leave college to lend support to their relatives (Zhou, 2016). The paradox of attending college weighed heavily on students' hearts and minds. On one hand, college was (and is) viewed as an opportunity to help the futures of Indigenous communities, and on the other hand, college distances oneself from the current struggles facing Indigenous communities.

Struggles over Native students' sense of belonging and simultaneous (in)visibility are also occurring on college campuses (Tachine et al., 2016). We employ Brayboy's (2004) use of (in)visibility to describe the constant interplay between visibility and invisibility, both within our control and out of our control, and the ways institutions, historical contexts, and sociopolitical structures interact with Native college students. For example, in May 2018, two Mohawk youths aged 17 and 19 drove several hours from New Mexico to Colorado State University (CSU) where they registered to be a part of a campus tour. They were both excited about the possibility of being students at CSU, but the visit was cut short.

The youths' dreams of becoming a CSU Ram were shattered when a parent within the tour called campus police, alleging that the boys were "definitely not part of the group" (para. 2), reinforcing conceptions of (in)visibility and ideologies of who belongs on campus and who does not (Keene & Tachine, 2018). In the audio, the parent described the two young men as standing out, having odd behavior, and as "creepy kids" (para. 2) who made her "feel sick" (para. 2) because of their quiet demeanor and rock band attire. After confirming the boys were preregistered to take part in the campus tour, CSU campus police deemed the boys were not threats and allowed them to return to the tour, but the damage was done. The youths missed the tour and turned around to drive the 7 hours back home. Research shows that Native college students represent 1% of college student populations nationwide and are also completing college degrees at rates significantly lower than their peers (Shotton et al., 2013). The most recent data indicates that the 6-year graduation rates of Native students is 35%, compared to 55% for the general population (NCES, 2017). It is estimated that for every 100 elementary Native students, 85 will graduate from high school, 11 will receive an associate degree, and 16 will receive a bachelor's degree, statistics which justify the enormity of increasing support for just one Native student (Salis Reyes & Shotton, 2018). These rates not only illustrate the low population of Native students on college campuses but also stress the isolation many Native students feel on a larger scale (Salis Reyes & Shotton, 2018).

When Native people are (in)visible from sociopolitical forces disrupting ideologies of belonging, how much more of an impact is felt and experienced when students are excluded from conversations as evidenced in the CSU example? With this understanding and the gap in traditional frameworks of campus racial climate, we offer a look at how Arizona State University (ASU) has engaged in ways to support Native students in times of sociopolitical challenges that are rooted in history and connection to place (land). More specifically, we explore what we learned from creating and building a magazine written for and by Native students titled *Turning Points: A Guide to Native Student Success* which reframes sense of place and belonging for Native students.

Traditional Frameworks of Campus Racial Climate and Alternative Frameworks of Place

To help contextualize our work, we look to traditional frameworks of campus racial climate (Hurtado et al., 1998). We then offer tribal critical race theory (TribalCrit) (Brayboy, 2005) and Indigenous Knowledge Systems (IKS) (Brayboy & Maughan, 2009) as alterNATIVE frameworks that intentionally engage sociohistorical/sociopolitical dynamics and connection to place/land which guided our work in creating *Turning Points: A Guide to Native Student Success*.[3]

Campus Racial Climate

Campus racial climate accounts for the interrelated dynamics of four dimensions that serve as a proxy of the institutional climate: historical, structural, psychological, and behavioral (Hurtado et al., 1998). Historical legacy of inclusion and exclusion accounts for the historical narrative of desegregation among racial/ethnic populations in enrollment, policies, and embedded norms and values of an institution. College and universities must be clear about an institution's past history and the effect that the history has had on the campus culture, with clear articulation of the ongoing plans for efforts to improve the climate. Structural diversity is the change in the enrollment of racial/ethnic students. Specifically, increasing the structural diversity of an institution will help improve the climate of the institution. Yet, increasing the enrollment of diverse students is not the only solution; other dimensions need to be accounted for, including, for example, the psychological and behavorial dimensions. The psychological dimension comprises the perceptions of group relations, racial conflict, and attitudes toward those from other racial/ethnic backgrounds. This dimension includes ensuring that clear policies and procedures are in place to confront and resolve incidents of harassment and discrimination, as well as implementing regular assessments of the campus climate for diversity for all members of the campus community. The behavioral dimension is the actual reporting of interactions and intergroup relations between and among individuals from different racial/ethnic groups. Faculty can support this dimension by engaging racial/ethnic diversity as part of course content, achievement, and opportunities in and out of the classroom. Missing from campus racial climate is the interplay between land/place, sociohistorical and sociopolitical forces, and a sense of belonging for Native students. To address these limitations, we supplement our framing of campus racial climate with TribalCrit (Brayboy, 2005) and IKS (Battiste, 2002; Brayboy & Maughan, 2009; Cajete, 1999, 2008) among Native college students.

AlterNATIVE Frameworks That Acknowledge Place and Belonging

TribalCrit was born out of the need to find a theoretical framework that honors being an Indigenous person. Brayboy (2005) outlined the theory and noted that for him, the creation of the theory was an attempt to create a custom-made theoretical idea, when he had previously been forced to create off-the-rack, patched-together theoretical ideas. He wrote of an encounter with a colleague who told him that people like him (as an Indigenous person) "told good stories" and further added that, because he told good stories, he might not be a "good theorist" (Brayboy, 2005, p. 446). Brayboy described his response to this encounter: "I was struck by the seeming disconnect between community stories and personal narratives and 'theory.'" (p. 426). He did what many Indigenous peoples do when confronted by a challenge; he called his mother. She asked him, "Baby, doesn't she know that our stories are our theories?" (Brayboy, 2005, p. 426). The articulation of stories as somehow separate from theory is profoundly troubling for Indigenous peoples. It is through stories that knowledge is passed down, a sense of goodness and of right or wrong is conveyed, and life lessons are established. Brayboy (2005) asserted, "Stories serve as a basis for how our communities work" (p. 427). We extend this by affirming that positioning theory as absent from stories is problematic, illustrating the value of stories and story sharing in our work with *Turning Points*.

TribalCrit offers nine tenets that highlight the liminal status of Indigenous peoples as both political and racialized individuals and communities and point to the centrality of colonization in their daily lives, arguing that the intersections between knowledge and power are multifaceted and profound. TribalCrit also recognizes that stories and tribal philosophies are an empirical approach to understanding Indigenous experiences asserting IKS. Through stories from an Indigenous worldview, individuals and communities are able to share experiences, divulge challenges, and collectively seek ways to eradicate systematic oppression (Brayboy, 2005). A TribalCrit framework foregrounds the historical, sociocultural, and structural forces of colonialism, offering a nuanced contextual explanation of forces shaping sense of belonging for Native students in higher education.

IKS are deeply and profoundly rooted in the lived experiences of peoples that have accumulated over time by generative teachings of peoples and places (land and water) (Battiste, 2002; Brayboy & Maughan, 2009; Cajete, 1999, 2008). IKS encompass epistemology (ways of knowing), ontology (ways of being), axiology (ways of valuing), and pedagogy (ways of teaching/doing). IKS are rooted in relationships, which require an acknowledgment of responsibility and reciprocity to others, beings, and place(s). IKS are also living, dynamic, multisensory, and ever evolving; they speak to the ways Indigenous peoples have survived, despite the onslaught of elimination from settler colonialism (Trask, 1993; Wolfe, 1999). Indigenous peoples are aware of the "ways that they know, come to know, and produce knowledges, because in many instances knowledge is essential for cultural survival and well-being" (Brayboy & Maughan, 2009, p. 3). Belonging is centered on an IKS paradigm, as connection (relationships) to people and places is a fundamental understanding of life and how we see and operate in the world around us. TribalCrit (Brayboy, 2005) and IKS (Battiste, 2002; Brayboy & Maughan, 2009; Cajete, 1999, 2008) serve as alterNATIVE frameworks that engage place as a way of belonging and an understanding of context (sociohistorical and sociopolitical) with visions toward self-determination (survival) and the sovereignty rights of Indigenous peoples (thriving). It is to the assertion of self-determination by students that we now turn.

Turning Points: Asserting Native Students' Sense of Place and Belonging at ASU

A few years ago, we were interested in getting a better sense of what the campus environment was like for Native students at ASU. Rather than rely on what we thought was happening, we spoke directly to students. We talked to hundreds of ASU Native college students to get a better sense of the challenges that they encountered at ASU and to acquire recommendations on what the institution can do to better support Native students' goals of receiving a college degree. From those discussions, we consistently heard that students felt isolated, invisible, lonely, marginalized in their academic programs, and unaware of the services provided for them. Simultaneously, many students were struggling with feelings of guilt, frustration, and anger over larger sociopolitical incidents that were impacting Native peoples and lands across the nation, further amplifying their sense of belonging in college. After these discussions, we asked ourselves what we could produce that the more than 3,000 Native students attending ASU could relate to and see that they are not alone. We decided to create a magazine written by and for Native students titled *Turning Points: A Native Student Guide for College*. The magazine provides content that addresses sociohistorical and political issues and connects Native students with other Native students and resources that align with tenets of TribalCrit and IKS. We offer elements of *Turning Points* which are guiding characteristics of the work that intentionally engage with belonging and place while centering the value of Indigenous lives' connection to the land and the world around us. Categories are Native visibility and belonging, affirming sense of place, Native aesthetics and design, asserting that stories matter, and giving back.

Native Visibility and Belonging

Society's depiction of Natives through media is largely outdated; grossly misrepresentative; negative; and can be credited to the stereotypical imagery and narratives depicted through film, television, and popular culture (Fryberg et al., 2008). Social commentary on Indigenous issues such as disparaging sports mascot imagery or team names, derogatory slurs, water/land/human rights, and social injustices often tells Native Americans to "get over it" and that what happened "was a long time ago." These issues directly impact Native students and how their non-Native peers may view them in the college setting. We understand these larger damaging perspectives and therefore worked with student writers to curate stories that share some of these challenges while providing strategies in navigating through them. As an example, an article titled "We're Still Here: Invisibility," by Diné students Megan Tom and Lejend Yazzie

(2018) covered the authors' personal experiences with the harmful notion that Natives are a thing of the past. Yazzie recalled a professor in her freshman year who discounted Natives from the classroom discourse about social and political issues by saying, "It was a long time ago" (p. 9). When Tom tabled at a campus event on behalf of a Native student organization, non-Native ASU students approached the table saying, "I thought you were all gone" (Tom & Yazzie, 2018, p. 9). Tom wrote, "My stomach dropped. Shaken, I replied, 'We're still here'" (Tom & Yazzie, 2018, p. 9). By sharing their personal narratives with others, Tom and Yazzie not only gave voice to this issue but also shared healthy resources and campus connections such as counseling centers, the American Indian Student Support Services, and Native student organizations to essentially help build cultural survival and attention to students' well-being, which are aspects of IKS (Brayboy & Maughan, 2009). One of the important drivers of *Turning Points* is that it both names issues and challenges and highlights resources to address these challenges.

Scholars, journalists, advocates, poets, filmmakers, and now Native college students themselves are reframing the narrative of Indigenous peoples. *Turning Points* strives to be aware of Native college student experiences and in turn create meaningful content with the intention to reframe narratives by reinforcing belonging in higher education. The magazine serves as a platform to tell Native college students that while their journeys will be fraught with barriers, they are not alone, because within each Indigenous student are teachings of resilience, persistence, and empowerment, seeds planted by ancestors affirming experiential knowledge (Battiste, 2002). This magazine strives to remind students of these teachings through visibility and stories rooted in a sense of belonging (Tachine et al., 2016).

Affirming Sense of Place

The state of Arizona is home to 22 of the 573 federally recognized Tribal Nations in the United States. ASU is located on the homelands of the Akimel O'otham and Pee Posh peoples, an acknowledgment cited by university President Michael Crow.[4] In the first issue of *Turning Points* published in fall 2017, we intentionally began with President Crow's statement:

> We must further enhance our capacity to leverage place, transform society, conduct use-inspired research, enable student success, work across disciplines, integrate Indigenous knowledge, and engage Indigenous issues globally. We are committed to providing access, retaining and graduating American Indian students in a climate that is welcoming and respectful of their languages and cultures. Foundational to these goals, we commit to

creating an environment of success and possibility for American Indian students at ASU. (Crow, 2017, p. 4)

We wanted students to know that the president of the university is acknowledging IKS and place at ASU, which affirms "concepts of culture, knowledge, and power" for Indigenous students (Brayboy, 2005, p. 437).

In addition to fostering belonging for Native college students at ASU, within the first issue was a campus-wide map created by the magazine's graphic designer Ravenna Curley (Diné) that highlights key locations and resources for Native students. For example, the American Indian Student Support Services and Native academic programs were highlighted, which is a simple yet powerful way to show Native students that these areas exist and are available. In the map, we explicitly stated that ASU resides on the land of the Akimel O'otham and Pee Posh peoples, as a reminder to Native students that they belong on campus because the land upon which ASU was built belonged to ancestral relatives of Indigenous peoples. Creating a map through an Indigenous lens benefits the Indigenous student body as it reinforces that Indigenous knowledge is inherently tied to land and place and that generative knowledges have been shared across time and space (Battiste, 2002).

Native Aesthetics and Design

When we were developing the magazine, we wanted to grab readers' attention and try to avoid reinforcing stereotypical imagery. Our team went through many iterations to try to represent the Native student body at ASU while staying within the bounds of the ASU brand. For the cover, we initially tried to create a collage of different Native students in the shape of a pitchfork (an ASU symbol) to represent the multiplicity of Native student faces at ASU. We wanted to place faces of Native students at ASU on the front of the magazine to address students' comments of feeling alone and isolated. However, we ran into problems with this idea and discovered challenges with ASU's library of stock photos. ASU offered us the use of photos in their stock library, a collection of photos that can be used university wide for ASU purposes. However, after reviewing thousands of pictures in the stock library, we found only a small number of photographs of Native students and faculty or events surrounding the ASU Native community. Moreover, we had a difficult time acquiring high-quality photos from Native students. We had to come up with something impactful and quick. With the deadline approaching, we found a photo via social media of an ASU Navajo student wearing a graduation cap that had been enhanced with a Navajo textile design made from glue and matches. She had her right hand up, glistening with turquoise jewelry, and her fingers formed into a pitchfork. The image was taken on Navajo land as mesas and vegetation of that place are evident. We knew immediately that this image conjured the impact we had hoped for. We contacted the student and received permission (and bought the rights) to use the photo. She was honored to be featured in our inaugural magazine (Figure 14.1), and we recognized that we were honored by her and her story. Taylor Notah wrote the story as an article published in the fall 2017 edition titled "Grounded to Home." Having a photo that valued contextual knowledge (Navajo textile mortarboard, jewelry, and localized in Navajo land) was part of Indigenous knowledges (Brayboy & Maughan, 2009).

Figure 14.1. The inaugural edition of *Turning Points.*

Note. Reprinted with permission.

The magazine highlights the vibrancy, beauty, and humor robustly found within Tribal nations and communities. *Turning Points* is housed on ASU's Tempe campus, on Akimel O'otham and Pee Posh homelands, and strives to share stories with Native college students that address all Tribal Nations and purposefully showcase imagery of the beautiful, diverse cultures and traditions of the student body and the homelands that they come from. *Turning Points* also provides students with stories and images that remind and circle back to home, which is "a circular worldview that connects everything and everyone in the world to everything and everyone" (Brayboy & Maughan, 2009, p. 13). This is incredibly important as home-going has been found to be a powerful strategy for Native students, affirming that home is a source of strength (Waterman, 2012). Overall, the aesthetics of the magazine were inspired by patterns and shapes that are familiar to Native experiences, such as those found in blankets, rugs, sand paintings, ceramics, landscapes, and other visual and textual designs.

Throughout the development of the aesthetic and design of the magazine, we sought feedback and guidance from Native students and colleagues. For example, at the onset of the initial magazine, we turned to Native students to help make a decision on the concept of *Turning Points*'s masthead. Their involvement was succesful, and they gave insightful critique as well as enthusiasm that energized the look and feel of the magazine. We also sought guidance and feedback from Native student center staff, the Center for Indian Education's staff and mentors, ASU's marketing team, and key people at ASU's Walter Cronkite School of Journalism and Mass Communication. Having a community to offer critique and expertise was invaluable. We recognized that this work would not be possible without a web of relationships that shares knowledges and responsibilities among itself (Battiste, 2002).

Asserting That Stories Matter

All of the stories in the magazine were written by Native college students at ASU; they were written for their student peers, although we realize that they may resonate with Native students at other institutions. Some students shared vulnerable stories, which makes *Turning Points* a unique college publication, as too often college conversations do not include the rich contexts and experiences of Native college students. As a team, *Turning Points* staff discusses potential story ideas based on their own experiences and being attuned to what is occurring among ASU's Native student population and Indian Country as a whole, reaffirming the value of experiential knowledge (Brayboy, 2005). For example, in the second edition of *Turning Points* released in the spring 2018 semester, we asked students to share difficulties they were dealing with and offer ways they were working through those hardships. A Diné juris doctor candidate wrote "Burnout: A Story of Reflection, Rest and Prayer" (Tso, 2018). *Turning Points* readers learned about the stressful phenomenon of burnout and how the author combatted external stresses in a highly competitive college environment with the aid of her traditional Navajo teachings. She urged readers to view her story "as a form of restoration and not loss" (Tso, 2018, p. 10) and to ensure that while students are pursuing a degree for their families and community they must not forget their personal reasons and should regularly take moments to reflect, pray, and rest. Stories are viewed as a legitimate source of being and knowing as components of TribalCrit (Brayboy, 2005) and Indigenous knowledges (Battiste, 2002; Brayboy & Maughan, 2009; Cajete, 1999, 2008).

By providing content that is specifically geared for students to succeed, the magazine is asserting that all stories matter—even those stories that are often not spoken about—and positioning those stories as theory and practice (Brayboy, 2005), *Turning Points* is also asserting the epistemological, ontological, axiological, and pedagogical strengths that reside in Native peoples. When working with students on these types of stories, we carefully and respectfully deliberate with the writers on what is appropriate to share. This magazine is not meant to get a hot story but crafted with the storyteller in mind, ensuring the safety of the writer. For example, another Diné graduate student contributed to the magazine's second issue where she addressed traumatic past experiences and how two blessings came her way: motherhood and art. Her deeply personal narrative, titled "Art Is Medicine," showcased the expression of art as a pathway for her ultimate self-care and well-being and also highlighted the local Phoenix community resources that students can take advantage of (Robbins, 2018, p. 12). *Turning Points* shows that the more Indigenous communities share stories, the more they are able to shed feelings of isolation and invisibility and reciprocate with an understanding that stories matter. It is the Native students themselves who are validating, affirming, and encouraging each other's endeavors in institutions that were not originally made for them but are now institutions where they see themselves and one another.

Connected to story sharing, Native writers and contributors also have input as to the best way the stories should be represented, also a way to showcase their other creative talents. With an impressive combination of photo, written text, and even artistic comics, students have shared stories in ways that are deeply meaningful. For example, in the second edition, a doctoral Isleta Pueblo student drew a comic titled "The Birth of a Native Scholar," in which she tells a story about a student wanting to conduct research that is rooted in traditional belief systems (Lucero, 2018, p. 16). The student calls her mother to seek advice and her grandmother chimes in with great wisdom including the power of generational pedagogies from elders, an example of IKS (Tachine, 2017).

Writing in the traditional Western paradigm typically involves strict boundaries around topic, voice, and representation. Students are usually writing for assignments that adhere to specific guidelines, which can limit the topics that Native students desire to share. *Turning Points* extends beyond these boundaries to tell stories that are raw, bold, and genuine. In a society where Native voices are often silenced, students are equipped with an empowering platform to share topics, issues, and experiences that matter deeply to them. With editing guidance, students remain in control of their narrative, enacting rhetorical sovereignty (Lyons, 2000), and are able to write stories that impact the Native student community at ASU.

Giving Back

By serving an underrepresented group within a college setting, the *Turning Points* team is giving back in a myriad of ways. One way is by sharing the inspirational stories of how other students are also giving back. In the second issue, one of the highlighted stories "Soul Sisters: Words of Wisdom," dives into the collegiate pursuits of five mothers and grandmothers of the Gila River Indian Community who were on the cusp of graduating with their master's degrees (Notah, 2018). Priscilla Espinoza, Edwardine Thomas, Starleen Somegustava, Marcella Hall, and Nina Allison were known as the "Soul Sisters" in the Gila River Culture and Language Teacher Cohort at ASU, a program that prepares educators to go back and work with their community. The Soul Sisters' collective goal upon graduating was to instill their Akimel O'otham language and culture back into their communities. In their story, they shared their experiences and struggles in returning to the classroom; however, the need of their community fueled their determination and higher education pursuits. They also shared advice with the *Turning Points* readership on setting goals and achieving them, keeping their community in mind, never doubting oneself, and reaffirming that Native students are not alone. Showcasing these types of stories is an example of giving back to the community that has shaped Native students' experiences and lifeways. That four of the five "Soul Sisters" are grandmothers is also important, as it shows Native peoples are always in the process of giving back.

Giving back also entails providing free publications to all 3,000 self-identified Native (undergraduate, graduate, and professional) students enrolled at ASU and to hundreds more key stakeholders. Working as a team, we considered places to send hard copies of the magazine that are beyond an ASU audience. Critically important was sending issues to Tribal and educational leaders in the state of Arizona and also across the United States. The demand for a physical copy surpassed our expectations, and we responded by putting the magazine online as well as employing social media platforms.[4] *Turning Points* has gained traction on social media and online, exemplifying the yearning for Indigenous-created content and reinforcing the powerful role of IKS's efforts in higher education.

Insights for Scholars and Researchers

Attention to the world around us is critically important, but often not taken seriously when referring to Native experiences in higher education. Hurtado et al. (1998) stated that "while research literature documents the effect of governmental policy, programs, and initiatives (particularly in financial aid), there are fewer studies of the influence of sociohistorical forces on the campus racial climate" (p. 282). Twenty years later, there is still no literature in higher education that explores sociohistorical forces on campus racial climate for Native students. That is not the purpose of this chapter, although we stress that empirical research on this phenomenon is warranted. We asked, How do sociopolitical and sociohistorical forces play into the lived experiences of students? How do these systemic conditions influence sense of belonging for students attending college? These questions come to our mind because of the development of *Turning Points*. We learned that sociopolitcal and sociohistorical forces do influence Native students' sense of belonging. Although the development of the magazine was not meant to be an empirical study, we see the value that such research would have in understanding Native students' experiences. Rather this chapter brought to light one institution's (ASU) response when Native students realized how sociohistorical and political forces were impacting their collegial experience. We offered a look at how ASU engaged to support Native students in times of sociopolitical challenges by building a magazine written for and by Native students, *Turning Points: A Guide to Native Student Success*, which reframes sense of place and belonging for Native students.

From a theoretical perspective, TribalCrit (Brayboy, 2005) and IKS (Battiste, 2002; Brayboy & Maughan, 2009; Cajete, 1999, 2008) provided a space for *Turning Points* to integrate questions about the importance of place. What does it mean when we acknowledge that the lands ASU rest upon are connected to indigeneity, Indigenous place, and belonging, and how do we give recognition to those who have come before us and who we are a part of?

Through TribalCrit and IKS, place was reframed to an understanding that there is more than one way of thinking about the world and our place in it. We believe that ASU and institutions of higher education have a responsibility to acknowledge the land it resides on and the history that it comes with. Thoretically, we see that there is room to expand upon campus racial climate and TribalCrit by including place/land and its interconnections with sociopolitical and sociohistorical conditions, while centering the effect of these influences on Native students' sense of belonging.

For practice, we encourage student affairs and administrators to take up an awareness to sociopolitical/historical conditions and their interplay with belonging for Native students. Tierney (1997) points out that "no policy can be isolated from the social arena in which it is enacted" (p. 177). We agree with Tierney's stance and suggest that our work in higher education must include being attuned to the lived experiences of Native peoples by resisting the pervasive narrative of (in)visibility. Universities can create more visibility through land acknowledgment and a meaningful relationship with Indigenous peoples and Native nations. The American Indian College Fund (2019) released a report that identified eight powerful declarations that colleges and universities should do to better support and make visible Native college students. The declarations cover the duty of colleges and universities to recognize the Native homelands on which their institutions were built and their duty to make visible, advocate for, and empower Native students' degree attainment. By practicing land acknowledgment, university administrators and staff must then understand that Indigenous existence continually experiences displacement and invalidation by non-Natives and the broader society. It is a common practice for Indigenous communities to honor guests and their hosts when visiting other nations and communities. When institutions do the same, it shows honor and gratitude and centers conversations on Indigenous peoples. We were grateful for the ability do this work at ASU, because ASU provided space to be creative in building a magazine that served Native students. Upper administrators, deans, faculty, designers, and media relations all helped in the evolution of the magazine, demonstrating to the all-Native *Turning Points* team that this work was important and valuable. As we mentioned earlier, there was a lack of Native stock photos in ASU's media library which impacted the larger branding of ASU. We directed attention to this concern, and ASU quickly responded and has effectively increased interest in capturing the lives of Native students through photos and videos. ASUNow, the university online news outlet, has more frequently added Native content to their stories. We often say that "teamwork makes the dream work" which truly captured our ideological perspectives when engaging in the development and execution of *Turning Points*. We encourage colleges to review their work, whether media or land acknowledgment practices, to see whether Indigenous perspectives are included. If not, work closely with Indigenous staff and students to address this in a meaningful way. We also point out that *Turning Points* explores beyond land acknowledgment statements in higher education institutions. What defines *Turning Points* as a viable and sustaining tool is that it continuously accumulates resources and university administrative support every semester with a focus on providing inclusion for Native students, staff, and faculty. It also takes responsibility for the care of Native students and their larger university community. Student affairs practitioners should consider how their practices are inclusive of Native perspectives and how, or whether, resources are provided to support these efforts.

For policy advocates, we pose questions that speak to land/place and sociopolitical conditions that impact Native peoples. Do institutional policies respect and support the land or waterways on which universities are located? Do institutional policies support students who are dealing with sociopolitical conditions that are impacting their world, such as excusing absences when students are dealing with trauma from settler colonial actions? When we spoke to Native students about the challenges that they were facing in college, one student described feeling "spiritually obliterated" (personal communication, March 1, 2017) upon hearing that President Trump made an executive order to allow for the Dakota Access Pipeline to continue destructing the land, waterways, and lifeways of peoples. Students and faculty are likewise feeling turmoil and stress over Mauna Kea and its threatened destruction because of the Thirty Meter Telescope project. What should institutions do to safeguard the land and waterways and create policies to support them?

When the magazine team reconvenes at the beginning of each semester, it turns to the storyboard to map out semester goals that are centered upon the words "By and for Native Students." That intention is in itself a centering of IKS. As Simpson (2017) states,

> If we want to create a different future, we need to live a different present, so that present can fully marinate, influence, and create different futurities. If we want to live in a different present, we have to center Indigeneity and allow it to change us. (p. 20)

This speaks volumes to how we engage in our work. What we do today and how we view the work we do today will influence the future.

Notes

1. Native students are a racialized and political group on college campuses, coming from specific cultural (ethnic) orientations, and frequently representing sovereign nations (Brayboy, 2005). Native should not be confused with the colloquial term of *native-born* where individuals claim being native to a particular place. Thus, we refer to Native students as a *racial/ethnic group* to highlight their marginalization along both racial and cultural spheres within predominantly White institutions (PWIs).

2. When we write of belonging here, we include the notion that students also matter. That is, they are seen by faculty, staff, and the policies that guide them as important, viable members of the community, and these individuals and policies recognize the unique needs of these students.

3. We were inspired by Ngā Pae o te Māramatanga, New Zealand's Māori Centre of Research Excellence's reference to alterNATIVE which provides an innovative forum for Indigenous scholars to set their own agendas, content, and arguments in hopes of establishing a standard of excellence in Indigenous scholarship.

4. *Turning Points* social media pages include Instagram: @ASUturningpointsmag, Facebook: @ASUturningpoints, Twitter: @ASUturningpoint, and Medium: ASU-Turning Points Magazine.

References

American Indian College Fund. (2019). *Creating visibility and healthy learning environments for Native Americans in higher education: Declaration of Native purpose in higher education: An Indigenous higher education equity initiative.* https://collegefund.org/about-us/media/publications/attachment/creating-visibility-and-healthy-learning-environments-for-natives-in-higher-education_web/

Battiste, M. (2002). *Indigenous knowledge and pedagogy in first nations education: A literature review with recommendations.* Indian and Northern Affairs Canada. https://www.afn.ca/uploads/files/education/24._2002_oct_marie_battiste_indigenousknowledgeandpedagogy_lit_review_for_min_working_group.pdf

Brayboy, B. (2004). Hiding in the ivy: American Indian students and visibility in elite educational settings. *Harvard Educational Review, 74*(2), 125–152. https://www.hepg.org/her-home/issues/harvard-educational-review-volume-74-issue-2/herarticle/american-indian-students-and-visibility-in-elite-e

Brayboy, B. (2005). Toward a Tribal Critical Race Theory in education. *The Urban Review, 37*(5), 425–446. https://doi.org/10.1007/s11256-005-0018-y

Brayboy, B., & Maughan, E. (2009). Indigenous knowledges and the story of the bean. *Harvard Educational Review, 79*(1), 1–21. https://doi.org/10.17763/haer.79.1.l0u6435086352229

Cajete, G. (1999). *Native science: Natural laws of interdependence*. Clear Light Publishers.

Cajete, G. A. (2008). Sites of strength in Indigenous research. In M. Villegas, S. R. Neugebauer, & K. R. Venegas (Eds.), *Indigenous knowledge and education: Sites of struggle, strength, and survivance* (pp. 204–207). Harvard Education Press.

Crow, M. (2017). President's letter. *Turning Points: A Guide to Native Student Success*, *1*(01), 4.

First Nations Development Institute & Echo Hawk Consulting. (2018). *Reclaiming Native truth: A project to dispel American's myths and misconceptions*. First Nations Development Institute.

Fryberg, S., Markus, H. R., Oyserman, D., & Stone, J. M. (2008). Of warrior chiefs and Indian princesses: The psychological consequences of American Indian mascots. *Basic and Applied Social Psychology*, 30, 208–281. https://doi .org/10.1080/01973530802375003

Hurtado, S., Milem, J. F., Clayton-Pedersen, A. R., & Allen, W. R. (1998). Enhancing campus climates for racial/ethnic diversity: Educational policy and practice. *Review of Higher Education*, *21*(3), 279–302. https://doi.org/10.1353/ rhe.1998.0003

Keene, A., & Tachine, A. (2018, May 7). Colorado State University tour incident is nothing new for Native students. *Teen Vogue*. https://www.teenvogue.com/story/ csu-incident-native-students-nothing-new-native-americans-in-united-states

Kostelecky, S. (2020, June 18). Sharing the mission voice: The Dakota Access Pipeline libguide. *Intersections: American Library Association*. http://www.ala .org/advocacy/diversity/odlos-blog/intersections-sharing-missing-voice-dakota-access-pipeline-libguide

Lucero, D. (2018). The birth of a Native scholar. *Turning Points: A Guide to Native Student Success*, *1*(02), 16.

Lyons, S. R. (2000). Rhetorical sovereignty: What do American Indians want from writing? *College Composition and Communication*, *51*(3), 447–468. https://www .joycerain.com/uploads/2/3/2/0/23207256/___lyons_rhetorical_sovereignty.pdf

Nagle, R. (2018, October 23). Invisibility is the modern form of racism against Native Americans. *Teen Vogue*. https://www.teenvogue.com/story/racism-against-native-americans

National Center for Education Statistics (2017). Table 104.20. Percentage of persons 25 to 29 years old with selected levels of educational attainment, by race/ethnicity and sex: Selected years, 1920 through 2017. *Digest of Education Statistics*. https:// nces/ed/gov/programs/disgest/d17/tables/dt17_104.20.asp?current=yes

Notah, T. (2017). Grounded to home. *Turning Points: A Guide to Native Student Success*, *1*(01), 26–27.

Notah, T. (2018). Soul sisters: Words of wisdom. *Turning Points: A Guide to Native Student Success*, *1*(02), 20–23.

Robbins, M. (2018). Art is medicine. *Turning Points: A Guide to Native Student Success*, *1*(02), 12–13.

Salis Reyes, N. A., & Shotton, H. J. (2018). *Bringing visibility to the needs and interests of Indigenous students: Implications for research, policy, and practice.* https://cece.sitehost.iu.edu/wordpress/wp-content/uploads/2017/02/Bringing-Visibility-to-the-Needs-and-Interests-of-Indigenous-Students-FINAL-2.pdf

Shotton, H. J., Lowe, S. C., & Waterman, S. J. (2013). *Beyond the asterisk: Understanding Native students in higher education.* Stylus.

Simpson, L. B. (2017). *As we have always done: Indigenous freedom through radical resistance.* University of Minnesota Press.

Tachine, A. R. (2017). Grandmother's pedagogy: Lessons for supporting students attending universities. In J. Frawley, S. Larkin, & J. A. Smith (Eds.), *Indigenous pathways, transitions, and participation in higher education: From policy to practice* (pp. 151–168). Springer.

Tachine, A. R., Cabrera, N. L., & Yellow Bird, E. (2016). Home away from home: Native American students' sense of belonging during their first year in college. *The Journal of Higher Education, 88*(5). http://doi.org/10.1080/00221546.2016.1257322

Tierney, W. G. (1997). The parameters of affirmative action: Equity and excellence in the academy. *Review of Educational Research, 67*(2), 165–196. https://doi.org/10.2307/1170625

Tom, M., & Yazzie, L. (2018). We are still here: Invisibility. *Turning Points: A Guide to Native Student Success, 1*(02), 8–9.

Trask, H. (1993). *From a native daughter: Colonialism and sovereignty in Hawai'i.* University of Hawai'i Press.

Tso, C. (2018). Burnout: A story of reflection, rest and prayer. *Turning Points: A Guide to Native Student Success, 1*(02), 10–11.

Waterman, S. (2012). Home-going as a strategy for success among Haudenosaunee college and university students. *Journal of Student Affairs Research and Practice, 49*(2), 193–209. https://urresearch.rochester.edu/fileDownloadForInstitutionalItem.action?itemId=27733&itemFileId=142116

Wolfe, P. (1999). *Settler colonialism.* A&C Black.

Zhou, J. (2016, September 14). Native American students protest Dakota Access Pipeline. *The Daily Evergreen.* https://dailyevergreen.com/7339/news/native-american-students-protest-dakota-access-pipeline/

15

REFLECTING ON MULTIRACIAL COLLEGE STUDENT IDENTITY THEORIES TO ADVANCE FUTURE HIGHER EDUCATION PRACTICE AND RESEARCH

Victoria K. Malaney Brown

Twenty years ago, higher education researcher Kristen A. Renn (2000) wrote in *The Review of Higher Education* that despite the increasing growth of multiracial students in the United States almost nothing is known about their college student development or racial identity experiences. Since then popular and political interest in the multiracial or "Two or More Races" (Jones & Bullock, 2012, p. 1) category has increased significantly. More specifically, data from the 2010 U.S. Census indicated that nearly nine million Americans checked more than one racial box. For the first time in U.S. decennial census history, statisticians were able to compare population figures from 2000 and 2010 (Jones & Bullock, 2012). The "face" (Root, 1992, p. 3) of the United States is transforming as racial mixing blurs the long-held ideology that preserved racial lines. The upcoming 2020 U.S. Census will provide yet another snapshot of the growing multiracial American community. In effect, the increasing numbers of multiracial families have created public recognition and affirmation of a diverse and vibrant community, whose children eventually become college students (Banks,

2003; Renn, 2004). Knaus (2006) argued that this increased awareness of multiracial people should encourage educators to question the racial categories and racial discourse in the United States. Yet, how have multiracial college students viewed their racial identity? What does the literature recommend? And what is missing from the theories to advance the future of the growing multiracial college student population?

The purpose of this chapter is to provide an overview of the historical development of multiracial identity theories written about multiracial college students while also critiquing the student affairs literature and discussing where we need to go next in supporting our diverse populations of multiracial students. The literature reviewed provides the context for how the past and current literature on multiraciality has been framed, and I argue how the theories can be used to inform practice within and outside of the American college context. First, I provide some key terms and present the historical framing of several events in U.S. history to contextualize the onset of multiracial identity theories. Second, I review three key categories of identity development theories written about multiracial individuals from different points of time (i.e., racial identity stage models, counseling theories, and higher education theories). Third, I discuss how the original critical race theory (CRT), while groundbreaking, was myopic in its development because it excluded the racialized realities of multiracial students. I further explain how Jessica C. Harris's (2016a) critical multiracial theory (MultiCrit) theory centers how multiracial student experiences are monoracialized (i.e., viewed as a single race) in higher education environments. I conclude the chapter with recommendations for practitioners and researchers that question and provoke how to push our field forward to advance the acknowledgment of the racialized experiences of multiracial collegians and also how to take action to support these students on our college campuses. Throughout this chapter, I synthesize theories and frameworks already developed for multiracial individuals and college students and I critique what is still missing from those identity theories to advance future higher education research and practice.

Key Terms

I begin by defining some key terms. *Biracial* "refers to a person whose parents are of two different socially designated racial groups, for example Black mother, White father" (Root, 1996, p. ix). *Mixed race* is defined as "people who are of two or more racial heritages. This may be the result of their parents being of different heritage from one another or from race mixing in the grandparent generation" (Root & Kelley, 2003, p. viii). Lastly, *multiracial* refers to "people who are of two or more racial heritages. It is the most inclusive term to refer to people across all racial mixes" (Root, 1996, p. xi). These key terms help provide clarity to the racial terms that the research literature uses interchangeably for the multiracial population.

A Concise Historical Context of Multiracial Identity Theories

To understand the development of past and current multiracial identity theories it is essential to remember a few significant historical events that influenced the development of theoretical research on multiracial American college students. The evidence of racial mixing in the United States is not a new concept to history. The categorizations of race or racial formation have long been contested (Omi & Winant, 1994). To understand theory, there needs to be an acknowledgment that each theory is written during a specific time and context. Since race is a social construct, the notion of race and its meaning change over time depending on the context (Chang, 2016; Omi & Winant, 1994; Shih & Sanchez, 2009).

The first historical event occurred in 1967, when the U.S. Supreme Court overturned antimiscegenation laws making interracial marriage legal. Richard and Mildred Loving's case against the state of Virginia set the foundation to permit interracial couples in the United States to marry legally in all 50 states (Evans & Ramsay, 2015). Root (1992) refers to the period after the Loving case as the "biracial baby boom" (p. 3). As attitudes toward interracial marriage shifted, so did the voice of multiracial population. In fact, by the 1990s in the United States there were

> more than 40 grassroots organizations representing the interest of this growing population of interracial couples and their offspring became the basis of a multiracial consciousness movement that lobbied for and successfully brought about changes in official racial classification (Daniel, 2003, p. 255).

As the voices of multiracial organizers and advocates lobbied against the U.S. government, more noticeable changes occurred in federal legislation, which resulted in more interracial couples having the freedom to marry and produce multiracial children (Morning, 2000, 2003; Root, 1996; Wijeyesinghe, 2001).

The second historical event occurred in 1997, when the United States Office of Management and Budget (OMB) responded to issued revisions to Directive 15, which changed the federal racial identification process to expand the number of racial categories and include the option for respondents to indicate more than one racial category on forms (White House, 1997). Modifications in U.S. Census practices, which began in 2000, coincided with Americans changing their thinking about the meaning of race (Pew Research Center, 2015; Shih & Sanchez, 2009).

However, it was the third historical event—the decision to allow Americans with two or more races to report multiple races in 2000—that was most controversial and debated. Morning (2005) recalled the fears of the Black and Hispanic community, stating that "the potential injury was twofold: first, a mixed-race exodus from the black community would constitute an insult if not outright betrayal; and second, lower head counts of blacks and Hispanics might have repercussions for their political clout" (p. 6). The fears that centered around the loss of mixed-race people from the Census numbers were focused more on the potential political and monetary impact on monoracial communities of color than allowing mixed-race people the ability to accurately classify their races. Notably, multiracial activists won the Census debate. Despite this monumental win, the OMB still required civil rights enforcement agencies to assign multiple-race respondents to single races for statistical purposes. For this reason, the government continued to deeply influence the educational system that upheld the practice of singular race classifications despite families selecting multiple races for their students. Morning (2005) discussed that the irony of the ostensible federal changes demonstrated,

> The fact that arguably the most important government users of race data—that is, the civil rights protection agencies continue to operate with single-race categories explains why so many of the dire predictions about the bureaucratic effects of multiple-race classification have proved unfounded. Its impact has been muted simply because the multiracial person does not yet truly exist for the machinery of government, which continues to use race data to implement single-race laws. (p. 8)

The powerful influence from this federal mandate continued to shape racial discourse, laws, and educational policy that presently impact multiracial students (Fernandes Williams & Namisi Chilungu, 2016; Root, 2003a). This succinct overview of the historical events that have influenced the identity development of multiracial college students provides the context needed to understand this racial population in higher education. With this in mind, universities and institutions of higher learning are "intimately involved in the production, contestation, and negotiation of racial identities" (Literte, 2010, p. 119), and it is through the development of racial identity theories that multiracial people and students have begun to voice their perspective about the messy and yet monoracial U.S. racial order. In the literature review to follow, I delineate and critique specific key theories of multiracial identity.

Three Categories of Multiracial Identity Development Theories

In the research literature, the first theories on racial identity were predominantly based on stage models that kept rigid and defined (mono)racial lines. Omi and Winant (1994) explained that most racial theory fails to centralize race in American life and politics. At the same time, it is important to remember that racial identity development models are influenced by the theorists during the time or period in which they were written. For example, Cross (1971) developed a racial identity for Black and African Americans, while Morten and Atkinson (1983) created the minority identity model (MIM), which provided a general overview of minority identity. However, the MIM was not applicable to all racial populations. Therefore, the pressure to name multiracial people arose from the multiracial organizers who quickly entered the racial identity theory discourse in the late 1990s. They were more vocal than ever in confronting the fact that racial classifications were still monoracially organized (Knaus, 2006; Root, 1992, 1996; Spickard & Daniel, 2004).

The Past: Counseling Biracial/Multiracial Identity Theories

Nearly 20 years after the first original racial identity development theories emerged (Cross, 1971; Erikson, 1968), biracial/multiracial identity development theories were published in psychology. The earliest theories of biracial identity development were advanced by theorists outside of higher education, specifically by psychologists. One of the first researchers to publish on biracial identity was W. S. Carlos Poston. Poston's (1990) developmental model, called the biracial identity model (BIM), focused on five stages of biracial identity:

1. Personal identity: The individual is young, typically a child, and recognizes their identity is becoming salient.
2. Choice of group categorization: The individual chooses usually one racial identity.
3. Enmeshment/denial: The individual feels confused or guilty about being in more than one racial group.
4. Appreciation: The individual begins to broaden their appreciation of their multiple racial identities.

5. Integration: The individual experiences wholeness and values all of their racial identities.

Although Poston's model was not developed for higher education it was influenced by Cross (1971) who developed the nigrescence model. When applying BIM to higher education, depending on the student's upbringing and understanding of their racial identity they could enter college being confused about their multiple racial groups. However, if the student received support in college through the student affairs staff or faculty members who acknowledged biracial students, the theory suggested that students could move toward acceptance and even to a full integration of valuing all of their biracial identity. Poston's original theory paved the way for additional biracial identity theories to develop.

George Kich's (1992) heuristic biracial identity model is called stages of biracial and bicultural identity development, and it was developed for multiracial people with Asian and European ancestry. Although Poston (1990) discussed five stages of identity development, Kich's model only had three stages. For both counseling psychologists, these racial identity theories suggested that the full achievement of identity development was positive self-acceptance of their biracial identity. Additionally, Kich included an added component called bicultural identity development in the third stage of his model. Kich's model comprised the following three stages:

1. An individual has initial awareness of difference and dissonance (age 3 through 10).
2. An individual undergoes struggle for acceptance from others (age 8 through late adolescence and young adulthood).
3. An individual achieves and assertion of a biracial and bicultural identity (late adolescence through adulthood.

Kich's theory was valuable to review as multiracial college students could possibly be between stage two and stage three upon entering college (Kich, 1992; Wilson, 1999). Together these identity theories created some understanding of biracial identity development, but they still did not address all multiracial individuals, much less all college students (Renn, 2000; Wijeyesinghe, 2001).

As these racial identity theories emerged so did the development of multicultural and cross-cultural counseling. The goals of multicultural and cross-cultural counseling were "to assist clients in developing their ability to use resources to effectively combat the debilitating effects of negative environmental forces" (Herring, 1995, p. 2). Psychologist Maria P. P. Root is one of the most important theorists to come from multicultural counseling, and her groundbreaking research deeply influenced the literature in multiracial identity development. Root (1992) was one of the first to suggest that "the multiracial person's understanding of her- or himself can enhance society's understanding of intra-and intergroup relations, identity, and resilience" (p. 10). Root (1996) shifted the deficit approach that commonly stated that multiracial people are fractured or fragmented. To assist in understanding the ongoing development of different theories for biracial and multiracial students, it is crucial to understand the development of theory that has shifted from a static racial identity development to theories that have begun to recognize the fluidity of a person's multiracial identity.

Multiracial Identity: A Complex and Fluid Life Spectrum

In the literature, bi/multiracial identity development is cited as more complex and can be an "undefined process" (Herring, 1995, p. 3; see also Renn, 2004). Overall, analyses of mixed race identity have revealed that "multiracial individuals may take a variety of identity paths, including occupying multiple racial identities simultaneously, engaging in situational identities, adopting a monoracial identity, asserting a multiracial identity" (Literte, 2010, p. 119), and refusing the categorization of race. The fluidity of racial identity for this racial population demonstrated a change from the former rigid linear identity development models (Cross, 1971; Erikson, 1968) to multiracial identities that have evolved and become more fluid over time. To illustrate this point, Root's (1996) theory has four parts that described how multiracial individuals negotiated their multiple identities. She defined the term *border crossings* as "the straddling of two worlds in a one-foot-in, one-foot-out metaphor that fractionalizes a multiracial person's existence" (Root, 1996, p. xxi). Root used this imagery to break down the following four developmental racial identity stages:

1. Accept the identity assigned by society.
2. Choose a monoracial identity.
3. Choose a mixed-race identity.
4. Create a new racial identity.

While Root's theory was not specifically developed for college students, the theory can be applied to understand the different racial identity paths that multiracial individuals can experience. Some multiracial students may be more comfortable choosing a monoracial identity to stay within society's defined monoracial frame (Korgen, 2016). Other multiracial students may create a new racial identity while in college or even opt to accept the identity that society assigns them.

In 2001, Charmaine L. Wijeyesinghe, another theorist, rejected the idea of allowing society to assign a race on a multiracial individual and created the theory factor model of multiracial identity (FMMI) as an alternative. The FMMI "assumes that there is no right or more appropriate choice of racial identity for each multiracial individual, as opposed to being assigned by other people or by society" (Wijeyesinghe, 2001, p. 131). This assumption provided a clear statement on this theory that addressed the external factors of identity in ways that were not envisioned before. The FMMI was created from a qualitative dissertation study of African American and European American multiracial adults. The model had the following eight factors which affected the racial choice of multiracial people:

1. Racial ancestry
2. Early experiences and socialization
3. Cultural attachment
4. Physical appearance
5. Social and historical context
6. Political awareness and orientation
7. Other social identities
8. Spirituality

These eight factors allowed for the multiracial individual to exist beyond their racial identity and instead considered a wide range of life experiences over a span of time or spectrum. At the center of the model is the "choice of racial identity" (Wijeyesinghe, 2001, p. 137). The benefits of the FMMI provided the multiracial person the freedom to change and choose their racial identity as they moved through life. While the FMMI theory was not developed using college students, it could help students understand that there are choices in racial identity and there is no right or wrong way to move along in racial identity development (Knaus, 2006).

Another significant model by Wijeyesinghe called the intersectional model of multiracial identity (IMMI) was developed in 2012, and it included a new concept which added intersectionality. Similar to the FMMI model, the IMMI placed more emphasis on the choice of racial identity based on time, and it considered the salience of other factors such as age, gender, class, and faith traditions for multiracial identity (Wijeyesinghe, 2012). The IMMI is more pertinent to the college context as Wijeyesinghe (2012) gave an example of a multiracial young woman with Black and White ancestry who identified as Black prior to college because of her physical appearance and socialization and because she grew up in the South. During college in California, the student became active in a campus group for multiracial students which gave her the confidence to shift her previously monoracial identity to a multiracial one. In higher education practice, the IMMI's ability to allow multiracial students to choose their racial identity based on intersecting social identities was promising. The IMMI emphasized the effect of time spent in college, which furthered the understanding that students can have a fluid multiracial identity that can and will be altered over time. While the earliest multiracial theories gave voice to multiracial individuals, the more contemporary and recent theories finally acknowledged that multiracial people have been here for centuries in the United States (Wijeyesinghe, 2001, 2012). However, it was not until the early 2000s that multiracial college student experiences began to be explored explicitly both in student affairs research and college student development theories.

The Present: Multiracial College Student Identity Theories

Contemporary racial identity theories about the multiracial student population emerged in mass in the 2000s mainly because of one important higher education scholar, Kristen A. Renn. Informed by Root's (1992) prolific work, Renn (2003) developed the ecology theory of mixed race identity. In 2003, Renn incorporated Bronfenbrenner's ecology model of human development and Root's (1992) ecological framework and applied them to the identity development of multiracial college students. However, what was unique about this approach is that the previous identity development models focused on the "outcomes of development (racial identities) than on the processes that lead to those outcomes, the ecology model incorporates both processes and outcomes" (Renn, 2003, p. 386). Building on processes that lead to racial identity development, the ecology model included the campus environment that helped explain the environmental messaging that multiracial students received about their identity development. In Renn's (2003) ecology model there are four main systems. First are microsystems, the venues on campus that the student is situated in (e.g., laboratories, residence halls, student organizations). Second are mesosystems, which transpire when "two or more microsystems interact" (Renn, 2003, p. 388). An example is when a student is within their college environment doing academic coursework, social activities, and work. Third are exosystems, which operate surrounding the individual and are influenced by the system. More specifically, higher education policy or institutional policies are examples of exosystems.

Fourth, the macrosystem is dependent on time, place, and culture and becomes most visible when the three systems (i.e., micro-, meso-, and exo-) collaborate together to make up the interconnected ecological system in the model. Renn's four systems can directly assist student affairs in understanding the different campus and familial environments that multiracial students navigate at college.

Another theory, called patterns of situational identity among biracial and multiracial students, was initially created by Renn in 2000 after she conducted a qualitative study at three different institution types with a total of 24 students (eight students from each institution). Subsequently in 2004, Renn expanded her previous qualitative studies on multiracial college students from 2000 and 2003. Renn's (2004) study identified the following five ways that multiracial college students illustrated the fluidity and variability of their mixed race identity:

1. They selected a monoracial identity based on their cultural knowledge influenced by family and their overall physical appearance.
2. They asserted a multiple monoracial identity in which the student labeled their identity based on their parental racial heritages.
3. They designated a multiracial identity which represented the student's unique mixed race heritage.
4. They selected an extraracial identity in which students opted out of any formal U.S. racial categorization.
5. They used a situational identity which described that students identified with their racial heritages depending on the different situational contexts (Renn, 2004, 2008, 2010).

Each of these theories was instrumental in creating the first multiracial identity theories that described college student development. Renn's (2000, 2003, 2004) multiple studies provided higher education institutions and student affairs practitioners with the foundation to better understand how multiracial students develop and describe their racial identities based on environmental factors and even how differing institutional types can change student experiences. Even though Renn's theories were developed at a specific point in time, her work helps build on and connect the previous multiracial identity theories which are now moving to effectively describe how the social forces of racism and White supremacy provide a new critical lens to understand both multiracial and monoracialized student experiences. By reexamining the current multiracial identity theories to include monoracism, this new theory will continue to impact multiracial and college student development (Abes, 2016; Johnston-Guerrero & Renn, 2016).

For instance, multiracial Americans often experience racial discrimination, but their experiences are habitually ignored or rendered invisible (Korgen, 2016). The existence of multiracial people is often not acknowledged because of the historically based structural positioning of Whites over Blacks (Thornton, 1996), due to racial passing, which occurs when a person of mixed heritage phenotypically can "pass" as another racial group because of their lighter White physical characteristics (i.e., hair color/texture, eye color/shape, and skin tone). To illustrate, multiracial individuals possess various racial features and characteristics that can cause confusion for others trying to monoracially classify them (Chang, 2016). As a result, the natural inclination for monoracial people to place their racial classification on multiracial people causes multiracial students to be misidentified because they are perceived as racially ambiguous. Researchers Johnston and Nadal (2010) termed this experience of subtle, everyday discrimination as *monoracism*. Expanding this concept further, Hamako (2014) defined *multiracial oppression* as "the systemic privileging of things, people, and practices that are racialized, as a single-race and or racially pure" (p. 81). The concept of monoracism is essential to understand when applied to the multiracial student population. As a result, students who do not fit the norm because of monoracialism experience unintended racial insults (i.e., microaggressions) against their multiracial identity. Monoracialism is described as "a social force shaping the monoracial paradigm while monoracism is the system of oppression that results from such paradigm" (Johnston-Guerrero & Renn, 2016, p. 140). While Renn's theories made an invaluable contribution to higher education student development theories about multiracial college students, monoracism was not developed yet when the theories were published, and it was Jessica C. Harris, a higher education professor, who began to connect and build on the multiracial oppression research of Johnston and Nadal (2010). She noticed that multiracial college students were not considered and were thereby missing or silent in research and literature, particularly when discussing the impact of CRT and racism on the multiracial college student population.

Drawing on CRT

In this section, I discuss drawing on CRT to unpack how CRT as a theory was limited and excluded the racialized realities of multiracial students in higher education. However, I believe this is because of the time and context of when CRT was created among a legal movement that began with attorneys, scholars, and activists in the mid-1970s that aimed to examine transforming the relationships among race, racism, and power. At its core, CRT centers the narratives of people of color and makes visible how racism has shaped U.S. culture (Delgado & Stefancic, 2001; Zamudio et al., 2011). In the late 1990s, Ladson-Billings (1998) argued that CRT would be helpful in "unmasking and exposing racism in its various permutations" (p. 12) in the field of education. CRT is an invaluable framework that acknowledges that racism is an endemic part of U.S. society (Patton et al., 2007). When applied to the context of higher education, CRT works to interrupt racist structures in the U.S. educational pipeline (Fraczek, 2013; Patton, 2016). CRT continues to emerge as a theoretical framework and a form of praxis to disrupt racism and oppression. To best understand CRT and how it can limit multiracial college students, it is important to review the original core tenets. Seven key tenets frame CRT: (a) the permanence of racism, (b) counterstorytelling and experiential knowledge, (c) interest convergence theory, (d) intersectionality, (e) Whiteness as property, (f) critique of liberalism, and (g) commitment to social justice (Delgado & Stefancic, 2001; McCoy & Rodricks, 2015). In research and scholarship, the tenets of CRT are not always used to describe its impact. Despite about 20 years of CRT scholarship focusing on race and racism in higher education, much more racial progress is still needed specifically in recognizing multiracial college students and how different forms of racism due to the White racial frame (Chang, 2016; Feagin, 2013; Knaus, 2006) affect them. While CRT has expanded its scope to include theories such as Latin@/x critical theory (LatCrit), Asian critical theory (AsianCrit), and Tribal critical race theory (TribalCrit) (Brayboy, 2005; Harris, 2016a; Liu, 2009; Perez Huber, 2010), it was not until 2016 that CRT was acknowledged to be inapt for use in describing multiracial students experiences. Jessica C. Harris (2016a), a self-identified multiracial higher education professor and researcher, published her study on MultiCrit examining the racialized experiences of multiracial collegians.

Contributing a New Theory for Multiracial Students: MultiCrit

It was only when Harris (2016a) proposed adapting CRT to include the multiracial perspective, essentially calling for an updated version of CRT, that CRT was expanded within higher education to include the racialized realities of the multiracial population. *MultiCrit* is defined as a "critique of the role that White supremacist structures play in the (re)construction of multiraciality, thus uncovering far more profound effects of racism for multiracial and monoracial people of color than 'a lack of place'" (Harris, 2016a, p. 4). MultiCrit also argues that higher education institutions need a better understanding of the historical context that surrounds multiracial students' present-day experiences to better understand how a monoracial view of racial identity directly impacts the lives of students who claim a multiracial identity (Harris, 2016a). In the college environment, racial identity and racism are interconnected. Drawing on this understanding, MultiCrit should be used moving forward and should be further expanded in higher education research and practice. According to Harris (2016a), "CRT is a framework that must be 'adopted and adapted' in higher education to expose (mono) racism for multiracial students as well as propose solutions for addressing these issues" (p. 4). Similar to CRT, MultiCrit also has several core tenets that were adapted from some, but not all, of Delgado and Stefancic's (2001) CRT tenets. Harris (2016a) later proposed the following adapted tenets in MultiCrit: (a) challenge to ahistoricism, (b) interest convergence, (c) challenge to dominant ideology, and (d) experiential knowledge. In the next section, I describe these four proposed tenet adaptions alongside the original core CRT tenets.

How CRT Binds Multiracial College Students

CRT originally provided educators with the framework to expose hidden and subtle forms of racism in higher education, but there are definite limitations to the theory when applied to multiracial students. First, CRT focuses more on the Black-White paradigm instead of pushing the theory to disrupt the monoracial binary (Valdes et al., 2002). The creation of the Black-White binary is complicated because it is connected to a larger systemic issue of law and society, which imposes racial identifications (i.e., monoracial) on multiracial individuals and families without considering the nuances of how they self-identify themselves (Onwuachi-Willig, 2013). Even in contemporary society, remnants of the one-drop rule continue to force students to choose a monoracial race in college,[1] especially when these students are asked to prove their ethnic membership to peers in order to feel included on campus (Literte, 2010). Second, CRT fails to interrogate its own historical foundation, since the United States continues to uphold the monoracial framework that it was founded upon (Fraczek, 2013; Knaus, 2006). Quite simply, because of the time and legal context in which CRT was developed, it was not able to articulate the multiracial experience. It had a rigid monoracial frame, which disallows for the recognition of people claiming a multiracial lived experience. Because of these limitations, Harris (2016a) argued that CRT "must be adopted and adapted in higher education to expose (mono)racism for multiracial students as well as propose solutions for addressing these issues" (p. 4). Therefore, CRT's monoracial approach limits its direct applicability to serve multiracial students in higher education.

Supporting this theory, in the past 5 years, new research on multiracial college student experiences with discrimination and prejudice has emerged.

Museus et al.'s (2016) qualitative study found seven themes that uniquely described multiracial college student experiences with discrimination and prejudice. The seven themes are: racial essentialization, invalidation of racial identities, external imposition of racial identities, racial exclusion and marginalization, challenges to racial authenticity, exoticization, and pathologizing of multiracial individuals. Museus et al.'s (2016) study findings demonstrates why the first original CRT tenet, permanence of racism, does not fully capture the racialized realities of multiracial students. Therefore, one recommendation is to expand the permanence of racism tenet (Delgado & Stefancic, 2001) to also include monoracism which manifests itself through differing forms of prejudice and discrimination. When Harris (2016a) proposed adapting CRT to MultiCrit, she further modified the tenet to "racism, monoracism, colorism" (p. 6). As evidenced by researchers, multiracial students, similar to their student of color peers, do not escape the effects of racism and discrimination on their college campuses (Harris, 2016b; Harris & BrckaLorenz, 2017; Johnston & Nadal, 2010; Johnston-Guerrero & Renn, 2016; Museus et al., 2016).

The second tenet of CRT is counterstorytelling and experiential knowledge. With counterstorytelling and experiential knowledge, CRT scholars value and recognize people of color's lived experiences instead of White dominant narratives when teaching about race and racism in education (Delgado & Stefancic, 2001; Knaus, 2006; McCoy & Rodricks, 2015). The original tenet does not explicitly include the stories of multiracial individuals. The second tenet suggests that the voices of silenced individuals should be called on to make sense of the world (Knaus, 2006), but multiracial voices are often not included in higher education counternarratives about race or racism. Chang (2016) offers an explanation for why—multiracial narratives counter the master narrative and disrupt the stories where monoracial identities seem natural.

To remedy this, one recommendation is for higher education practitioners to reexamine their multicultural affairs support resources and disrupt the monoracial programming. Multicultural centers still tend to create cultural programming that may not be inclusive of multiracial students. Harris (2016a) suggested that "exploring the experiential knowledge of multiracial students centers their voices as well as challenges dominant ideologies concerning race and multiraciality" (p. 6). Literte (2010) noted that higher education cultural centers formed during the 1960s were created originally to give voice to students of Color. Thus, multiracial students do not feel as welcomed because their existence can challenge cultural centers' focus on Native American, Latin@/x, Black, and Asian (i.e., monoracial) students. Simply put, the cultural centers were not designed to address students with multiple racialized identities (Literte, 2010). Another recommendation to change multiracial students not feeling welcome at cultural centers is to create a multiracial peer liaison program. Yale University's students proposed creating a peer liaison program to offer support to multiracial students to make them feel more welcome on their campus while recognizing each of their racial identities and not just one (Wang, 2016).

As a byproduct of monoracism, multiracial students commonly voice experiencing feelings of not being "enough" of a certain race to join a cultural club (Johnston-Guerrero & Renn, 2016; Malaney & Danowski, 2015; Ozaki & Johnston, 2008; Renn, 2000, 2004). Unfortunately, cultural student organizations tend to lean toward upholding a monoracial frame (Ozaki & Johnston, 2008). Allowing multiracial students the space to share their racialized narratives in university programming or even in course assignments will "reduce alienation for members of excluded [multiracial student] groups, while offering opportunities for members of the majority group [monoracial students] to meet them halfway" (Delgado & Stefancic, 2001, p. 44). Counterstorytelling and experiential knowledge, the second tenet, should also include opportunities for multiracial college students to share their voices. Higher education institutions can continue to expand student programming and academic courses that teach about the history of multiracial people and the fluidity of race (Hamako, 2014). When given the opportunity, the powerful narratives that multiracial students share call attention to how current racial discourse still consistently upholds the monoracial system and affects students as a result.

The third tenet of CRT is interest convergence theory. An example of interest convergence is when racial equity advances only when it benefits White people (Harris, 2016a; McCoy & Rodricks, 2015). Keeping this in mind, interest convergence for multiracial people is when multiracial people are viewed as the racialized ideal or the poster children for living in a postracial society (Johnston & Nadal, 2010; Johnston-Guerrero, 2016). In the college context, Harris (2016a) provided another example of interest convergence when a multiracial student was selected to be an orientation leader because she was "very diverse" (p. 8) and the university wanted to show prospective students and families that their institution was diverse. The different interpretations of interest convergence suggest that this CRT tenet must be expanded to be accurately applied to multiracial college students. As such, another suggestion is to redefine how interest convergence is being enacted on campus for multiracial students. It is not uncommon for institutional research offices to allow multiracial students to check more than one race box in admissions, but they rarely disaggregate the data in campus climate assessments, which can regrettably misrepresent multiracial students on campus whose racial identities are fluid and have been demonstrated to change over time (Guillermo Wan & Johnston, 2012; Kellogg & Niskodé, 2008; Wijeyesinghe, 2012).

The fourth core tenet, intersectionality, is related to racialization, the idea that each race has its own history (Delgado & Stefancic, 2001). When intersectionality is examined, race, sex, class, national origin, and sexual orientation are also simultaneously included (Delgado & Stefancic, 2001). Out of all of CRT's original core tenets, this tenet is the most promising for actually being inclusive of multiracial students. The concept of intersectionality is sometimes difficult to comprehend because U.S. society is organized along binaries (McCoy & Rodricks, 2015). However, multiracial students continue to disrupt the binary because they do not hold a single identity. Harris (2016a) adapted the core tenet, intersectionality, to "intersections of multiple racial identities" (p. 6). She further described it as "allow[ing] for an exploration beyond the intersection of singular social identities and examin[ing] the intersections of multiracial students' racial heritage(s)" (p. 6). If higher education practitioners could break free from using binary practices and instead use an intersectional framework when working with multiracial students, it would allow staff to also consider how their students' marginalized and oppressed identities are affected (Harris, 2016b). By expanding beyond the Black-White binary of CRT, multiracial stories that center an analysis of intersectionality "place value on the multiple oppressions that are specific to multiracial students" (Chang, 2016, p. 709). Colleges and universities need to be challenged to examine intersectionality. To best understand intersectionality, developing a keener critical analysis of the multiple levels of oppression is needed—not only in the view of racial mixing, but also around class, sexuality, religion, and citizenship (Jolivette, 2014).

The fifth core tenet of CRT is Whiteness as property. The concept of Whiteness as property was first introduced by Cheryl Harris in 1993 (Delgado & Stefancic, 2001). Whiteness is viewed as property because of the color binary lines that separated White people from people of Color. Associating with Whiteness is an asset to seek and protect (Johnson, 2005) which is related to White supremacy and legal systems such as antimiscegenation laws that were meant to keep people from racially mixing. In the context of education, Whiteness is used in exchange for power, social capital, and access to high-paying jobs (McCoy & Rodricks, 2015). Multiracial college students' university experiences are marked by a "Sea of Whiteness" (McCoy & Rodricks, 2015, p. 21), in which multiracial students are socialized not to think about racial inequality. Accordingly, multiracial students are explicitly taught not to think of race and racism through a curriculum that centers on Whiteness, students are reminded . . . by an overarching assumption that guided their K–12 schooling, college, and peer interactions that all people are, or should be, monoracial. (Knaus, 2006, p. 66)

Understanding the deep-rooted nature of Whiteness as a property, higher education needs to become more inclusive of multiracial students. For instance, faculty could teach the hidden history of being mixed-race in the United States (Hamako, 2014), including the recognition of ahistorical time periods, pointing out the consequences for multiracial people, helping students understand why antimiscegenation laws were implemented, and acknowledging that interracial couples continue to face racism could allow multiracial students to challenge the commonly presented binary of Whiteness (Fernandes Williams & Namisi Chilungu, 2016; McCoy & Rodricks, 2015; Spickard, 2004). Another recommendation for this tenet is to include the perspective that there are multiracial individuals who have White heritage. Multiracial students can face challenges with developing their racial identity because of the differential treatment they may receive, which depends on their skin tone and how they are perceived in society (Dawkins, 2012; Delgado & Stefancic, 2001).

The sixth core tenet of CRT is critique of liberalism. Critique of liberalism characterizes color blindness as a belief that race and skin color do not matter (Delgado & Stefancic, 2001; McCoy & Rodricks, 2015). This tenet implies that the United States is a postracial society, when in fact that is clearly untrue. Multiracial students are racialized and affected by multiracial microaggressions (Johnston & Nadal, 2010) based on their physical appearance, and assumptions are made about their backgrounds and skin color. While it could be easy to make the assumption that being mixed or multiracial means that they are equal, it does not account for ways that race can be ignored in U.S. society (McCoy & Rodricks, 2015).

The seventh and final core tenet of CRT is commitment to social justice. This tenet is described as by critical race scholars as both a process and a goal. McCoy and Rodricks (2015) contend that a commitment to social justice is "emancipatory in nature [and] is grounded in a consistent commitment to resist the racialized and gendered inequality and injustice marking access to social, political, economic, and cultural resources" (p. 14). Higher education practitioners and faculty must encourage multiracial collegians and help these students understand that they also have a voice. They must also demonstrate their commitment to self-reflection and education about racial and social justice (Malaney Brown, 2020).

Overall, these suggested recommendations further expand CRT and provide more of a systemic and critical analysis of multiracial students' racial realities when using MultiCrit in higher education rather than the original core CRT tenets. While CRT has certainly created an analysis of race, racism, and power, further adaptation of these core tenets is needed because the growing multiracial student populations at American higher education institutions and their awareness of multiracial oppression need to be reconciled. Understanding these key contributions of MultiCrit provides researchers and practitioners with additional frames to continue to push research and practice to better support multiracial college students who are increasingly experiencing and learning about racism on their college campuses (Harris, 2016b; Museus et al., 2016).

Pushing Toward the Multiracial Future: Recommendations for Higher Education Research and Practice

The fact remains that multiracial college students are not going anywhere. While less than 1% of higher education research literature focuses on multiracial students, the work of the groundbreaking racial identity theorists reviewed have begun to provide much-needed voices to legitimize the racialized lives of multiracial college students (Museus et al., 2015). Although it is clear that multiracial identity theories have evolved over the past 2 decades, there is much more to learn about history to understand multiracial American college students. Higher education research needs to address multiraciality while also providing various types of research methodologies to best understand the complexity of race. All of the theories reviewed were qualitative (Kich, 1992; Poston, 1990; Renn, 2000, 2003, 2004, 2010; Root, 1992, 1996; Wijeyesinghe, 2001, 2012). Future research should also theorize how racism influences racial identity formation (Harris, 2016a; Johnston-Guerrero & Renn, 2016) and how to analyze campus environments using the White racial frame (Feagin, 2013) to better understand multiracial students (Renn, 2003) and monoracism (Johnston-Guerrero & Renn, 2016). Therefore, more intentional critical qualitative research (Marshall & Rossman, 2016) and critical quantitative studies will be needed to tease apart the long-standing complexities of multiracial students to better understand how they develop their racial identity while attending college. While research on the subtle racisms that multiracial students face is emerging (Hamako, 2014; Harris, 2016b; Johnston-Guerrero & Renn, 2016; Museus et al., 2015), additional inquiries into understanding if these subtle racisms can influence the racial identity development of multiracial students requires more investigation.

The earliest reviewed theories demonstrated a linear approach to multiracial identity (Kich, 1992; Poston, 1990), but Renn (2003, 2004) determined that multiracial identity for college students is contextual and situational. It is no longer viewed as static but can be fluid and dynamic (Wijeyesinghe, 2001, 2012). The increased awareness and affirmation of the voices of the bi/multiracial student population will continue to challenge student programming that situates itself only from the perspective of monoracial student services (Kellogg & Niskodé, 2008; Literte, 2010). As such, it will be essential for different higher education institutional types to understand how multiracial students choose to engage with their racial identities in college (Shivers, 2011), especially at historically Black colleges and universities (Harris & BrckaLorenz, 2017), minority-serving institutions, and Hispanic-serving institutions (Garcia, 2019), which continue to be understudied. An additional recommendation for practice is providing better training for student affairs professionals to learn how to improve assessment opportunities for multiracial students (Hamako, 2005; Herring, 1995). Wilson (1999) stated that student affairs administrators need to be educated to meet multiracial students where they are at within their recognition of racial identity. Student affairs professionals play a key role in encouraging and educating multiracial college students to become more actively involved.

The literature review of this chapter's multiracial identity theories revealed several notable gaps in higher education research, particularly the need for more multiracial identity studies to investigate the fluidity of multiracial identity and whether multiracial identity development can change based on the student's geographic region in the United States. Increased focus on how multiracial students are impacted by racism and monoracism within their college environments is also needed. In line with the growth of the multiracial and college student population (Literte, 2010; Pew Research Center, 2015), more research will need to focus on how multiracial students enter college and are racialized in the campus climate (Guillermo-Wann & Johnston, 2012). Another needed area of research includes theorizing how students could change their racial identity when they return home to their interracial families after several years of college (Renn, 2003; Renn & Shang, 2008). Notably, multiracial identity theories do not make distinctions among different mixed-race combinations. While the experiences of multiracial individuals could be similar, the specific combination of multiple racial heritages could create different dynamics (Renn, 2010). More research is required to determine if racism, racial hypodescent, and physical appearance (e.g., Black and Asian, Black and White, or White Asian students) could influence the racial identity development of multiracial students. Even more exploration is needed to understand if there are gender differences between multiracial men and women.

In conclusion, reviewing the current literature that addresses multiracial college student identity reinforces the idea that in order to understand the development of racial identity theories in the U.S. college context, history, time, place, and culture must be taken in account (Renn, 2003). Without reflecting on the past, higher education may lose sight of the challenges that multiracial students are presently facing. Indeed, valuing history is key; Root (2003b) described the concept of identity simply as "dynamic and informed by one's life experiences in a historical context" (p. 17). The values of higher education institutional structures historically hold the understanding of race and social identity norms that are transmitted through "social status, resource distribution, economic attainment, and residential patterns" (Miller, 1992, p. 35). By centering multiracial identity more critically to disrupt monoracism in higher education practice, we can advance the past and present multiracial college identity development theories toward the future (Combs, 2018; Johnston & Nadal, 2010; Texeira, 2003).

Questions for Practitioners to Consider

1. What resources are available on your campus to support multiracial students?
2. How do you count your multiracial students in your racial demographics?

Questions for Researchers to Consider

1. What can you do as researcher to center the voices of multiracial students in qualitative or quantitative research?
2. How can theorists account for the time and place that can at times limit the applicability of racial identity theory in an educational context?

Note

1. The one drop rule was "historically used to define anyone with any 'drop' of black blood as black" (Khanna, 2010, p. 96).

References

Abes, E. S. (Ed.). (2016). Situating paradigms in student development theory. In E. S. Abes (2016) *Critical perspectives on student development theory* [Special Issue] (New Directions for Student Services, no. 154, pp. 9–13). Wiley. http://doi .org/10.1002/ss.2071

Banks, J. A. (2003). Foreword. In M. P. P. Root & M. Kelley (Eds.), *Multiracial child's resource book: Living complex realities* (pp. x–xiii). Mavin Foundation.

Brayboy, B. M. J. (2005). Toward a tribal critical race theory in education. *The Urban Review, 37,* 425–446. http://doi.10.007/s11256-005-0018-y

Chang, A. (2016). Multiracial matters—disrupting and reinforcing the racial rubric in educational discourse. *Race Ethnicity and Education, 19*(4), 706–730. http://doi.org/10.1080/13613324.2014.885427

Combs, L. (2018). *Racial justice & decolonization can't happen without disrupting monoracism.* ACPA Convention 2018. http://convention.myacpa.org/houston2018/racial-justice-decolonization/

Cross, W. E. (1971). The Negro-to-Black conversion experience: Toward a psychology of Black liberation. *Black World, 20*(9), 13–27.

Daniel, G. R. (2003). Multiracial identity in global perspective: The United States, Brazil, and South Africa. In L. I. Winters & H. L. DeBose (Eds.), *New faces in a changing America: Multiracial identity in the 21st century.* (pp. 247–287). SAGE.

Dawkins, M. A. (2012). *Clearly invisible: Racial passing and the color of cultural identity.* Baylor University Press.

Delgado, R., & Stefancic, J. (2001). *Critical race theory: An introduction.* New York University Press.

Erikson, E. (1968). *Identity: Youth and crisis.* Norton.

Evans, A. M., & Ramsay, K. (2015). Multiracial and biracial individuals: A content analysis of counseling journals, 1991-2013. *Journal of Multicultural Counseling and Development, 43*(4), 262–274. http://doi.org/10.1002/jmcd.12020

Feagin, J. R. (2013). *The White racial frame: Centuries of racial framing and counterframing* (2nd ed.). Routledge.

Fernandes Williams, R., & Namisi Chilungu, E. (2016). Multiracial students and educational policy. In K. O. Korgen (Ed.), *Multiracial Americans and race policy* (pp. 123–137). University of Chicago Press.

Fraczek, C. (2013). Re(thinking) race: Positioning multiracial representations within critical pedagogy. In J. S. Brooks (Ed.), *Confronting racism in higher education: Problems and possibilities for fighting ignorance, bigotry, and isolation* (pp. 161–180). Information Age.

Garcia, G. A. (2019). *Becoming hispanic-serving institutions: Opportunities for colleges and universities.* Johns Hopkins University Press.

Guillermo-Wann, C., & Johnston, M. P. (2012, November 1–4). *Investigating theory and research on multiracial college students in a "post-racial" era: Towards an integrative model of multiraciality in the campus climate for diversity.* Paper presented at the Critical Mixed Race Studies Conference, Chicago, Illinois.

Hamako, E. (2005). For the movement: Community education supporting multiracial organizing. *Equity & Excellence in Education, 38*(2), 145–154. http://doi.org/10.1080/10665680590935124

Hamako, E. (2014). *Improving anti-racist education for multiracial students* [Doctoral dissertation, University of Massachusetts Amherst]. Scholar Works. http://scholarworks.umass.edu/dissertations_2/90

Harris, J. C. (2016a, April). Toward a critical multiracial theory in education. *International Journal of Qualitative Studies in Education, 8398*, 1–19. http://doi.org/ 10.1080/09518398.2016.1162870

Harris, J. C. (2016b, November). Multiracial college students' experiences with multiracial microaggressions. *Race Ethnicity and Education, 3324*, 1–17. http://doi .org/10.1080/13613324.2016.1248836

Harris, J. C., & BrckaLorenz, A. (2017). Black, White, and biracial students' engagement at differing institutional types. *Journal of College Student Development, 58*(5), 783–789. http://doi.org/10.1353/csd.2017.0061

Herring, R. D. (1995). Developing biracial ethnic identity: A review of the increasing dilemma. *Journal of Multicultural Counseling and Development, 23*(1), 29–38. https://doi.org/10.1002/j.2161-1912.1995.tb00264.x

Johnson, A. G. (2005). *Privilege, power, and difference* (2nd ed.). McGraw-Hill.

Johnston, M. P., & Nadal, K. (2010). Multiracial microaggressions: Exposing monoracism in everyday life and clinical practice. In D. W. Sue (Ed.), *Microaggressions and marginality: Manifestation, dynamics, and impact* (pp. 123–144). Wiley & Sons.

Johnston-Guerrero, M. P., & Renn, K. A. (2016). Multiracial Americans in college. In K. O. Korgen (Ed.), *Race policy and multiracial Americans* (pp. 139–154). University of Chicago Press.

Jolivette, A. (2014). Critical mixed race studies: New directions in the politics of race and representation. *Journal of Critical Mixed Race Studies, 1*(1), 149–161. https:// escholarship.org/uc/item/62p3p25p

Jones, N., & Bullock, J. (2012). *The two or more races population: 2010.* Census 2010 Brief. U.S. Census Bureau #C2010BR-13. https://www.census.gov/prod/ cen2010/briefs/c2010br-13.pdf

Kellogg, A., & Niskodé, A. S. (2008). Student affairs and higher education policy issues related to multiracial students. In K. A. Renn & P. Shang (Eds.), *Biracial and multiracial students* [Special Edition] (New Directions for Student Services, no. 123, pp. 93–103). Wiley. https://doi.org/10.1002/ss.290

Khanna, N. (2010). If you're half black, you're just black: Reflect appraisals and the persistence of the one-drop rule. *Sociological Quarterly, 51*(1), 96–121. https:// doi.org/10.1111/j.1533-8525.2009.01162.x

Kich, G. K. (1992). The developmental process of asserting a biracial, bicultural identity. In M. P. P. Root (Ed.), *Racially mixed people in America.* (pp. 304–317). SAGE.

Knaus, C. (2006). *Race, racism, and multiraciality in American higher education.* Academica Press.

Korgen, K. O. (2016). *Race policy and multiracial Americans.* University of Chicago Press.

Ladson-Billings, G. (1998). Just what is critical race theory and what's it doing in a nice field like education? *Qualitative Studies in Education, 11*(1), 7–24. https:// doi.org/10.1080/095183999823863

Literte, P. E. (2010). Revising race: How biracial students are changing and challenging student services. *Journal of College Student and Development, 51*(2), 115–134. http://doi.org/10.1353/csd.0.0122

Liu, A. (2009). Critical race theory, Asian Americans, and higher education: A review of research. *InterActions: UCLA Journal of Education and Information Studies, 5*(2), 1–12. http://doi.org/10.5811/westjem.2011.5.6700

Malaney, V. K., & Danowski, K. (2015). Mixed foundations: Supporting and empowering multiracial student organizations. *Journal Committed to Social Change on Race and Ethnicity, 1*(2), 55–85. https://doi.org/10.15763/issn.2642-2387.2015.1.2.54-85

Malaney Brown, V. K. (2020). *Exploring multiracial consciousness: Voices of multiracial students at a predominantly White institution* [Doctoral dissertation, University of Massachussets Amherst]. Scholar Works. https://scholarworks.umass.edu/dissertations_2/1852

Marshall, C., & Rossman, G. B. (2016). *Designing qualitative research* (6th ed.). SAGE.

McCoy, D. L., & Rodricks, D. J. (2015). Critical race theory in higher education: 20 years of theoretical and research innovations. *ASHE Higher Education Report, 41*(3), 14–16. http://www.wiley.com/WileyCDA/WileyTitle/productCd-1119111927.html

Miller, R. L. (1992). The human ecology of multiracial identity. In M. P. P. Root (Ed.), *Racially mixed in America* (pp. 24–36). SAGE.

Morning, A. (2000). Who is multiracial? Definitions and decisions. *Sociological Imagination, 37*(4), 209–222. https://www.researchgate.net/profile/Ann_Morning/publication/288006373_Who_is_multiracial_Definitions_and_decisions/links/57742e7108aead7ba06e610b/Who-is-multiracial-Definitions-and-decisions.pdf

Morning, A. (2003). New faces, old faces: Counting the multiracial population past and present. In H. L. DeBose & L. I. Winters (Eds.), *New faces in a changing America: Multiracial identity in the 21st century* (pp. 41–67). SAGE.

Morning, A. (2005). Multiracial classification on the United States census: Myth, reality, and future impact. *Revue Européenne Des Migrations Internationales, 21*(2), 2–19. http://doi.org/10.4000/remi.2495

Morten, G., & Atkinson, D. R. (1983). Minority identity development and preference for counselor race. *The Journal of Negro Education, 52*(2), 156–161. http://doi.10.2307/2295032

Museus, S. D., Lambe Sariñana, S. A., Yee, A. L., & Robinson, T. E. (2016). A qualitative analysis of multiracial students' experiences with prejudice and discrimination in college. *Journal of College Student and Development, 57*(6), 680–697. https://doi.org/10.1353/csd.2016.0068

Museus, S. D., Sariñana, S. A. L., & Ryan, T. K. (2015). A qualitative examination of multiracial students' coping responses to experiences with prejudice and discrimination in college. *Journal of College Student Development, 56*(4), 331–348. http://doi.org/10.1353/csd.2015.0041

Omi, M., & Winant, H. (1994). *Racial formation in the United States: From the 1960s to 1990* (2nd ed.). Routledge.

Onwuachi-Willig, A. (2013). *According to our hearts: Rhinelander v. Rhinelander and the law of the multiracial family.* Yale University Press.

Ozaki, C., & Johnston, M. P. (2008). The space in between: Issues for multiracial student organizations and advising. In K. A. Renn & P. Shang (Eds.), *Biracial and multiracial students* [Special Edition] (New Directions for Student Services, no. 123, pp. 53–61). Wiley. https://doi.org/10.1002/ss.286

Patton, L. D. (2016). Disrupting postsecondary prose: Toward a critical race theory of higher education. *Urban Education, 51*(3), 315–342. http://doi.org/10.1177/0042085915602542

Patton, L. D., McEwen, M., Rendón, L., & Howard-Hamilton, M. F. (2007). Critical race perspectives on theory in student affairs. In S. R. Harper & L. D. Patton (Eds.), *Responding to the realities of race* (New Directions for Student Services, no. 120, pp. 39–54). Wiley.

Perez Huber, L. (2010). Using Latina /o critical race theory (LatCrit) and racist nativism to explore intersectionality in the educational experiences of undocumented Chicana college students. *Educational Foundations, 24,* 77–96. https://files.eric.ed.gov/fulltext/EJ885982.pdf

Pew Research Center. (2015). *Multiracial in America: Proud, diverse and growing in numbers.* http://www.pewsocialtrends.org/2015/06/11/multiracial-in-america/

Poston, W. S. (1990). The biracial identity development model: A needed addition. *Journal of Counseling & Development, 69,* 152–155. https://doi.org/10.1002/j.1556-6676.1990.tb01477.x

Renn, K. A. (2000). Patterns of situational identity among biracial and multiracial college students. *The Review of Higher Education, 23*(4), 399–420. http://doi.10.1353/rhe.2000.0019

Renn, K. A. (2003). Understanding the identities of mixed race college students through a developmental ecology lens. *Journal of College Student Development, 44,* 383–403. http://doi.10.1353.csd.2003.0032

Renn, K. A. (2004). *Mixed race students in college: The ecology of race, identity, and community.* SUNY Press.

Renn, K. A. (2008). Research on biracial and multiracial identity development: Overview and synthesis. In K. A. Renn & P. Shang (Eds.), *Biracial and multiracial students* (New Directions for Student Services, no. 123, pp. 13–21). Jossey-Bass. https://doi.org/10.1002/ss.282

Renn, K. A. (2010). Multiracial identity development. In N. J. Evans, D. S. Forney, F. M. Guido, L. D. Patton, & K. A., Renn (Eds.), *College student development in college: Theory, research, and practice* (2nd ed., pp. 288–304). Jossey-Bass.

Renn, K. A. & Shang, P. (Eds.). (2008, Fall). *Biracial and multiracial students* (New Directions for Student Services, no. 123). Jossey-Bass. https://doi.org/10.1002/ss.284

Root, M. P. P. (1992). *Racially mixed people in America.* SAGE.

Root, M. P. P. (1996). *Multiracial experience: Racial borders as the new frontier.* SAGE.

Root, M. P. P. (2003a). Multiracial families and children: Implications for educational research and practice. In J. A. Banks & C. A. McGee Banks (Eds.), *Handbook of research on multicultural education* (2nd ed., pp. 110–124). Jossey-Bass.

Root, M. P. P. (2003b). Five mixed-race identities: From relic to revolution. In L. I. Winters & H. L. DeBose (Eds.), *New faces in a changing America: Multiracial identity in the 21st century* (pp. 3–20). SAGE.

Root, M. P. P., & Kelley, M. (2003). *Multiracial child resource book: Living complex realities.* Mavin Foundation.

Shih, M., & Sanchez, D. T. (2009). When race becomes even more complex: Toward understanding the landscape of multiracial identity and experiences. *Journal of Social Issues, 65*(1), 1–11. http://doi.org/10.1111/j.1540-4560.2008.01584.x

Shivers, M. S. (2011). *How do I choose?: Biracial postsecondary choice of historically Black colleges and universities or predominantly White institutions* [Doctoral dissertation, University of Georgia]. https://getd.libs.uga.edu/pdfs/shivers_melissa_s_201108_phd.pdf

Spickard, P. (2004). The power of Blackness: Mixed-race leaders and the monoracial ideal. In P. Spickard & G. R. Daniel (Eds.), *Racial thinking in the United States: Uncompleted and independence* (pp. 103–123). University of Notre Dame Press.

Spickard, P., & Daniel, G. R. (2004). *Racial thinking in the United States: Uncompleted and independence.* University of Notre Dame Press.

Texeira, M. T. (2003). The new multiracialism: An affirmation of or an end to race as we know it? In L. I. Winters & H. L. DeBose (Eds.), *New faces in a changing America: Multiracial identity in the 21st century* (pp. 21–37). SAGE.

Thornton, M. C. (1996). Hidden agendas, identity theories, and multiracial people. In M. P. P. Root (Ed.), *The multiracial experience: Racial borders as the new frontier* (pp. 101–120). SAGE.

Valdes, F., McCristal-Culp, J., & Harris, A. P. (2002). *Crossroads, directions, and a new critical race theory.* Temple University Press.

Wang, M. (2016, February 3). Students propose multiracial peer liaison program. *Yale Daily News.* http://yaledailynews.com/blog/2016/02/03/multiracial-peer-liaison-program-to-launch/

White House. (1997, March 30). *Revisions to the standards for the classification of federal data on race and ethnicity.* https://www.whitehouse.gov/wp-content/uploads/2017/11/Revisions-to-the-Standards-for-the-Classification-of-Federal-Data-on-Race-and-Ethnicity-October30-1997.pdf

Wijeyesinghe, C. L. (2001). Racial identity in multiracial people: An alternative paradigm. In C. L Wijeyesinghe & B. W. Jackson III (Eds.), *New perspectives on racial identity development: A theoretical and practical anthology* (pp. 129–152). New York University Press.

Wijeyesinghe, C. L. (2012). The intersectional model of multiracial identity: Integrating multiracial theories and intersectional perspectives on social identity. In C. L. Wijeyesinghe & B. W. Jackson III (Eds.), *New perspectives on racial identity development: Integrating emerging frameworks* (2nd ed., pp. 81–107). New York University Press.

Wilson, T. (1999). You know that I'm triracial right? Multiracial college student identity development and the college experience. In K. Manning (Ed.), *Giving voice to critical campus issues: Qualitative issues in student affairs* (pp. 113–133). University of America Press.

Zamudio, M. M., Russell, C., Rios, F. A., & Bridgeman, J. L. (2011). *Critical race theory matters: Education and ideology.* Routledge.

16

THE MULTIDIMENSIONALITY OF MULTIRACIAL IDENTITY IN THE POST– CIVIL RIGHTS ERA

Patricia E. Literte

I am the son of a Black man from Kenya and a White woman from Kansas. I was raised with the help of a White grandfather who survived a Depression . . . and a White grandmother who worked on a bomber assembly line at Fort Leavenworth. . . . I am married to a Black American who carries within her the blood of slaves and slave-owners—an inheritance we pass on to our two precious daughters. I have brothers, sisters, nieces, nephews, uncles and cousins, of every race and every hue, scattered across three continents, and for as long as I live, I will never forget that in no other country on Earth is my story even possible.

—Barack Obama (2008, para. 7)

In Barack Obama's speech on race relations, given in Philadelphia during his first presidential campaign, he spoke extensively about the racial tensions and inequalities of U.S. society and presented his multiracial, multicultural background as an example of the possibilities and promise of finding common ground across the racial divide. He framed the United States as a nation-state that provided a unique setting and ideological tools to build on this common ground. Contrary to some pundits' commentary suggesting that Obama's election marked the beginning of a postracial era, racism, race, and what his presidency represented to different racial groups were defining features of his presidency (Pettigrew, 2009). Although he embraced his multiracial background, Obama identified as Black and was subjected to unceasing anti-Black racism throughout his presidential campaigns and two-term presidency (Joseph, 2011; Wingfield & Feagin, 2013). These dynamics illustrate that Obama is representative of the complexities of race in the post–civil rights era and the simultaneously fundamental and fluid nature of race in U.S. society.

Obama's personal and political engagement with multiraciality is reflective of a larger and growing population of people who challenge the traditionally accepted "monoracial" or single-race categories of Black/African American, Latinx, Native American, Asian American, and White (Jeffries, 2012). The increasing desire of some multiracial people to be recognized in U.S. society was most clearly reflected in the debate over the potential addition of a multiracial category to the 2000 Census (Perlman & Waters, 2002). The proposal and ensuing debate exemplified multiraciality's significance to not only the general population but also the political landscape, political organization/mobilization, and resource allocation. The creation of a multiracial category was proposed by a coalition of mixed-race identity organizations, prominently headed by Project RACE (Reclassify All Children Equally), whose leader was Susan Graham, a White woman with Black/White biracial children (DaCosta, 2007; Williams, 2006). The multiracial category was opposed by nearly every monoracial civil rights, political, and legal organization, including the National Association for the Advancement of Colored People (NAACP), the Mexican American Legal Defense Fund (MALDEF), and the National Asian Pacific American Legal Consortium (NAPALC), which viewed "the multiracial box as a wrecking ball aimed at affirmative action" (Wright, 1994, p. 26), the fiscal health and survival of communities of color, and enforcement of civil rights protections (Espiritu & Omi, 2000). Civil rights organizations were further alarmed by the political right's support for a multiracial category (including Speaker of the House Newt Gingrich), which was perceived as indicative of the right's quest to propagate a "beyond race" or color-blind ideology denying the importance of race in U.S. society. After extensive debate, the House subcommittee decided in favor of multiple racial identifications—thus, for the first time in U.S. history, respondents could mark more than one box for racial identification on the 2000 Census, with the options of White, Black or African American, American Indian and Alaska Native, Asian, or Native Hawaiian and Other Pacific Islander, and Some Other Race (Grieco & Cassidy, 2001; Sundstrom, 2001; Williams, 2006; Zack, 1993). Illustrating the gap which can exist between "official" racial categories and people's lived experiences, Hispanic was and is not a racial category on the Census, as it is characterized as "ethnicity," in spite of the majority of Hispanics people's assertion that being Hispanic "is, at least in part, their race" (Parker et al., 2015, p. 8).

The contentious debate over U.S. Census categories is a reflection of the rising construct of multiracial identity in concert with changing demographics and social attitudes. It exemplifies the simultaneous fluidity and constancy of race in U.S. society and "illustrates the awkward historical moment we currently inhabit. It is a moment in which we acknowledge that race is a social construct (as opposed to a biological reality), but a construct that has real and measurable consequences" (Rockquemore et al., 2009, p. 14). And of course, everyone is racially mixed and there are no biologically "real" racial groups (Daniel, 2002). All categorizations of race, including "multiracial," are social constructs. However, the socially constructed nature of race should not be mistaken for unimportance, as race and racism are foundational to U.S. society. As Omi and Winant (2015) noted, "Race is a concept which signifies and symbolizes social conflicts and interests by referring to different types of human bodies" (p. 110). That is, race is much more than a Census category or data collection point—it is a manifestation and reflection of the deepest, foundational fractures in U.S. society, rooted in colonialism and slavery, which continue to produce racial inequalities in lived experiences and social institutions.

The Youthful and Growing Multiracial Population

The data that emerged from the 2000 Census, as well as data collected in subsequent years by the U.S. Census Bureau, shed light on the growing population of people who identify as more than one race. In the 2000 Census, 2.4% of the population (6.8 million people) reported more than one race. By 2010, the self-identified multiracial population had increased by roughly one third to 2.9% of the population (9 million people). Out of this population, more than one million people identified with one of the following combinations: (a) Black and White; (b) some other race and White; (c) Asian and White; and (d) American Indian and Alaska Native. People identifying as Black and White and Asian and White are among the fastest growing biracial populations. According to official Census data, from 2000 to 2010, the number of Black-White biracial Americans doubled, and the amount of Asian-White biracial Americans grew by 87% (Jones & Bullock, 2012). Yet findings from the Pew Research Center (Parker et al., 2015) present different data from that of the Census, as Pew asked respondents to self-identify, as well as report the race of their parents and grandparents. Based on these data, Pew estimates that 6.9% of the population is multiracial, as opposed to the Census-reported 2.9% (Parker et al., 2015). Regardless of what definitions are used, the growth of the multiracial population is significant compared to the general population. Conclusive findings from the 2010 Census data showed that the population of people who self-identify as more than one race is growing at a faster rate than the population of people who identify as a single race (Jones & Bullock, 2012). However, identification with more than one racial category on government forms should not be conflated with identification as multiracial. According to the 2015 Pew study, 61% of respondents who stated they had a racially mixed background did not identify as multiracial (Parker et al., 2015).

Those Americans who claim mixed race ancestry and/or identify as multiracial are disproportionately young, and the population raises compelling questions about how social institutions, including institutions of higher education, address issues of race (Chang, 2016; Jones & Bullock, 2012; Parker et al., 2015). Census data about the "two or more races population" show that "Americans younger than 18 accounted for 23% of the total population in 2013, but they were 46% of the multiracial population. The younger the age group, the higher its share of multiracial Americans" (Parker et al., 2015, p. 30). Given this demographic profile, there are significant numbers of multiracial persons who are of traditional college-going age (18 years to 22 years old), and it is important to consider how these students' experiences may or may not differ from their monoracially identified counterparts. The significance of such considerations is compounded when the population of students identifying as multiracial is likely to grow larger, and multiraciality is negatively correlated with education. More specifically, multiracial people are less likely to complete their bachelor's degree (23%) than the general population (31%) (Parker et al., 2015). This suggests that there are challenges retaining this population in higher education, although it is unclear to what degree this attrition is tied to multiracial identity or the experiences of multiracial students. Simultaneously, intriguing data about marriages show that interracially married couples are more likely to have attended college. Livingston and Brown (2017) noted that "in 2015, 14% of newlyweds with a high school education or less were interracially married, while 18% and 19% of newlyweds with some college and with a bachelor's degree, respectively, were interracially married" (p. 8). Data on U.S. newlyweds and educational attainment indicate that the higher the educational attainment, the higher the likelihood that people will intermarry, which in turn may suggest that their children will be more likely to attend college (Cataldi et al., 2018; Livingston & Brown, 2017). Therefore, although colleges and universities may not have a critical mass of multiracial students yet, it is likely that in the coming years multiracial students will be attending in larger numbers.

Beyond demographic data, ample research and evidence illustrate the relevance of multiracial people and identities within higher education contexts.

Researchers have delved into a range of topics pertaining to multiracial students' experiences, including identity development, interactions with peer groups, microaggressions, inclusion/exclusion from curricula, availability of programs and services, access to space, and perceptions of President Obama (Ford & Malaney, 2012; Harris, 2017; Jeffries, 2012; Renn, 2000; Rockquemore et al.; Sims, 2016; Tran et al., 2016). One of the most well-known individual examples of the connection between multiraciality and college students is the case study of Matt Kelley. While a student at Wesleyan University in Connecticut, Kelley began *Mavin*, a magazine that explored the mixed race experience (Davila, 2005). *Mavin* eventually grew into a full-fledged nonprofit organization, with programs and publications ranging from the Matchmaker Bone Marrow Program (Iwasaki, 2004; Smith, 2005) to the *Multiracial Child Resource Handbook* (Root & Kelley, 2003). Although his is merely one case that illustrates a student using their college experience as a springboard into a career centered on identity, Kelley is an example of how students' assertion of multiracial identity can have significance long after leaving their home institution of higher learning. Hence, understanding multiracial students' experience has implications far beyond the college campus.

Chapter Focus

In this chapter, I present an interdisciplinary theoretical framework, drawing on critical race theory (CRT), racial formations, and Black feminist thought, which can be utilized to understand multiracial students' identities and lived experiences, as well as how social structure and the institution of higher education circumscribe these identities and realities. This framework most aligns with social identity development theories in the field of student affairs, which examines "social identity as an organizing concept of the self within higher education" (Patton et al., 2016, p. 95). These theories focus on themes of privilege and oppression along the lines of race, class, gender, sexuality, disability, and so on (Patton et al., 2016). In order to lay the foundation for the theoretical framework, I first discuss the history of multiracial people in the United States, the social construction of multiracial identity, and theorizing around multiraciality. I group our discussion of the history of multiracial people and multiraciality theorizing together, as the theories are intimately tied to the social and political dynamics of different eras. I conclude this chapter with recommendations for practitioners and educators to improve the collegiate experiences of multiracial students.

History of Multiracial People in the United States

Contrary to much of the literature and discourse that characterizes people of mixed race as part of a so-called new generation, mixed-race people have always existed in the United States (Bost, 2003; Morning, 2003). What is new are the U.S. Census categorizations and a significant number of people who identify as biracial or multiracial, take pride in their backgrounds, and/or seek specific recognition of their identities. For the bulk of U.S. history, this was not the case, and people of mixed-race ancestry were socially and legally marginalized.

Multiraciality as Pathology

As early as the colonial era, hypodescent and the one-drop rule were used to "group" multiracial people with people of color, as a means to preserve White supremacy and privilege by reinforcing the boundaries between Whites and non-Whites. Hypodescent refers to the process "whereby biracial individuals are assigned the status of their socially subordinate parent group" (Ho et al., 2011, p. 492). The one-drop rule "provides that one drop of Black blood makes a person Black" (Hickman, 1997, p. 1163). These means of identification have altered in deployment over time; for example, the one-drop rule was eventually internalized by African Americans and embraced as a mechanism for Black solidarity (Hickman, 1997).

Since the first contact between Whites, Blacks, Mexicans, and Indigenous peoples in the colonial era, and then the United States, there has been intermixing. Intermixing was often used as a tool of oppression and control, constituted by rape, sexual assault, and coerced sex. However, a small number of racially mixed families lived in anonymity or quietly involved themselves in causes for racial justice, such as abolitionism (Forbes, 1993; Nash, 2010). Sexual interaction between Blacks and Whites was a common occurrence during slavery. White enslavers, as well as other Whites, frequently raped and sexually assaulted Black women (Collins, 2000). Hence, a population of racially mixed persons of Black and White heritage emerged early on in U.S. history (Davis, 2001). The Census in the 1800s utilized terms such as *mulatto, quadroon,* and *octoroon* to identify those with Black ancestry (Hickman, 1997). Yet interracial contact resulting in biracial and multiracial children were not solely confined to Blacks and Whites. In the West during the early 1900s, interracial mixing occurred between Whites and Asian immigrants, although such mixing was rare and viewed as an abomination. Native American and White forced, coerced, and consensual relationships also occurred from the time of initial contact, and given their close social standing and geographical proximity in some areas of the United States,

African Americans and Native Americans engaged in interracial relationships (Brooks, 2002; Forbes, 1993; Perdue, 2005).

Given the strict U.S. racial hierarchy, the children who were born of interracial relationships were often viewed with outrage, disgust, and fascination. Reflecting racist sentiments of the time, early scholarly literature pathologized multiracial people, their experiences, and their identities. Rockquemore et al. (2009) characterize this literature as adopting the problem approach, which

> encompasses all work on racial identity development that takes as its basic tenet the idea that being a mixed-race person in a racially divided world is, in and of itself, a problematic social position that is inevitably marked by tragedy. (p. 16)

In his 1928 article "Human Migration and the Marginal Man," Robert Park argued that one of the inevitable results of migration was the mixing of disparate populations. This mixing process would manifest individuals of mixed racial, ethnic, and cultural backgrounds. Park (1928) asserted that "the man of mixed blood is one who lives in two worlds, in both of which he is more or less a stranger and exhibits the characteristics of spiritual instability, intensified self-consciousness, restlessness and malaise" (p. 893). Building upon Park's work, Stonequist (1935) described people of mixed race as subject to "pride and shame, love and hate, and other contradictory sentiments," which "mingle uneasily in his nature," resulting in "increased sensitiveness, self-consciousness and race-consciousness, an undefinable malaise, inferiority and various compensatory mechanisms" (p. 6). Park's and Stonequist's work reflected the notion that the mixing of the races resulted in people who were inherently deficient and dysfunctional, due to both their psyche and the impossibility of fitting in to the existing racialized social structure.

Understanding Multiracial Identity as Non-White Identity

The social and political changes that began with the civil rights movement in the 1950s and continued with the cultural nationalist movements in the late 1960s to early 1970s offered alternative ways to theorize people of mixed race. The civil rights movement promoted a belief system that encouraged people to look beyond race and recognize shared humanity (Jackson, 2006). The recognition of shared humanity served as the foundation for racial equality, which affirmed the value of all people, including those of mixed race. The cultural nationalist movements of the 1960s and early 1970s, such as the Black Power Movement, emphasized self-determination and racial pride among non-Whites (Gutierrez, 1998; Ogbar, 2005). In doing so, this altered understandings and conceptualizations of multiracial people. Rockquemore et al. (2009) noted that

> theorists working in the context of the Civil Rights and Black Power movements reoriented their thinking about Blackness and the one-drop rule. Researchers assumed that (Black/White) mixed-race people were part of the Black population and, as such, there was no need to draw such distinctions (referring back to the one-drop rule). Importantly, in this era, mixed-race people were expected to develop a positive sense of Black identity just like any other Black person. (p. 17)

Consequently, identity development models for people of color were presumed to be applicable to those of mixed-race ancestry.

Institutions of higher education and college students played central roles in both the civil rights and cultural nationalist movements. Students' activism included demanding that colleges and universities become more racially equitable and meet the needs of students of color through the implementation of ethnic studies courses, enrollment of more students of color, and hiring more faculty of color (Chavez, 2002; Joseph, 2003; Umemoto, 1989). However, advancements in theorizing identity development for students of color were relatively slow and incremental. For example, Arthur Chickering's (1969) seminal book, *Education and Identity*, while foundational to the study of student development, did not substantively explore how the seven vectors of development (developing competence, managing emotions, developing autonomy, developing mature interpersonal relationships, establishing identity, developing purpose, and developing integrity) could be impacted by race, ethnic culture, and/or the larger sociopolitical forces which manifest racial inequity. With minimal attention paid to non-White monoracial identities, multiracial identities were for the most part disregarded as a legitimate basis for rethinking development models.

The Shift: Laying the Groundwork for Multiracial Identity

The social progress driven by the civil rights movement and cultural nationalist movements ultimately contributed to an increase in the multiracial population and the proportion of this population identifying in nonmonoracial terms. First, the movements opened up both literal and symbolic areas of integration, such as colleges, where Whites and non-Whites slowly, but increasingly, began to engage in romantic interracial relationships (Root, 1996, 2003). Second, antimiscegenation laws were deemed unconstitutional with the Supreme Court ruling in the 1967 case *Loving v. Virginia* (Sollors, 2000). While the Loving case did not immediately lead to a flood of interracial marriages, it opened an important legal door. In 1967, only 3% of newly married couples were interracial couples. By 1980, the rate of interracial marriage had risen to 7%, and by 2015, it was 17% (Livingston & Brown, 2017). Third, in concert with legalization of interracial marriages and increasing integration, social approval of interracial relationships and marriages grew. Fourth, the growth in interracial relationships and marriages led to a notable increase in birthrates of multiracial babies. From 1980 to 2015, the number of U.S. infants born to interethnic or interracial couples tripled from 5% to 14% (Livingston & Brown, 2017).

Yet the rapid growth in interracial marriages and a multiracial baby boom still does not fully explain why calls for social, psychological, governmental, legal legitimation of mixed-race identity have recently emerged. Thus, we must turn to two political and intellectual factors. First, in the political realm, we have witnessed an increase in the importance attached to racial/ethnic designations as instrumental to public policy, which is rooted in great society and civil rights legislation (Williams, 2003, 2006). For example, public, governmental racial categorizations have been key in tracking the enforcement of civil rights legislation, as well as civil rights violations (Omi & Winant, 1994). Racialized political groups have increasingly recognized governmental legitimation of racial categories as tied to the groups' social status, public identity, and access to resources (DaCosta, 2003; Espiritu & Omi, 2000; Williams, 2003). This, in part, explains the mixed-race identity movement's focus on Census categories. Second, race theorizing has changed, increasingly recognizing the fluid and socially constructed nature of race. From social constructionism, to Whiteness studies, to postmodernism, to color-blind ideology, monoracialism, and the very meaning of race, has been aggressively interrogated, yielding intellectual space to explore deviations from monoracialism (Bonilla Silva, 2003; Korgen, 1998; Spickard, 2003; Winant, 2002). Together, these political and intellectual shifts further set the stage for new understandings of multiraciality and its relationship to identity and institutions, including that of higher education.

Pride and Self Determination: Multiracial Identity Rises

The social, political, and legal changes driven by the movements of the 1950s through 1970s ultimately contributed to a continual increase in the population of multiracial people and the emergence of literature which approached the experiences and identities of multiracial people with an analytical lens decidedly different from the lenses of pathology or racial solidarity utilized by previous scholars. During the 1990s, the dominant theoretical strain in the literature on multiracial people argued that biracial/multiracial identity progressively challenges monoracialism and, in so doing, challenges the racist sensibilities and ideologies on which biological theories of race were built. That is, it makes race more fluid, correctly identifies people, and discourages racism (Root, 2003; Wright, 1994; Zack, 1993). In their challenge of monoracialism, multiracialists—advocates for the recognition of multiracial identity—have often framed biraciality multiraciality as an issue of the individual. Exemplified by activists' emphasis on the "right" of a person to identify as biracial/multiracial, these writers pushed existing boundaries to urge institutions to recognize biracial multiracial identities and legitimize the personal narratives of people of mixed race (Root, 1994).

Moreover, in the 1990s, psychological concerns about multiracial children's self-esteem served as the basis for new identity development models that contested previous eras' characterization of multiracial people as "marginal" and/or as individuals who should be grouped with people of color for the sake of racial solidarity (Dalmage, 2000; Frazier, 2002). More psychologically oriented literature further reinforced an individualist understanding of multiracial identity. For instance, Poston (1990) proposed a biracial identity development model entailing the following five stages:

1. Personal identity: Children's racial identity and attitudes are not developed and/or are inconsistent. Identity is primarily derived from "self-esteem and feelings of self-worth that they develop and learn in the family" (p. 153).
2. Choice of group categorization: Individuals feel forced to choose one identity, which may result in alienation and marginalization.
3. Enmeshment/denial: Individuals feel confusion and guilt for choosing one identity.
4. Appreciation: Individuals begin to appreciate their full background, although they still only identify with one group.
5. Integration: Individuals recognize and value all identities and begin to feel secure in the multiplicity.

These stages contrast with earlier models of mixed-race identity that centered racial embattlement. This newer model "emphasizes the individual's need to value and integrate multiple cultures" and multiple racial identities (Poston, 1990, p. 154). However, such models generally did not take into consideration the role and reality of social institutions outside of the family, such as colleges and universities, which may influence how individual racial identities are constructed and enacted.

Whether psychological or more social in nature, literature in this vein decidedly characterized the development and assertion of a multiracial identity as positive and healthy. For example, Maria P. P. Root's numerous and influential writings constantly reiterate positive conceptualizations of multiraciality, with works ranging from *Love's Revolution: Racial Intermarriage* in 2001 to the *Bill of Rights for Racially Mixed People* in 1994, which has become a rallying cry for multiracial organizations. In her work *Five Mixed Race Identities: From Relic to Revolution*, Root (2003) presented five identities which mixed race people can assume: "(a) accept the identity society assigns . . . (b) choose a single identity . . . (c) choose a mixed identity . . . (d) choose a new race identity . . . (e) choose a White identity" (pp. 13–15). While Root critically analyzed each identity formation, the language in her texts revealed a preference for multiracial identities as optimal and characterization of monoracial identities as potentially problematic. For example, Root (2003) made several cautionary statements regarding the single identity choice, asserting that "actively choosing a monoracial or monoethnic identity does not guarantee that one will be spared racial authenticity tests or 'hazing'" and "sometimes the active choice of a single identity of a minority group reflected family dysfunction" (p. 14). While Root (2003) mentioned the drawbacks of the mixed-race identity, which include similar forms of "hazing and authenticity tests" (p. 15) she emphasized more the positive aspects of mixed-race identity, such as being loved by parents of different races and the purported ability to "transcend color" (p. 15).

Contemporary Higher Education Multiracial Identity Theories and Models

More recent literature from the 2000s contests the views that multiracial identity, and multiracial students' experiences in particular, can be thoroughly explained using traditional psychological development theories, which posit a specified beginning and end to identity development, where the end is constituted by proudly embracing a multiracial identity (Renn, 2008). Central to this literature is the rejection of linear, individualistic models of development and the contention that multiracial individuals can and will assert a range of identities, which may or may not change over time (Renn, 2000; Rockquemore et al., 2009). Identity development is viewed in an ecological context in which students' backgrounds, families, friends, institutions of higher education, student organizations, and classes shape the ways in which multiracial students make meaning of their experiences (Museus et al., 2015)

Fluidity of racial identity among students of multiracial backgrounds is a common theme throughout the current literature. Harper (2014) noted that the majority of multiracial students in her study changed their racial identification over the course of their undergraduate careers. Renn (2000, 2004) both built upon and departed from Root's (2003) work with her five identity constructs/patterns that multiracial people may hold: monoracial, multiple monoracial, multiracial, extraracial, and situational identities. With the monoracial identity, students chose their nondominant ancestry, and it was not until they were in college that their peer systems affected the degree to which they asserted their monoracial identity. The multiple monoracial identity entails equal acknowledgment of both parents' heritage. The students' propensity to identify with more than one monoracial group was dependent on their peers. Multiracial identities are those outside of the monoracial categories and include labels like multiracial, biracial, Hapa, and/or mixed. These students seemed to be most active in advancing multiracial initiatives on campus. Extraracial students opted out of racial categories all together. Lastly, situational identities were those that vary depending on space and place, making them fluid and contextually driven.

The literature suggests that adoption of any of Renn's (2000, 2004) identity constructs is substantively influenced by the nature of the interaction between students of mixed race and monoracially identified peers. Interactions can be shaped by questions of authenticity, physical appearance, cultural knowledge, education, and microaggressions. Peer cultures and student organizations may play instrumental roles in fostering a sense of belonging for multiracial students (Kellogg & Liddell, 2012). Student-led multiracial organizations and communities have been shown to positively impact multiracial students' experiences on college campuses (Museus et al., 2015; Wong & Buckner, 2008). Furthermore, participation in student organizations can shape and affirm students' identities, even if the institution does not (Kellogg & Liddell, 2012; Literte, 2009). In Harper's (2014) study, "joining a racial or ethnic student organization was predictive of a sustained multiracial designation and a sustained single-race designation" (pp. 942–943). Museus et al. (2015) also found that students themselves exercised agency and "sought and constructed support networks for multiracial college students" (p. 338). Ultimately, most of the spaces that provided affirming experiences were "student-initiated multiracial organizations" (Museus et al., 2015, p. 345).

Some campus interactions may present challenges or opportunities to multiracial students. One of the most frequent interactions that multiracial students experience is when they are explicitly asked about their racial identity (Tran et al., 2015). Multiracial students often find themselves to be objects of curiosity, pressured to continually answer questions, such as, "What are you?" (Kellogg & Liddell, 2012, p. 533). Responses to such inquiries run the gamut with some students viewing these as opportunities to express pride in their multiracial backgrounds, while others view them as microaggressions (Jeffries, 2012). Museus et al. (2015) found that multiracial students often took it upon themselves to educate others "about their racial backgrounds and engage in activity to spread awareness about multiracial issues toward the end of addressing prejudice and discrimination experienced by this population" (p. 338).

For some students, the question of "What are you?" is indicative of and is often followed by antagonistic challenges to their identity, whether they are identifying as multiracial or monoracial. For example, multiracial students who seek to identify with students of color may have their "authenticity" questioned (Museus et al., 2015). Authenticity assessments may include questioning students' cultural knowledge and evaluation of physical appearance (Chang, 2016; Renn, 2000; Sims, 2016). Evaluation of physical appearance as a measure of racial authenticity and identification has a long and fraught history. Historically, the one-drop rule ensured that no matter how "light" a person's skin was, they would be identified as Black. Multiracial students with racially ambiguous physical features may engage in "body work" (p. 571), such as altering one's hairstyle, which can in turn, change how they are perceived (Sims, 2016). A multiracial student with ambiguous racial features or appearing to be of a different racial group than that of which they are claiming membership, may experience monoracial students questioning their racial identity.

Cultural knowledge and behaviors are other measures utilized to evaluate multiracial students' authenticity. As Chang (2016) noted, we use racial rubrics that encompass a wide array of variables to assess others' racial authenticity:

> Racial rubrics exist because we recognize, through our approaches to racial labeling and differentiation that our phenotype, customs, movements, linguistic characteristics, class, sexuality, religion/spiritual beliefs, eating habits, schooling, interests, hobbies, educational background, family relationships, choices and nuances position us in distinct, often separate, boxes in the continuum of racial authenticity. (p. 718)

These racial rubrics exemplify the multidimensional standards of authenticity that multiracial students may be held to by their monoracial counterparts. That is, authenticity tests may go well beyond body work and evaluations of students' phenotypes and include assessments of culture, knowledge, personal interests, and other identities.

Peer interactions, as well as the perpetuation of "authentic" forms of cultural knowledge and behaviors, occur within institutional contexts that can shape multiracial students' experiences in college. The impact of institutional contexts begins even before students arrive on campus. Demographic data collection processes may or may not include those students who identify as multiracial or more than one race. Yet this would be an important first step to assessing and evaluating the multiracial student population's particular needs (Kellogg & Liddell, 2012). The racial categories used in demographic data collection are indicative of most universities' continued reliance on monoracial categories as a means for institutional organization. These practices publicly convey tacit legitimization of monoracialism. Monoracial categories are drawn upon in not only institutional research and admissions but also the organization of ethnic studies departments, cultural centers, student service offices, and most student clubs. For some students, the ways in which the institution is organized around race, and in particular monoracialism, amplifies the salience of race for them (Kellogg & Lidell, 2012). Furthermore, the institutional reliance on monoracialism is connected with larger sociopolitical forces. For example, the elimination of affirmative action in California's public institutions imbued a heightened sense of vulnerability among race-based student service offices. Under threat, some of these offices have been focused on merely surviving or serving their traditional student populations, not investing resources into implementing programming for small populations of multiracial students (Literte, 2010).

A Note Regarding Biracial Categorizations

As reflected in the literature on multiracial identity and peoples, *multiracial* is frequently used as an umbrella term that includes biracial people, as well as those who identify as more than two races. The U.S. Census reports also reflect this approach, using the terminology "Two or More Races." However, understanding multiraciality merits a discussion of literature that focuses specifically on biracial people, which tends to be based on the experiences of people with Black and White parentage or people of Asian and White parentage.

Black and White biracial identity has received most of the attention in research and literature due to the centrality of White supremacy and Black slavery in U.S. history. In the modern era, Whites and Blacks continue to be seen as the most socially distant racial groups, hence interracial relationships between the two elicit greater attention. As previously discussed, White people's desire to ensure a racial caste system during and after slavery resulted in the development of the concepts of hypodescent and the one drop rule. These concepts were coopted and internalized by the Black community as a means for racial solidarity and recognition of Blackness as a master status. In Cross's (1991) compelling work on Black identity, he argued that "the social science literature on Negro identity written between 1936 and 1967 reported that self-hatred and group rejection were typical of Black psychological functioning" (p. ix). His model, known as nigrescence, is a psychological model that describes the process of becoming Black. In spite of the significant number of African Americans/Blacks with White heritage, the closest Cross (1991) came to a focus on multiracial self-identification was through a multicultural perspective derived from "a *bicultural* reference group orientation from their nigrescence experience" (p. 213). Cross's and others' research followed the social and intellectual trends of the 1960s and 1970s, which applied Black identity development models to Black-White biracial people. However, over time, researchers began to consider that there might be differences in the experiences of Black-White biracial people and their monoracially Black identified counterparts. Research from Daniel (2002) did examine Black-White biracial identity formation and proposed three identity types: (a) synthesized identity, (b) functional identity/European American, and (c) African American functional identity. This typology indicated that Black-White identity can be integrative; pluralistic; and, depending on background and environment, mixed-race individuals may choose how to identify.

Different from the Black and White biracial narratives, Asian and White identity allows for more self-identification and social flexibility. *Hapa* is a Hawaiian word that literally means part, fragment, fraction, and so on, and it has been used to refer to Hawaiians with racially mixed backgrounds. While Hapa was originally a derogatory label, it is now used in a neutral or positive fashion. Its usage has spread to the mainland and has been adopted by some people of Asian American-White parentage (Edles, 2003). The assertion of this identity is rooted in "the growth of the Asian American population and, concurrently, intermarriages involving Asian America, in a time when racial attitudes toward minorities have become more tolerant" (Xie & Goyette, 1997, p. 54). Vast intermarrying between Whites and Asian Pacific Americans has been occurring since the 1960s. In particular, the passage of the 1965 Immigration Act yielded a large flow of Asian immigration. Educated Asian immigrants rapidly began to intermarry with Whites (Kitano & Daniels, 2005). Today such intermarriages are so common that some Asian ethnic groups, such as Japanese Americans, out-marry more than they in-marry (Alba & Nee, 2005; Qian et al., 2001).

Stereotypes of Asian Pacific Americans may also be contributing factors to the acceptance of Asian-White individuals. More specifically, Asian Pacific

Americans are often viewed as pseudo-White, model minorities who are passive, exceptionally intelligent, and work diligently to advance in U.S. society (Lee, 1996). These purported characteristics are much different from those ascribed to African Americans and Latinxs, who are frequently perceived as minorities unjustifiably looking for economic support from the government (Entman & Rojecki, 2001). Therefore, because Asian Pacific Americans are typically viewed as being socially closer to Whites than African Americans or Latinxs, they are also more likely to intermarry with Whites. Although children from interracial relationships involving Blacks are historically not allowed to claim Whiteness or any social identity which places them equally close to both their White and non-White parentage, children from Asian-White unions may be regarded more flexibly and allowed to claim both identities in the form of a Hapa identity because Whiteness and Asianness are perceived as somewhat compatible. Such racial identity processes among Asian Pacific American multiracials appear to be supported by literature which argues that biracial children of White and Asian American descent have racial options when identifying (Saenz et al., 1995; Xie & Goyette, 1997).

Though Black and White and Asian and White parentage are not the only biracial pairings, they are the largest biracial groups and the most discussed in literature. They are examples of how the biracial experience can be vastly different from group to group. It is important then to honor and understand the nuanced and complicated history of racial fluidity in the United States and how this plays out in local contexts and in educational settings. It is especially important to keep this in mind when applying multiracial identity theories and models.

Overview of CRT, Racial Formations Theory, and Black Feminist Thought Principles

The multiracial experience has a long history and is characterized by complexity and nuance, adding to the need for student recognition, space, and culturally competent educators and administrators in higher education. Traditional student development theories have been "raceless," and therefore inadequate for understanding the experiences of multiracial students (Patton et al., 2007). Conversely, monoracial student development theories focus on specific non-White groups and these students' experiences. The preponderance of evidence suggests that race plays a role in multiracial students' experiences, although the significance of its role may vary. It is a challenge to theorize multiracial identity, because multiraciality in itself is such a porous and fluid experience. People who are multiracial or identify as multiracial share the characteristic of being from a background in which the parents are of different racial groups or identities. But beyond this starting point, diversity abounds; multiracial people may come from a variety of racial backgrounds, as well as a range of class statuses, family structures, genders, sexual identities, cultures, and so on. The multiracial category clumps together many different people who may have very little in common. A student of Native and White parentage who is fair skinned, an upper-class suburban resident, and does not participate in any Native cultural practices is placed in the same category as a student of Black, Asian, and White ancestry who appears racially ambiguous, is a middle-class resident of a major urban center, and consistently engages in Asian and Black cultural practices. Considering most variables, these students are more different than they are similar. These differences contribute to the range of racial identities observed among multiracial students; multiracial students may identify as multiracial or monoracial or may have fluid identities, which are situational or change over time. Given the extraordinary diversity among multiracial students, whether any particular student's racial identity is psychologically "healthy" is truly dependent on the individual.

Given the complexities of multiraciality, as opposed to a specific identity development theory, I propose that a synthesis of CRT, racial formations theory, and Black feminist thought provides a more holistic understanding of multiraciality and can serve as a guide for educators and practitioners working with multiracial students. This interdisciplinary framework allows us to situate and understand how multiracial students' experiences are shaped in relation to larger historical and sociopolitical forces and institutions of higher education. This type of macro analysis of multiracial students' experiences is still underdeveloped in the literature, which tends to focus most on individual identity development and interactions with others on campus. This theoretical framework allows for an enhanced multidimensional analysis of multiracial identity, including the interplay among social structure, institutions of education, and students' lived experiences. In the following, the key tenets of each theory are reviewed, followed by an application of the theoretical framework to multiracial students.

CRT

CRT originated with legal scholars in the 1980s, with the premise that race is embedded in and fundamental to U.S. legal and social institutions (Crenshaw et al., 1995). CRT scholars argue that purportedly color-blind and meritocratic legislation conceals systematic institutional racism—Whiteness and White privilege—which is manifested in property rights. In CRT, first-person narratives from communities of color are viewed as valid and valuable ways to critique institutional racism. Furthermore, CRT is social justice oriented, contending that CRT scholarship must work toward social change and justice (Ladson-Billings & Tate, 1995). Dixson and Rousseau (2005) advanced the parameters and themes presented in CRT for specific application to education. They asserted that CRT in education:

1. argues that racial inequity in education is the logical outcome of a system of achievement premised on competition;
2. examines the role of education policy and educational practices in the construction of racial inequity and the perpetuation of normative Whiteness;
3. rejects the dominant narrative about the inherent inferiority of people of color and the normative superiority of White people;
4. rejects ahistoricism and examines the historical linkages between contemporary educational inequity and historical patterns of racial oppression;
5. engages in intersectional analyses that recognize the ways that race is mediated by and interacts with other identity markers (i.e., gender, class, sexuality, linguistic background, and citizenship status);
6. agitates and advocates for meaningful outcomes that redress racial inequity (it does not merely document disparities). (Dixson & Rousseau, 2005, p. 123)

Racial Formations Theory

Michael Omi and Howard Winant (2015) constructed racial formations theory in response to the weaknesses inherent in race theories of biologism, ethnicity, class, and nation. They argue that these theories fail to treat race as a fundamental axis around which our social, political, and economic lives turn. In an attempt to remedy such theoretical decentering of race, Omi and Winant (2015) defined *racial formations theory* as

> the socio-historical process by which racial categories are created, inhabited, transformed, and destroyed. . . . Racial formation is a series of historically situated projects in which human bodies are represented and organized. A racial project is simultaneously an interpretation, representation, or explanation of racial dynamics, and an effort to redistribute resources along particular racial lines. (p. 109)

Omi and Winant illuminate how the paradoxical fluidity and constancy of race inform the ways in which race, racial identity, and racial meanings are negotiated among and between the state, social institutions, and the general populace. Omi and Winant also asserted that race manifests as "a constituent of the individual psyche and of relationships among individuals; it is also an irreducible component of collective identities and social structures" (p. 138). Racial formations therefore recognizes the multiple planes on which race and racial identities may exist—both within individual psyches and social structures.

Omi and Winant (2015) specifically highlighted multiraciality as an example of racial formations at the micro level:

> One of the first things we notice about people when we meet them (along with their sex) is their race. We utilize race to provide clues about who a person is. This fact is made painfully obvious when we encounter someone whom we cannot conveniently racially categorize—someone who is, for example "racially mixed" or of an ethnic or racial group we are not familiar with. Such an encounter becomes a source of discomfort and momentarily a crisis of racial meaning. (p. 59)

The micro is inextricably attached to the macro in that "our ability to interpret racial meanings depends on preconceived notions of a racialized structure" (Omi & Winant, 1994, p. 59). At the institutional level, higher education is a compelling site for the study of racial formations and corollary political activity due to its unique historic and contemporary role as a flashpoint for volatile racial discourses and racial protest over the distribution of resources. Colleges and universities are shaped by larger social structures and, in turn, shape students' experiences at the microlevel.

Black Feminist Thought

Patricia Hill Collins's (1989) Black feminist thought comes from a longstanding tradition of Black women's resistance and resilience. It highlights the intersecting systems of oppression (race, gender, and class), or matrix of domination, enacted on Black women. Collins articulates an epistemological legacy and perspective of Black feminism that stems from a dialectical relationship between the suppression of Black women as knowledge producers, thinkers, and intellectuals and the activism of Black women who reject and resist their oppression. She identifies three interdependent oppressive structures for Black women. The first structure is economic; the second structure is the political dimensions of oppression; and the third is ideological, manifested in controlling images of Black women. Black feminist thought, and in particular, Collins's (2000) concept of the matrix of domination provides the tools to analyze the intricacies of multiracial students' experiences, which may entail occupation of both the spaces of the oppressed and the oppressor.

Using CRT, Racial Formations, and Black Feminist Thought to Understand Multiracial Students' Experiences

Reflecting the complexities of multiraciality, no one theory is sufficient for scholars or practitioners to understand multiracial students' experiences. I propose that multiracial students' experiences can be better understood by drawing upon CRT, racial formations, and Black feminist thought. The argument presented here about multiracial students' experiences reconfigures student development theories to illustrate the relationships among multiracial students' microlevel experiences, the social institution of higher education, and macrolevel racial forces and dynamics. Figure 16.1 visually presents the synthesis of these theories. First, the circle surrounding the "multiracial student" indicates that there is no defined beginning or end to multiracial students'

Figure 16.1. Multidimensional and integrative model of multiracial identity.

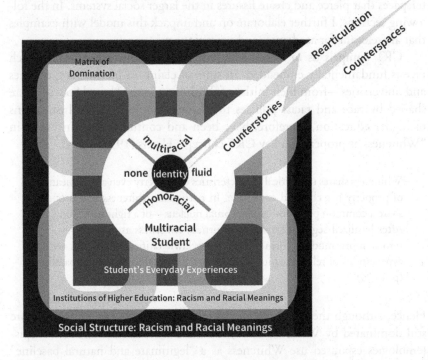

development. Multiracial students may identify as monoracial, multiracial, fluidly racial, or as no race at all. However, as indicated by the "x," students may travel back and forth across these identities, changing them according to time and circumstances; they also may occupy multiple identities at once, illustrating intersectionality. At this micro level, students reflect the racial formations process of inhabiting, transforming, and destroying racial categories. The fluidity of these identity formations is shaped and circumscribed by not only the student's experiences but also the larger social institution of higher education and social structure. The majority of higher education institutions are still engaging in racial formations, whereby they "inhabit" monoracial categories in large part, because, as CRT contends, race is embedded in the existing social structure. More specifically, monoracialism is embedded in the social structure and institutions of society, as the historical racial projects of colonialism and slavery relied on strict monoracial boundaries and distinctions. Furthermore, the matrix of domination, which creates interlocking systems of oppression along the lines of race, class, gender, and sexuality, bleeds into each level of this model—from the microlevel of students' experiences to the macrolevel of social structure. Despite the rigidity of the social structure and institutions of higher education, multiracial students still have the agency to leverage their identities and experiences to create counterstories and counterspaces that pierce and create fissures in the larger social systems. In the following sections, I further elaborate on and unpack this model with examples that are relevant for academics and practitioners.

CRT compels us to view higher education as an institution in which race is fundamentally embedded. In spite of claims of meritocracy, colleges and universities—from their initial establishment in the United States—were shaped by race and racist policies to exclude people of color. Institutions of higher education, therefore, have been and continue to be investors in "Whiteness as property," a key CRT concept. Harris (1993) stated,

> Whiteness shares the critical characteristics of property even as the meaning of property has changed over time. In particular, whiteness and property share a common premise—a conceptual nucleus—of a right to exclude. . . . After legalized segregation was overturned, whiteness as property evolved into a more modern form through the law's ratification of the settled expectations of relative white privilege as a legitimate and natural baseline. (p. 1714)

Hence, although the Jim Crow era has passed, colleges and universities are still dominated by White students, staff, and administrators, and the epistemologies espoused use Whiteness as a "legitimate and natural baseline"

(Harris, 1993, p. 1714) In doing so, institutions exclude or marginalize not only students of color but also multiracial students, who are often subject to or adopt the tenets of hypodescent and the one-drop rule.

However, the identity complexities and diversity of the multiracial student population are such that not all students will be marginalized or identify with students of color; the non-White/White binary is analytically insufficient. Here, racial formations theory is instructive in helping us better discern these complexities in identity and how multiracial students may interact with colleges and universities grounded in Whiteness. Omi and Winant (2015) define *racial formations theory* as "the socio-historical process by which racial categories are created, inhabited, transformed, and destroyed. . . . Racial formation is a series of historically situated projects in which human bodies are represented and organized" (p. 307). Racial formations theory thus emphasizes the fluidity, as well as the constancy, of race at micro- and macrolevels. As extensive research indicates, the identities among multiracial students are extremely fluid and can include identifying as multiracial, monoracial, or raceless. Identities can also be circumstantial and change over time. This framework allows for the recognition of all of these identity formations' existence, including multiracial students with White ancestry, who may attempt to claim their "Whiteness as property" and "normative Whiteness" because they are making a conscious or unconscious decision to ally themselves with the dominant group or simply because they identify with Whites more than non-Whites.

The identity formation process is not one that simply begins and ends with a student's arrival on campus and eventual graduation. How students self-identify; the communities to which they lay claim; and how they relate to the institution, particularly upon matriculation, are in part the result of the matrix of domination and racial projects to which students are exposed long before they arrive on campus. Collins's (2000) matrix of domination rejects "additive models" (p. 221) of oppression which view racism, classism, sexism, and homophobia as systems of oppression that function independently. Under additive models, Black women experience one oppression— racism—and then another oppression—sexism—that is added on separately. The matrix of domination instead views "race, class, and gender as interlocking systems of oppression" which "fosters a paradigmatic shift of thinking inclusively about other oppressions, such as age, sexual orientation, religion, and ethnicity" (Collins, 2000, p. 223). Racial formations allows for an understanding of how a multiracial student may engage "Whiteness as property." Black feminist thought provides a lens to further understand the complexities of multiracial students, particularly those with White parentage or ancestry, because as Collins asserted "depending on the context, an individual may be an oppressor, a member of an oppressed group, or simultaneously the oppressor and oppressed" (p. 224). The matrix of domination illuminates the reality that multiracial students can interact with larger systems of oppression, in which their multiple racial identities, class statuses, sexual orientations, and gender may situate them as oppressor, oppressed, or both depending on the circumstances.

Racial projects can be executed within the matrix of domination or weaponized to challenge the matrix. Omi and Winant (2015) define a *racial project* as "simultaneously an interpretation, representation, or explanation of racial dynamics, and an effort to redistribute resources along particular racial lines" (p. 125). Racial projects can occur at structural, institutional, and individual levels (Omi & Winant, 2015). Political efforts to pass more restrictive immigration laws can be considered a racial project, as can, for example, the activism of small groups of individuals who leave water in the desert for migrants who are attempting to cross the U.S.–Mexico border. Omi and Winant (2015) argue that these racial projects, big and small, are significant, as each one "attempts to reproduce, extend, subvert, or directly challenge" (p. 125) the social system's patterning of race. The multiracial student who identifies as White may have grown up exposed to a racial project of school funding implementation laws that exacerbate racial inequality yet are characterized as color-blind and fair. The understanding of "Whiteness as property" in a literal sense is also relevant here, as these students may come from "predominantly White communities who resent paying for a public school system whose clientele is largely non-White and poor" (Ladson-Billings & Tate, 1995, p. 53). The multiracial student who proudly asserts a multiracial identity may have been exposed to the racial project of the mixed-race identity movement, which celebrates multiraciality and the right to self-determination. Understanding the multitude of racial projects to which students have been exposed thus helps us understand how larger social and political forces shape identity.

Multiracially identified students can and do exercise agency by seeking to engage in racial projects that challenge institutions' perpetuation of the matrix of domination and, more specifically, institutions' deployment of monoracialism. In other words, colleges and universities are not only historically grounded in Whiteness but also perpetuate racial formations which put forth the notion that people can only belong to one race. When multiracial students seek to disrupt monoracialism and seek affirmation of their experiences and identities, they appear to manifest CRT's tenet of social activism as a part of any CRT project to improve the educational experiences of people of color (Dixson & Rousseau, 2005). Yet what this CRT activism should be is unclear when the issue at hand is multiraciality and multiracial people's experiences. In the contemporary era, the quest of organizations representing particular segments of the multiracial population to secure a "multiracial" category on the U.S. Census is the most notable example of activism that seeks to validate the identities and experiences of multiracial people. This particular effort can be considered part of the larger racial project of the multiracial identity movement, which interprets the racial dynamics of the U.S. as fluctuating and progressively changing because of an increase in interracial marriages and relationships which produce mixed-race offspring (Root, 2003; Zack, 1993). In turn, the movement believes that there must be new forms of representation for multiracial people, such as the creation of governmental classifications for multiracial people (Williams, 2006). The movement has also paired pursuits such as the creation of another racial classification/category with aims to redistribute resources; for example, mixed-race activists have argued that mixed-race people often have unique health needs due to their mixed-race background (Winters & DeBose, 2003). However, as previously discussed, major civil rights organizations opposed such a change, which was viewed as a move to deracialize the Census and impede access of communities of color to resources. CRT's extensive critique of color-blind ideology's influence on the law and legal system suggests that CRT principles align with the civil rights groups in this case. However, there is a sincerely held belief among some multiracially identified individuals that governmental validation of multiracial identity is not only just but also supportive of multiracial peoples' psychological health. There is an apparent conflict then between CRT-rooted activism to improve the ideological and material conditions of racial inequality for communities of color and the expressed need of some multiracial individuals to have their identities affirmed.

Although the applicability of CRT's mandate for social activism to multiracial students' experiences is unclear, student testimonials and creating supportive organizations and networks are reflective of the value CRT places on people's experiential knowledge, intersectional identities, and need to create and engage in counterstories and counterspaces. First-person narratives were central in the shift away from literature which pathologized multiracial people and multiracial identities, and they continue to be impactful today.

The counterstories and counternarratives constructed by students are derivative of their personal experiences, as well as their interactions with social institutions and structure. Various racial movements and projects foster *rearticulation*, which Omi and Winant (2015) defined as "a practice of discursive reorganization or reinterpretation of ideological themes and interests already present in subjects' consciousness, such that these elements obtain new meanings or coherence" (p. 165). The counterspaces, counterstories, and student organizations that multiracial students establish exemplify an effort to rearticulate understandings of multiraciality.

Furthermore, CRT's recognition of experiential knowledge is also reflected in more current literature focusing on multiracial people's experiences and identities, which challenges the notion that adoption of a multiracial identity is always the most desirable, most optimal, and healthiest choice for multiracial people. Instead, based on the viewpoints of multiracial people themselves, this literature finds extensive fluidity of identity, with multiracial people expressing that they may identify as multiracial, monoracial, or change their identity based on circumstance or over time. Out of this multitude of identities, one is not held up as the "ideal" for multiracial people; instead, greater importance is placed on preserving and advancing multiracial people's agency and right to identify as they wish.

CRT's legitimation of experiential knowledge and personal narratives serves as the foundation for multiracial people's engagement with intersectionality and counterspaces. Kimberlé Crenshaw (1991) coined the term *intersectionality* to recognize the ways in which race, class, gender, and so on can simultaneously shape people's lived experiences. She unpacked the concept further with a typology of intersectionality, which includes structural intersectionality (the ways in which groups' intersectional identities and corresponding social location yield different experiences from majority groups, which merit different institutional responses), political intersectionality (the ways in which intersectional identities may place people between various political entities that pursue conflicting political agendas), and representational intersectionality. In their study of African American students' experiences, Solórzano et al. (2000) described counterspaces as "sites where deficit notions of people of color can be challenged and where a positive collegiate racial climate can be established and maintained" (p. 70). First-person narratives are reflected in the current literature on multiracial students and illustrate the diverse range in identities. With its emphasis on the voice and agency of marginalized groups, CRT speaks to the importance of challenging the sentiment that a multiracial identity is desirable, healthy, or optimal and legitimizing multiracial students' multiple identity formations.

Recommendations for Practitioners

Renn (2004) recommended that higher education practitioners enhance multiracial students' campus life by affecting change in the following areas: assessments, policy change, programs, structural diversity, curriculum, and boundary crossing. Assessment entails accurately determining the number of multiracial students at a given institution and assessing the campus climate from the viewpoint of multiracial students. Policy change can include alterations in how local college and university policies racially categorize students or national governmental policies like the ability to report more than one race to the U.S. Department of Education. Programs that have the potential to enhance students' experiences include welcome space initiatives, student-led organizations, orientation presentations, multiracial speakers, awareness campaigns, and cultural events. Structural diversity, in the form of multiracial faculty, administrators, and staff, provides role models to whom students can turn for guidance. Curriculum can include information about multiracial issues and identities in the classroom, which challenge historic assumptions about the purportedly biological nature of race and rethinking the social construction of race. Lastly, institutionally sanctioned boundary crossing injects environments that encourage respectful cultural exchanges in spaces like orientation, advising groups, and leadership retreats. Though Renn (2008) proposed these recommendations just over a decade ago, we have yet to make advances in these areas on a large scale. Therefore, in the following discussion a few key recommendations are reiterated along with proposals for how institutions and personnel can facilitate multiracial students' development, and in so doing, enrich the collegiate experiences of these students.

Assessment

If we do not collect data on multiracial students, then we cannot begin to understand the scope of this student population's needs. According to Omi and Winant (1994),

> How one is categorized is far from a merely academic or even personal matter. Such matters as access to employment, housing, or other publicly or privately valued goods; social program design and the disbursement of local, state, and federal funds; or the organization of elections (among many other issues) are directly affected by racial classification and the recognition of 'legitimate' groups. (p. 3)

We cannot claim to work toward equity and inclusion without representation. And even if we suspect the multiracial student numbers are low at our respective institutions, the research indicates that the population of multiracial students is steadily growing.

Many institutions still do not offer students a multiracial option on forms or the option to mark more than one race. Following the practice of the U.S. Census, colleges and universities should engage in a racial formations process, whereby students are offered the option of marking more than one race on college forms. This approach to data collection is preferred over the inclusion of a multiracial category because high-quality assessments are in part contingent on the precision of data. A multiracial category is limited in its usefulness, as it groups together students of a wide array of racial backgrounds. It can include biracial students, as well as those students who have one great-great grandparent of a different race; it can include students of Black and White parentage, as well as Asian American and White parentage. If students are given the option of marking more than one race, it gives institutional research the opportunity to aggregate and disaggregate data. Alternatively, institutions could not only allow students to mark more than one racial category but also have a question that asks if students identify as multiracial. The racial formations process tells us that racial categories and racial identities are fluid; however, racial formations also indicates that racial categories and individual identities are not the same. A student might mark multiple racial categories on a form, but it does not mean that they *identify* as multiracial. Either of these changes to data collection conveys that institutions recognize the significance of race on both an institutional and personal level, as well as the fluid, intersectional identities students may possess. With these data, colleges and universities will have the ability to better understand the racial landscape of the student population, including the size of the student population that identifies as more than one race. Moreover, institutions can track the growth of the population over time.

Demographic data collection should be followed by a climate survey to investigate the degree to which the multiracially identified population has specific needs for resources, opportunities, and support that they would like the institution to address. It is crucial that students' voices are heard, and although institutionally implemented, a survey provides students the opportunity to share counterstories and engage in self-authorship. Looking for and listening to counterstories is essential to understand multiracial students' experiences. One should not assume that multiracial students, regardless of their population size, have racialized needs or concerns that warrant an institutional response. As the literature indicates, there are many multiracial students who are quite comfortable in monoracial environments. However, if students do express needs or desires for representation or specific services, colleges and universities must be responsive if they wish to be culturally sensitive and engaged in progressive racial projects that seek to distribute resources more equally. However, institutions may be limited in their capacity to respond fully or instantaneously, dependent on the availability of resources, personnel, and space. When institutions are unable to meet students' direct requests, adaptations to existing programs and services can still be implemented to illustrate that the institution recognizes and validates multiracial students' perspectives. For instance, a university may not have enough funds to fulfill students' requests for the establishment of a multiracial student services office or center. However, the university can still be responsive by creating a climate in which student service offices and programs are encouraged to collaborate. First, multicultural centers should implement programming which helps students make meaning of their experiences and recognizes multiracial people's identities (e.g., screening films/documentaries that focus on multiracial people, holding panels during which multiracial faculty or staff discuss their experiences). Second, monoracially based student services offices (e.g., Center for Asian Pacific American Students) can be encouraged or even required to create joint programming that recognizes multiracial identities. This type of programming can also potentially be validating for students who are not necessarily multiracial but who have other intersectional identities or life experiences, such as being transracially adopted.

Curricula

Validation of multiraciality needs to take place on both sides of the higher education "house"—student affairs and academic affairs. Although less studied than student services, the literature does indicate that classes, especially ethnic studies, can have an impact on multiracially identified students' experiences. Harper (2014) argued that "among the remaining college-level variables, living on campus, taking an ethnic studies course or racial/cultural awareness workshop, and discussing politics 'frequently' were all predictive of changing to a multiracial designation as seniors" (p. 943). While ethnic studies programs continue to face unyielding attacks from proponents of the racial project of color blindness, colleges and universities should require ethnic studies, which should include multiracial experiences. Bringing to light the untold legacy of multiracial people in the United States is an important component of institutionalizing counterstories, such that eventually they become simply stories.

Programs that have both a student affairs and an academic orientation have the potential to be the most impactful type of programming, as they can offer the opportunity for students to reexamine their identities in relation to others and the larger social structure. Programs, facilitated by appropriate faculty and staff, in which students from different backgrounds come together to eat and discuss topics of contention and importance are necessary for the advancement of mutual understanding and increased intercultural exposure for students of any race. Intergroup dialogue prepares students for diverse lives outside of institutions of higher learning and workforce environments. Ford and Malaney (2012) studied the effect of intergroup and intragroup dialogue courses on multiracial students and students of color at a historically White institution. They confirmed the importance of institutionalizing such courses about race, as opposed to assuming that cross-racial interactions among students will somehow occur organically.

Cultural Competency Training

The implementation of recommendations such as those described in the preceding section may be dependent on not only political will and resources but also appropriately trained, culturally competent faculty, administrators, and staff. Just as assumptions should not be made about multiracial students, we should not assume that administrators, faculty, and staff have a strong understanding of multiraciality, including its history and relationship to racial formations processes and the matrix of domination. Educators must avoid making assumptions about multiracial students and their identities and recognize that multiracial students' identities may vary widely. Students' identities may change dependent on the people surrounding them, location, circumstances, and time. Their racial identities may or may not be their master status. It is also important for educators to not reinforce the notion that there is a specific identity which is "best" or "healthiest" for multiracial students. The racial identity that is "best" or "healthy" will change from individual to individual. Additionally, multiracial students' experiences prior to arrival on campus may differ widely. For example, the racial projects to which they have been exposed, experiences growing up in a segregated or integrated neighborhoods, and family racial dynamics may vary substantially from student to student. Furthermore, multiracial students possess intersectional identities along the lines of race, class, gender, sexual orientation, and so on. Given these complexities and the relative newness of the legitimization of multiracial identities, colleges and universities should ensure that any cultural sensitivity or diversity training provided to administrators, faculty, and staff be inclusive of multiraciality.

Empowerment of Multiracial Students

The recommendations offered thus far have focused on the ways in which institutions can better acknowledge, validate, and serve multiracial students. Yet multiracial students themselves can also exercise their own agency in a way that will contribute to a more affirming environment. Numerous studies have illustrated the importance of peer groups and student organizations that advance students' counterstories and also offer counterspaces. Given the funding restraints of some institutions, personnel can still provide intentional guidance for multiracial students by offering to assist or advise them in the creation of student organizations and process of accessing available resources designated for student clubs.

In today's era, technology may be one of the most powerful tools that students can independently leverage to create a sense of belonging. Gasser (2008) noted, "The proliferation of multiracial groups on social networking sites shows that students look to online portals for a shared experience and supportive community" (p. 63). The most notable digital terrains include social networking sites, wikis, blogs, and video sites among others. These digital platforms can be a part of the mission fulfillment of CRT's call to support students' moves toward self-identification, occupying counterspaces, telling counterstories, and a rearticulation of the understandings of multiraciality. Digital campaigns like 500 Queer Scientists, an LQBTQ+ STEM visibility campaign, is a perfect example of storytelling and representation. Similar multiracial campus or national visibility initiatives may also be useful in increasing multiracial student representation.

Conclusion

As more multiracial students attend institutions of higher learning, we must do better to prepare for them and serve their needs within our limits. We must take responsibility as educators and staff to make sure multiracial students feel seen, heard, and represented. Doing so involves understanding that multiracial students are not empty vessels when they arrive on campus but are full human beings who are shaped by racial formations, racial projects, and the matrix of domination long before they arrive on campus. They will then be shaped by how the colleges and universities they attend deploy and engage in racial formations, racial projects, and the matrix of domination, as well as the extent to which they provide the literal and symbolic space for multiracial students to explore their identities and grow.

The literature on multiracial students continues to grow rapidly, but more can be done to help institutions better serve these students, and the natural place to start is with those institutions that are engaging in cutting edge or innovative practices. To that end, future research should further explore and engage in a comparative analysis of institutions of higher education that collect data on multiracial students, administer multiracial student services, have curricula that includes multiracial narratives, and implement cultural competency training for faculty and staff which addresses multiracial issues. Conversely, more research should be conducted on those institutions that have attempted to address multiraciality on their campuses but were not successful. Furthermore, longitudinal studies of students would greatly increase our understanding of multiracial students' diverse experiences over time and help us to identify how college impacts these students. In turn, academics and practitioners would develop a better sense and fuller view of these students that could inform student services and curricula. Finally, professional organizations such as National Association of Student Affairs Administrators in Higher Education (NASPA), the premier professional organization for student affairs professionals, can continue to support the work of entities such as the MultiRacial Knowledge Community. This NASPA community seeks to "stimulate education, develop knowledge, and promote resources and networking opportunities related to multiracial and transracial adoptee identity" (NASPA, 2019, para. 1). Moreover, in an effort to develop data and knowledge, these communities can work with groups from academic organizations, such as the American Psychological Association and American Sociological Association, to pool resources in order to execute more studies.

Institutions of education possess the power "to create, shape, and regulate social identities" and employ particular "institutional norms and procedures . . . to maintain a racial order," framing "how we see ourselves and others in a racial hierarchy" (Ferguson, 2001, p. 19). Thus, it is evident that examining colleges and universities as sites for the production, contestation, and negotiation of racial identities, including multiracial identity, will continue to be important given the unique standing of institutions of higher education as flashpoints for incipient political organization and mobilization around race.

References

Alba, R., & Nee, V. (2005). *Remaking the American mainstream: Assimilation and contemporary immigration.* Harvard University Press.

Bonilla Silva, E. (2003). *Racism without racists: Colorblind racism and the persistence of racial inequality in the United States.* Rowman and Littlefield.

Bost, S. (2003). *Mulattas and mestizas: Representing mixed identities in the Americas, 1850-2000.* University of Georgia Press.

Brooks, J. F. (Ed.). (2002). *Confounding the color line: The Indian-Black experience in North America.* University of Nebraska Press.

Cataldi, E. F., Bennett, C. T., & Chen, X. (2018). *First generation students: College access, persistence, and postbachelor's outcomes.* National Center for Education Statistics.

Chang, A. (2016). Multiracial matters—disrupting and reinforcing the racial rubric in educational discourse. *Race Ethnicity and Education, 19*(4), 706–730. http://dx.doi.org/10.1080/13613324.2014.885427

Chávez, E. (2002). *"¡Mi raza primero!" Nationalism, identity, and insurgency in the Chicano movement in Los Angeles, 1966-1978.* University of California Press. http://dx.doi.org/10.1080/13613324.2014.885427

Chickering, A. W. (1969). *Education and identity.* Jossey-Bass.

Collins, P. H. (1989). The social construction of Black feminist thought. *Signs: Journal of Women in Culture and Society, 14*(4), 745–773. https://doi.org/10.1086/494543

Collins, P. H. (2000). *Black feminist thought: Knowledge, consciousness, and the politics of empowerment.* Routledge. http://dx.doi.org/10.4324/9780203900055

Crenshaw, K. (1991). Mapping the margins: Intersectionality, identity politics, and violence against women of color. *Stanford Law Review, 43*(6), 1241–1249. http://dx.doi.org/10.2307/1229039

Crenshaw, K., Gotanda, N., Peller, G., & Thomas, K. (Eds.). (1995). *Critical race theory: The key writings that formed the movement.* The New Press.

Cross, W. E. (1991). *Shades of Black: Diversity in African-American identity.* Temple University Press.

Dacosta, K. M. (2007). *Making multiracials: State, family, and market in the redrawing of the color line.* Stanford University Press.

Dalmage, H. M. (2000). *Tripping on the color line: Black-White multiracial families in a racially divided world.* Rutgers University Press.

Daniel, G. R. (2002). *More than black?: Multiracial identity and the new racial order.* Temple University Press.

Davila, F. (2005, January 17). Race isn't as clear as black and white. *The Seattle Times.* https://archive.seattletimes.com/archive/?date=20050117&slug=mixed17m

Davis, F. J. (2001). *Who is black?: One nation's definition.* Pennsylvania State University Press.

Dixson, A. D., & Rousseau, C. K. (2005). And we are still not saved: Critical race theory in education ten years later. *Race Ethnicity and Education, 8,* 7–27. http://dx.doi.org/10.1080/1361332052000340971

Edles, L. D. (2003). "Race," "ethnicity," and "culture" in Hawai'i: The myth of the "model minority" state. In L. I. Winters & H. L. Debose (Eds.), *New faces in a changing America: Multiracial identity in the 21st century* (pp. 222–246). SAGE. http://dx.doi.org/10.4135/9781452233840.n12

Entman, R. M., & Rojecki, A. (2001). *The black image in the white mind: Media and race in America.* University of Chicago Press. http://dx.doi.org/10.7208/chicago/9780226210773.001.0001

Espiritu, Y., & Omi, M. (2000). 'Who are you calling Asian?': Shifting identity claims, racial classifications, and the Census. In P. M. Ong (Ed.), *The state of Asian Pacific America: Transforming race relations* (pp. 43–101). LEAP Asian Pacific American Public Policy Institute and UCLA Asian American Studies Center.

Ferguson, A. A. (2001). *Bad boys: Public schools in the making of black masculinity.* The University of Michigan Press.

Forbes, J. D. (1993). *Africans and Native Americans: The language of race and the evolution of red-black peoples.* University of Illinois.

Ford, K. A., & Malaney, V. K. (2012). "I now harbor more pride in my race": The educational benefits of inter- and intraracial dialogues on the experiences of students of color and multiracial students. *Equity & Excellence in Education, 45*(1), 14–35. http://dx.doi.org/10.1080/10665684.2012.643180

Frazier, S. (2002). *Check all that apply: Finding wholeness as a multiracial person.* InterVarsity Press.

Gasser, H. S. (2008). Being multiracial in a wired society: Using the internet to define identity and community on campus. In K. A. Renn & P. Shang (Eds.), *Biracial and multiracial students* [Special Issue] (New Directions for Student Services, no. 123, pp. 63–71). Wiley. http://dx.doi.org/10.1002/ss.287

Grieco, E., & Cassidy, R. (2001). Overview of race and Hispanic origin. *Census 2000 Brief,* C2KBR/01-1. U.S. Census Bureau.

Gutierrez, D. (1998). *CASA in the Chicano movement: Ideology and organizational politics in the Chicano community, 1968-1973.* Stanford Center for Chicano Research, Stanford University.

Harper, C. E. (2014). Pre-college and college predictor of longitudinal changes in multiracial college students' self-reported race. *Race Ethnicity and Education, 19*(2016), 927–949. http://dx.doi.org/10.1080/13613324.2014.911161

Harris, C. I. (1993). Whiteness as property. *The Harvard Law Review, 106*(8), 1707–1791. http://dx.doi.org/10.2307/1341787

Harris, J. C. (2017). Multiracial college students' experiences with multiracial microaggressions. *Race Ethnicity and Education, 20*(4), 429–445. http://dx.doi.org/10.1080/13613324.2016.1248836

Harvey Wingfield, A., & Feagin, J. R. (2013). *Yes we can? White racial framing and the Obama presidency.* Routledge. http://dx.doi.org/10.4324/9780203078730

Hickman, C. B. (1997). The devil and the one drop rule: Racial categories, African Americans, and the U.S. census. *Michigan Law Review, 95*(5), 1161–1265. http://dx.doi.org/10.2307/1290008

Ho, A. K., Sidanius, J., Levin, D. T., & Banaji, M. R. (2011). Evidence for hypodescent and racial hierarchy in the categorization and perception of biracial individuals. *Journal of Personality and Social Psychology, 100*(3), 492–506. http://dx.doi.org/10.1037/a0021562

Iwasaki, J. (2004, March 24). Foundation helps those of mixed race. *Seattle Post-Intelligence Reporter.* http://seattlepi.nwsource.com/local/165661_mixedrace20.html

Jackson, T. F. (2006). *From civil rights to human rights: Martin Luther King, Jr., and the struggle for economic justice.* University of Pennsylvania Press.

Jeffries, M. P. (2012). 'Mutts like me': Multiracial students' perceptions of Barack Obama. *Qualitative Sociology, 35,* 183–200. http://dx.doi.org/10.1007/s11133-012-9226-4

Jones, N. A., & Bullock, J. (2012). The two or more races population: 2010. *2010 Census Briefs.* C2010BR-13, U.S. Census Bureau.

Joseph, P. E. (2003). Dashikis and democracy: Black studies, student activism, and the Black Power movement. *The Journal of African American History, 88*(2), 182–203. http://dx.doi.org/10.2307/3559065

Joseph, R. L. (2011). Imagining Obama: Reading overtly and inferentially racist images of our 44th president, 2007–2008. *Communication Studies, 62*(4), 389–404. http://dx.doi.org/10.1080/10510974.2011.588074

Kellogg, A. H., & Liddell, D. L. (2012). "Not half but double": Exploring critical incidents in the racial identity of multiracial college students. *Journal of College Student Development, 53*(4), 524–541. https://doi.org/10.1353/csd.2012.0054

Kitano, H. H., & Daniels, R. (2005). *Asian Americans: Emerging minorities.* Prentice Hall.

Korgen, K. O. (1998). *From black to biracial: Transforming racial identity among Americans.* Praeger Publishers.

Ladson-Billings, G., & Tate, W. F. (1995). Toward a critical race theory of education. *Teachers College Record, 97,* 47–68. https://www.researchgate.net/publication/279676094_Toward_a_Critical_Race_Theory_of_Education

Lee, S. J. (1996). *Unraveling the model minority stereotype: Listening to Asian American youth.* Teachers College Press.

Literte, P. (2009). "We have created our own meaning for Hapa identity": The mobilization of self-proclaimed Hapas within institutions of higher education. *Amerasia Journal, 35*(2), 191–212. http://dx.doi.org/0.17953/amer.35.2.983647568174q020

Literte, P. (2010). Revising race: How biracial students are changing and challenging student services. *Journal of College Student Development, 51*(2), 115–134. http://dx.doi.org/10.1353/csd.0.0122

Livingston, G., & Brown, A. (2017). *Intermarriage in the U.S. 50 years after Loving v. Virginia.* Pew Research Center.

Morning, A. (2003). New faces, old faces: Counting the multiracial population past and present. In L. I. Winters & H. L. DeBose (Eds.), *New faces in a changing America: Multiracial identity in the 21st century* (pp. 41–67). SAGE.

Museus, S. D., Sariñana, S. A. L., & Ryan, T. K. (2015). A qualitative examination of multiracial students' coping responses to experiences with prejudice and discrimination in college. *Journal of College Student Development, 56,* 331–348. http://dx.doi.org/10.1353/csd.2015.0041

Nash, G. B. (2010). *Forbidden love: The hidden history of mixed-race America* (rev. ed.). Berkeley: University of California Press.

NASPA. (2019). *NASPA multiracial knowledge community.* https://www.naspa.org/division/multiracial

Obama, B. (2008, March 18). *Transcript: Barack Obama's speech on race.* National Public Radio. https://www.npr.org/templates/story/story.php?storyId=98455533

Ogbar, J. O. G. (2005). *Black power: Radical politics and African American identity.* Johns Hopkins University Press.

Omi, M., & Winant, H. (1994). *Racial formation in the United States: From the 1960s to the 1990s* (2nd ed.). Routledge.

Omi, M., & Winant, H. (2015). *Racial formation in the United States: From the 1960s to the 1990s* (3rd ed.). New York: Routledge.

Park, R. E. (1928). Human migration and the marginal man. *American Journal of Sociology, 33*(6), 881–893. http://dx.doi.org/10.1086/214592

Parker, K., Horowitz, J. M., Morin, R., & Lopez, M. H. (2015, June 11). *Multiracial in America: Proud, diverse and growing in numbers.* Report prepared for Pew Research Center. https://www.pewsocialtrends.org/2015/06/11/multiracial-in-america/

Patton, L. D., McEwen, M., Rendon, L., & Howard-Hamilton, M. F. (2007). Critical race perspective on theory in student affairs. In S. R. Harper & Lori D. Patton (Eds), *Responding to the realities of race on campus* (New Directions for Student Services, no. 120, pp. 39–53). http://dx.doi.org/10.1002/ss.256

Patton, L. D., Renn, K. A., Guido, F. M., & Quaye, S. J. (2016). *Student development in college: Theory, research and practice* (3rd ed.). Jossey-Bass.

Perdue, P. (2005). *Mixed blood Indians: Racial construction in the early South.* University of Georgia Press.

Perlman, J., & Waters, M. C. (2002). *The new race question: How the Census counts multiracial individuals.* Russell Sage Foundation.

Pettigrew, T. (2009). Post-racism?: Putting President Obama's victory in perspective. *Du Bois Review: Social Science Research on Race, 6*(2), 279–292. http://dx.doi .org/10.1017/S1742058X0999018X

Poston, W. C. (1990). The biracial identity development model: A needed addition. *Journal of Counseling & Development, 69*(2), 152–155. http://dx.doi .org/10.1002/j.1556-6676.1990.tb01477.x

Qian, Z., Blair, S. L., & Ruf, S. D. (2001). Asian American interracial and interethnic marriages: Differences by education and nativity. *International Migration Review, 35*(2), 557–586. http://dx.doi.org/10.1111/j.1747-7379.2001.tb00029.x

Renn, K. A. (2000). Patterns of situational identity among biracial and multiracial college students. *The Review of Higher Education, 23*(4), 399–420. http://dx.doi .org/10.1353/rhe.2000.0019

Renn, K. A. (2004). *Mixed race students in college: The ecology of race, identity, and community on campus.* State University of New York Press.

Renn, K. A. (2008). Research on biracial and multiracial identity development: Overview and synthesis. In K. A. Renn & P. Shang (Eds.), *Biracial and multiracial students* [Special Issue] (New Directions for Student Services, no. 123, pp. 13–21). http://dx.doi.org/10.1002/ss.282

Rockquemore, K. A., Brunsma, D. L., & Delgado, D. J. (2009). Racing to theory or retheorizing race? Understanding the struggle to build a multiracial identity theory. *Journal of Social Issues, 65*(1), 13–34. http://dx.doi.org/10.1111/j.1540-4560.2008.01585.x

Root, M. P. P. (1996). *The multiracial experience: Racial borders as the new frontier.* SAGE. http://dx.doi.org/10.4135/9781483327433

Root, M. P. P. (2003). Five mixed-race identities: From relic to revolution. In L. I. Winters & H. L. DeBose (Eds.), *New faces in a changing America* (pp. 3–20). SAGE. http://dx.doi.org/10.4135/9781452233840.n1

Root, M. P. P., & Kelley, M. (2003). *Multiracial child resource book: Living complex identities.* Mavin Foundation.

Saenz, R., Hwang, S. S., Aguirre, B. E., & Anderson, R. N. (1995). Persistence and change in Asian identity among children of intermarried couples. *Sociological Perspectives, 38*(2), 175–194. http://dx.doi.org/10.2307/1389289

Sims, J. P. (2016). Reevaluation of the influence of appearance and reflected appraisals for mixed-race identity: The role of consistent inconsistent racial perception. *Sociology of Race and Ethnicity, 2*, 569–583. https://doi.org/10.1177/2332649216634740

Smith, C. (2005, December 26). Sister as donor match thrilled another family. *Seattle-Post Intelligence Reporter.* http://seattlepi.nwsource.com/local/253436_mednicoleforweb26.html

Sollors, W. (2000). *Interracialism: Black-white intermarriage in American history, literature, and law.* Oxford University Press.

Solórzano, D., Ceja, M., & Yosso. T. (2000). Critical race theory, racial microaggressions, and campus racial climate: The experiences of African American college students. *The Journal of Negro Education, 69*(1/2), 60–73. https://www.middlesex.mass.edu/RLOs/748/Critical-Race-Theory.pdf

Spickard, P. (2003). Does multiraciality lighten? Me-too ethnicity and the whiteness trap. In L. I. Winters & H. L. DeBose (Eds.), *New faces in a changing America: Multiracial identity in the 21st century* (pp. 289–300). SAGE. http://dx.doi.org/10.4135/9781452233840.n14

Stonequist, E. V. (1935). The problem of the marginal man. *American Journal of Sociology, 41*(1), 1–12. https://doi.org/10.1177/144078337601200212

Sundstrom, R. R. (2001). Being and being mixed race. *Social Theory and Practice, 27*(2), 285–308. https://doi.org/10.5840/soctheorpract200127213

Tran, A. G. T. T., Miyake, E. R., Martinez-Morales, V., & Csizmadia, A. (2016). "What are you?" Multiracial individuals' responses to racial identification inquiries. *Cultural Diversity and Ethnic Minority Psychology, 22*(1), 26–37. http://dx.doi.org/10.1037/cdp0000031

Umemoto, K. (1989). "'On strike!' San Francisco State College strike, 1968-69: The role of Asian American students." *Amerasia Journal, 15*(1), 3–41. https://doi.org/10.17953/amer.15.1.7213030j5644rx25

Williams, K. M. (2003). From civil rights to the multiracial movement. In L. I. Winters & H. L. DeBose (Eds.), *New faces in a changing America: Multiracial identity in the 21st century.* SAGE. http://dx.doi.org/10.4135/9781452233840.n5

Williams, K. M. (2006). *Mark one or more: Civil rights in multiracial America.* University of Michigan Press. http://dx.doi.org/10.3998/mpub.17441

Winant, H. (2002). *The world is a ghetto: Race and democracy since World War II.* Basic Books.

Winters, L. I., & DeBose, H. L. (Eds.). (2003). *New faces in a changing America: Multiracial identity in the 21st century.* SAGE.

Wong, M. P. A., & Buckner, J. (2008). Multiracial student services come of age: The state of multiracial student services in higher education in the United States. In K. Renn & P. Shang (Eds.), *Biracial and multiracial students* (New Directions for Student Services, no. 123, pp. 43–51). Wiley. http://dx.doi.org/10.1002/ss.285

Wright, L. (1994, July 24). One drop of blood. *The New Yorker,* 46–55. https://www.newyorker.com/magazine/1994/07/25/one-drop-of-blood

Xie, Y., & Goyette, K. (1997). The racial identification of biracial children with one Asian parent: Evidence from the 1990 Census. *Social Forces, 76*(2), 547–570. https://doi.org/10.2307/2580724

Zack, N. (1993). *Race and mixed race.* Temple University Press.

ALTERNATIVE FRAMEWORKS AND MODELS FOR NONTRADITIONAL COLLEGE STUDENT POPULATIONS

17

DUAL ANCHORING

Advancing a Framework for Nontraditional Doctoral Degree Student Success

Derrick Robinson

A ttainment of the doctoral degree remains a rare accomplishment. Statistically, as of 2015, approximately 1.7% of U.S. citizens and .716% of citizens worldwide, ages 25 and older, possessed a doctoral degree (UNESCO, n.d.). While certainly still a small group, trends have shown significant growth of earned doctorates over the last decade in the United States. In mathematics and computer sciences and physical and earth sciences, the last 10 years have shown 42.4% and 33.4% growth, respectively, as shown in Table 17.1. Growth trends in earned doctoral degrees have looked particularly promising for women in the last decade, particularly in the fields of engineering, physical and earth sciences, and life sciences (National Science Foundation, 2017a). However, although women are 50.8% of the U.S. population, they represented only 46.1% of doctoral recipients in 2016 (National Science Foundation, 2017a; U.S. Department of Commerce, 2016). Despite tremendous growth, the gender profile of the doctoral recipient still leans toward men.

Trends have also shown growth in the racial and ethnic diversity of the recipients of doctoral degrees. In the last 10 years, Hispanic and African-American doctoral recipients have grown by 53.6% and 31.4%, respectively, as shown in Table 17.2. While these numbers are promising, they reveal how small the percentage, in proportion to the population, is of earned doctorates held by marginalized persons of color. Hispanic, African American, and American Indian populations represent 17.8%, 13.3%, and 1.3% of the U.S. population, but they only represent 5.2%, 6.5%, and .2% of doctoral recipients, respectively (National Science Foundation, 2017b; U.S. Department

TABLE 17.1

**Percent Change of Doctorate Recipients by Sex
and Field of Study (2006–2016)**

General Field of Study			
	Total (%)	*Men (%)*	*Women (%)*
Life sciences	29.5	20.3	38.3
Physical and earth sciences	33.4	29.1	44.3
Mathematics and computer sciences	42.4	44.6	36.2
Psychology and social sciences	25.5	22.0	28.3
Engineering	31.8	27.0	51.0
Education	–15.8	–27.2	–9.6
Humanities and arts	2.9	–1.5	7.4
Total	20.4	18.4	23.0

Note. Data retrieved from National Science Foundation, National Center for Science and Engineering Statistics, Survey of Earned Doctorates, Table 15; National Science Foundation (2017a). *Doctoral recipients by sex and major field of study: 2006-2016* [Table 15]. Washington DC: National Center for Science and Engineering Statistics, Survey of Earned Doctorates

TABLE 17.2

Doctorate Recipients by Race and Ethnicity, 2006–2016

Race/Ethnicity	*Growth (%)*	*Percentage of Recipients (%)*
American Indian/Alaska Native	10.6	.2
Asian	20.9	25.6
Black/African American	31.4	5.2
Hispanic	53.6	6.5
White	14	52.4
Total	20.4	-

Note. Data retrieved from National Science Foundation, National Center for Science and Engineering Statistics, Survey of Earned Doctorates, Table 19; National Science Foundation (2017b). *Doctoral recipients by ethnicity, race, and citizenship status: 2006-2016* [Table 19]. Washington DC: National Center for Science and Engineering Statistics, Survey of Earned Doctorates

of Commerce, 2016). In the United States, the racial profile of the average doctoral recipient in 2016 was White or Asian.

This chapter focuses on the growing but underrepresented population of doctoral recipients in American, Westernized universities. In its initial discourse, this population will be referred to as *nontraditional doctoral degree students*. It is important to note that this description of this population emerges from Western research literature on the topic of their success or attrition in their educational attainment.

Who Is the Nontraditional Doctoral Degree Student?

According to literature, this population is part-time, more diverse, mostly women, older than 30 years old, married with children or dependent parents, works full-time, and is self-funded (paying for tuition out of pocket or through student loans) (Offerman, 2011). Although research finds it difficult to fully define a part-time student, this population is generally considered to be part-time, doctoral degree students, with a full-time professional life (Bates & Goff, 2012; Gardner & Gopaul, 2012; Mills et al., 2014). Further, research on the part-time doctoral degree student positions a small, but growing, population of older students who are challenged to balance professional life and academic life. In Canada, the number of part-time doctoral students has doubled since the turn of the 21st century (Bates & Goff, 2012). In the United States, part-time doctoral degree students represented 38% of doctoral student enrollment in public and private research universities (Allum, 2014).

Traditional

Examining age in concert with field study and demographic characteristics helps provide a profile of the nontraditional doctoral degree student. Offerman (2011) also provided a profile of the so-called traditional doctoral student. This student is predominantly White, male, enrolled full-time, 22 years to 30 years old, single, childless, preparing to be a scholar in higher education, focusing on the research doctorate (i.e., PhD), typically a graduate assistant, and funded through tuition waivers or stipends. Accounting for age, statistics allow us to see and determine a profile of what could be considered the nontraditional doctoral degree student. As demonstrated in Table 17.3, we conclude that older, female, and marginalized minority populations pursue doctorates in education and the social sciences, creating the nontraditional student profile (National Science Foundation, 2017c).

Positioning the Nontraditional

The nontraditional doctoral degree student is framed as living on the periphery of the doctoral experience. Because the general assumption of the doctoral student is that of a young, White, male, full-time student, students who

TABLE 17.3
Doctorate Demographics Compared to Field of Study

	Demographics	Average Age (Years)	Older Than 30 (%)	Older Than 40 (%)
Field of Study	All	31.6	55.8	13.1
	Life Sciences	30.9	49.8	10.0
	Physical and Earth Sciences	29.5	33.4	3.0
	Mathematics and Computer Sciences	30.3	43.8	6.1
	Psychology and Social Sciences	32.5	63.6	14.0
	Engineering	32.5	38.8	4.5
	Education	38.6	74.5	26.3
	Humanities and Arts	34.1	71.0	10.4
Sex	Men	31.3	53.1	10.4
	Women	32.0	58.8	16.1
Citizenship Status	U.S Citizen or Permanent Resident	32	58.3	16.9
	Temporary Visa Holder	31	50.2	4.7
Race and Ethnicity	American Indian/Alaska Native	39.2	85.7	41.3
	Asian	31.4	54.4	11.5
	Black/African American	35.9	76.7	33.1
	Hispanic	32.7	62.2	17.8
	White	31.8	56.6	15.9

Note. Data retrieved from National Science Foundation, National Center for Science and Engineering Statistics, Survey of Earned Doctorates, Table 27; National Science Foundation (2017c). *Median age and age distribution of doctoral recipients by broad field of study, sex, citizenship status, ethnicity, and race: 2006-2016* [Table 27]. Washington DC: National Center for Science and Engineering Statistics, Survey of Earned Doctorates

do not meet these assumptions are positioned as *invisible* (Bates & Goff, 2012; Neumann & Rodwell, 2009; Teeuwsen et al., 2014). Advancing the idea of legitimate peripheral participation, Teeuwsen et al. (2014) positioned nontraditional students as existing on the periphery of the academic community and challenged by the strain of shifting mindsets from professional to student. While access through distance education has increased the opportunities for nontraditional doctoral degree students, it also positions them as strangers to the context of the university campus life. This assertion is supported through the integration of the work of Gardner and Gopaul (2012), Mills et al. (2014), and Teeuwsen et al. (2014), which further suggests that nontraditional doctoral degree students are less engaged in scholarly work and opportunities afforded through informal networks that result from participation in the academic community.

Adopting a Framework for Study

The adoption of a framework is essential for identifying, assessing, and providing agency for the nontraditional doctoral degree student. Frameworks and conceptual models provide us with a lens for understanding the subject and context of our study. In studying American and Westernized colleges and universities, Western frameworks are assumed to be *traditional*. Indigenous or non-Western frameworks are, therefore, positioned as *alternative* frameworks. In this section, we provide a quick overview of traditional and alternative frameworks for examining the nontraditional doctoral degree student.

Traditional Frameworks

We use the discourse of *traditional frameworks* to be understood as *White Western thought*. The convergence of the two is itself an example of White Western thought, a hegemonic construction of society in favor of Western European ideals, which also includes White America. However, our purpose here is to examine how traditional frameworks for understanding, approaching, and assessing doctoral degree students is framed in White Western literature and practice. The two guiding frameworks for this exploration are Bean and Metzner's (1985) conceptual model of nontraditional undergraduate student success and Berger and Milem's (1999) causal model of student persistence.

Student Success
The conceptual model of Bean and Metzner (1985) serves as an elaboration of Tinto's (1975) assertion that academic success is contingent upon the individual's ability to integrate academically and socially in the college environment. Their conceptual model forms the basis of current research on understanding and predicting student success in higher education (University of Maryland University College, 2015). While asserting that it is difficult to frame a prototype nontraditional undergraduate student, the

model presented by Bean and Metzner describes general characteristics of nontraditional undergraduate students as women, ethnic minoritized persons, students over 25, and those who attend part-time. The conceptual model of nontraditional undergraduate student attrition examines the interacting variables at play that contribute to the dropout rate of nontraditional undergraduate students.

Bean and Metzner (1985) examine background variables, the achieved and ascribed characteristics of students, academic and environmental variables associated with school and home, and academic and psychological outcomes that contribute to college dropout. Congruent with White Western thought, Bean and Metzner (1985) begin their model with the background of students as the defining variables for understanding student attrition. It is important to note that two of the three variables, student background and environmental variables, are both noninstitutional and framed as direct and most important to college dropout. Moreover, of the five subtopics within the academic variable, only two, academic advising and course availability, can be positioned as institutional. It can be concluded, therefore, that the institution, as structural support or administrator of faculty actors, has a minimal role in student dropout.

Findings supporting the development of this model suggest that age, when associated with family responsibility and hours of employment, might have an association with student attrition. Studies supporting the development of this model have produced mixed results on race and gender attrition rates (Alfred, 1973; Bennett & Bean, 1984; Nelson et al., 1984). Bean and Metzner (1985) found that while most studies report lower persistence rates for Black students compared to White students, a few studies have found the reverse. Gender, particularly for women, is likely to have indirect effects on attrition when associated with environmental variables, family responsibility, and opportunity to transfer. Of the structural variables noted in the model, Bean and Metzner (1985) found *academic advising* provided minimal to inconsistent results on student attrition while course availability was found to be a direct factor in dropout. Student success at White Western campuses is primarily the product of individual factors.

Student Persistence

Berger and Milem's (1999) model of student persistence emerged as an elaboration on earlier theories of involvement. Under the theory of involvement, student success or departure from college is explained by their level of integration in their first year. Berger and Milem (1999, 2000) elaborated on the theory of involvement by merging the concept of interaction as a means of explaining student persistence. Therefore, the level to which a student commits, becomes involved, and integrates within the system—in other words, becomes *interactive*—will determine whether they will persist in the higher education environment.

It is important to note that according to the undergraduate persistence model, student persistence is almost exclusively the function of ascribed and achieved characteristics of the individual. Race, gender, and family income, as ascribed characteristics of the individual, are the initial variables that impact student persistence in this model. Political view, high school grade point average, and whether the institution was a top choice of the student, as achieved characteristics, are also positioned as initial variables that impact student persistence. The remaining variables and models are based upon student perceptions of their involvement and integration into college life. The institution, as structural support or faculty and administrative actors, is viewed as minimal in the understanding of student persistence.

Findings from studies within the model suggested that race, particularly being African American, and political views, particularly holding a liberal worldview, had a negative effect on persistence (Milem & Berger, 1997; Pascarella & Terenzini, 1991). Likewise, gender, particularly being female, and income, particularly having a higher family income, added positive effects on interaction and involvement, thereby increasing persistence. This model of student persistence, as framed by Berger and Milem (1999) suggested that "students who are most likely to persist are those who have values, norms, and establish patterns of behavior that are congruent with the dominant values, norms, and establish patterns . . . that are already in existence on campus" (p. 661). Therefore, students on White Western university campuses must reflect, possess, or be willing to assimilate to the values of White Western dominant practices to persist in higher education.

Alternate Frameworks

For the moment, as with traditional frameworks, we will use the term *alternative frameworks* to be understood as *Indigenous or non-Western thought*. It is understood that the convergence of the two is a reification of White Western thought, which positions anything other than traditional as exotic and secondary. However, this chapter asserts that frameworks framed as alternative are as legitimate as those considered traditional. Moreover, the observed increase in diversity in society, and in the context of this study, suggests that alternative frameworks may be more appropriate to understand the nontraditional doctoral degree student. The two guiding frameworks for this exploration are Singh et al.'s (2016) *Indigenous and non-Western theoretic-linguistic knowledge* and Shockley and Frederick's (2010) *constructs and dimensions of Afrocentric education.*

Theoretic-Linguistic Knowledge

The adoption of theoretic-linguistic knowledge is a framework that implies an epistemological view that is grounded in a transcultural, nonlinear approach to knowledge construction. The integration of the scholarship of Singh et al. (2016) and Mampaey and Zanoni (2016) suggests the inclusion of Indigenous and non-Western theory, literature and research, and language and discourse as a legitimate proclamation of diversity. Theoretic-linguistic knowledge, as established by Singh et al. (2016), includes the "concepts, metaphors and images which Indigenous and other non-Western scholars introduce into research from their home cultures, or knowledge produced using linguistic or cultural elements of their home countries" (p. 57). The acknowledgment of intellectual property and discourse of Indigenous and non-Western populations, supported by Mampaey and Zanoni's (2016) critique of monocultural suppression of non-Western culture, provides an opportunity to employ a plurality of understandings of knowledge and people.

The work of Singh et al. (2016) supports the adoption of a transcultural approach to the construction of knowledge and the authentic support of diversity. The transcultural approach counters knowledge hierarchies and arrogance with epistemological openness and curiosity. Rather than adopting a singular view of what is truth and knowledge, this approach acknowledges the importance of context to expand conceptions of a doctoral degree student. Singh et al.'s (2016) transcultural assertion of blending theoretic and linguistic knowledge means reexamining the power of language and the authorship of ideas and knowledge construction. Theoretic-linguistic knowledge implies not only interrogating what is meant by the terms *traditional* and *nontraditional* students but also observing how such discourse impacts the actions of university administration, faculty, and students. This approach also means expanding research approaches to include the lived experiences and perspectives of nontraditional doctoral degree students. Finally, the transcultural approach supports multilingual coresearch and coconstruction of knowledge rather than a multidimensional form of institutional racism that thrives on "nonaggressive acts of discrimination" (Mampaey & Zanoni, 2016, p. 928).

Employing theoretic-linguistic knowledge does not mean exalting Indigenous and non-Western thought as more authentic than others. Rather, it implies rethinking and reconceptualizing intellectual influence to fit a global society in which White, male, and Western are not the standard-bearers of truth claims. Unlike the frameworks that characterize White Western thought's individualistic construction of higher education students, the theoretic-linguistic knowledge framework supports the institutional, structural responsibility of providing entry and expanded conception of knowledge and lived experiences.

Afrocentric Education

The integration of Shockley and Frederick's (2010) constructs and dimensions of Afrocentric education and Johnson's (2001) Nguzu Saba African American college student development serves as a guiding elaboration of Afrocentrism applied to educational practices. Afrocentricity is framed as a collective epistemology that departs from Eurocentric epistemology, often characterized as *linear*. The work of Asante (1998) on Afrocentricity places the African throughout the diaspora of the world as the subject, or center, in the analysis of their respective culture. This implies that any analysis of any culture of people must be centered through the authentic lens of that individual. Moreover, the individual must also be viewed as in harmony with and connected to a lineage and the future. Shockley and Frederick (2010) asserted five constructs of Afrocentric education: (a) identity, centering the Black student as African; (b) pan-Africanism, connecting Black peoples of the world to Africa; (c) culture, aligning the Black student to a sustaining tradition of self and community; (d) African ethos, transmission of African values through the educational process; and (e) Black Nationalism, collective agency and community empowerment. Johnson (2001), in promoting African student worldview, advanced three basic tenets: (a) harmony with nature, the right to be; (b) survival of the tribe, responsibility to the integrity of community; and (c) spirituality, a sense of connection greater than self.

Afrocentric education, as a framework for understanding the higher education student, is a collective and an individual effort to develop an affirming identity. This affirming identity can only be compared and connected to its larger cultural group. Employing this perspective, the nontraditional doctoral student represents a lineage of those before them and a connection to those yet to come. Comparing the nontraditional doctoral degree student to the traditional doctoral degree student presents incongruence, as they are not the same; such comparisons represent a Westernized, linear attempt to exalt one over the other. As with the Afrocentric educational framework, the nontraditional doctoral degree student has a culture and ethos that must be promoted as valuable and dignified. Further, Afrocentric education recommends a collective sense of agency and purpose that extends beyond the individual.

Employing an Afrocentric education-based framework enables institutions and institutional actors to contribute to the nontraditional doctoral degree student. Institutions, particularly universities and employers, can help change or redefine the concept of nontraditional. Under a linear model, this language positions that student and their identity as lesser than traditional conceptions of students. Institutions and institutional actors can also create spaces where students can connect to a larger community during both conventional and unconventional work hours. Where employers can adopt more liberating policies to allow the student to engage in campus life on their terms, students will reaffirm their harmony, or right-to-be, with the university. Likewise, universities could also host and participate in collective events that incorporate shared learning and cultural experiences of the student. Such efforts on the behalf of institutions will support the collective agency of the student's doctoral journey.

Departing From Traditional Frameworks

The traditional frameworks used to assess student success and persistence in higher education focused primarily on the undergraduate experience, with an emphasis on the first year of college (Bean & Metzner, 1985; Milem & Berger, 1997). Few, if any, speak to the experiences of the nontraditional doctoral degree student. Without this focus, the use of these frameworks fails to capture the dynamics of age, maturation, gender, race, professional experience, and environmental variables that differentiate nontraditional doctoral degree students from nontraditional undergraduate students. To accept the frameworks as true on the premise that adopting the values and norms, as well as establishing patterns, are factors in success and persistence would be rendered useless for nontraditional doctoral degree students, as they have already demonstrated success and persistence in reaching the doctoral level.

White Western thought, upon which traditional frameworks of student success and persistence in higher education are currently based, places all responsibility on the individual regardless of structural impact to the individual. Under the idea of meritocracy, success or failure is primarily due to the individual's ascribed and achieved characteristics. Those who are in nontraditional or minority groups are positioned as failing to adopt the values and practices of the traditional or majority group. These assertions are supported through the research of Mampaey and Zanoni (2016), which noted the creation of monocultural school practices discursive acts and cultural models to frame nontraditional students as outsiders, noncommitted, and thereby disposable.

Monocultural suppression of non-Western language or intellectual contribution is observed even while the claim of diversity is promoted. Even as Western universities acknowledge diversity as reality, White Western thought "still position[s] difference as a deficit or threat, or as exotica for intellectual appropriation" (Singh et al., 2016, p. 57). Claiming to practice diversity while suppressing non-Western intellectual knowledge production creates a superficial form of diversity that accepts the physical presence of Indigenous and non-Western students, as long as their research and intellectual property are used to reinforce a Western epistemology. This form of intellectual gatekeeping, as posited by Singh et al. (2016), promotes what they term *nice White intellectual colonialism*. Nice White intellectual colonialism is understood to be promotion of inclusion that remains dominated by White voices, with the slow, incremental addition of voices of color.

Dynamic Dual Anchoring

This chapter advances the idea of *dynamic dual anchoring* as a framework to understand and support the nontraditional doctoral degree student. The essential premise is that the nontraditional doctoral degree student is anchored in two worlds, often competing for the same space. Unlike the conception of the traditional doctoral degree student, the nontraditional student is immersed in a dual context in which to navigate identity, responsibility, and aspirations. Inside this context, as shown in Figure 17.1, we find many variables that moderate and mediate the success and persistence of the nontraditional student.

Figure 17.1. The dynamic dual anchoring framework.

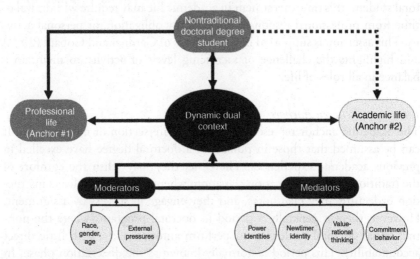

Anchors

The term *anchors* conjures in the mind the image of large ships. The anchor is used to hold the ship steady and grounded. Like ship anchors, anchors for the nontraditional doctoral degree student are the grounding existence in which they find identity, productivity, and actualization. For the nontraditional doctoral degree student, there are two essential anchors: professional life and academic life.

Professional Life

The anchor of professional life for the nontraditional doctoral degree student represents an existence in which the student has been heavily invested in for some time. Given the general age profile of the nontraditional doctoral student, it is reasonable to believe that 15 to 20 years or even more have been invested into their professional life (Offerman, 2011). Moreover, previous investments in education have helped these students reach the status in which they are presently anchored. The professional life of the nontraditional doctoral student has an established culture, network, and expectations that exist independent of their academic life.

Academic Life

The anchor of academic life for the nontraditional doctoral degree student represents a new, yet familiar, existence in which the student is expected to reinvest time, time which may already be allotted to professional life and external responsibilities (e.g., children and families, career advancement, caregiving for parents). Given the general profile of the nontraditional doctoral student, this time investment in academic life may require withdrawal of time from professional responsibilities, family obligation, or personal activity. This assertion is supported in the findings of Gardner and Gopaul (2012) and highlights the challenge of sacrificing levels of activity to maintain a balance in all roles of life.

Interaction Between Anchors

The academic anchor represents a complex intersection of new and old. It can be assumed that those in pursuit of a doctoral degree have excelled in previous academic experiences. Therefore, they may relish the comfort of the traditional higher education classroom where a professor delivers instruction or lecture, they take notes, and they engage in success by assignment. However, there is generally a period in doctoral programs where the nontraditional doctoral student must perform autonomously, with little direct accountability. This period is normally known as the dissertation phase. In addition, the nontraditional doctoral degree student enters even the familiar classroom environment while in a new stage of life. For example, a teacher completing a master's degree in education leadership in their late 20s or early 30s may be single or married, with emerging family, and have moderate professional responsibilities. As a transition from one role, teaching, to a greater role, leadership, they may recognize over time the desire or need to pursue more education for further career advancement. They then enter the doctoral classroom in their mid to late 30s or early 40s with greater professional and family responsibilities than their previous higher education experience.

Push Factors

The professional and academic anchors of the nontraditional doctoral degree student can be a push or pull factor for the pursuit of an advanced degree. The desire to escape their professional life in exchange for another, a push factor, may motivate the student to pursue an advanced degree, thereby increasing the allure of academic life. In that existence, the nontraditional doctoral student recognizes that they no longer wish to exist, or advance, within that professional field. In this scenario, the anchor of this specific professional life is weakened, and the academic life strengthened, as the pursuit of an advanced degree as framed as a bridge to another professional life.

Pull Factors

Likewise, the desire to advance, as a *pull* factor, within their professional life may motivate the student to pursue a terminal degree, thereby increasing the *push* of academic life. In that existence, the nontraditional doctoral degree student recognizes that the pursuit of an advanced degree will enhance the status, power, and compensation within that professional field. In this scenario, the anchor of this specific professional life is strengthened, and the element of time to degree completion creates a sense of urgency, which weakens the academic anchor. This assertion may support the findings of Neumann and Rodwell (2009), which suggest that younger nontraditional students, meaning early 40s and presumably in career advancement stages of employment, are more likely to complete their program faster than their traditional doctoral degree counterparts. This sense of urgency incentivizes the nontraditional doctoral student to rush through their academic pursuit, and they may fail to establish research, networks, or depth within the academic experience.

Dynamic Dual Context

Unlike the traditional doctoral student, who was afforded the time and space to exist in the singular world of the college campus, the nontraditional doctoral degree student exists in a complex, dynamic world that vacillates between professional and academic life. Success in this dynamic dual context requires the additional challenge of juggling responsibilities of work, family, and academic pursuits. In this dynamic dual context, demands converge and diverge in unpredictable ways, which heightens the importance of time management and resiliency for the nontraditional student. When demands compete for their time, the nontraditional doctoral degree student is met with the challenge of balancing life's anchors without exhaustion or compromise. When demands converge and present overlapping opportunities, the nontraditional doctoral degree student must have the energy and skill to take advantage of these moments. This assertion is supported in the findings of Mills et al. (2014), Bates and Goff (2012), and Prince-Embury (2011). When integrated, these findings suggest that the abilities to handle competing demands and capitalize on overlapping opportunities are regulated by, and supported through, a sense of relatedness, mastery, and emotional reactivity.

Triumphs or trials in this dynamic dual context are contingent on the nontraditional doctoral degree student's ability to successfully navigate the mediators and moderators inherent in this environment. Our perceptions, and thereby actions, within the mediators and moderators are governed by our frameworks for addressing them. In White Western thought, mediators and moderators are threats and obstacles to the individual, as they represent challenges to White male dominance. In non-Western transcultural approaches, mediators and moderators are coconstructive for individuals, as they represent a unique insight that is brought to a community of academics and practitioners.

Mediators

In the dynamic dual context, the successful anchoring of professional and academic life is mediated by power identities, newtimer identity, value-rational thinking, and commitment behavior. As mediators, these four variables help explain the relationship between professional and academic life in the dynamic dual context for the nontraditional doctoral degree student. The perceptions of these mediators, and thereby our approaches to them, are guided by the frameworks we use to construct knowledge.

Power identities.   The nontraditional doctoral degree student in the dynamic dual context experiences a level of power dynamics not experienced by their traditional counterpart. In balancing professional and academic anchors, the nontraditional doctoral degree student moves between professional and student mindsets. Mills et al. (2014) highlighted this observation as power asymmetries in which the student derives a sense of power and control in their professional life and a degree of powerlessness as a student in their academic life. Balancing the need to be assertive and committed in their professional capacity and the need to be receptive of new knowledge in their academic capacity can be challenging for this group of students. The integration of research from Mills et al. (2014) and Teeuwsen et al. (2014) advance a context where the commitments to employment and scholarship, the professional and academic anchors, are brought into question. The lack of employer support, for example, forces the nontraditional doctoral degree student to sacrifice time off work to meet academic goals, and the strain of professional demands and reduced university research opportunity alienates them from exercising "participation as a way of knowing" (Teeuwsen et al., 2014, p. 683).

From a White Western thought framework, this is problematic for the individual. The individual must choose either the professional or academic anchor. Applying an Indigenous non-Western framework, this observation presents an opportunity for collective community response to create and strengthen a third space where the student can become dually anchored and successful.

Newtimer identity.   In addition to balancing power identities, the nontraditional doctoral student also balances their identity as both a *newcomer* and an *old-timer* in the dynamic dual context. Termed *newtimer*, this student has the lived experience of being a college student while also experiencing the new reality of the doctoral experience. Unlike master's programs in which a master's thesis may be required, the doctoral program presents the student with the challenge of the classroom experience, the dissertation experience, and the promotion of research publication within the academic community. Through the integrated analysis of Mills et al. (2014), Teeuwsen et al. (2014), and Gardner and Gopaul (2012), the nontraditional doctoral degree student, as a working professional, is now faced with a resocialization and career development opportunity that incorporates a new academic research identity. Simply put, in addition to becoming a student again, this group must now navigate how this academic pursuit will enhance future identification within their profession.

In the White Western thought framework, success and persistence is determined by the individual's ability to acquiesce to institutional values of the university and the workplace. When those sets of values are in conflict, linear thinking suggest that the individual must choose one or the other. White Western thought is limited in its ability to see two things occupy the same space. Indigenous non-Western frameworks suggest that there can be a creative space where both institutional values can be harmoniously rethought to strengthen the nontraditional doctoral student's right-to-be (Johnson, 2001). The newtimer identity, therefore, can be reframed away from serving as a mediator to student success.

Value-rational thinking.   A significant mediator in the success of the nontraditional doctoral degree student in the dynamic dual context is value-rational thinking. Value rationalization, as a form of social action, forces an individual to assign importance to an object, action, or idea. When choices appear to compete for the individual's attention, time, and effort, the value-rational thinker chooses the action, object, or idea that provides the best value or end. This assertion of value-rational thinking is supported by the works of Weber et al. (1978) who noted that "value-rational action always involves 'commands' or 'demands' which, in the actor's opinion, are binding on him" (p. 25). Problematic in value-rational thinking is the binding pressure to seek immediate or expedient values or ends, which invariably places time as a variable to consider. Therefore, in comparing the value of the professional anchor to the academic anchor, the professional anchor can be viewed as offering the most immediate payoff, in the form of financial compensation. Value-rational thinking is also observed as a mediator in balancing of the dynamic dual context through the allocation of time toward the doctoral experience, which signals a sense of investment (Gardner & Gopaul, 2012). Simply put, how a student allocates time to study, write, and participate in their doctoral journey is representative of their valuation toward this pursuit. It does not say that the student does not value academic life; rather, it demonstrates a value-rational choice when other interests are competing for the same time.

In the White Western thought framework, value-rational thinking surfaces as the individual's choice between two things that cannot coexist. This linear level of thinking asserts that professional and academic life exist on competing extremes and that the individual may find it difficult to successfully navigate both. Therefore, success and persistence in higher education require the immersion of the student into their academic life. Failure to succeed or persist is assessed as the individual placing higher value on something other than academic life. This assertion is supported by Berger and Milem's (1999) conclusion that students who drop out of school are those who chose not to get involved in school. Through an Indigenous non-Western thought framework, the value of the object, action, or idea can be replaced by the values of coconstruction, collective agency, and sense of connection to a power greater than self. Under such a framework, as promoted through the integration of Singh et al. (2016), Shockley and Frederick (2010), and Johnson (2001), there is opportunity for the university, the student, and the workplace to support a space where academic and professional anchors overlap. These overlapping spaces should work to resolve value-rational thinking as a time-bound selection of objects, actions, or ideas.

Commitment behavior. As an elaboration on the concept of organizational citizenship behavior, commitment behaviors mediate the performance of the nontraditional doctoral degree student in the dynamic dual context. Commitment behaviors represent the doctoral student's willingness, or reluctance, to go above and beyond formal conceptions and expectations of a student. As an elaboration on organizational citizenship behavior, the integrated work of Somech (2016) and Sesan and Basim (2012) provides foundational components of commitment behavior. Their work promotes the framing of commitment behaviors as both context and disposition are built on desire, need, and obligation. This suggests that the nontraditional doctoral degree student possesses not only an inclination, or personal disposition, toward scholarly activity but also environmental circumstances, or context, that are either supportive or prohibitive of existence in this dynamic dual context. Moreover, the convergence of desire, need, and obligation motivates the student to extend beyond what may be considered typical. Those with high levels of commitment behavior are simply the right people in the right situation with a sense of destiny. This can be observed in their self-imposed rigor toward research, presentation, and application of knowledge in both their professional and academic life. Likewise, the absence of those foundational components is observed in work quality, absence, and self-talk.

Applying White Western thought, as a framework, to commitment behaviors would frame student success and persistence as the individual's natural inclination toward academic life, regardless of context. Failure to succeed or persist in higher education would be purely a product of ascribed and achieved characteristics. Whether the environment is promotive or inhibitive, successful and persistent students in higher education are successful because they have the right background, which can be read to mean race, gender, age, and worldview. These assertions are supported through Bean and Metzner's (1985) conceptual model of nontraditional undergraduate student attrition and Berger and Milem's (1999) causal model of student persistence. Applying an Indigenous non-Western thought framework to commitment behaviors would frame student success and persistence as a result of collective agency and knowledge coconstruction. Failure to succeed or persist would be viewed as disharmony and a collective failure to affirm the individual's right-to-be

(Johnson, 2001; Singh et al., 2016). Placing success and persistence as contextual harmony empowers the nontraditional doctoral degree student with a desire, need, and obligation to their professional and academic anchors, as well as the collective anchors of others.

Moderators

In the dynamic dual context, the successful anchoring of professional and academic life is moderated by race, gender, age, and external pressures. As moderators, these variables affect or alter the relationship between professional and academic life in the dynamic dual context for the nontraditional doctoral degree student. Like mediators, the frameworks we use to construct knowledge shape perceptions and approaches to these moderators.

Race, gender, and age.   The integration of status congruence, an elaboration of role congruity theory, helps explain how members of a social group will be evaluated in a role or position based on previous conceptions of that group's societal role (Triana et al., 2017). In examining the nontraditional doctoral degree student, we discover that they are generally an ethnic nonmajority, women, and an older demographic. As a doctoral student, they are positioning themselves in a role that is traditionally considered the role of a White, male, young adult. Therefore, race, gender, and age play a moderating role in assessing these nontraditional students' status. This assertion is supported through an integrated assessment of Garner and Gopaul (2012) and Triana et al. (2017), who each recognize that race, gender, and age increase the scrutiny of the performance of nontraditional doctoral degree students and subordinates their status. While not always posing a direct barrier, race, gender, and age add to the challenge of fitting the mold of the doctoral degree student (Gardner & Gopaul, 2012). Their research may be viewed as so-called liberal slants, race sermons, niche, outdated, or less academic simply because of their demographic status.

White Western thought, as a framework for assessing student persistence and success, clearly expresses that student background characteristics such as race, gender, and age can have negative direct or indirect effects on the success of higher education students (Bean & Metzner, 1985; Berger and Milem, 2000). As these frameworks primarily studied undergraduate students, they assume even worse outcomes, as it relates to race, gender, and age, for nontraditional doctoral degree students who balance work, family, and academics. For their success, under White Western thought frameworks, there must be total abandonment of their values in exchange for the values and practices of the nonethnic majority. Such thinking, particularly as it notes that just "being African-American is the one direct effect on persistence

Figure 17.2. Racial hierarchy in White Western thought.

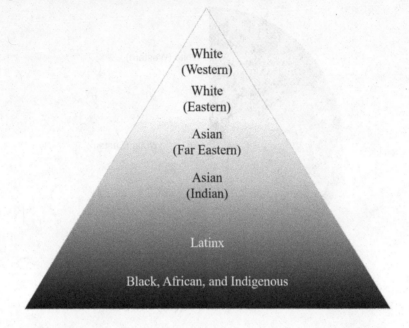

and it is negative" (Berger & Milem, 1999, p. 653), both promotes and reproduces racial hierarchies in academic and social pursuits, as visualized in Figure 17.2.

As Western academics rendered cultural difference as problematic, Indigenous non-Western frameworks promote the incorporation of shared cultural experiences as welcomed theoretic-linguistic knowledge (Shockley & Frederick, 2010; Singh et al., 2016). Adopting a transcultural framework as a counterapproach to monocultural school practices promotes a new narrative where cultures can meet in a non-subordinate context to enable coconstruction of new knowledge and nonhierarchical approaches to status, as suggested in Figure 17.3.

External pressures. As a working adult student, the nontraditional doctoral degree student is more likely to be affected by external pressures. Unlike the profile of the traditional doctoral student, the nontraditional doctoral degree student is more likely to grapple with balancing school, work, and family. The integrated work of Gardner and Gopaul (2012), Mills et al. (2014), and Offerman (2011) supports the assertion that work-life balance is more critical to the nontraditional doctoral degree student. Financial constraints, family commitments, professional responsibilities, and academic competition

Figure 17.3. Non-Western racial thought.

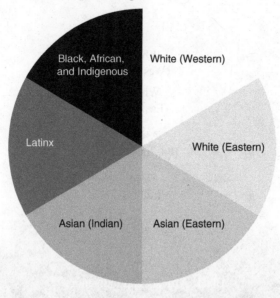

can offer both promotive and inhibitive perspectives of the nontraditional doctoral degree student. From one perspective, they can be viewed as potentially less effective and less productive in both professional and academic anchors, as they may be overextended. Another perspective, however, can frame the nontraditional doctoral degree student as strong, resilient, and driven because of navigating this dynamic dual context.

Using White Western thought as a lens, external pressures are the byproducts of the ascribed and achieved characteristics of the nontraditional doctoral degree students. Under this lens, their lack of success and persistence in higher education is explained by personal choices that place them in the position of being overextended. Simply put, their background, history, and unwillingness to assimilate combine to make poor choices. This assertion is affirmed in the models of persistence and attrition promoted through the integrated understanding of Bean and Metzner (1985) and Berger and Milem (1999), which suggests that students who fail to persist are plagued by patterns of behavior that are not congruent with dominant values. Under an Indigenous non-Western lens, the presence of external pressures are challenges that strengthen individuals and are also responsibilities of the collective community to resolve and reestablish harmony with nature (Johnson, 2001). A collective agency view of external pressures, through this lens, activates those within the professional and academic lives of the nontraditional doctoral degree student to provide physical, emotional, and cognitive space as a source of support. This assertion is supported by the research of Gardner and Gopaul (2012) and Shockley and Frederick (2010) who note collective community and institution building as a process of family, employer, and coworker support for the nontraditional doctoral degree student.

Navigating the Dynamic Dual Anchoring Framework

The promotion of the dynamic dual anchoring framework for understanding nontraditional doctoral degree students is most positive when viewing it as an extension of Indigenous non-Western thought, often positioned as alternative frameworks. It is of little use, or less promotive, when viewed through the lens of White Western thought. Under the lens of White Western thought, promoting the nontraditional doctoral degree student is the equivalent of attempting to fit square pegs into round holes. Moving forward with dynamic dual anchoring as an extension of Indigenous non-Western thought, it is necessary to engage in theoretic-linguistic knowledge practices by changing the discourse of nontraditional doctoral degree students to academic professional students. Signaling their dynamic balance of academic and professional life, the academic professional student, with the collective agency of institutions, stands on the shoulders of a long tradition of scholars who merge research and craft knowledge.

Insights for Research, Practice, and Policy

Promoting the dynamic dual anchoring framework as an extension of Indigenous non-Western thought has insights and implications for research, practice, and policy. This framework offers institutions the opportunity to view and support academic professional students, once viewed as invisible nontraditional doctoral degree students. Moving forward in support of the academic professional student, this work promotes insight for collective agency and responsibility.

Theoretical Insights

Few models of student success and persistence have focused on doctoral degree students, particularly those framed as academic professionals. The prevailing models offered by Bean and Metzner (1985) and Berger and Milem (1999) were almost exclusively grounded in the study of first-year undergraduates in higher education. As newer, more global research has taken into consideration the full-time working, doctoral degree student, advancing the dynamic dual anchoring framework will move beyond profiling the challenges and benefits of this once invisible population. This framework has the potential to aid scholars and researchers in supporting a truly asset-based perspective of academic professionals in the overlapping institutions that can support them.

Practical Insights

As student affairs administrators and officials seek to address student retention, their efforts can be extended to the doctoral level with a greater understanding of the academic professional. The dynamic dual anchoring framework can provide a synthesized lens for understanding the complexity and dedication of this group of students. Student affairs administrators and officials, through this lens, can find ways to highlight the scholarly participation of academic professionals through directly addressing mediators and moderators in the dynamic dual context. Research supports the promotion of the cohort experience as a way to build community, overcome feelings of isolation through the online learning experience, and improve the structure and sequencing of coursework (Fields et al., 2016; Neumann & Rodwell, 2009; Offerman, 2011).

This understanding is not only limited to university student affairs administrators and officials at academic institutions. It should also apply to professional institutions, as this framework recognizes the role of professional life as an anchor. This framework suggests an opportunity for partnership and collaboration to create overlapping spaces for the academic professional to exercise high-performance in both institutions. Present research suggests that academic professionals feel supported by employers who find ways to merge their academic contributions to the professional workplace (Mills et al., 2014).

Authentic Insights

The understanding of the academic professional experience, as framed by the dynamic dual anchoring framework, can improve the andragogical practices of higher education faculty. As higher education faculty understand the profiles and challenges of academic professional students, the next step is to utilize their teaching, research, and service to collaborate directly with professional institutions in support of their students. This creates ample opportunities for the faculty member, as well as the academic professional student. The promotion of this framework also supports higher education faculty dispositional change from White Western thought, grounded in individualism and false meritocracy, to Indigenous non-Western thought, which supports coresearch and coconstruction of knowledge and agency. Higher education faculty members can create a mutually empowering learning community, merge course assignments with academic professional research agendas, and enlist dissertation and research by assignment to improve completion rates and work quality.

Policy Insights

Policymakers, in understanding the dynamic dual anchoring framework, can construct clear and concise practices for both professional and academic institutions in support of the academic professional. Where time and financial constraints can challenge academic professional pursuits, policy can be reimaged and reconstructed to relieve moderators and mediators of student access and support. Redefining leave policies in the workplace to not punish academic professionals for knowledge acquisition that ultimately supports the organization is an example of policy insight informed by this framework. Reconstructing tuition waivers and tuition payment plans to support the academic professional's ability to stay on track with course sequencing is an example of institutional and state policy insight informed by this framework. Moreover, as this framework promotes collective agency and responsibility toward the academic professional student, it must be backed by policy that promotes overlapping physical, emotional, and cognitive spaces for the academic professional. This assertion is supported by the integrated analysis of Offerman (2011), Somech (2016), and Sesan and Basim (2012) in which contextual foundations can promote a new design of the doctorate program to increase the commitment behaviors of the academic professional.

Concluding Recommendations

The ability and right to define one's own reality and cultural knowledge, and also protect it from being exploited and maligned by paternalistic outsiders, is at the heart of Indigenous non-Western thought (Singh et al., 2016). The construction of the dynamic dual anchoring framework for understanding the academic professional student represents an extension of an Indigenous non-Western lens. As a member in the long tradition of academic professional students, I share in insights and perspectives gained from this diverse college student population. The dynamic dual anchoring framework recommends that institutions, via university and professional actors, reimagine the academic professional student and collectively create supportive spaces for their success. Part of creating those collective supportive spaces also requires that the academic professional student both speak and be heard in the defining of their reality. The promotion of academic professional cultural knowledge through this framework recommends coconstruction and coresearch support from the academic community as a means of recognizing and shaping policy for the academic professional student. It is the desire that the dynamic dual anchoring framework be a contributing model for such work.

References

Alfred, R. L. (Ed.). (1973). Student attrition: Strategies for action. In R. L. Alfred (Ed.), *GT-70 Conference Proceedings* (pp. 27–51). Metropolitan Junior College District. https://files.eric.ed.gov/fulltext/ED085064.pdf

Allum, J. (2014). *Graduate enrollment and degrees: 2003 to 2013*. Council of Graduate Schools.

Asante, M. K. (1998). *The Afrocentric idea*. Temple University Press.

Bates, P. J., & Goff, L. (2012). The invisible student: Benefits and challenges of part-time doctoral studies. *Alberta Journal of Educational Research, 58*(3), 368–380. https://journalhosting.ucalgary.ca/index.php/ajer/article/view/55628

Bean, J. P., & Metzner, B. S. (1985). A conceptual model of nontraditional undergraduate student attrition. *Review of Educational Research, 55*(4), 485–540. https://doi.org/10.3102/00346543055004485

Bennett, C., & Bean, J. P. (1984). A conceptual model of Black student attrition at a predominantly white university. *Journal of Educational Equity and Leadership, 55*(4), 173–188. https://doi.org/10.2307/1170245

Berger, J. B., & Milem, J. F. (1999). The role of student involvement and perceptions of integration in a causal model of student persistence. *Research in Higher Education, 40*(6), 641–664. https://doi.org/10.1023/A:1018708813711

Berger, J. B., & Milem, J. F. (2000). Organizational behavior in higher education and student outcomes. In J. C. Smart (Ed.), *Higher education: Handbook of theory and research* (Vol. 15, pp. 268–338). Agathon.

Fields, A., Lai, K., Gibbs, J., Kirk, A., & Vermunt, J. (2016). The transformation of an online learning community from an organized facility to an organic fraternity. *Distance Education, 37*(1), 60–72. https://doi.org/10.1080/01587919.2016.1158769

Gardner, S. K., & Gopaul, B. (2012). The part-time doctoral student experience. *International Journal of Doctoral Studies, 7,* 63–78. https://doi.org/10.28945/1561

Johnson, V. D. (2001). The Nguzo Saba as a foundation for African-American college student development theory. *Journal of Black Studies, 31*(4), 406–422. https://doi.org/10.1177/002193470103100402

Mampaey, J., & Zanoni, P. (2016). Reproducing monocultural education: Ethnic majority staff's discursive constructions of monocultural school practices. *British Journal of Sociology of Education, 37*(7), 928–946. https://doi.org/10.1080/01425692.2014.1001059

Milem, J. F., & Berger, J. B. (1997). A modified model of college student persistence: The relationship between Astin' s theory of involvement and Tinto' s theory of student departure. *Journal of College Student Development, 38*(4), 387–400.

Mills, S., Trehan, K., & Stewart, J. (2014). Academics in pursuit of the part-time doctorate: Pressures and support issues associated with the career development of business and management academics. *Human Resource Development International, 17*(4), 438–458. https://doi.org/10.1080/13678868.2014.928136

National Science Foundation. (2017a). *Doctoral recipients by sex and major field of study: 2006-2016* [Table 15]. National Center for Science and Engineering Statistics, Survey of Earned Doctorates.

National Science Foundation. (2017b). *Doctoral recipients by ethnicity, race, and citizenship status: 2006-2016* [Table 19]. National Center for Science and Engineering Statistics, Survey of Earned Doctorates.

National Science Foundation. (2017c). *Median age and age distribution of doctoral recipients by broad field of study, sex, citizenship status, ethnicity, and race: 2006-2016* [Table 27]. National Center for Science and Engineering Statistics, Survey of Earned Doctorates.

Nelson, R. B., Scott, T. B., & Bryan, W. A. (1984). Precollege characteristics and early college experiences as predictors of freshman year persistence. *Journal of College Student Personnel, 25*(1), 50–54

Neumann, R., & Rodwell, J. (2009). The 'invisible' part-time research students: A case study of satisfaction and completion. *Studies in Higher Education, 34*(1), 55–68. https://doi.org/10.1080/03075070802601960

Offerman, M. (2011). Profile of the nontraditional doctoral degree student. (New Directions for Adult & Continuing Education, no. 129, pp. 21–30). Wiley. https://doi.org/10.1002/ace.397

Pascarella, E. T., & Terenzini, P. T. (1991). *How college affects students.* Jossey-Bass.

Prince-Embury, S. (2011). Assessing personal resiliency in the context of school settings: Using the resiliency scales for children and adolescents. *Psychology in Schools, 48*(7), 672–685. https://doi.org/10.1002/pits.20581

Sesen, H., & Basim, N. H. (2012). Impact of satisfaction and commitment on teachers' organizational leadership. *Educational Psychology, 32*(4), 475–491. https://doi.org/10.1080/01443410.2012.670900

Shockley, K. G., & Frederick, R. M. (2010). Constructs and dimensions of Afrocentric education. *Journal of Black Studies, 40*(6), 1212–1233. https://doi.org/10.1177/0021934708325517

Singh, M., Manathuga, C., Bunda, T., & Qi, J. (2016). Mobilizing Indigenous and non-Western theoretic-linguistic knowledge in doctoral education. *Knowledge Cultures, 4*(1), 56–70. https://sotl-south-journal.net/?journal=sotls&page=article&op=view&path%5B%5D=138

Somech, A. (2016). The cost of going the extra mile: The relationship between teachers' organizational citizenship behavior, role stressors, and strain with the buffering effect of job autonomy. *Teachers and Teaching, 22*(4), 426–447. https://doi.org/10.1080/13540602.2015.1082734

Teeuwsen, P., Ratković, S., & Tilley, S. A. (2014). Becoming academics: Experiencing legitimate peripheral participation in part-time doctoral studies. *Studies in Higher Education, 39*(4), 680–694. https://doi.org/10.1080/03075079.2012.729030

Tinto, V. (1975). Dropout from higher education: A theoretical synthesis of recent research. *Review of Educational Research, 45*(1), 89–125. https://doi.org/10.3102/00346543045001089

Triana, M. D. C., Richard, O. C., & Yücel, İ. (2017). Status incongruence and supervisor gender as moderators of the transformational leadership to subordinate affective organizational commitment relationship. *Personnel Psychology, 70*(2), 429–467. https://doi.org/10.1111/peps.12154

UNESCO. (n.d.). *Educational attainment of the population aged 25 and older, 2017.* United Nations Educational, Scientific and Cultural Organization, UNESCO Institute for Statistics. http://data.uis.unesco.org/Index.aspx?DataSetCode=edulit_ds

University of Maryland University College. (2015, January 6). *Predictive analytics for student success: Developing data-driven predictive models of student success* [Final Report]. University of Maryland University College, Kresge Foundation. http://www.umuc.edu/documents/upload/developing-data-driven-predictive-models-of-student-success-final.pdf

U.S. Department of Commerce. (2016). *Quick facts: United States population estimates* [July 2017]. U.S. Department of Commerce, United States Census Bureau. https://www.census.gov/quickfacts/fact/table/US/PST045217

Weber, M., Roth, G., & Wittich, C. (1978). *Economy and society: An outline of interpretive sociology.* University of California Press.

18

THE PARADOX OF COMMUNITY COLLEGES

Latino Men and the Educational Industrial Complex

Pavitee Peumsang, Jorge M. Burmicky, Victor B. Sáenz, and Emmet Campos

I n the United States, the long history of racist ideas and racism has highly influenced—and continues to influence—many educators' and policy-makers' collective decision-making processes in higher education (Kendi, 2019; Singleton, 2015). As a result, many color-blind policies are developed without much thought to their potential impact (Felix et al., 2015; Singleton, 2015). Unfortunately, one adverse consequence from this is the ability to predict the racial and gender disparities across any academic discipline or institutional type (Singleton, 2015; Villarosa et al., 2010). For this reason, we focus particularly on Latino men, who are more likely to enroll within the community college system (CCS) (Peña, 2017; Excelencia in Education, 2019). For example, in California, Latino men are more likely to enroll in the CCS than 4-year colleges or universities, and 84% enroll with goals to transfer to obtain a bachelor's degree (Crisp & Nuñez, 2014; Peña, 2017). Despite their high aspirations, studies indicate Latino men's transfer and bachelor's degree attainment outcomes do not equitably reflect their initial enrollment rates (Georgetown University Center on Education and the Workforce, 2018; Lundberg et al., 2018).

In the past decade, some scholars have developed a range of conceptual and theoretical frameworks (C&TFs) to better understand how Latino men's academic and social experiences impact their academic outcomes in higher education (Delgado Bernal, 2002; Kezar, 2014). Traditionally, a majority of C&TFs are interpreted from a dominant White Eurocentric perspective (DWEP) that primarily focuses on Latino men's racial, gender, and cultural identities as factors to explain their low achievement rates (Malágon, 2010;

Solórzano, 1997; Tinto, 1982). Alternatively, emerging scholars offer C&TFs that amplify Latino men's narratives and that attempt to understand their dynamics of identity development (Carrillo, 2016; Sáenz et al., 2013), sense of belonging (Strayhorn, 2012), and social and cultural capital (Arámbula Ballysingh, 2016; Strayhorn, 2010). More recently scholars have called for faculty members, administrators, and staff (FMAS) and researchers to become more systems focused (Dowd & Bensimon, 2015; Wood, 2018). These scholars emphasize the need to critically understand the role of FMASs' racial identities, mindsets, and institutional policies and their impact on students' academic outcomes (Malcom-Piqueux & Bensimon, 2017; Ramaley, 2014).

Therefore, the purpose of this chapter is to offer an alternative systems-focused C&TF by utilizing concepts from the military industrial complex, prison industrial complex, and education industrial complex as guiding frameworks (Davis, 2012; Giroux, 2007; 2008; Janiewski, 2011). More specifically, the frameworks seek to understand the paradox of the CCS that is designed to structurally operate as a community college complex (CCC) (Brint & Karabel, 1989; Giroux, 2008). This CCC framework focuses specifically on forces that impact Latino men's academic experiences and outcomes such as (a) the power dynamics of FMAS's decision-making processes, (b) the CCS organizational culture, and (c) how FMAS engage in policy implementation procedures (e.g., course curriculum, office hours). Ultimately, we emphasize that the purpose of the CCC framework is not intended to uphold a deficit paradigm around Latino men or the CCS. Instead, the purpose is to emphasize that systemic barriers and institutional racism involve the power dynamics of FMAS and their individual and collective responsibility for the academic outcomes that result at the CCC (Michael, 2015; Singleton, 2015).

Over the years, the prison industrial complex and its emphasis on systemic racism has called for more contributions to the education industrial complex to intentionally include racial analysis (Davis, 2003, 2012; Giroux, 2008; Shakur, 2001). Some scholars explain the complex dynamics of the prison industrial complex and its driving institutional forces of color-blind racism, neoliberalism, and capitalistic profit that structurally operate to disproportionally adversely impact Black and Brown men (i.e., racialized neoliberal subjects) (Alexander, 2012; Brewer & Heitzeg, 2008; Davis, 2003). The development of the education industrial complex has primarily reflected the structures of prison industrial complex which is also driven by the dynamics of the institutional forces of neoliberalism and capitalistic profit (Giroux, 2009). However, the education industrial complex's emphasis on the notions of economic and social mobility that primarily benefit groups of higher socioeconomic status dismisses the need to include a racial analysis (Bowles & Gintis, 1976, 2002; Davis, 2012).

Additionally, the education industrial complex emphasizes the paradox of education systems that offer access to economic and social mobility yet often fail groups of lower socioeconomic status (Bowles & Gintis, 2002). For example, García and De Lissovoy (2013) pointed out how "the school, as an institution within the state, serves to produce the subjects that are required for the novel social conditions of the neoliberal era" (p. 50). In other words, in the education industrial complex, Latino men represent racialized neo-liberal subjects and enroll in the CCS that is marketed as providing them socioeconomic mobility (Davis, 2012; Shakur, 2001). However, because Latino men are more likely to come from working-class households, upon community college enrollment they immediately encounter forces of racial stigmatization and economic stratification that limit their access to resources (Giroux, 2007, 2008; Solórzano, 1997). Thus, for Latino men, the CCS becomes a paradox which markets notions of accessible opportunities while forces of color-blind racism and capitalism are designed to systematically and disproportionately fail them (Giroux, 2008; Nevarez & Wood, 2010).

Thus, this chapter serves as an urgent call for educational leaders, schol-ars, and policymakers to engage in difficult and truthful conversations about power structures of race, racism, and late capitalism/neoliberalism. It is criti-cal to understand that these organizational structures continue to adversely impact Latino men's experiences and outcomes (Arámbula Ballysingh, 2016; Sáenz et al., 2015; Singleton, 2015).

Contextual and Historical Background

Prior to identifying and understanding the education industrial complex as a C&TF within the CCS, it is important to understand the origins and evo-lution of the military industrial complex (Davis, 2003; Dunne & Sköns, 2010). The fruition of the military industrial complex was introduced by for-mer President Dwight D. Eisenhower through a politically and economically driven rhetoric which focused on the allocation of military budget (Dunne & Sköns, 2010). These interests helped designed a foundation for the United States government and private corporations to build relationships with the correctional and media institutions which led to the establishment of the prison industrial complex (Davis, 2003). Over time, the process of strategic political and economic partnerships helped strengthen the military indus-trial complex and evolved to the mass construction of private prisons and mass incarceration in the United States as manifested by the prison industrial complex (Alexander, 2012; Bury, 2013; Davis, 2003; Janiewski, 2011). Thus, the structural operations of the education industrial complex are often reflective of the structural operations driven by racist policies that adversely impact Black and Brown bodies supported by funding from military, law enforcement, and private corporation institutions (Alexander, 2012; Davis, 2003; Kendi, 2019; Prados, 2015).

The Military Industrial Complex: Post-WWII Era and Dwight Eisenhower

On January 17, 1961, Eisenhower delivered a historically pivoting farewell address to a television and radio audience from the Oval Office (Kutler, 2003). In his speech, he highlighted the need for the United States to keep its interest to restrain the power of the military industrial complex (Janiewski, 2011). Simultaneously, Eisenhower advised Americans to accept the need for a large military infrastructure while working toward international coop-eration (Kutler, 2003). However, Eisenhower urged elected officials not to seek excessive profits through military contractors and to avoid endangering market freedoms. These presidential speeches demonstrated the ongoing political rhetoric loaded with contradictions, tensions, and ambiguity in the government's policies and practices (Janiewski, 2011). In this farewell address, Eisenhower stated,

> This conjunction of an immense military establishment and a large arms industry is new in the American experience. The total influence economic, political, even spiritual—is felt in every city, every state house, every office of the Federal government. . . . In the councils of government, we must guard against the acquisition of unwarranted influence, whether sought or unsought, by the military-industrial complex. (as cited in Kutler, 2003, p. 434)

There are two important takeaways from these historical remarks. First, it is important to recognize the country's stances and executive branch deci-sions that made the U.S. military the recession-proof, multibillion-dollar industry that it is today. This is important to acknowledge given the corpo-ratization we see across educational sectors today (Janiewski, 2011). Second, we recognize that the decisions made by the federal government have a pro-found impact on the general public. The influence granted by the executive office has had a tremendous—and often irreversible—influence in the coun-try's approach to several industries over the years.

Eisenhower's speech left a permanent mark on how we approach military spending today. For example, as publicized by the Department of Defense website, the requested fiscal year 2018 base budget amounted to $574.5 billion, not including the Overseas Contingency Operations (OCO) budget which supports continued operations such as the fight against ISIS in the Middle East, totaling an additional $64.6 billion. This is by far the most that any country in the world spends on military. In contrast, the federal government simply does not prioritize the education sector to the same extent. For example, in an effort to "simplify" funding for higher education (U.S. Department of Education, 2018), the president's fiscal year 2018 budget requested that the U.S. Department of Education set the budget for TRIO at $808.3 million and for GEAR UP at $219 million. This is a $193 million decrease from the previous year. Further, because local schools often rely on local property taxes for most of their funding, most areas in the United States end up spending less money on low-income students than high-income students. Once again, the same neoliberal mindset that prioritizes profit and traditional structures of power (e.g., military) deeply affects the way in which marginalized students are granted (or denied) access to education.

The Prison Industrial Complex

Recent publications such as *The New Jim Crow* (Alexander, 2012) and *Just Mercy* (Stevenson, 2014) have brought attention to the pervasive issue of mass incarceration, particularly with U.S.-born Black men who are denied political and human rights that democracy offers, such as voting and making the laws that govern their own communities. However, it would be a disservice to dismiss the countless efforts by many activists and scholars who have worked diligently for decades to draw attention to this very significant issue affecting racially minoritized communities. For example, since the civil rights movements, antiprison activists such as Angela Davis were already dismayed by the prodigious amount of people living in prison cells. In her book *Are Prisons Obsolete?*, Davis (2003) indicated that in the 1960s there were close to 200,000 people in prison with a disproportionately higher rate of Black and Brown bodies. Davis (2003) added that "had anyone told me that in three decades ten times as many people would be locked away in cages, I would have been absolutely incredulous" (p. 11). Most importantly, Davis (2003) drew attention to the prison industrial complex to debunk the myth that increased levels of crime were the sole reason for higher rates of imprisonment. This particular belief was prevalent during the Reagan Era and the intensified so-called tough-on-crime stances coming from the White House (Brewer & Heitzeg, 2008).

Davis (2003) shifted these narrow-minded narratives by singling out the mass construction of prisons (often by private corporations) and the drive to fill these new structures with human bodies, often motivated by racist and profit-driven ideologies. In fact, both Davis (2003) and Alexander (2012) point out that many corporations often rely on prisons as an important source of labor and profit, even in areas of the country where crime rates have actually dropped. Alexander (2012) elaborates on the "media bonanza" (p. 5) experienced during Reagan's "War on Drugs" (p. 5), which deliberately exploited images of Black "crack whores . . . crack dealers . . . and crack babies" (p. 5) which inevitably fueled the racial disparities we see in today's prison population. As a result, Davis (2003) stated, "antiracist and social justice movements are incomplete with[out] attention to the politics of imprisonment" (p. 85). These politics of imprisonment, which are built on market-driven decisions and racist structures consequentially shape the DWEP of Latino men in the CCS.

Historical Connections to the Education Industrial Complex

According to Brightman and Gutmore (2002), there are striking similarities between the conceptual framework of the military industrial complex, prison industrial complex, and the present-day education industrial complex. For example, from a very young age, schoolchildren are subjected to commercialism in the classroom. From in-school advertisements to corporate-sponsored materials, apparel, contests, and giveaways, consumerism has become a central part of children's educational experiences (Brightman & Gutmore, 2002). In addition, through certain pedagogical and disciplinary practices, educational institutions transmit corporate values and norms that prepare students for conditions they will encounter in the workplace or prison (García & De Lissovoy, 2013). As referenced by Eisenhower (Prados, 2015), the total influence of economic, political, and even spiritual forces of the military industrial complex (and arguably the education industrial complex) are felt in every single household of the country. Just as military dominance has controlled America's budget for decades, so have consumerism and commercialism controlled the budget in the educational sector. Davis (2003) placed a particular emphasis on antiracist movements paired with the pervasive issue of mass incarceration and corporations' desire to maximize profit often at the expense of Black and Brown bodies.

As we examine how the education industrial complex can be applied as an alternative framework to critically examine the CCS, it is important to keep in mind the historically rooted structures and mechanisms that have been designed to exclude Communities of Color (Malcom-Piqueux & Bensimon, 2017; Valenzuela, 1999). Moreover, it is vital to be aware of the

Figure 18.1. The industrial complex metaphor.

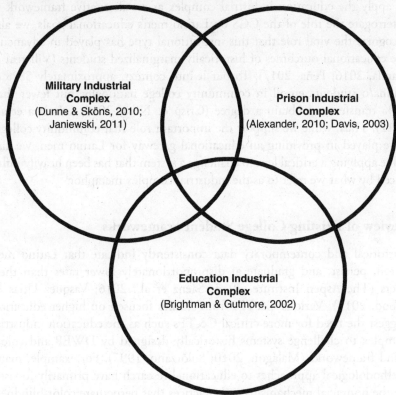

ways in which consumerist tendencies influence the educational pipeline. As such, by providing the historical context about the evolution of the education industrial complex and the various forces that define it, we can now set the stage for understanding Latino men's structural reality within the CCS. This seeks to forge an alternative framework that can be critically applied to examine their experiences.

Figure 18.1 visually summarizes how we conceptualized the industrial complex metaphor after outlining some of its historical context. In the following section, we examine existing C&TFs that have traditionally been suggested to conceptualize Latino men's educational journeys. While many of these C&TFs are still emerging, they have certainly provided a "starting point" to contextualize Latino men's experiences. Next, we explain how the education industrial complex works as an alternative framework to move the conversation a step further and examine the role of the CCS for Latino men navigating the higher education system.

Before we transition, it is important to acknowledge that while we seek to apply the education industrial complex as an alternative framework to interrogate the role of the CCS on Latino men's educational goals, we also recognize the vital role that this institutional type has played in advancing the educational outcomes of historically marginalized students (Villareal & García, 2016; Peña, 2017). To put it into context, approximately 58% of Latina/o students enroll in community college nationally, but fewer than 20% transfer and obtain a degree (Crisp & Nora, 2010; Gándara et al., 2012). Thus, while we support the important role that community colleges have played in providing an educational gateway for Latino men, we also value applying a critical lens to challenge a system that has been heavily influenced by what we refer to as the industrial complex metaphor.

Review of Existing College Student Frameworks

Historical and contemporary data consistently indicate that Latino men enroll, persist, and graduate at disproportionately lower rates than their peers (The Aspen Institute, 2013; Sáenz et al., 2016; Vasquez Urias & Wood, 2015). Various C&TFs from studies focused on higher education suggest the need for more critical C&TFs such as the education industrial complex to challenge systems historically designed by DWEP and color-blind frameworks (Malágon, 2010; Solórzano, 1997). For example, many methodological approaches to educational research have primarily focused on the nonracial mechanisms and practices that perpetuate color-blindness and structural racism (Bonilla-Silva, 2014; Lewis, 2001). In the following sections, we seek to move beyond the traditional interpretations from a DWEP.

Additionally, the call for a more critical framework is not intended to imply that the understandings of the education industrial complex remain abstract for intellectual theorizing. Simultaneously, the understandings of the education industrial complex are a call for FMAS, policymakers, and researchers to take self-responsibility for their roles and capacities to challenge those in power to become collectively accountable for their decision-making in policy implementation and practices.

Dominant White Eurocentric and Color-Blind Frameworks

Historically, many studies in education that sought to "close the gaps" among students' academic outcomes often applied deficit-oriented DWEPs to suggest outcomes were primarily influenced by "the fault" of students, families, and Communities of Color (Carrillo, 2016; Harper, 2010; Sáenz et al., 2016). Consequently, many studies rarely identified problems with the organizational structures and education systems that failed to serve and graduate students (Dowd & Bensimon, 2015; Harper & Kuykendall, 2012). As a result, DWEP and color-blind frameworks such as theories of student departure (Tinto, 1975) and social and cultural reproduction (Bourdieu, 1986) were developed to better understand how college students' academic and social experiences impact their academic outcomes. However, when color-blind frameworks are analytically applied to understand Latino men, they are often interpreted to fit the DWEP, which inevitably puts them at a disadvantage (Alemán & Alemán, 2010). Similarly, theories from the DWEP also adversely impact racially minoritized students, particularly Latino men, which helps maintain the DWEP.

Although Tinto's (1975) and Bourdieu's (1986) theories were intended to explore solutions to better serve college students, they unintentionally normalized deficit notions of Latino men and racially minoritized students. For example, Tinto's (1975) theory of college student departure hypothesized that student persistence is determined by the *individual's* motivation and their ability to engage with their academic and social environments. As a result, this suggests only individuals are responsible for their academic and social experiences which excludes external dynamics that shape human experiences (Strayhorn, 2012). Therefore, the CCS systematically operates with dominant DWEPs that uphold the institutional expectations and value individualistic and meritocratic ideologies (Carrillo, 2016; Delgado Bernal, 2002). Altogether, Bourdieu's (1986) and Tinto's (1975) theories often adversely impact the understanding of racially and socially marginalized student groups given the lack of opportunity for students to contribute their social and cultural traditions.

Thus, the power relationship that is associated with greater access to educational and professional capital for students from upper-middle- and upper-class households continues to place value on White Eurocentric norms and expectations of competition and merit (Ábrego, 2011; Bourdieu, 1986). Overall, both Tinto's (1975) and Bourdieu's (1986) emphasis on the ideology of individuality and students' household income contributes to the color-blind discourse. Consequently, this dismisses the need to intentionally identify the power relationship between higher education systems and the role of race, gender, and sociocultural experiences.

Frameworks Centering Men of Color in Higher Education

Over the years, emerging studies that intentionally center Men of Color and their academic and social experiences in higher education have introduced frameworks such as antideficit achievement (Harper, 2010) and sense of belonging (Strayhorn, 2012). From a national study across 42 colleges and universities, Harper (2010) collected data from 219 Black undergraduate men. This study intentionally developed guiding questions that sought to transform deficit-oriented research questions that often place responsibility on the individual student for their academic outcomes. Specifically, Harper (2010) reframed research questions in an antideficit manner to interrogate systems to better understand the influences that support the persistence of Black men enrolled in undergraduate science, technology, engineering, and math (STEM) disciplines.

Additionally, Strayhorn (2012) sought to understand Latino students' academic persistence at predominantly White institutions (PWIs). He challenged Tinto's (1975) DWEP model of student departure. Findings from this study revealed that Latino students are more likely to develop a positive sense of belonging at PWI when they feel validated and valued in their relationships with peers and faculty members. Harper's (2010) and Strayhorn's (2012) frameworks capture the experiences of Men of Color in higher education which in turn helps researchers and practitioners explore alternative strategies to encourage institutions to learn from Men of Color and amplify their sociocultural wisdom, thus promoting an inclusive learning environment among peers and professors.

Although Harper's (2010) and Strayhorn's (2012) frameworks critically challenge the deficit-oriented DWEP that often stereotype and stigmatize Men of Color in higher education, some theoretical gaps remain. The antideficit frameworks amplified the potentials and strengths that Men of Color contribute to their academic and social environment (Harper, 2010; Strayhorn, 2012) with a primary focus on students' social interactions on- and off-campus and their influence on their academic retention and outcomes. However, there is a gap in understanding the power dynamics among students' on-campus interactions, particularly FMAS. This suggests antideficit C&TFs have not yet fully explored the ways in which the CCS (e.g., decision-making, culture, policy, etc.) impacts Men of Color's academic outcomes, particularly those of Latino men.

Frameworks Centering Latino Men in Higher Education

There are two theories, Latino critical theory (LatCrit) (Delgado Bernal, 2002) and mestiz@ theory of intelligence (MTI) (Carrillo, 2013, 2016), that focus intentionally on Latina/o student populations and contribute to the antideficit C&TF gap.

LatCrit

Many empirical studies focused on Black and Latino boys and men in the P–20 education system indicate they remain one of the most adversely impacted populations academically and socially (Noguera et al., 2012; Perez Huber et al., 2015; Sáenz et al., 2016). These scholars also highlight that many Black and Latino men share similar familial, educational, and sociocultural experiences. It is critical to recognize the ways in which race, ethnicity, and skin complexion often shape their distinct gendered experiences in the higher education system (Harper, 2010; Strayhorn, 2012; Yosso, 2005). Past studies have expanded on critical race theory (CRT) from the school of law to the field of education (Ladson-Billings, 2011; Solórzano, 1997). The evolution of CRT in education led to additional frameworks such as Tribal CRT (Brayboy, 2006), Asian critical theory (AsianCrit) (Iftikar & Museus, 2018), and Latina/o critical theory (Delgado Bernal, 2002) to better understand students' nuanced experiences in education among different Indigenous, racial, and ethnic groups.

Therefore, LatCrit is utilized to understand Latina/o/x college students' experiences and also include their panethnic group experiences (Solórzano & Delgado Bernal, 2001). Additionally, LatCrit helps theorize about issues around race, ethnicity, gender, culture, immigration, and sexuality differences that shape Latino men's academic and social experiences (Delgado Bernal, 2002). Delgado Bernal (2002) particularly emphasized that LatCrit "is a theory that has a tradition of offering a strong gender analysis" (p. 108). Despite LatCrit's contribution to the field of education, it remains underutilized for better understanding Latino men's experiences within the CCS.

MTI

Similar to LatCrit, the MTI challenges DWEPs in the field of education (Carrillo, 2013, 2016; Delgado Bernal, 2002). Carrillo (2016) defined *MTI* as "[centering] the identities of individuals that navigate multiple cultural worlds and creatively negotiate often vastly different and contradictory sociocultural and political contexts all while achieving academic excellence" (p. 160). Therefore, MTI also suggests the need to intentionally include race, racism, and gender to understand students' holistic experiences in education (Carrillo, 2016). However, these conversations are often avoided and excluded from DWEPs (Delgado Bernal, 2002; Singleton, 2015). Furthermore, MTI explained how constructs of intelligence are rooted in DWEPs that are interconnected within a network of power, Whiteness, and middle-class cultural capital (Carrillo, 2016).

Carrillo (2013) utilized MTI to better understand the experiences of four Latino men who attended 4-year universities. These men also shared the experience of living in working-class urban communities prior to college. Findings suggested these men represent a significantly low percentage of Latinos who obtain a degree within their departments. Despite this, their narratives expressed a sense of empowerment and presented the power dynamics they negotiated as Latino men from working-class urban communities. Overall, MTI is a critical framework that helps shift from a deficit-oriented DWEP that often labels many young Latino boys/men as school "dropouts" and criminals (Carrillo, 2013; Malágon, 2010; Singleton, 2015).

Although MTI helped amplify Latino men's experiences at PWIs, understandings of Latino men's experiences in the CCS remain marginalized (Carrillo, 2013, 2016; Excelencia in Education, 2019). It is critical to consistently expand and adapt C&TFs to understand nuanced experiences of marginalized community college students, particularly Latino men (Goldrick-Rab, 2010; Karabel, 1977; Peña, 2017). Therefore, the following sections seek to utilize LatCrit (Delgado Bernal, 2002; Solórzano & Delgado Bernal, 2001) and MTI (Carrillo, 2013, 2016) as guiding C&TFs to better understand the ways in which Latino men are impacted by organizational structures of the CCS that subtly operate in paradoxical ways.

Educational Industrial Complex: Latino Men and Community Colleges

In 2013, The Aspen Institute published a guide for leaders across sectors (e.g., education, healthcare) who were interested in developing and implementing strategies to eliminate racial divisions and disparities. The first lesson suggested to the following institutional leaders—in this case FMAS—that

> starting with data shows how racial disparities occur regularly, systematically, and cumulatively across all sectors, and across the country. Data alone, however, cannot speak for themselves, and so it is crucial to look at them in context—both contemporary and historically. (p. 2)

In other words, it is critical to understand the ways historical and contemporary policies continue to disproportionately impact Latino men's experiences and outcomes in the CCS. To do this, we highlight significant milestones to illustrate the evolution of the education industrial complex that designed systems of inequities in today's CCS (Bensimon, 2007; Wood, 2018).

In 1901, the United States established Joliet Junior College in Illinois as the first public community college (Joliet Junior College, 2019). By 1921, California passed legislation which authorized Modesto Junior College to become the first-ever community college district (Winter, 1964). Over time, external socioeconomic and political demands contributed to the exponential development of community colleges nationwide (Bowles, 1977). Despite this, racial segregation of students of Mexican ancestry/descent remained legal in California public schools until the passage of *Mendez v. Westminster* in 1947 (United States Courts, n.d.a). Later, the 1954 *Brown v. Board of Education* Supreme Court case declared legal racial segregation of any student in U.S. public schools to unconstitutional (United States Courts, n.d.b). Altogether, the historical context of racist policies in CCSs suggests that FMAS have the power to redesign organizational structures to improve Latino men's experiences and outcomes (Bensimon, 2007; Wood, 2018).

Over the past 6 decades, the legal racial exclusion and overt racist policies have evolved and manifested in more subtle ways in the CCS (Kendi, 2019; Wood, 2018). For example, they often show up in the ways FMAS engage in decision-making, behaviors, and institutional norms and expectations (Bensimon, 2007; Wood, 2018). As emerging alternative C&TFs develop that better understand Latino men's academic experiences and outcomes, there remains a gap in understanding the systems-level impact (Carrillo, 2016; Delgado Bernal, 2002). Therefore, we utilize the military industrial complex and prison industrial complex as guiding C&TFs to apply the education industrial complex—or CCC—to help analyze the power dynamics of FMAS and the ways in which they impact Latino men's academic outcomes in the CCS (Davis, 2012; Janiewski, 2011). However, the education/CCC framework is not intended to critique any individual FMAS or students. Rather, the purpose of the education/CCC framework is to gain more understanding of FMAS' collective roles and responsibilities to transform CCS to achieve equitable institutional outcomes (Felix et al., 2015).

Paradox of Community College and Enrollment

The CCS and CCC are designed by the same driving forces of the military industrial complex and the prison industrial complex such as systemic racism and capitalistic exploitation, often dominated by White leadership (Davis, 2012; Giroux, 2008). For example, community college outreach and recruitment efforts often hyperrecruit Black and Latino men, which mirrors the hyperrecruitment of Black and Latino men to the military industrial complex and prison industrial complex (Manges Douglas & Sáenz, 2013). Often,

Black and Latino working-class communities are central to hyperoutreach and recruitment efforts by CCS and military recruiters (Advancement Project, 2010; Sáenz et al., 2016).

The Latino men who enroll in CCS are also more likely to be placed in developmental education courses (Goldrick-Rab, 2010). Immediately, Latino men encounter the paradox in which the CCS is perceived as a pathway to obtain bachelor's degrees (Attewell et al., 2006), but Latino men enrolled in developmental courses, particularly in math, are less likely to persist and take an average of 8 years to obtain a college degree (Attewell et al., 2006; Silva & White, 2013). Although the DWEP promotes the notion of equal opportunity, it dismisses the structural reality of some men who were incarcerated or have undocumented immigration status and limited economic resources (Manges Douglas & Sáenz, 2013). This demonstrates how the CCS engages Latino men in capitalistic exploitation; the CCS is marketed as affordable, yet Latino men (often working class) are forced to pay tuition which profits various corporate systems (Karabel, 1977; Shakur, 2001).

Paradox of Retention and Persistence

According to Apple (2004), the hidden curriculum is the process of socialization where education systems impose dominant White Eurocentric norms, values, and dispositions in students' school experiences to ensure the reproduction of society ideals. García and De Lissovoy (2013) extend this concept of the hidden curriculum and propose a notion of *school time,* building on Michael Hardt's (1997) notion of *prison time* that prepares students for "incorporation into familiar spaces of labor and citizenship" (p. 50). Moreover, they argue that when this notion of school time is considered in the context of concrete practices of teaching, high-stakes testing, and certain disciplinary practices (zero-tolerance policies), the education industrial complex functions to "injure and demoralize students in addition to disciplining them" (García & De Lissovoy, 2013, p. 50). Additionally, Valenzuela (1999) argues that schooling serves to divest racially minoritized students of their cultural assets, social capital, and identity, thus racializing classroom instruction. These schooling practices leave racially minoritized students progressively susceptible for school systems to fail them.

In response, if FMAS collaborate across academic departments to critically understand their institutional data, this offers the opportunity to gain understanding about the nuanced needs of diverse student groups (Dowd & Bensimon, 2015). The collective collaboration of FMAS also offers the opportunity to share alternative strategies (e.g., curriculum, activities, etc.) that seek to promote racially and socially inclusive environments. Also,

FMAS who explore innovative approaches may be facilitators of Latino men's sense of belonging and empowerment (Delgado Bernal, 2002; Strayhorn, 2012). In turn, this would help disrupt the routine of prison time culture that often prevents Latino men from sharing their diverse perspectives and knowledge in the classroom.

Systems Shift: Collective Responsibility of Community Colleges

While there are increasing efforts at the local level (in various higher education institutions across the nation), there are still scant initiatives across the nation that unapologetically focus specifically on Latino men. For this reason, we provide one example of a Texas statewide initiative that is slowly expanding its effort across the nation.

The Texas Education Consortium for Male Students of Color (Consortium) grew out of the challenges articulated in this chapter to initiate a statewide network and build solidarity for creating strong higher education pathways for young Men of Color. Headquartered at The University of Texas at Austin (UT), the Consortium is a direct response to the state and national policy mandates that have raised significant questions about the various challenges facing Men of Color as they navigate the educational pipeline. The Consortium represents a strategic research partnership between the two state flagship institutions—UT and Texas A&M University, College Station (TAMU)—along with school districts, community colleges, and 4-year institutions across the state using culturally responsive and antideficit approaches to address these challenges. As a result, the Consortium deliberately forges cross-sector partnerships to address the racial and gender disparities in academic outcomes among Men of Color.

As a critical intervention in pedagogy and curriculum that contests the hidden curriculum in educational institutions that positions students as neoliberal subjects, Project MALES (n.d.), a mentoring and research initiative at UT, created the IMPACT 113P course as an interdisciplinary curriculum that introduces undergraduate students to emergent research on Latino males in K–12 and higher education. The course introduces undergraduate students to the complexities involved in studying the multiple cultural, social, economic, and linguistic factors that influence how people of diverse backgrounds learn. Students develop a more nuanced understanding of challenges that Boys/Men of Color face in a U.S. Latina/o/x context using critical theories and methodologies that also employ Chicana feminist intersectional analyses.

Although we propose the CCC as an alternative framework to inform how the CCS can equitably serve Latino men, it is important to emphasize that intentional conversations around race and racism with strategic action-oriented plans at the institutional level are necessary to truly achieve racial equity across students' academic outcomes (Dowd & Bensimon, 2015; Harper & Kuykendall, 2012). If researchers, educational leaders, and policymakers intentionally commit to this—through ongoing assessment and evaluation—then race will no longer be a predictor of outcomes in education (Villarosa et al., 2010).

References

Ábrego, L. J. (2011). Legal consciousness of undocumented Latinos: Fear and stigma as barriers to claims-making for first- and 1.5-generation immigrants. *Law & Society Review, 45*(2), 337–370. https://doi.org/10.1111/j.1540-5893.2011.00435.x

Advancement Project. (2010). *Test, punish, and push out: How "zero tolerance" and high-stakes testing funnel youth into the school-to-prison pipeline.* https://b.3cdn.net/advancement/d05cb2181a4545db07_r2im6caqe.pdf

Alemán, E., Jr., & Alemán, S. M. (2010). Do Latin@ interests always have to "converge" with White interests? (Re)claiming racial realism and interest-convergence in critical race theory praxis. *Race Ethnicity & Education, 13*(1), 1–21. https://doi.org/10.1080/13613320903549644

Alexander, M. (2012). *The new Jim Crow: Mass incarceration in the ages of colorblindness.* The New Press.

Apple, M. W. (2004). *Ideology and curriculum* (3rd ed.). Routledge Falmer.

Arámbula Ballysingh, T. (2016). Caballeros making capital gains in college: The role of social capital in first-year persistence at predominantly white 4-year institution. In V. B. Sáenz, L. Ponjuán, & J. López Figueroa (Eds.), *Ensuring the success of Latino males in higher education: A national imperative* (pp. 152–173). Stylus.

The Aspen Institute. (2013). (2013). *Ten lessons for taking leadership on racial equity.* The Aspen Institute Roundtable on Community change. https://www.aspeninstitute.org/publications/ten-lessons-taking-leadership-racial-equity/

Attewell, P., Lavin, D., Domina, T., & Levey, T. (2006). New evidence on college remediation. *Journal of Higher Education, 77*(5), 886–924. https://doi.org/10.1080/00221546.2006.11778948

Bensimon, E. M. (2007). Presidential address: The underestimated significance of practitioner knowledge in the scholarship on student success. *The Review of Higher Education, 30*(4), 441–469. https://doi.org/10.1353/rhe.2007.0032

Bonilla-Silva, E. (2014). *Racism without racists: Color-blind racism and the persistence of racial inequality in America.* Rowman & Littlefield.

Bourdieu, P. (1986). The forms of capital. In J. Richardson (Ed.), *Handbook of theory and research for the sociology of education* (pp. 241–251). Greenwood.

Bowles, S. (1977). Unequal education and the reproduction of the social division of labor. In J. Karabel & A. H. Halsey (Eds.), *Power and ideology in Education* (pp. 137–153). Oxford University Press.

Bowles, S., & Gintis, H. (1976). *Schooling in capitalist America: Educational reform and the contradictions of economic life.* Basic Books.

Bowles, S., & Gintis, H. (2002). Schooling in capitalist America revisited. *Sociology of Education, 75*(1), 1–18. https://doi.org/10.2307/3090251

Brayboy, B. M. J. (2006). Toward a tribal critical race theory in education. *The Urban Review, 37*(5), 425–446. https://doi.org/10.2307/3090251

Brewer, R. M., & Heitzeg, N. A. (2008). The racialization of crime and punishment: Criminal justice, color-blind racism, and the political economy of the prison industrial complex. *American Behavioral Scientists, 51*(5), 625–644. https://doi .org/10.1177/0002764207307745

Brightman, H. J., & Gutmore, D. (2002). The educational-industrial complex. *The Educational Forum, 66*(4), 302–308. https://doi.org/10.1080/00131720 208984848

Brint, S., & Karabel, J. (1989). American education, meritocratic ideology, and the legitimation of inequality: The community college and the problem of American exceptionalism. *Higher Education, 18,* 725–735. https://doi.org/10.1007/ BF00155663

Bury, H. (2013). *Eisenhower and the military-industrial complex : "Open Skies" and the Cold War arms race.* I. B. Tauris.

Carrillo, J. F. (2013). The unhomely in academic success: Latino males navigating the ghetto nerd borderlands. *Culture, Society & Masculinities, 5*(2), 193–207. https://doi.org/10.3149/CSM.0502.193

Carrillo, J. F. (2016). I grew up straight 'hood: Unpacking the intelligences of working-class Latino male college students in North Carolina. *Equity & Excellence in Education, 49*(2), 157–169. https://doi.org/10.1080/10665684.2015.1086247

Crisp, G., & Nora, A. (2010). Hispanic student success: Factors influencing the persistence and transfer decisions of Latino community college students enrolled in developmental education. *Research in Higher Education, 51*(2), 175–194. https:// doi.org/10.1007/s11162-009-9151-x

Crisp, G., & Nuñez, A. M. (2014). Understanding the racial transfer gap: Modeling underrepresented minority and nonminority students' pathways from two-to-four-year institutions. *The Review of Higher Education, 37*(3), 291–320. https:// doi.org/10.1353/rhe.2014.0017

Davis, A. Y. (2003). *Are prisons obsolete?* Seven Stories Press.

Davis, A. Y. (2012). *The meaning of freedom: And other difficult dialogues.* City Lights Books.

Delgado Bernal, D. (2002). Critical race theory, Latino critical theory, and critical raced-gendered epistemologies: Recognizing students of color as holders and creators of knowledge. *Qualitative Inquiry, 8*(1), 105–126. https://doi .org/10.1177/107780040200800107

Dowd, A. C., & Bensimon, E. M. (2015). *Engaging the "race question": Accountability and equity in U.S. higher education.* Teachers College Press.

Dunne, J. P., & Sköns, E. (2010). The military industrial complex. In A. T. H. Tan (Ed.), *The global arms trade* (1st ed., pp. 281–292). Routledge. https://doi .org/10.4324/9780203851456-20

Excelencia in Education. (2019). *Early College High School (ECHS) Initiative.* https:// www.edexcelencia.org/programs-

Felix, E. R., Bensimon, E. M., Hanson, D., Gray, J., & Klingsmith, L. (2015). Developing agency for equity-minded change. In E. L. Castro (Ed.), *Understanding equity in community college practice* [Special Issue] (New Directions for Community Colleges, no. 172, pp. 23–42). Wiley. https://doi.org/10.1002/cc.20161

García, J., & De Lissovoy, N. (2013). Doing school time: The hidden curriculum goes to prison. *Journal for Critical Education Policy Studies, 11*(4), 49–69. http:// www.jceps.com/wp-content/uploads/PDFs/11-4-03.pdf

Gándara, P., Alvarado, E., Driscoll, A., & Orfield, G. (2012). *Building pathways to transfer: Community colleges that break the chain of failure for students of color.* Civil Rights Project/Proyecto Derechos Civiles.

Georgetown University Center on Education and the Workforce. (2018). *Our separate & unequal public colleges: How public colleges reinforce White racial privilege and marginalize Black and Latino students.* https://files.eric.ed.gov/fulltext/ ED594576.pdf

Giroux, H. (2007). *The university in chains: Confronting the military-industrial-academic complex.* Routledge.

Giroux, H. (2008). Education and the crisis of youth: Schooling and the promise of democracy. *The Education Forum, 73*(1), 8–18. https://doi.org/10.1080/ 00131720802539523

Goldrick-Rab, S. (2010). Challenges and opportunities for improving community college student success. *Review of Educational Research, 80*(3), 437–469. https:// doi.org/10.3102/0034654310370163

Hardt, M. (1997). Prison time. *Yale French Studies, 91,* 64–79. https://doi.org/ 10.2307/2930374

Harper, S. R. (2010). An anti-deficit achievement framework for research on students of color in STEM. (New Directions for Institutional Research, no. 148, pp. 63–74). Wiley. https://doi.org/10.1002/ir.362

Harper, S. R., & Kuykendall, J. A. (2012). Institutional efforts to improve Black male student achievement: A standards-based approach. *Change: The Magazine of Higher Learning, 44*(2), 23–29. https://doi.org/10.1080/00091383.2012. 655234

Iftikar, J. S., & Museus, S. D. (2018). On the utility of Asian critical (AsianCrit) theory in the field of education. *International Journal of Qualitative Studies in Education, 31*(10), 935–949. https://doi.org/10.1080/09518398.2018 .1522008

Janiewski, D. E. (2011). Eisenhower's paradoxical relationship with the "military-industrial complex." *Presidential Studies Quarterly, 41*(4), 667–692. https://doi .org/10.1111/j.1741-5705.2011.03909.x

Joliet Junior College. (2019). *Home page.* https://www.jjc.edu/about-jjc/history

Karabel, J. (1977). Community colleges and social stratification: Submerged class conflict in American higher education. In J. Karabel & A. H. Halsey (Eds.), *Power and ideology in education* (232–254). Oxford University Press.

Kendi, I. X. (2019). *How to be an antiracist.* One World.

Kezar, A. (2014). *How colleges change: Understanding, leading, and enacting change.* Routledge.

Kutler, S. I. (2003). *Dictionary of American history* (3rd ed). Gale Division of Cengage Learning Inc.

Ladson-Billings, G. (2011). Race . . . to the top, again: Comments on the genealogy of critical race theory. *Connecticut Law Review, 43*(5), 1441–1457. https://opencommons.uconn.edu/law_review/121

Lewis, A. E. (2001). There is no "race" in the schoolyard: Color-blind ideology in an (almost) all-white school. *American Educational Research Journal, 38*(4), 781–811. https://doi.org/10.3102/00028312038004781

Lundberg, C. A., Kim, Y. K., Andrade, L. M., & Bahner, D. T. (2018). High expectations, strong support: Faculty behaviors predicting Latina/o community college student learning. *Journal of College Student Development, 59*(1), 55–70. https://doi.org/10.1353/csd.2018.0004

Malágon, M. C. (2010). All the losers go there: Challenging the deficit educational discourse of Chicano racialized masculinity in a continuation high school. *Education Foundations, 24,* 59–76. https://files.eric.ed.gov/fulltext/EJ885932.pdf

Malcom-Piqueux, L., & Bensimon, E. M. (2017, Summer). *Taking equity-minded action to close equity gaps* [Peer review]. Association of American Colleges & Universities.

Manges Douglas, K., & Sáenz, R., (2013). The criminalization of immigrants & the immigration-industrial complex. *The Journal of the American Academy of Arts & Sciences, 142*(3), 199–227. https://doi.org/10.1162/DAED_a_00228

Michael, A. (2015). *Raising race questions: Whiteness & inquiry in education.* Teachers College Press.

Nevarez, C., & Wood, J. L. (2010). *Community college leadership and administration: Theory, practice, and change* (Vol. 3). Peter Lang.

Noguera, P., Hurtado, A., & Fergus, E. (2012). *Invisible no more: Understanding the disenfranchisement of Latino men and boys.* Routledge.

Peña, M. I. (2017). *The role of community college first-year experience programs in promoting transfer among Latino male students* (ProQuest ID: Penn_ucla_0031D_1598) [Doctoral dissertation, University of California, Los Angeles]. ProQuest Dissertations and Theses Global.

Perez Huber, L., Malágon, M. C., Ramirez, B. R., Camargo Gonzalez, L., Jimenez, A., & Velez, V. N. (2015). Still falling through the cracks: Revisiting the Latina/o education pipeline. *UCLA Chicano Studies Research Center Research Report, 19,* 1–23. https://www.chicano.ucla.edu/files/RR19.pdf

Prados, J. (2015). Eisenhower and the cold war arms race: "Open skies" and the military-industrial complex. *Journal of Cold War Studies, 17*(3), 232–233. https://doi.org/10.1162/JCWS_r_00569

Project MALES. (n.d.). *Advancing equitable educational outcomes for male students of color.* https://diversity.utexas.edu/projectmales/

Ramaley, J. A. (2014). Educating for a changing world: The importance of an equity mindset. *Metropolitan Universities, 25*(3), 5–15. https://journals.iupui.edu/index.php/muj/article/view/20578/20178

Sáenz, V. B., Lu, C., Bukoski, B. E., & Rodriguez, S. (2013). Latino males in Texas community colleges: A phenomenological study of masculinity constructs and their effect on college experiences. *Journal of African American Males in Education, 4*(2), 82–102. http://journalofafricanamericanmales.com/wp-content/uploads/2013/11/Saenz-et-al-2013.pdf

Sáenz, V. B., Ponjuán, L., & López Figueroa, J. (2016). *Ensuring the success of Latino males in higher education: A national imperative.* Stylus.

Sáenz, V. B., Ponjuán, L., Segovia, J. J., & Del Real Viramontes, J. (2015). Developing a Latino mentoring program: Project MALES (Mentoring to Achieve Latino Educational Success). In C. S. Turner (Ed.), *Mentoring as transformative practice: Supporting student and faculty diversity* [Special Issue] (New Directions for Higher Education, no. 171, pp. 75–85). Wiley. https://doi.org/10.1002/he.20144

Shakur, A. (2001). *Assata: An autobiography.* Lawrence Hill Books.

Silva, E., & White, T. (2013). *Pathways to improvement: Using psychological strategies to help college students master developmental math.* Carnegie Foundation for the Advancement of Teaching.

Singleton, G. E. (2015). *Courageous conversations about race: A field guide for achieving equity in schools* (2nd ed.). Corwin A. Sage Company.

Solórzano, D. G. (1997, Summer). Critical race theory, racial stereotyping, and teacher education. *Teacher Education Quarterly, 24*(3), 5–19.

Solórzano, D. G., & Delgado Bernal, D. (2001). Examining transformational resistance through a critical race and LatCrit theory framework: Chicana and Chicano students in an urban context. *Urban Education, 36*(3), 308–342. https://doi.org/10.1177/0042085901363002

Stevenson, B. (2014). *Just mercy: A story of justice and redemption* (1st ed.). Spiegel & Grau.

Strayhorn, T. L. (2010). When race and gender collide: Social and cultural capital's influence on the academic achievement of African American and Latino males. *The Review of Higher Education, 33*(3), 307–332. https://doi.org/10.1353/rhe.0.0147

Strayhorn, T. L. (2012). Sense of belonging and Latino students. In T. L. Strayhorn (Ed.), *College students' sense of belonging: A key of educational success for all students* (pp. 27–38). Routledge.

Texas Education. (n.d.) *About us.* https://diversity.utexas.edu/projectmales/about-us/

Tinto, V. (1982). Limits of theory and practice in student attrition. *The Journal of Higher Education, 53*(6), 687–700. https://doi.org/10.1080/00221546.1982.11780504

Tinto, V. (1975). Dropout from higher education: A theoretical synthesis of recent research. *Review of Educational Research, 45*(1), 89–125. https://doi.org/ 10.3102/00346543045001089

United States Courts. (n.d.a). *Background - Mendez v. Westminster Re-enactment.* https://www.uscourts.gov/educational-resources/educational-activities/back-ground-mendez-v-westminster-re-enactment

United States Courts. (n.d.b). *History - Brown v. Board of Education re-enactment.* https://www.uscourts.gov/educational-resources/educational-activities/history-brown-v-board-education-re-enactment

U.S. Department of Education. (2018). *FY education budget fact sheet.* https://www2 .ed.gov/about/overview/budget/budget18/index.html?src=search

Valenzuela, A. (1999). *Subtractive schooling: U.S.-Mexican youth and the politics of caring.* State University of New York Press.

Vasquez Urias, M., & Wood, J. L. (2015). The effect on non-cognitive outcomes on perceptions of school as a feminine domain among Latino men in community college. *Culture, Society & Masculinities, 7*(1), 22–32.

Villarreal, M. de Lourdes., & García, H. A. (2016). Self-determination and goal aspirations: African American and Latino males' perceptions of their persistence in community college basic and transfer-level writing courses. *Community College Journal of Research and Practice,* 1–16. https://doi.org/10.1080/10668926.2015 .1125314

Villarosa, L., Cohen, R., Potapchuk, M., & Williams, L. (2010). Marking progress: Movement toward racial justice. *Philanthropic Initiative for Racial Equity, 3,* 1–46.

Winter, C. G. (1964). History of the junior college movement in California. *Bureau of Junior College Education, 20,* 3–43. https://files.eric.ed.gov/fulltext/ED346902. pdf

Wood, J. L. (2018). *Advancing equity for students of color* [PowerPoint presentation]. https://depts.valleycollege.edu/professional/opening-day-presentation-pt1-8-10-18.pdf

Yosso, T. J. (2005). Whose culture has capital? A critical race discussion of community cultural wealth. *Race Ethnicity and Education, 8*(1), 69–91. https://doi .org/10.1080/1361332052000341006

CONCLUSION

Future Direction and Concluding Thoughts

Fred A. Bonner II, Rosa M. Banda, Stella L. Smith, and aretha f. marbley

Kurt Lewin's (1936) interactionist equation B = f(P x E) remains as salient today as it did decades ago as we chart the future direction of college student development. As we seek outcomes geared to promote the success of our college student cohorts, it is imperative to begin with what Stephen Covey (1989) has advanced in his work: The end in mind. Thus, it is important to ask ourselves the following critical questions:

- Who are our college students?
- What set of experiences do our students bring to the higher education context?
- What role have their environments/contexts (i.e., home, P–12, community, family, peer groups, mentors) played in our student's lives?
- What impact have intervening variables (i.e., race, oppression, power) had on their experiences?
- What strategies do they use to overcome developmental obstacles?
- How do they define success?
- How do they know they have achieved success?

Evans et al. (2010) share a robust list of recommendations for the future, many of which have widespread implications for the direction of advancing alternative college student development frameworks. Their recommendation that development must be considered in a more holistic and less linear manner provides a greater range of developmental motion for those students who do not start the postsecondary process right out of high school, or for those who do not initiate this journey from traditional P–12 schooling experiences. Thus, traditional models that assume that college students are typical 18-year olds from the typical elementary and secondary school context potentially belie the engagements of diverse student cohorts.

Another recommendation states that researchers must examine what development looks like for various student populations independent of dominant cultural models. Abes (2009), who foregrounded Anzaldúa's scholarship in her research on lesbian identity development, spoke to the urgent need to use multiple frameworks, many of which have not historically been on the developmental theory "radar," to scaffold greater authenticity regarding the diverse college student experience. So, too, does Tanaka's (2002) treatise about development as it relates to the reflexive turn in higher education speak to the need to seek frameworks that are meaningful to the populations to which they are applied.

> In times of fragmentation linked to rapidly changing student racial demographics and heightened awareness of difference based on race, gender, and sexual orientation, a culturally neutral perspective may overlook differential impacts from participation by diverse groups and fall short of providing the data policymakers will need to foster meaning and harmony across groups. (Tanaka, 2002, p. 264)

Another recommendation asserts educators must remember that all theory reflects the values of its authors and the times in which they live. According to Jones and Abes (2011), "When thinking about identifying and applying theories to practice, it behooves student affairs educators to look inward and consider how their own experiences, biases, and assumptions may predispose them to one set of theories over others" (p. 12). Hence, the very selection of theory is a process that has both political and power dimensions (Apple, 1995; Foucault, 1983); in essence, the student development researcher and practitioner must be aware of their positionality. It is common practice for scholars engaged in qualitative research to devote considerable energy and time to framing a researcher's positionality statement. This statement serves as a self-reflective tool that requires the researcher to galvanize key past engagements and experiences that could potentially influence the outcomes of the intended investigation. Perhaps what is needed for those tasked with the implementation of college student development theory is a similar document and process that requires the creation of an educator's/practitioner's positionality statement. The process of developing this statement would allow these individuals to reflect on their assumptions, biases, and motivations as they relate to college student populations in general and their application of college student development theory in particular.

Yet another key recommendation advances that unacknowledged and underacknowledged representations of groups in our theory base must be given appropriate voice. The primary focus of this tome, *Square Pegs and Round Holes,* is to shine a light on the dark areas of college student development and the attendant theorizing that has tended to leave certain collegiate cohorts, particularly diverse student groups, in the shadows. While the previous sections have peeled back the layers of college student development and diversity as they relate to race, gender, and sexual identity, an area of future exploration that will demand attention is college student development among the international college student population. According to Kim (2012), "Despite their growing presence, international students are left out of much of the literature on college student development theory in the United States" (p. 3). Hence, forcing college students who are nonnatives to American education cultures, mores, and traditions to fit into domestic student development frameworks is at best inappropriate and at worst damaging. Kim (2012) added:

> As international students, challenge and (re)-examine their sense of self and their status as international students, their identity can be validated, redefined, and reinforced. Given the critical role of student affairs professionals, and faculty in college student development, these university personnel need to be cognizant of ways to help international students with unique challenges, academic and cultural backgrounds, to understand their overall development and help them to adjust to new learning environments. (p. 16)

Finally, educators must challenge themselves to be creative in the use of theory. Abes (2009) deftly used and introduced the concept of bricolage in her discussion of how college student development theorists must disrupt the common practice of using theory singularly to explain multilayered and complex college student development processes. She shared, "Kincheloe and McLaren (2005) have advocated for the border-crossing notion of bricolage, which is typically understood to involve the process of employing . . . [multiple] methodological strategies as they are needed in the unfolding context of the research situation" (p. 316). Therefore, for educators to address this recommendation, it is necessary to think outside of the box and to seek alternative frameworks that are both daring and creative.

A key strategy to alter prevailing thought processes related to the selection of college student development theory is to "flip the approach." Instead of using the theory to frame student development, use student development to frame theory. Said differently, who our college students are and what they present as essential elements in their learning, growth, and development should guide our choices and application of theory—not the reverse.

References

Abes, E. S. (2009). Theoretical borderlands: Using multiple theoretical perspectives to challenge inequitable power structures in student development theory. *Journal of College Student Development, 50*(2), 141–156. https://doi.org/10.1353/csd.0.0059

Apple, M. W. (1995). *Education and power* (2nd ed.). Routledge.

Covey, S. R. (1989). *The seven habits of highly effective people.* Simon & Schuster.

Evans, N. J., Forney, D. S., Guido, F. M., Patton, L. D., & Renn, K. A. (2010). *Student development in college: Theory, research, and practice.* John Wiley & Sons.

Jones, S. R., & Abes, E. S. (2011). The nature and uses of theory. *Student services: A handbook for the profession* (5th ed., pp. 149–167). Jossey-Bass.

Kim, E. (2012). An alternative theoretical model: Examining psychosocial identity development of international students in the United States. *College Student Journal, 46*(1), 99–113.

Lewin, K. (1936). *Principles of psychological topology.* McGraw-Hill.

Foucault, M. (1983). The subject and power. In H. L. Dreyfus & P. Rabinow (Eds.), *Beyond structuralism and hermeneutics* (pp. 208–226). The University of Chicago Press.

Tanaka, G. (2002). Higher education's self-reflexive turn: Toward an intercultural theory of student development. *The Journal of Higher Education, 73*(2), 263–296. https://doi.org/10.1353/jhe.2002.0024

AFTERWORD

For decades, experts have attempted to predict the future of higher education. The pundits' many assertions about the forthcoming events in the field often revolve around various financial and operational aspects of the higher education enterprise. Although it is necessary for every higher education leader to be concerned about the business aspects of delivering on their campus mission, one can argue that just as much attention, if not more, should be placed on closely examining students' experiences. The undeniable fact for everyone in higher education is that without students, there can be no successful colleges of any kind.

This is a critical moment for higher education institutions to intentionally couple relevant instruction and holistic support, both of which are essential to students' success in college and their navigation of the world that awaits after college. This book, *Square Pegs and Round Holes: Alternative Approaches to Diverse College Student Development Theory*, opens with a call for alternative frameworks for addressing students' development in college, frameworks that create new contexts for discussions rather than solely relying on existing ones. The plea is followed by a seven-part series of models that elevate and affirm the diversity of today's student populations.

Previous examinations of student development theory have prompted scholars, researchers, policymakers, and practitioners to better understand the myriad ways in which students' learn and engage. This book expands on those prior examples and creates new areas for discussion and inquiry. For example, as America continues to grapple with the many racial injustices and inequities that permeate the fabric of nearly every industry, this is the perfect time for a volume that uses critical race theory as a central frame. The selected topics stress the importance of not forcing conversations about students' development into previous models but instead reframing the dialogues in new and more appropriate ways. *Square Pegs and Round Holes: Alternative Approaches to Diverse College Student Development Theory* definitely fills a void in the literature by providing an abundance of approaches that help practitioners better understand the nuances of students' progress. The effect should be a cadre of professionals who can make more precise adjustments to policies and procedures and thus positively impact student outcomes.

McNair et al. (2016) argued that colleges should strive to be student ready, the result of which will be institutional commitments to inclusion, student-centered practices, and positive postcollege outcomes for all learners. The work of student affairs professionals is central to the process, as students' development is highly connected to their various out-of-classroom experiences. Offices such as advising, counseling, and health and wellness are integral to students' matriculation through college, and this book's dedicated focus on underaddressed theories prompts student services professionals to interrogate their role in delivering the comprehensive resources that students deserve.

The concept of a student-ready college is also best suited to institutions that acknowledge how every professional, irrespective of their role, does work that in some way contributes to students' success. This book aligns well with such a concept because learning happens everywhere and students' development is not limited to a certain type or number of environments. Although the primary audiences for this book are student affairs educators and faculty, the frameworks also provide context for professionals who engage with students in other areas of the campus. For example, Grafnetterova and Banda address identity development of Latinx student athletes, which can help coaches and other athletic department administrators make thoughtful operational decisions that are attuned to students' lived experiences.

Another ideal outcome of this book is that it will help professionals who are responsible for analyzing student performance data. For example, Henke et al. (2018) stated that in the next 10 years, there will be an increased demand for professionals who can serve as data translators. The translator role requires one to have knowledge of the industry, the ability to interpret the results of analyses, and project management skills. Imagine if those tasks were completed by higher education professionals who periodically refer to *Square Pegs and Round Holes*. The influence of the translator role, and any other position that leverages analytics for decision-making, would be more dynamic, as the student development models would provide a fuller description of students' college journey.

In this time of continued uncertainty regarding how the field of higher education will transform to address new demands and unanticipated challenges, professionals need an evergreen resource that focuses on students' development. This book's arrival could not be timelier, as the pressure on both campuses and students to succeed is arguably higher than ever. The approaches included in this volume certainly answer the call for new models and, in some ways, provide a glimpse of the kinds of interactions that are possible when students are consistently placed at the center of campus strategies. This book contains a remarkable blend of historical contexts, current paradigms, and future aspirations and offers a means for connecting student populations that have traditionally received less attention in published scholarly works.

It is urgent that institutions demonstrate their capacity to deliver personalized experiences to students, particularly those who are expecting their college experience to result in greater financial stability and social mobility. As professionals respond to those expectations, the frameworks included in *Square Pegs and Round Holes* offer a foundation to provoke them to acknowledge, welcome, and support students whose identities need to be visible and prioritized every day. Regardless of what the future holds, those who refer to this book often will have a reliable guide to make students' experience the most optimal possible, which is a goal that every institution should have today and beyond.

Amelia Parnell
NASPA – Student Affairs Administrators in Higher Education

References

Henke, N., Levine, J., & McInerney, P. (2018, February 21). You don't have to be a data scientist to fill this must-have analytics role. *Harvard Business Review.* https://hbr.org/2018/02/you-dont-have-to-be-a-data-scientist-to-fill-this-must-have-analytics-role

McNair, T. B., Albertine, S., Cooper, M. A., McDonald, N., & Major, T. (2016). *Becoming a student-ready college: A new culture of leadership for student success.* Jossey-Bass.

Zarrina Talan Azizova, PhD, is an assistant professor of higher education at the University of North Dakota. Her research uses qualitative and quantitative research methods and social theory to understand and mitigate inequalities in college access, student experiences, and outcomes in (inter)national contexts of higher education. Her works have examined the role of various forms of capital, institutional differences, and educational practices in college access and student success of diverse students at all levels of postsecondary education. Her research calls for a departure from deficit-oriented deterministic views and for a shift toward a better understanding of student agency.

Rosa M. Banda, PhD, is assistant professor of educational leadership at Texas A&M University-Corpus Christi. Formerly, Banda was a research associate to the Samuel DeWitt Proctor Chair in Education in the Graduate School of Education at Rutgers University. Banda earned her PhD in higher education administration and human resource development from Texas A&M University-College Station. A critical social justice advocate, Banda's primary research interests include high-achieving Latinas in engineering, gifted poor students of color, faculty diversity, and qualitative research.

Fred A. Bonner II is professor and endowed chair of educational leadership and counseling in the Whitlowe R. Green College of Education at Prairie View A&M University. He also serves as the founding executive director and chief scientist of the Minority Achievement Creativity and High Ability (MACH-III) Center. His research foci illuminate the experiences of academically gifted African American males across the P–20 pipeline, diverse faculty in academe, and diverse populations in science, technology, engineering, and math (STEM). He is coeditor of two books with Stylus Publishing, *Building on Resilience: Models and Frameworks of Black Male Success Across the P–20 Pipeline* (2014) and *Diverse Millennials Students in College: Implications for Faculty and Student Affairs* (2011). Bonner is currently developing a theoretical framework, mascusectionality, that will explore the engagements of Black men.

Bryan McKinley Jones Brayboy (Lumbee) is President's Professor of Indigenous Education and Justice in the School of Social Transformation at Arizona State University (ASU). He is also senior adviser to ASU's president, director of the Center for Indian Education, and coeditor of the *Journal of American Indian Education*. He is the author of more than 90 scholarly documents in which he examines the role of race and diversity in higher education and the experiences of Indigenous students, staff, and faculty in institutions of higher education. He is a fellow of the American Educational Research Association and a member of the National Academy of Education.

Jorge M. Burmicky serves as a research coordinator at Project MALES (Mentoring to Achieve Latino Educational Success), a research and mentoring initiative at The University of Texas at Austin (UT-Austin) committed to men of color in education. Through a scholar-practitioner approach, his research is focused on understanding the leadership pipeline of minoritized populations in higher education. Burmicky holds a doctorate in educational leadership and policy from UT-Austin and a master's degree in student affairs and higher education from Ball State University.

Emmet E. Campos, PhD, directs Project MALES (Mentoring to Achieve Latino Educational Success) and the Texas Education Consortium for Male Students of Color in the Division of Diversity and Community Engagement at The University of Texas at Austin (UT-Austin). Campos serves as the chief operations officer for Project MALES/Consortium activities and is responsible for communications and engagement with key partners. He received his BA in ethnic/third world studies and his PhD in cultural studies in education/curriculum and instruction from UT-Austin. He is also a lecturer at UT-Austin and previously taught at St. Edward's University and Austin Community College in the education and English departments.

Karina Chantal Canaba, EdD, is a research assistant professor in the Department of Educational Leadership and Foundations and associate director of the Campus Office of Undergraduate Research Initiatives (COURI) at the University of Texas at El Paso (UTEP). Her scholarship seeks to better understand issues of equity in K–12 and higher education through a critical lens by incorporating subaltern research methodologies. Recently her work has focused on examining the experiences of faculty of color at minority-serving institutions. Canaba has over a decade of experience working in higher education and student support services.

Jason Chan is the fellowship and career adviser at the Center for Career and Professional Advising at Haverford College. His research interests are in race and diversity in higher education with a focus on environmental and contextual influences on college students' understanding of race and racial identity. Chan earned his PhD in higher education and organizational change at the University of California, Los Angeles.

Mitchell J. Chang is a professor of education at the University of California, Los Angeles. His research focuses on diversity-related issues and initiatives on college campuses. He has written more than 100 publications, some of which have been cited in U.S. Supreme Court rulings concerning the use of race-conscious admissions practices. Chang was elected in 2016 as a Fellow of the American Educational Research Association and is the editor–in-chief of the Journal of Higher Education.

G. Christopher Cutkelvin is a program coordinator for the Division for Diversity and Community Engagement at The University of Texas at Austin (UT-Austin). He earned his master's degree in in higher education leadership at UT-Austin 2019, and he earned his bachelor's degree from Texas Southern University. He is currently pursuing a doctorate in educational leadership and policy. He is a founding member of the Collegiate 100 in Houston and has served in leadership roles for the NAACP and Alpha Phi Alpha.

Sequoia Lynn Dance is a member of the Shoshone-Bannock Tribes and a direct descendant of the Assiniboine Red Bottom Band. She received her BA in human development from Washington State University and her MA in social and cultural pedagogy from Arizona State University. She joined the *Turning Points Magazine* team in the summer of 2017 and worked on contributing with the magazine for 2 years. She developed a passion for storytelling and story sharing throughout the process that continues to fuel the work that she does. Dance is currently serving at Lewis-Clark State College as the director of college assistant migrant program.

Sattik Deb, EdD, has been an educator for nearly 20 years. He currently directs student academic services at New York University Center for Urban Science and Progress. Prior to this appointment, Deb served as the director of student services at Rutgers University School of Management and Labor Relations. He has taught courses in American history, labor studies, social justice, and leadership. He earned his master's degree and doctorate of education from Rutgers University.

Alonzo M. Flowers III, PhD, is an associate professor and PhD program director in the School of Education at Drexel University. Flowers specializes in educational issues including academic identity development of men of color (MoC) in science, technology, engineering, and math (STEM) education. He also focuses on issues including diversity, teaching and learning, and college student development in higher education. Specifically, Flowers's research focuses on the academic experiences of academically gifted African American male students in the STEM disciplines. Flowers is also the managing coeditor of the *Journal of African American Males in Education* (*JAAME*).

Nikola Grafnetterova, EdD, is athletic academic coordinator at Texas A&M University-Corpus Christi. Grafnetterova earned an EdD in educational leadership with a cognate in higher education from Texas A&M University-Corpus Christi. Primary research interests include Latinx college athletes, leadership and administration within college athletics, and athletic academic services.

Mary F. Howard-Hamilton is the Coffman Distinguished Research Professor and chair of the Department of Educational Leadership at Indiana State University. She received the Presidential Medal from the Association for the Study of Higher Education in 2018 and was a recipient of the Contribution to Knowledge Award from the American College Personnel Association in 2017. Indiana State University awarded her with the Presidential Medal for Exemplary Teaching and Scholarship and the Theodore Dreiser Distinguished Research and Creativity Award in 2015. Howard-Hamilton has published more than 90 articles and book chapters and coauthored *Multicultural and Diversity Issues in Student Affairs Practice: A Professional Competency-Based Approach* (Charles C. Thomas Pub Ltd, 2019).

Nicholas D. Hartlep holds the Robert Charles Billings Endowed Chair in Education at Berea College where he chairs the Education Studies Department. *Diverse: Issues in Higher Education* named him a 2019 Emerging Scholar. Author of 23 books, his most recently published book is *Racial Battle Fatigue in Faculty: Perspectives and Lessons from Higher Education* (Routledge, 2019), published in Fred A. Bonner II's Diverse Faculty in the Academy Routledge book series. In 2020 he was named an Emerging Scholar by *Diverse: Issues in Higher Education.*

Christy Heaton, PhD, is the assistant vice chancellor of student transitions and family engagement at the University of Colorado Denver (CU Denver), where she also serves as a lecturer in the School of Education. Her doctoral research centered on the exploration of undergraduate transgender students' experiences at institutions of higher education in the southern United States. Other areas of work focus include college student transition, first-generation students, and leadership development. Prior to CU Denver, she spent 10 years at the University of New Orleans where she worked primarily with areas that focused on orientation, transition, and retention.

Patricia E. Literte is associate professor of sociology at California State University, Fullerton. Her areas of specialization are race and ethnicity, higher education, and urban sociology, and her work has been published in the *Journal of College Student Development*, *Journal of African American Studies*, *Journal of Negro Education*, and *Amerasia Journal*. Literte is the program director of the federally funded Ronald E. McNair Post-Baccalaureate Achievement Program, which prepares undergraduate students from low-income, first-generation, and underrepresented backgrounds for entrance into doctoral programs.

Victoria K. Malaney Brown currently serves as the inaugural director of academic integrity for undergraduates at Columbia University. She earned her bachelor of arts degree in an interdepartmental English-Spanish program and minors in dance and Latin American studies from Skidmore College. Malaney Brown received her higher education doctorate from the College of Education at the University of Massachusetts Amherst. Her qualitative dissertation explored critical consciousness in the narratives of multiracial collegians at a predominantly White institution. A scholar-practitioner, Malaney Brown's research interests focus on the racialized experiences of multiracial undergraduate students in higher education, intergroup dialogue, college student activism, and academic integrity.

aretha f. marbley is a professor and coordinator of clinical mental health counseling in counselor education and interim director of women and gender studies at Texas Tech University. She is an academic counselor and a critical humanist, womanist educator, storyteller, activist, servant, morally engaged researcher, and transdisciplinary scholar with a commitment to helping people and communities. Her scholarship focuses on critical global multicultural-social justice activism, organic connections, and literacy advocacy across cultures, social structures, and social identities in mental health and communities. She has received numerous awards including national human rights, social justice, anti-oppression, and multicultural research awards.

Saralyn M. McKinnon-Crowley is a PhD candidate in higher education at The University of Texas at Austin (UT-Austin). She earned a BA with majors in religious studies and linguistics from Indiana University Bloomington; an MA in religious studies from Northwestern University; and an MEd in college and university student personnel administration from UT Austin, where she won the Dr. Sharon H. Justice Student Leadership Award in 2017. She has previous work experience in residence life and in student conduct and works as a graduate research assistant with Huriya Jabbar and Lauren Schudde. Her research interests include financial aid policy and practice in the United States, community colleges, and gender in the academy.

Jesse P. Mendez, PhD, JD, is a dean and professor of higher education of the College of Education at Texas Tech University. Throughout his academic career, he has served as both a faculty member and administrator within urban and rural universities, a land-grant institution, a community college, and two Hispanic-serving institutions. Mendez's research explores the dynamics of postsecondary access and policy issues in higher education.

Samuel D. Museus is professor of education studies at the University of California, San Diego (UCSD) and founding director of the National Institute for Transformation and Equity (NITE). Prior to joining UCSD, he taught at Indiana University Bloomington, the University of Denver, the University of Hawai'i at Mānoa, and the University of Massachusetts Boston. His research agenda is focused on diversity and equity, social movements and activism, transforming systems to be more inclusive and equitable.

Vanessa S. Na is a Khmer American doctoral student in education studies at the University of California, San Diego (UCSD) and a research associate for the National Institute for Transformation and Equity (NITE). Her research examines institutional equity and justice in higher education with a focus on illuminating the experiences of Southeast Asian American students and understanding the solidarity and coalition efforts of students of color.

Mariama N. Nagbe is a proud Detroit, Michigan, native; University Council for Educational Leadership (UCEA) Jackson Scholar; and PhD candidate in higher education at The University of Texas at Austin (UT-Austin). A critical organizational scholar, her research interests seek to examine the socialization structures, policies, culture, and practices of doctoral programs from an organizational theory perspective. She earned a bachelor's and two master's degrees from the University of Michigan-Ann Arbor. Nagbe plans to pursue a tenure-track position at a leading research institution, and she hopes to use her scholarship to transform how institutional practices and policies of graduate programs center social/organizational justice and equity in their structures and approaches, while mentoring young scholars to increase underrepresented groups in academia.

Taylor Notah is a Diné multimedia journalist and wordsmith originally from St. Michaels, Arizona, on the Navajo Nation. She is senior editor of Arizona State University's Native American student publication titled *Turning Points: A Guide to Native Student Succes.* Notah is a cum laude graduate of Arizona State University (ASU) with a BA in journalism and is a member of the Native American Journalists Association. Through her writing, Notah aims to accurately illustrate the beauty and issues of Indian Country and share diversified stories in media through a Native lens.

Mike Hoa Nguyen is assistant professor of higher education at the University of Denver. His research examines the benefits and consequences of public policy instruments in expanding and constraining the academic operations of colleges and universities, with a specific focus on federal diversity initiatives. Prior to earning his doctorate, Nguyen served as a senior staff member in the United States Congress.

Pavitee Peumsang is a PhD candidate in the Department of Educational Leadership and Policy at The University of Texas at Austin. Her dissertation applies both critical race studies and critical Whiteness studies to explore how faculty members shape the racial dynamics of community college mathematics classroom environments. Peumsang began her higher education pathway as a nontraditional community college student at East Los Angeles College. She earned a BA in sociology with a minor in labor and workplace studies (2015) and an MA in education with a concentration in race and ethnic studies (2016) at the University of California, Los Angeles.

Chavez Phelps is an assistant professor of school psychology at Indiana State University. He teaches courses in socioemotional assessment and intervention, ethics and law in school psychology, and child trauma. His research interests include child trauma as a form of social justice. Phelps offers professional development in trauma-informed care for school districts across the state of Indiana. He is a member of the National Association of School Psychologists (NASP) Government and Professional Advocacy Committee, where he represents the central region of the United States. From 2009 to 2017, he functioned as a school-based practitioner in New Orleans, Louisiana, working in nontraditional school settings such as juvenile correctional facilities, adolescent mental health hospitals, and alternative high schools.

Richard J. Reddick is an associate professor and associate dean for equity, community engagement, and outreach in the College of Education at The University of Texas at Austin, where he is affiliated with the Department of African and African Diaspora Studies. Reddick is also faculty cochair of the Harvard Institute for Educational Management. Reddick's research focuses on the experiences of Black faculty and faculty of color at predominantly White institutions and mentoring relationships between faculty and Black students.

Kristen A. Renn is professor of higher, adult, and lifelong education at Michigan State University where she also serves as associate dean of undergraduate studies for student success research. With a background in student affairs administration, she has for the last 20 years focused her research on the identities, experiences, and development of college students. Through her work on mixed-race college students, leaders in identity-based student organizations, women's colleges and universities around the world, and LGBTQ college student success, she has contributed to the growing literature on minoritized students in higher education.

Derrick Robinson, PhD, is an assistant professor of educational leadership at the University of Memphis. He received his BA from Morehouse College, an MBA from Johns Hopkins University, a master of educational leadership from Wingate University, and a PhD in curriculum and instruction with a focus on urban education from the University of North Carolina at Charlotte. Robinson has 22 years of teaching and leadership experience in urban schools from Prince George's County, Maryland; Washington DC; and Charlotte, North Carolina. Robinson's research examines the contextual nature of school climate and culture, leadership effectiveness, and teacher effectiveness in urban settings.

Petra A. Robinson, PhD, is director for faculty affairs and professional development in the College of Human Sciences and Education. Robinson is also an associate professor in the School of Leadership and Human Resource Development. She received her PhD in educational administration and human resource development from Texas A&M University with a focus on adult education. She is keenly interested in issues related to colorism; nontraditional, critical literacies; diversity and social justice; global lifelong learning; and professional development in the academy.

Victor B. Sáenz is a professor and chair of the Department of Educational Leadership and Policy at The University of Texas at Austin (UT-Austin). He holds courtesy appointments in the Center for Mexican American Studies; the University of California, Los Angeles (UCLA) Higher Education Research Institute; and various other research centers. In 2010 Sáenz cofounded an award-winning initiative called Project MALES, a multipronged effort focused on advancing educational outcomes for male students of color through research, mentoring, and a statewide consortium. Sáenz earned his PhD in higher education and organizational change from UCLA in 2005. He also earned a master's degree in public affairs (1999) and a bachelor's degree in mathematics (1996) from UT-Austin.

Brian Skeet is an Indigenous (Diné) designer born in Tuba City, Arizona, and raised on the rim of the Grand Canyon. Skeet is a multidisciplinary designer who strives to cultivate Indigenous initiatives through design, research, technology and innovation. Strategically, Skeet's work focuses on energizing future Indigenous creatives to illuminate systemic issues, disentangle bureaucratic dependence and cultivate culturally centered solutions within their community. Skeet holds a bachelor's degree in industrial design and design management and an associate degree in graphic design. Skeet is also the cocreator and designer for IndigeDesign Collab, coowner of C&B Designs, and owner of Brian Skeet Design.

Stella L. Smith, PhD, is the associate director for the Minority Achievement, Creativity and High-Ability (MACH-III) Center and an adjunct instructor in the Department of Educational Leadership and Counseling at Prairie View A&M University. A qualitative researcher, her scholarly interests focus on the experiences of faculty and administrators of color in higher education; African American females in leadership in higher education; access and inclusion of underserved populations in higher education; and P–20 educational pipeline alignment. For the entirety of her professional career, she has worked in areas that promote access for underrepresented populations to higher education. Smith is a strong advocate for social justice and passionate about creating asset based pathways of success for underserved students. Smith was recognized with a 2014 Dissertation Award from the American Association of Blacks in Higher Education and as part of the 2019 Class of 35 Outstanding Women Leaders in Higher Education by *Diverse Issues in Higher Education*. She serves as the managing editor for the *Journal for Minority Achievement, Creativity, and Leadership* and an associate editor of the *Journal of Family Strengths*. Smith earned her PhD in educational administration with a portfolio in women and gender studies from The University of Texas at Austin.

Terrell L. Strayhorn is provost and senior vice president of academic affairs and professor of urban education in the Evelyn Reid Syphax School of Education at Virginia Union University, where he also serves as director of the Center for the Study of HBCUs. He is a faculty affiliate at Rutgers University's Center for MSIs and several other research institutes. An internationally recognized education equity expert, Strayhorn's research commitments center on the social psychological determinants of student success for minoritized and other vulnerable populations. His pioneering research on college students' sense of belonging has informed state policy reform, transformed campus/school practices, and advanced theory and intervention testing. Strayhorn is associate editor of *Social Sciences & Humanities*, specialty chief editor of *Frontiers in Education*, and author of more than 200 scholarly publications.

Daniel K. Suda possesses nearly 8 years of higher education experience, ranging from orientation and student activities to alumni relations. His professional areas of expertise include strategic planning, event planning, and programming. Suda's research interests include racial identity, higher education fundraising, and policy impacts on philanthropy. Suda earned his undergraduate degree from Texas A&M University and an MS in college student personnel administration from Illinois State University. Currently, he's pursuing a PhD in higher education from the University of North Texas.

Amanda R. Tachine is Diné from Ganado, Arizona. She is Náneeshtéézhí Táchii'nii (Zuni Red Running Into Water clan) born for Tłizilani (Many Goats clan). An assistant professor of higher education in the Mary Lou Fulton Teachers College at Arizona State University, her research centers on exploring college access, persistence, and sense of belonging among Indigenous college students using qualitative Indigenous research methodologies. She is drawn to contribute to research that focuses on systemic and structural barriers that disenfranchise college access for Indigenous and marginalized populations.

Howard A. Thrasher is a resident director at Boston University. He earned his master's degree in higher education leadership at The University of Texas at Austin in 2019, and he earned his bachelor's degree from Auburn University. His interests are in housing and residence life, building student leaders of color, transfer students and nontraditional students, the use of technology, queering leadership, and campus safety.

Latana Jennifer Thaviseth is a doctoral student in the Higher Education and Organizational Change Program at the University of California, Los Angeles. Her research focuses on the educational and occupational trajectories of Southeast Asian American college students. She is currently the assistant director of the Asian American Activities Center at Stanford University.

Saundra M. Tomlinson-Clarke, PhD, is professor and chair in the department of educational psychology at Rutgers Graduate School of Education. She is a licensed psychologist and Fellow, American Psychological Association, Division 17 (The Society of Counseling Psychology). Her research explores the influence of identity and culture on psychological well-being with a focus on multicultural and strength-based approaches that advance equity in education and training.

Hannah Hyun White is a Korean transracial/transnational adoptee doctoral student and Education Studies Fellow at the University of California, San Diego (UCSD). Her research concentrates on understanding colonial paradigms within transracial/transnational adoptee communities and student engagement and experiences in social/political student movement groups in higher education.